JOSEPH HALL

A Study in Satire
and Meditation

JOSEPH HALL
A Study in Satire
and Meditation

RICHARD A. McCABE

CLARENDON PRESS . OXFORD

1982

Oxford University Press, Walton Street, Oxford OX2 6DP
London Glasgow New York Toronto
Delhi Bombay Calcutta Madras Karachi
Kuala Lumpur Singapore Hong Kong Tokyo
Nairobi Dar es Salaam Cape Town
Melbourne Auckland
and associate companies in
Beirut Berlin Ibadan Mexico City

Published in the United States by
Oxford University Press, New York

British Library Cataloguing in Publication Data
McCabe, Richard A.
Joseph Hall: a study in satire and meditation.
1. Hall, Joseph—Criticism and interpretation
I. Title
828'.309   PR2283.H7
ISBN 0-19-812807-X

Library of Congress Cataloging in Publication Data
McCabe, Richard A. (Richard Anthony), 1954—
Joseph Hall: a study in satire and meditation.
Bibliography: p. 343
Includes index
1. Hall, Joseph, 1574–1656—Criticism and interpretation.
I. Title.
PR2283.H7Z77   828'.309   81-22443
ISBN 0-19-812807-X   AACR2

Type set by Burgess & Son (Abingdon) Ltd, Station Road, Abingdon, Oxfordshire
and printed in Great Britain
at the University Press, Oxford
by Eric Buckley
Printer to the University

For

MY MOTHER

Maugre the peevish Worlds complaint
Here lies a Bishop and a Saint
Whom Ashby bred, and Granta nurs'd
Whom Halsted, and old Waltham first
To rouz the stupid World from sloth,
Heard thund'ring with a Golden Mouth,
Whom Wor'ster next did dignifie
And honoured with her Deanry:
Whom Exon lent a Mitred wreath,
And Norwich where he ceas'd to breath.

These all with one joint voice do cry,
Death's vain attempt, what doth it mean?
My Son, my Pupil, Pastor, Dean
My rev'rend Father cannot die.

Deaths Alarum

The violent obtaine heaven, onely the meeke
are worthy to inherit the earth.

Contemplations

PREFACE

> I First adventure, with fool-hardie might
> To tread the steps of perilous despight:
> I first adventure: follow me who list,
> And be the second English Satyrist.

Such was the bold declaration with which Joseph Hall (1574–1656) greeted his public at the outset of his literary career in 1597. The spirit of the age breathes in the lines: adventure, primacy, and challenge. Explorers had revealed a vast new world, the humanists a new cultural ideal, the Reformers a new approach to God, and Hall himself was soon to emerge as a great literary pioneer in an age of restless aesthetic innovation. Yet the era of 'enlightenment' remained far off even for someone so aware of the significance of the new discoveries, so immersed in the learning of Greece and Rome, and so passionately committed to the ideals of religious reform. In England in particular, medieval systems of thought displayed an amazing tenacity and new ideas were linked as surely with the past as were the men who espoused them. Had not Solomon's fleet sailed westwards towards the fabled isles of Ophir? Had not Seneca predicted the discovery of America in his *Medea*?

> Venient annis
> Secula seris, quando Oceanus vincula rerum
> Laxet, et ingens pateat tellus.
> *(Mundus Alter et Idem, p. 11)*

Such questions preoccupied contemporary scholars. Theirs was less an age of 'discovery' in the absolute sense than of excavation, of finding things lost, of fulfilling oracles and prophecies. At what precise point emulation overtook imitation it is difficult to say. At the beginning of the Renaissance Petrarch revitalized the literary world by discovering Cicero's letters neglected and unnoticed in the library of a monastery; a century or so later scholars such as Lorenzo Valla began to analyse original Greek and Hebrew texts in an attempt to supplant the claims of tradition by those of truth; in 1506, just two years before Michelangelo began work on the Sistine Chapel roof, the astonishing Laocoon group was dug up amid the ruins of the Emperor Titus' villa. The past exercised a powerful influence on the present. The reformers of Wittenberg and Geneva claimed not to have established a new religion but to have rediscovered the original, to have restored Christianity to its pristine purity thereby fulfilling the prophecies of Revelation. Such was the complex intellectual heritage of Joseph Hall who describes himself in the preface to his *Characters of Vertues and Vices* (1608) as one who 'in worthy examples hold imitation better than invention'. Yet he has followed the path of Theophrastus with 'an higher and wider step' for to him the truth has been divinely revealed whereas the philosopher received only 'the Acts of an inbred law, in the Sinai of Nature'.

We think of the Elizabethan age as one of expansion and change, and so undeniably it was, but it was also an age labouring under a sense of hubris and guilt. New ways of thought were emerging but were not yet fully born. The advancement of learning which so heartened Bacon also inspired Marlowe's handling of the legend of Faust:

> Whose fiendful fortune may exhort the wise
> Only to wonder at unlawful things,
> Whose deepness doth entice such forward wits,
> To practise more than heavenly power permits.

Leonardo da Vinci kept his notebooks in a personal code and was commonly believed to be possessed. Cornelius Agrippa had a reputation for necromancy, and while Hall was still a fellow at Emmanuel College, Cambridge, Giordano Bruno was burned by the Inquisition. The sixteenth century saw the emergence of a new 'scientific' approach to astronomy, but it was also the age of the great witch-craze, an intolerant age of which the Council of Trent is as typical as the voyaging of Columbus and Cavendish. New ideas were not easily received. Even serious cartographers such as Ortelius and Mercator still decorated tracts of unexplored country with pictures and legends reminiscent of the Hereford Mappa Mundi. Donne's 'new philosophy' called less in doubt than one might imagine. The soul of Elizabeth Drury passes to heaven in the traditional way without stopping to notice whether the element of fire is there or not. For Joseph Hall the new astronomy was to mean very little. 'Nothing is more evident', he conceded, 'than that there have been further discoveries made of the visible and materiall heavens ... but into the spirituall Heaven, in vaine shall we expect any further insight, then the already-revealed will of the Father hath vouchsafed to open to us.' In his *Mundus Alter et Idem* the new geography provided him with an excellent vehicle for assailing the moral failings of the old world.

Like most Reformers, Hall stiffly opposed himself to what he regarded as the 'superstitions' of popery, yet he retained a firm belief in witchcraft, lycanthropy, and exorcism. Whereas we commonly interpret his age as a turning-point in human history, he saw it as the sad culmination of a sequence of events begun by the Fall and destined to end in a cosmic cataclysm. For him the pivotal moment in human history was that of the Incarnation. He identified the Pope with the Antichrist and expected the end of the world if not in his own lifetime at least in that of his children. In reading his works, therefore, we must try to see the world through his eyes, the eyes of a Calvinist minister assured of his own salvation who adhered to a strictly providential view of history and interpreted everything in severely moral terms. Yet his was a subtle, witty, and complex intelligence. A fiery denouncer of the enormities of his day, he was also a spiritual adventurer, a great traveller in the realms of divine meditation where the mind admits 'of all material objects, as if they were so altogether transparent, that through them I might see the wonderfull prospects of another world'. For him, as for so many of the great contemporary mystics and contemplatives,

the material world was itself a sort of 'allegory', a divinely
written 'book' whose every word and line pointed to a deeper
level of meaning beyond. His attitude was that of the
'contemptus mundi': contempt for the frailties and evils of
human life, which as a Calvinist minister he felt obliged to
condemn, combined with an insistence upon purely spiritual
values, the values of the 'invisible world' to which he felt
mysteriously drawn. Not surprisingly, therefore, meditation
and complaint form the two most prevalent modes of his
literary output. I have attempted a study of both, at first
separately, and then of their fusion in the homily, the genre
perhaps best suited to Hall's genius. To the details of his
biography I have paid less attention, believing with his friend
and physician Sir Thomas Browne that 'his owne works are
the best monument, and character of himself.' In my
introductory remarks, however, I have endeavoured to place
his religious and devotional attitudes in the context of
contemporary debate and to supply such biographical and
historical information as I believe to be essential to an
understanding of the literary works. After his own fashion I
have attempted to observe a 'wise moderation' in the use of
such background material. In every case I have tried to let the
texts themselves determine my method.

My study falls into three sections. The first is concerned
with the satiric writings: the *Virgidemiarum, Mundus Alter et
Idem*, the *Characters of Vertues and Vices*, and some of the
controversial tracts. The second takes as its theme the
predominantly contemplative works, in particular the various
collections of 'extemporal' and 'deliberate' meditations and the
great series of *Contemplations* on the Bible. The final section
concerns itself exclusively with the sermons, considered
principally as vehicles for the fusion of satire and meditation.
Much of my work involves a complete reassessment of the
importance of Hall not merely as an 'influence'—for this has
always been recognized—but as a creative artist in his own
right, as an important figure in the development of English
satire, and a prime-mover in the great contemplative revival of
the seventeenth century. What I hope will emerge from this
reassessment is first of all a new awareness of the intrinsic
excellence of Hall's satiric writings together with their

relevance to the religious, social, and political problems of their time. Secondly I hope to rescue the meditations and contemplations from certain misinterpretation at the hands of a few recent critics, and undeserved neglect at the hands of most. Finally and perhaps most important of all, I hope that the homilies may once again take their deserved place alongside those of Andrewes and Donne as among the most outstanding productions of English pulpit oratory.

Having explained the purpose and scope of this work, I would also like to take this opportunity of acknowledging its debt to the many distinguished scholars without whose liberal advice and assistance it could never have been written. In particular I wish to express my deep gratitude to my teacher and friend, Dr Howard Erskine-Hill, for his generosity, guidance, and patience. More than anyone else he has helped to give a sense of purpose and direction to my studies and has remained throughout a source of inspiration and encouragement. Secondly, I am much indebted to Professor Ian Jack for first introducing me to the works of Joseph Hall and for the interest he has always shown in the development and success of my research. Thirdly, to Professor Fitzroy Pyle, of Trinity College, Dublin, I can only express my sincerest gratitude for favours too numerous to mention. I have also greatly benefited from the constructive criticism of Dr J. C. A. Rathmell, Professor Dominic Baker-Smith, Mr R. R. Bolgar, and Professor G. R. Elton. Finally, a special word of thanks to the Master and Members of the Drapers' Company of London for their generous patronage, and to the Master and Fellows of Pembroke College, Cambridge for electing me into the Drapers' Research Fellowship which has enabled me to write this book: *Nec procurabo malum domui aut sociis.*

CONTENTS

ILLUSTRATIONS

Terra Australis Incognita from *Mundus Alter et Idem* (1605?) by kind permission of the Master and Fellows of Pembroke College, Cambridge

facing p. 86

Abraham Ortelius, *Epitome of the Theater of the Worlde* (1603), Map One, by permission of the Syndics of Cambridge University Library

facing p. 87

ABBREVIATIONS

The following abbreviations have been used throughout for the various collected editions of Hall's works.

Works i   *The Works of Joseph Hall B. of Exeter* (London, 1634)

Works ii   *The Second Tome: Containing The Contemplations upon the History of the New Testament, now complete: Together with Divers Treatises not hitherto reduced to the greater Volume: And Some others never till now Published* (London, 1634)

Works iii   *Divers Treatises, Written upon severall Occasions, By Joseph Hall late Bishop of Norwich, The Third Tome. Now first collected into one Volume, and digested in the Order designed by the Author* (London, 1662)

Olive-Tree   *The Shaking of the Olive-Tree, The Remaining Works of that Incomparable Prelate Joseph Hall . . . with Some Specialities of Divine Providence in his Life Noted by His own Hand. Together with His Hard Measure: Written also by Himself,* 2nd edn. (London, 1660)

Works ed.   *The Works of Joseph Hall, D.D.,* 12 vols. (Oxford,
P. Hall   1837–9)

Works ed.   *The Works of the Right Reverend Joseph Hall, D.D.,* 10
P. Wynter   vols. (Oxford, 1863)

Poems   *The Poems of Joseph Hall,* ed. Arnold Davenport (Liverpool, 1949)

Seventeenth-century spelling and punctuation have been preserved throughout, and every effort has been made to quote from either the first or best contemporary edition of each work. In the interest of clarity, however, contractions have normally been expanded, and modern orthography has been adopted for 'u' and 'v'.

Further Abbreviations:

ELN   *English Language Notes*

HLQ   *Huntington Library Quarterly*

MLR   *Modern Language Review*

PMLA   *Publications of the Modern Language Association of America*

RES   *Review of English Studies*

STC   *Short-Title Catalogue*

INTRODUCTION: THE MAN AND HIS IDEAS

Once a writer of enormous popularity, Joseph Hall has now been almost totally eclipsed by the revival of interest in his contemporaries, Andrewes and Donne. Surprisingly, modern studies of the metaphysical and meditative schools have left his work virtually untouched, yet this neglect is comparatively recent. During the last century, there appeared no fewer than three editions of his voluminous collected works together with two full-length biographies. He was even the subject of an historical novel by Emma Marshall.[1] Today, however, Hall's writings, though frequently referred to, are seldom read, and he is remembered principally as the author of the *Virgidemiarum* and the antagonist who provoked Milton's invaluably autobiographical *Apology* during the Smectymnuan debate. Indeed there can be few literary figures of equivalent stature who remain so obviously underrated. In his own day Hall was acknowledged as a great literary innovator, a leader of fashion. He pioneered the development of formal verse satire during the 1590s, began the long tradition of the Theophrastan character, produced the first collection of 'familiar' epistles, fostered the great contemplative revival of the early seventeenth century, and together with Lord Bacon, helped to effect one of the most important changes in the direction of English prose style. He was also one of the most outstanding preachers of his time and his influence is duly acknowledged, if infrequently examined, in most studies of Jacobean and Caroline homiletics. Indeed students in all the fields I have mentioned acknowledge Hall's influence *en passant*, and this in itself is part of the problem. He has dwindled to an 'influence', with the result that knowledge of his own career and achievements is fragmentary and inconclusive. He is the subject of chapters rather than books. He has been studied in relation to the history of various important themes and genres, but a thorough examination of his own work has yet to appear. Despite his importance in ecclesiastical affairs there is no modern biography, and such studies as are available are all of the rather generalized 'life and works' variety.[2] Little if any attempt has been made to assess his importance as a literary artist. This is the purpose of the present study.

The range of the extant material is dauntingly wide: the last edition of the collected *Works* ran to some ten weighty volumes. In an age when variety was an acknowledged aesthetic principle Hall could well feel proud of the incredible diversity of his own literary output. In dedicating the first collection of his works to James I he remarks that:

seldome any man hath offered to your Royall hands a greater bundle of his owne thoughts . . . nor perhaps more varietie of discourse: for here shall your Majestie finde Moralitie, like a good handmaid, waiting on Divinitie; and Divinitie, like some great Lady, every day in severall dresses; Speculation interchanged with experience; Positive Theologie with Polemicall; Textuall with discursorie; Popular with Scholasticall.[3]

With so much to choose from, and so many profitable avenues of inquiry, I have decided to concentrate upon the works of satire and meditation not in an attempt to diminish in any way the rich diversity of Hall's writings but in order to suggest their underlying unity. Satire and meditation reflect the two most prevalent modes of his moral and religious outlook, and for the better expression of both he introduced to English letters a variety of new literary forms. Yet it was in the ancient form of the homily that he achieved the perfect fusion of the two modes, and that his writing attained its finest balance.

In the strict sense of the terms Hall was neither philosopher nor theologian, but an impassioned devotionalist deeply convinced of the moral efficacy of imaginative literature. Though aesthetically an irrepressible innovator, he remained to the end theologically orthodox and conservative. Essentially he was a lifelong contemplative. 'I shame not to professe', he tells us, 'that I have passed my most, and best hours in quiet Meditation; wherein I needed not bend mine edge against any

Adversarie, but Satan, and mine own corruptions: These controversorie points I have rather crost in my way, then taken along with me.'4 Yet despite this disclaimer Hall was a man of blazing indignation—as the greatest contemplatives so often are. His childhood was spent among convinced Puritans, and however he came to differ from them later in matters of ecclesiastical polity, he retained to the end their sense of elect isolation in a sinful world, their determined resolution to bear witness to the truth despite the cost. When he meets with a 'froward generation' he must call it so, and even in his moments of contemplative retirement he 'bends his edge' against his own corruptions.5 Complaint and satire force themselves upon him, disrupting the tranquillity of his private devotions. In 'holy Rage' he must 'chide the world, that did my thoughts offend'.6 Under the influence of Calvin, he came to regard 'fraternal castigation' as a Christian duty. As a minister he exhorted the 'sonnes of Levi' to 'consecrate' their hands in the 'holy slaughter of vice', to let their voice 'bee both a trumpet to incite, and a two-edged sword to wound and kill'.7 The imagery is worth noting. For Hall, life was a relentless battle against the stratagems of Satan in a world rapidly approaching its dissolution. Such dim glimpses of the eternal city as were enjoyed atop the 'mount of contemplation' served rather to fortify the Christian warrior against his spiritual enemies, than to inspire a self-imposed, and from Hall's point of view 'monkish', retirement from the material world. Unlike Hamlet he revelled in the task of putting to rights a world so grossly out of joint:

What if we cannot turne the streame? Yet wee must swim against it: even without conquest, it is glorious to have resisted: in this alone they are enemies, that doe nothing. Thus, as one that delights more in amendment, than excuse, I have both censured and directed.8

Hall's devotional and meditative works complement his works of satire and controversy. Together they display the positive and negative aspects of the one outlook, the two facets of the ancient 'contemptus mundi'. In his own epistle 'Of the contempt of the world' Hall teaches how 'to distinguish wisely, betwixt a Stoicall dulnesse, and a Christian contempt'. 'What is fame', he asks, but smoak? and metall, but drosse? and pleasure, but a pill in sugar? Let some Gallants condemne this, as the voice of a Melancholike Scholler: I speake that which they shall feele, and shall confesse . . . All these earthly delights, if they were sound, yet how short they are! and if they could be long, yet how unsound! . . . This ground beares none but maples, hollow and fruitlesse; or, like the banks of the dead Sea, a faire apple, which under a red side containes nothing but dust . . . Goe then, ye wise idolatrous Parasites, and erect shrines, and offer sacrifices to your God, the world, and seek to please him with your base and servile devotions: it shall be long enough ere such religion shall make you happy. You shal at last forsake those alters, emptie and sorrowfull. How easy is it for us Christians, thus to insult over the worldling, that thinks himselfe worthy of envie? How easie to turne off the world with a scornfull repulse; and when it makes us the Devils profer, *All these will I give thee*, to returne *Peters* answer, *Thy silver and thy gold perish with thee?* . . . Fasten your eyes upon your future glory, and see how meanly you shall esteeme these early graces.[9]

'Censure' and 'direction' belong together: 'who but a *Caine* is not his brothers keeper?'. The writing of satire was a necessary consequence of Hall's concept of verity. 'Truth', he explains, 'is when we speak as we think, and think as it is.'[10] Meditation discovers the reality, satire explodes illusion. 'Truth be thy speed, and Truth thy Patron bee', says the prologue to the *Virgidemiarum*.[11] Similarly in sermon after sermon Hall apologizes for focusing upon unpleasant realities in such a vehement, forthright manner, but he does so, he tells us, after the example of one of the greatest contemplatives of them all, St Bernard of Clairvaux. Like him, he must speak 'plaine truth, in a plaine fashion, *nuda nude*'.[12] Indeed the moral duty of reprehension is the subject of many of his own extemporal meditations, and the aesthetic manifestation of such reprehension, one remembers, is satire or complaint:

I see Iron first heated red hot in the fire, and after beaten and hardened with cold water. Thus will I deale with an offending friend: first heat him with deserved praise of his vertue, and then beat upon him with reprehension: so good nurses, when their children are fallen, first take them up and speake them faire, chide them afterwards: Gentle speech is a good preparative for rigor. He shall see that I love him, by my approbation; and that I love not his faults by my reproofe. If he love himselfe, he will love those that mislike his vices; and if he love not himselfe, it matters not whether he love me.[13]

To us, the worlds of satire and meditation may seem distant, if not mutually exclusive. Satire is assured, aggressive, and public, meditation self-analytic, devotional, and private. Yet consider the careers of the great Puritan leaders of the sixteenth and seventeenth centuries whose relentlessly introspective diaries shed such revealing light upon their stern, assertive, public images.[14] The men who denounce are commonly the men who mediate and analyse. Their convictions are born of conflict, their strength of character is the product of ceaseless wrestling with their own recalcitrant nature. So it was with Joseph Hall, and we must therefore know something of the man before we can hope to come to grips with the work. A clear understanding of his religious convictions helps greatly towards an appreciation of his aesthetic achievement: he was an unashamedly didactic author.

In Hall's age the literary form which afforded perhaps the best opportunities for the self-justification so many seemed impelled to supply, was the spiritual autobiography, and writing the account of his own life, Hall tells us that

some that sate at the sterne of the Church, had me in great Jelousie for too much favour of Puritanisme ... under how dark a Cloud I was hereupon, I was so sensible, that I plainly told the Lord Archbishop of *Canterbury* [William Laud] that rather then I would be obnoxious to those slanderous tongues of his misinformers, I would cast up my Rochet; I knew I went right wayes ...[15]

This powerful sense of personal assurance and destiny pervades and unifies all of Hall's writings, but in order to understand how it developed we must first examine his background and upbringing.

Joseph Hall, successively Bishop of Exeter and Norwich, was born at Bristow Park, Ashby-de-la-Zouch on 1 July 1574. His father, as he tells us himself, held the 'government' of the town of Ashby under Henry Hastings, third Earl of Huntingdon, President of the Council of the North, and for a short time gaoler of Mary Queen of Scots. Since the Earl was of staunchly

Puritan sympathies, so of necessity was the town.[16] Its incumbent was Anthony Gilby, a celebrated Marian exile and one deeply suspected by the authorities, who impressed himself strongly upon Hall's mother, and whom the bishop was later to recall as one of the 'godfathers' of the presbyterian system of lay-eldership against which he wrote some of his most forceful controversial tracts, including the famous *Episcopacie by Divine Right* (1640).[17] But undoubtedly the strongest influence on the young Hall was that of his family.

Being intensely religious, Hall's parents apparently 'devoted' him to the ministry from an early age. His mother he remembered as a saint whose constant theme was 'Temptations, Desertions, and Spiritual Comforts'. It was she who was chiefly responsible for his religious education. 'Never any lips', he wrote, 'have read to me such feeling Lectures of piety; neither have I known any Soul, that more accurately practised them, then her own.'[18] No less devout was the father whose resignation in the face of death became for his son a supreme example of the confidence of the elect.[19] Together, Hall's parents aspired to the ideal of the godly Protestant family, and under Gilby's guidance, and Huntingdon's patronage lived to see many of their most cherished ambitions fulfilled. For them at least, Ashby was the perfect environment. The famous Grammar School in which their son received his first education was run by a 'series of radical Protestant masters'.[20] Among its many distinguished alumni was Hall's close contemporary, William Bradshaw, author of *English Puritanisme* (1605), one of the most important statements of the dissenting point of view. For a short period in the early 1590s Hall returned to teach at Ashby himself, but undoubtedly its most celebrated master was his brother-in-law, John Brinsley, whom another former pupil, the astrologer William Lilly, remembered as 'a strict Puritan, not conformable wholly to the Ceremonies of the Church of *England*'.[21] Brinsley was the author of *Ludus Literarius: or, The Grammar Schoole* (1612), an extremely enlightened educational tract for which Hall wrote a commendatory preface. His son accompanied Hall, then Dean of Worcester, to the Synod of Dort in 1618 as his amanuensis and receives great praise for his defence of pedobaptism in one of the later theological works.[22]

Despite the relative poverty of his family—there were nine other children to be provided for—Hall's father decided to send him to Cambridge. Naturally he chose the recently established Puritan stronghold of Emmanuel College, in which the Hastings family took a direct interest.[23] Here, Hall moved in exactly the same sort of circles as he had just left. His tutor was Nathaniel Gilby, the Ashby preacher's son, and he met and engaged in theological discussion with William Perkins (1558–1602), one of the most influential Puritans of his day, and a foremost exponent of the 'plain' style of preaching.[24] But his real spiritual mentor was Richard Greenham (1535?–1594), the celebrated preacher of Dry Drayton who enjoyed the patronage of Huntingdon's wife.[25] Hall refers to him as 'that Saint of ours', and seems to have particularly approved of his *Treatise of the Sabbath*, a work banned by Archbishop Whitgift.[26] Since Greenham was also one of the first Protestant Englishmen actively to encourage the practice of divine meditation, his influence upon his young disciple must have been considerable. It cannot be mere coincidence that Hall was destined to distinguish himself most in the field of meditation. Greenham, he tells us, 'excelled in experimentall divinitie', the same sort of divinity promoted by his mother, and it therefore seems likely that he is largely responsible for the strong emphasis upon 'practical' Christianity which runs throughout Hall's entire canon, for his insistence that 'religion . . . is not a schoole of Learning, but a discipline of living.'[27] His *Resolutions and Decisions of Divers Practicall Cases of Conscience* (1649) owes not a little to Greenham's known pastoral methods, although the influence of Perkins is undoubtedly strong here also.[28]

With one short break Hall stayed at Emmanuel, first as a student and then as a fellow, from 1589 to 1601. His reputation for scholarship was universally acknowledged, and for two consecutive years he was chosen to the rhetoric lectureship in the university.[29] During the same period he wrote his first literary works: the *Virgidemiarum* (1597–1598), a collection of six books of formal verse satires after the Roman manner, and *Mundus Alter et Idem* (not published until 1605) a prose satire in the form of an imaginary journey to the Antipodes. They represent his first reaction to the highly ungodly world outside his own small circle, a world he was soon called upon to enter.

Scarcely a year after his ordination in 1600, Hall became chaplain to Sir Robert Drury of Hawstead in Suffolk, reputedly one of the wealthiest men in England. His wife Anne was the granddaughter of Lord Keeper Bacon, and, therefore, niece of Sir Francis. By inviting Hall to accompany him on a visit to the Continent in 1605, her brother Sir Edmund Bacon gave him his first real introduction to the bugbears of his childhood: Roman Catholicism, the Jesuits, and the Inquisition.[30] Indeed so far as Hall was concerned, this was the sole purpose of the journey. He went to have his prejudices confirmed and returned entirely successful. Never after could he contemplate 'peace with Rome'.[31] The prospect of the Spanish match filled him with horror, and the historian and letter writer, James Howell, tells us that he went so far in his support for the Elector Palatine, giving him the title of King of Bohemia in his 'Pulpit-Prayer', that 'he had a check for his pains'.[32]

The same year in which he journeyed to the Continent Hall published his first two 'centuries' of *Meditations and Vowes, Divine and Morall*. So well were they received that they gained him entrance to the Court of Prince Henry, the eldest son of James I, who invited him, through his governor Sir Thomas Chaloner, to become his chaplain.[33] The offer was entirely welcome. Hall had long entertained great hopes of Henry upon the occasion of whose birth in 1594 he had composed a pastoral modelled upon Virgil's famous fourth *Eclogue* predicting the return of the golden age. The poem does not appear to have been published and unfortunately has not survived but Hall was careful to alert the public to its existence in 1603 when he published *The Kings Prophecie: or Weeping Ioy*, an accomplished, tactful poem marking both the death of Elizabeth and the accession of her successor. Acceptance of the prince's offer constituted a turning-point in Hall's life. Moving in the unfamiliar surroundings in which he now found himself he soon made the acquaintance of a wide variety of courtiers, scholars, and divines, and perhaps for the first time fully emerged from the rather sheltered Puritan atmosphere of his upbringing. His writings reflect the change. The

Epistles (1608–1611) are addressed to such noted public figures as Sir John Harington, the third Earl of Essex, the ageing actor Edward Alleyn, Sir David Murray, Bodley's first librarian, Thomas James, and the founder of Charterhouse, Thomas Sutton. About the same time Hall also made the acquaintance of Fulke Greville, a man with whom he shared many religious attitudes, and one of whose closest friends, Samuel Burton, Archdeacon of Gloucester, was his cousin.[34]

While still in attendance upon Prince Henry, Hall, now a married man, left Hawstead due to a disagreement with Sir Robert concerning his stipend. Instead he accepted Sir Edward Denny's offer of Waltham Holy Cross in Essex.[35] This proved to be one of the most fateful decisions of his life. At one stroke he gained a powerful patron and lifelong friend. Denny, who was created first Earl of Norwich in 1626, was an influential man with powerful connections. His son-in-law was James Hay, a particular favourite of James I who created him first Earl of Carlisle. Hall accompanied Hay's rather flamboyant embassy to Paris in 1616.[36] Lady Denny was the daughter of Thomas Cecil, eldest son of Lord Burghley and first Earl of Exeter, and it may well have been this Cecil connection which secured for Hall the bishopric of Exeter in 1627. He must have enjoyed some influential support since the Duke of Buckingham apparently desired the position for a candidate of his own choosing.[37] That Hall was indeed supported by the Cecils seems all the more likely since the wife of the second Earl, William Cecil, was Sir Robert Drury's sister. The disagreement over the stipend does not seem to have embittered either party, and when Elizabeth Drury died in 1610 Hall wrote two prefatory poems to Donne's *Anniversaries*. Thereafter he remained one of Donne's closest friends, and presumably a close friend of Drury's also. The 'witty and bold Atheist, one Mr. Lilly', who caused him such problems during his early days at Hawstead was none other than Donne's brother-in-law.[38]

Meanwhile Hall's literary reputation was climbing steadily. While the *Meditations* sped through a series of editions, the appearance of *The Arte of Divine Meditation* (1606) consolidated their author's position at the head of the great contemplative revival. Soon afterwards the publication of the

Characters of Vertues and Vices (1608) and the *Epistles* (1608–1611) assured his place in literary history by adding two new genres to English letters. Between the years 1612 and 1634 he was engaged upon his most ambitious project yet, the enormously popular *Contemplations upon the Principall Passages of the Holy Storie.* In all departments of ecclesiastical life he was rapidly becoming one of the best-known churchmen of his day. Soon after his introduction to court he received the prestigious invitation to preach at Paul's Cross, delivering his first sermon, *Pharisaisme and Christianity,* in 1608. Two years later he dedicated his first full-length controversial tract, *A Common Apologie of the Church of England, against the unjust challenges of the over-iust sect, commonly called Brownists,* to the Archbishop of Canterbury, George Abbot. The work is a defence of all things established and we may well pause to inquire how it came to be written by a native of Ashby-de-la-Zouch, a parishoner of Anthony Gilby, and a fellow of Emmanuel College. What did Hall actually believe?

The usual answer is that he was a 'moderate', that his was a 'via media' between the extremes of Laud and Cartwright, and so far as it goes this is undoubtedly correct. 'Hee was one', says John Whitefoote, 'whose *moderation was known to all men.*'[39] Indeed it was quite celebrated, and it is at least arguable that had like-minded churchmen prevailed, English history might have followed a far different course. This much is clear. The difficulty is that descriptions of Hall's moderation are usually couched in such negative terms that what he did not believe emerges far more clearly than what he did.[40] All too frequently he is made to appear a man of little original thought, a tireless compromiser whose beliefs are pieced together from the convictions of others. Even at the distance of almost four hundred years it is amazing how potent the propaganda of the Civil War still remains. Today to call Hall an episcopalian Calvinist, which is exactly what he was, seems a contradiction in terms: after all Puritans were Calvinists and bishops were Arminians. Yet the moment one begins to examine the matter more closely such bland generalizations suddenly collapse. No less a Puritan than John Milton came to espouse the views of Arminius, while many of the bishops were in fact far more Calvinist than those who opposed them.[41] It was perfectly

possible to accept Calvin's views on the nature of the deity and
the sacraments without also accepting as universally binding
the Genevan system of Church government. Not even upon
the Continent did it enjoy such unchallenged acceptance.
Different systems operated in Strassbourg, Basle, Zurich,
Wittenberg, and almost all the other major centres of the
Reformation. What Gilby had objected to was not bishops but
Lord bishops, the 'Romish' combination of spiritual and
temporal power.[42] In his own controversial writings, Hall is
therefore quick to distinguish between temporal authority
conferred as a mark of honour by the sovereign, and spiritual
authority conferred directly by Christ and his Apostles.[43] Only
the latter he deems essential to episcopacy. As Patrick
Collinson points out, Gilby's position at Ashby was itself
episcopal in all but name, and even so noted a Puritan as Sir
Walter Mildmay, founder of Emmanuel College, opposed
Parliamentary attempts to introduce the Presbyterian system
of Church government in the 1580s.[44] Hall's position, therefore, was by no means anomalous. Like Archbishop Abbot he
was a Calvinist in theological outlook while remaining at the
same time a confirmed supporter of the established episcopal
system.[45]

Hall's Calvinism pervades his biblical *Contemplations*. Here
he is preoccupied with the doctrine of election, with the
mysterious will of a supremely transcendent God. As a result
he is also fascinated by techniques of meditation and self-
analysis, by the art of detecting within oneself the signs of
election or reprobation. Yet he is careful to shun the fanatical
doctrines of the Antinomians. We must live, he tells us, *as if*
everything depended upon our own efforts: 'Ita ergo nos
gerere debemus in tota vitae nostrae institutione, et in
operando salutem nostram, acsi nulli occulto Dei decreto
subessemus . . . Sic itaque fidei, paenitentiae, bonisque operi-
bus danda est opera, quasi ab illis unice penderet salus, et
immunitas ab omni reprobationis periculo.'[46] Good works are
the sign, though not the cause, of election. 'The way not to
presume upon salvation', he warns, 'is, in an humble modesty
to content our selves with the clearly revealed will of our
Maker; not prying into his counsells, but attending his
commands . . . It is for the heavenly Angels to climbe downe

the ladder from heaven to earth: It is for us onely to climbe up from earth to heaven.'[47] To begin 'at Gods eternall decree of our election, and thence descend to the effects of it in our effectuall calling' is a course 'saucily preposterous':

Wee have his word for this; that if wee do truly beleeve, repent, obey, persevere, wee shall bee saved . . . What need wee to look any further, than conscionably and cheerefully to do what we are enjoyned; and faithfully and comfortably to expect what hee hath promised?[48]

Everywhere he insists upon the importance of faith: 'faith is the grace that assents to, apprehends, applyes, appropriates Christ, and hereupon the uniting grace, and (which comprehends all) the saving grace.'[49] Reprobation is never overstressed. In a letter to Herman Hildebrandt of Bremen he writes that the sole cause of damnation is sin. To suggest otherwise is to attribute tyranny to God—a hateful way of speaking ('odiosae hujusmodi loquendi formulae'). Foreknowledge imposes no sort of compulsion upon the sinner.[50]

Such ideas as these exercised a profound effect upon Hall's attitude towards ecclesiastical polity. While acknowledging that the sole cause of reprobation was sin, he also warned against arrogating to oneself the judicial function of God. Appearances are deceptive: Eli misjudged Hannah, thereby demonstrating that a man can know only his own heart.[51] Therefore, by propounding impossible ideals of purity, and plunging themselves into a recurrent nightmare of excommunications and schisms, the Separatists had violated Christian charity. They were no better than the proud Pharisee in the parable. In striking contrast Hall felt entirely satisfied that a complete and thorough Reformation had occurred in the days of Edward VI and Elizabeth I. His image of the Church was not that of a small select group condemning the world from a pure parlour in Amsterdam, but of a vast 'drag-net' in which both good and evil mingle until God separates them.[52] To his way of thinking, such imperfections as the Church militant undoubtedly displayed were the necessary consequences, not of popish corruption, but of mortality. Perfection was attainable only in the world beyond, here there could be no Utopia: 'this power to purge out all corruptions, Christ hath not given us.'[53] Although his hatred of Rome was paramount, he was consequently unwilling to depart further from its ways than it had departed from its original purity: 'nihilo longius a Romana discedere Ecclesia, quam illa a se, a primigenia puritate discessisse deprehendatur.'[54] In so far as they had destroyed the 'foundation' of the faith the 'innovations' of the Papacy had, of course, to be rejected, but it was first essential to discover the exact nature of such innovations. Otherwise, one ran the risk of subverting Christ's own intentions. Following this line of thought, Hall went so far as to assert that despite its manifold corruptions the Church of Rome remained a 'true, visible Church'—and this although he repeatedly identified the Pope with the Antichrist. Predictably this involved him in heated controversy, especially after the publication in 1628 of *The Olde Religion*, a work in which he asserted that 'the true Principles of Christianitie, which it [the Roman Church] maintaines, maintaine life in that Church; the errors which it holds, together with those Principles, struggle with that life, and threaten an extinction . . .'[55] In order to quell the storm of protest, he produced an apology entitled *The Reconciler* (1629) complete with the supporting testimonies of Thomas Morton, John Davenant, Gilbert Primrose, and John Prideaux.[56] Also, in an 'advertisement' added to *The Olde Religion* itself, he explained that by 'true, visible Church', he did not intend 'a true-beleeving Church', a sense 'as far wide from my words, or thoughts, as from truth it selfe':

That she is truely visible, abates nothing of her abhominations: For who sees not, that, *Visible*, referres to outward profession; True, to some essentiall principles of Christianitie, neither of them to soundnesse of beleefe; So as these two may too well stand together, a true visible Church, in respect of outward profession of Christianity; and an hetericall, Apostaticall, Anti-christian Synagogue in respect of doctrine and practice; Grant the Romanists to bee but Christians, how corrupt soever, and wee cannot deny them, the name of a Church: Outward visibility gives them no clayme either to truth, or Salvation.[57]

But the hub of the dispute, as everyone knew, was not Rome but the Church of England. As Hall himself said, his crime lay not in what he had written, but in his elevation to the episcopacy.[58] It suited the Puritans' aims wilfully to misunder-

stand his attitude towards Rome, thereby suggesting that all
bishops were popish. Upon this issue, however, Hall's views
were entirely consistent. Whatever may have been the reason
for his refusal of the see of Gloucester in 1625 it cannot have
been one of conscience, since he had publicly defended
episcopacy as early as 1610, repeating King James's dictum,
'No bishop, no King.'[59] It is very noticeable that in all
controversies concerning ceremony and ritual what he emphasizes is the duty of civil obedience, the right of the monarch to
dictate the form though not the substance of religious practice.
With the question of episcopacy, however, he deals differently.
Here it is a matter of divine authority, and in this belief he
himself accepted the bishopric of Exeter in 1627 and
welcomed his translation to Norwich in 1641. With the
publication of *Episcopacie by Divine Right* the previous year
and his subsequent contributions to the Smectymnuan debate,
he emerged as one of the most forceful defenders of the
established system. Episcopacy, he pointed out, was almost as
old as Christianity itself and could be traced back to the days
of the Apostles. On the other hand, the Genevan system of lay-
eldership was an 'innovation' as vicious as any perpetrated by
Rome. Gilby was quite wrong to suggest otherwise, and in any
case a city state could not become the model for a monarchy.
Then again, how equal was Calvin to the other Genevan
presbyters? To all intents and purposes he was himself the
Bishop of Geneva: in fact 'no Bishop in *England* swayed more,
then he did in that Church.'[60]

In Hall's opinion the principle of hierarchy was essential to
the well-being of the Christian community, yet he was very
careful not to condemn the continental Churches. Instead he
attributes their differences to a wide range of historical causes,
and contents himself with the conclusion that though imperfect from the point of view of ecclesiastical organization, they
remain nevertheless true Reformed Churches in the eyes of
God.[61] In this respect his arguments strike some of the most
rational notes of the controversy. They might have sounded
even more convincing, and certainly more acceptable to his
opponents, had Laud allowed them to pass uncensored.
However, as Prynne was quick to point out at the Archbishop's trial, he did not.[62] He objected to Hall's identification of

the Pope with the Antichrist, and insisted that episcopacy differed from the priesthood in order rather than merely in degree. Unwisely Hall acquiesced, but the very existence of such corrections illustrates the differences between the two men. Laud had never trusted him and their former association had not been happy. Archiepiscopal spies had infiltrated Hall's diocese and he was three times on his knees before Charles I. Even when no charge could be found against him, Laud's records sometimes display only a grudging acknowledgement of his conformity.[63] As we have seen, he finally threatened to resign rather than continue under such circumstances.

In his own way the Archbishop was just as extreme as the Puritans he persecuted, and who in their turn persecuted him, but Hall's outlook had always been different. He came into conflict with the Arminians as early as 1617 when he accompanied King James to Scotland in order to impose conformity, including episcopacy, upon a highly suspicious Kirk. It was the time of the projected Spanish match and his colleagues were Bishops Montague, Andrewes, Neile, and Neile's chaplain, William Laud—Arminians all, and all unpopular. Only Hall was well received, and perhaps for this very reason left Scotland before any of the others at his own request. Recriminations, however, were quick to follow, and he soon found himself charged with an 'over plausible Demeanure and doctrine to that already prejudicate people.'[64] In order to clear himself he wrote a letter at the king's request to William Struthers defending the Five Articles of Perth, albeit in highly conciliatory terms. His emphasis falls upon civil obedience: 'one King may . . . prescribe to two Churches, whereof he is head . . . authority may presse the use of things indifferent.'[65] He never speaks of the intrinsic worth of ceremonies, only of 'holy decency' in approaching a transcendent God.[66] Nor does he ever seem to have fully approved of the administration of the oath *ex officio mero* whereby defendants in the High Commission were forced either to incriminate themselves or be held in contempt of court. Prior to the fall of Laud Hall's statements on this issue are cautious and restrained, but it becomes quite clear from a later work that he finds the whole procedure repulsive. One point, however, he makes consistently: he was never himself a member of the High Commission.⁶⁷ On the issue of episcopacy he believed just as strongly as did Laud in his own 'divine right', but his style of Church government was entirely different. On coming to Exeter, he tells us, he used 'all fair and gentle means' to win over the disaffected, with the result that after a short while he 'had not one Minister professedly opposite to the anciently received orders (for I was never guilty of urging any new Impositions) of the Church in that large Diocess'. Not surprisingly, complaints of 'my too much Indulgence to persons disaffected' arose on all sides, but Exeter itself seems to have enjoyed a unique calm.⁶⁸

A striking illustration of Hall's leniency and its consequences is supplied by *A Letter Lately sent by A Reverend Bishop From The Tower To A private Friend: and By him thought fit to be published* (1642). This document was the result of Hall's brief incarceration in the Tower from December 1641 to May 1642 and answers perfectly to the needs of the time by presenting a clear and forthright statement of his attitude towards his own role as a bishop. Here he tells us that he has used his clergy 'as if they had been all Bishops with me, or I onely a Presbyter with them' (p. 3). Here too he absolutely denies having ever suppressed preachers, imposed innovations either liturgical or ceremonial, administered offensive oaths, or arrogated to himself the trappings of temporal power. Even more interesting, however, is the reply by his unidentified correspondent Mr H.S. who expresses his astonishment at the treatment now being meted out to the bishop by those whom he had defended and protected with much danger to himself during the Laudian ascendancy. 'It is not full two yeares ago', he says,

when in that innovating age you suffered under storms and threats from over-busie instruments: every step waited on by intrapping spyes and informers; and brought so far into the mouth of danger, that that *Accuser, Kilvert,* durst openly threaten you, to be the next man designed for his Inquisition. How often have you stood as a shield betweene those men and danger, who can now complain you are a Bishop; when, if you had not been so, where had they been at this houre? How many of those Antiprelaticall men, even the most rigid of them, have we heard blessing God for such a Diocesan, by whose provision and government, great hath been the company of

Preachers; and acknowledging the Sun of the Gospel, with your approach, setting in your Western Sea, or rather rising there, in more perfect lustre, when the world justly complained it went downe in some other parts of the Kingdome? What prayers, what praises, what wishes were then, on all sides, poured out for you?[69]

Not the least fascinating aspect of this purposefully straightforward statement of the facts is the allusion to Richard Kilvert (d. 1649), the rather unsavoury tool in the Laudian attempt to destroy Bishop Williams. Kilvert was the man who discredited Williams's principal witness when he was arraigned on a trumped-up charge of betraying state secrets in 1634, and Kilvert was the man who profited so handsomely from the condemnation of the bishop three years later following the publication of the allegedly unorthodox treatise *The Holy Table,* a contribution to the controversy concerning the positioning of the altar. There can be no clearer indication of the danger in which Hall stood—and deliberately stood— then that he should have become the object of the open threats of this unscrupulous, mercenary lawyer.

Hindsight facilitates condemnation. Today it is easy to attack Hall for not completely repudiating Laud's emendations, for not speaking out clearly at such a critical moment in the Church's history. In reality, however, the issues were far less clear-cut than may now appear. *Episcopacie by Divine Right* had a long and complex history which illustrates better than anything else the difficulty of Hall's position. It began in October 1639 when, in a letter addressed to Laud, he professed himself scandalized at the repudiation of the whole episcopal system by George Graham, former Bishop of Orkney. He suggests the calling of a General Synod 'wherein all the reverend bishops, the chief of the learned and dignified clergy, and the professors, and some other eminent doctors of all the universities in all the said kingdoms, may be assembled, to pass their judgement (after free and full expectation) of these schismatical points, determined thus proudly and rashly by our northern neighbours.' This suggestion was respectfully rejected, but instead Laud urged Hall to undertake the defence of episcopacy himself.[70] Undoubtedly he felt that a clear declaration of support for the established system by a man hitherto so respected in Puritan circles would carry much weight. A more cynical view, however, might be that he was attempting to capitalize on whatever sympathy his own known hostility to Hall had undoubtedly generated in disaffected circles. After all, according to Smectymnuus, Hall was one of those bishops who *'have beene labouring these twelve yeeres to get off the name of Puritan, and yet it will not doe,* and because of this have beene printed *Tantum non in Episcopatu Puritani'*— Puritans in all but episcopacy![71]

In his reply to Laud's request Hall doubted the wisdom of assigning the task to any one individual for 'what will the vulgar be more apt to say than This is but one doctor's judgement?' The work should be accomplished, he suggests, by a committee of bishops composed of Archbishop Ussher, and Bishops Bedell, Leslie, Morton, Davenant, and Hall himself if Laud so desired it.[72] The selection is significant: it includes not a single Arminian. The Archbishop, however, was not to be deterred from his original plan and Hall finally agreed to write *Episcopacie by Divine Right.* But at this stage he also made the suggestion that his work should at least be proof-read by Laud's chaplains and that the Archbishop, should have power to amend it for, 'the more and the more judicious eyes pass upon it the better.'[73] Terrified of causing yet further schism, he was anxious to produce an *agreed* document. He even suggested that a synopsis of the work should be sent to all the other bishops to receive their signature of assent. His subsequent correspondence with Laud is quite fascinating, for nowhere is the conflict between moderation and extremism more clearly marked. At one point, for example, Hall concedes that, 'Your Grace observes truly some mitigation in stating the cause, which I confess to have purposely used out of a desire to hold as good terms with our neighbour churches abroad as I safely might.'[74] At another we hear that 'for that point of the degree or order of episcopacy, although I well knew the weight of it, yet I did purposely intend to waive it here, because both it fetcheth a great and learned part of the school upon us, and because I found it to be out of my way, since these factions with whom we deal deny both a several order and a several degree.' Nevertheless, he concludes, 'our tenet is doubtless most defensible.'[75] One

wonders, however, how 'doubtless' is to be interpreted. Laud
had to mention the matter twice, and even in the completed
version he finds Hall's emphasis still unsatisfactory: '[what]
you seem to pass by, as not much material in the question, is,
in our judgement here, the very main of the cause; and it is,
whether Episcopacy be an Order or Degree. An order
certainly, if it be of Divine and Apostolical institution.'[76] In the
event the emendation was made, and Hall's work was indeed
proof-read by another bishop, but not by any of those whose
names he had himself put forward. Matthew Wren, Laud's
strongest supporter in pursuing the policy of 'Thorough', was
its reader and critic.[77] One can only speculate upon Wren's
reaction to Hall's later, uncensored pronouncements—Laud
himself having warned of the dangers of an imprecise manner
of speaking, 'as if the Bishop's were but the title of honour,
and the same calling with a Priest.'[78] In *The Peace-Maker*
(1645), however, Hall asserts that Timothy, the hub of so
much episcopal debate, was chosen by the 'College of
Presbyters, to be the President of them, and that not without
some authority over the rest, but yet such as have the due
bounds and limits'. If the name 'bishop' displease, he
continues, 'let them call this man a Moderator, a President, a
Superintendent, an Overseer; Only for the fixednesse or
change of this person, let the ancient, and universall practise of
Gods Church be thought worthy to over-sway.'[79]

Apparently Hall had originally hoped that even despite
Laud's emendations, his own known antipathy towards Rome,
and mild manner of ecclesiastical government would carry the
day. When it became increasingly clear that this was not the
case, he allowed himself a far greater measure of freedom.
Laud, now a prisoner in the Tower, had manifestly failed, and
it was left to such survivors as himself to salvage as much of the
Anglican Church as possible. In one of the later contributions
to the Smectymnuan debate he assures his opponents that
there are many on the episcopal bench 'no lesse zealously
conscionable, though better tempered, then your selves' who
'conspire' with them in their opposition to 'loud Musick,
uncouth, and unedifying Anthems; a pompous superstitious
Altar-service'.[80] 'Particular incroachments' and 'innovations in
some few hands' are not, therefore, to be attributed to 'the

whole Church of *England*'.[81] This determination not to appear
a party man must be seen not merely as a matter of
compromise, but of fundamental conviction. Hall was one of
the first to realize that the Church stood in danger of tearing
itself apart, and he saw his own role as that of peacemaker. His
call for a Synod was a bid for unity not further division. In a
sermon appropriately entitled *The Mischief of Faction* delivered before the court in 1641, he made one of the most
courageous and impassioned protests against the party system
ever delivered by a member of the Caroline episcopal bench:

Good Lord what uncharitable censure [*sic*] are men apt to passe
upon each other; let a man be strict and austere in moral and divine
duties though never so peaceable, he is a Puritan, and every Puritan
is an Hyppocrite: Let him be more free, and give more scope to his
conversation though never so conscionable he is a Libertine; let him
make scruple but of any innovated forme, he is a Schismatick; let him
stand for the antiently received rites and government, he is a time-
serving Formalist; This is a *Diotrephes,* that an *Aerius,* this a scorner,
that a flatterer: In the mean time who can escape free? Surely, I that
taxe both shall be sure to be censured of both: shall be? yes am, to
purpose; and therein I joy, yea and will joy: What? a *neuter,* saies one,
what on both sides, sayes another; This is that I look't for; yes truly
brethren, ye have hit it right; I am and professe to be as the termes
stand, on neither, and yet of both parts; I am for the peace of both,
for the humour of neither; how should the morter or cement joyn the
stones together if it did not lie between both?[82]

It was this attitude perhaps more than anything else which
infuriated Milton. 'You would seem', he objects, 'not to have
joyn'd with the worst, and yet keep alooff off from that which
is best. I would you would either mingle, or part, most true it is
what *Savanarola* complaines, that while hee endeavour'd to
reforme the Church, his greatest enemies were still these
Lukewarm ones.'[83] But Hall could neither 'mingle' nor 'part':
such was the dilemma of the episcopalian Calvinist. His
'moderation' was not the result of deliberate trimming—although he does, of course, counsel compromise in matters
indifferent—but an essential element of his thought. He was
many years ahead of his time in the assertion that God allows
'much *latitude* in the free use of all . . . not prohibited.'[84]
Personally he thanks God that he has 'vouchsafed to keepe me

within the due lines of Devotion; not suffering me to wander into those two extremes, which I see and pitty in others.'[85] Theologians of the end of the century were to applaud his good sense. His tirelessly repeated message is that the essential tenets of Christianity are few and clear, and that all else is a matter for the individual conscience. Strangely enough, he would not consent to calling this the doctrine of *Adiaphora,* a term which for him implied a lack of concern for the truth.[86] Yet it cannot be denied that Martin Bucer's ideas are close to his own. 'I know no booke so necessary for these times', he writes, 'as that *De paucitate credendorum.*'[87] So it was that he favoured James I's abortive project for the establishment of a school of controversy at Chelsea, a sort of anti-heresy task force, to which all contentious matters might safely be relegated. He displayed equal enthusiasm for Charles I's restrictions on freedom of theological discussion. At all costs what he terms 'the *Belgick* disease' must not be allowed to spread to England.[88]

In every facet of theological controversy Hall holds fast to one principle: that the truth lies in moderation and is betrayed by extremes. In *A Plain and Familiar Explication of Christ's Presence in the Sacrament of his Body and Blood* he tells us that 'it is requisite we should here walk with a wary, and even foot as those that must tread in the midst betwixt profanenesse, and superstition; not affixing a deity upon the Elements on the one side, nor on the other sleighting them with a common regard.'[89] Similarly in *Cheirothesia,* a pamphlet on confirmation, we must 'walke with an even foot in the mid-way betwixt Romish Superstition, and profane neglect'.[90] In *Holy Decency in the Worship of God* 'wise Christians sit down in the mean' and it is 'meet for us to hold a midle way betwixt superstition, and neglect'.[91] In *Resolutions and Decisions of Divers Practicall Cases of Conscience* 'a Meane would do well betwixt two extremes' and we frequently 'walke in a middle way'.[92] In all cases of controversy the rule, enunciated most clearly in *Pax Terris* (1648), is the same:

A Christian man must walk with caution, and constantly preserve a middle way; shunning, on the one hand, that vague liberty of interpretation, which submits to no restraints of pious moderation;

and, on the other hand, those narrow limits of theological definition, within which some of our harsher legislators would utterly confine the enquiries of the Christian mind.[93]

But it is undoubtedly in *Christian Moderation* that Hall gives the most profound statement of this mode of thought. Here it emerges not merely as the guiding principle of Christian life, but as the principle of universal cohesion. By observing the rules of moderation man brings his thoughts and actions into line with the cosmic forces whereby creation continues to subsist. Without moderation he is 'so far from being a Christian, that he is not himselfe':

It is . . . Moderation, by which this inferiour world stands: since that wise and great God, who hath ordained the continuance of it, hath decreed so to contemper all the parts thereof, that none of them should exceed the bounds of their owne proportion, and degree, to the prejudice of the other. Yea, what is the heaven it selfe, but . . . as a great clock regularly moving in a equall sway of all the Orbes, without difference of poyse, without variation of minutes, in a constant state of eviternall eavennesse, both of beeing and motion: Neither is it any other, by which this little world of ours, (whether of body or minde) is upheld in any safe, or tolerable estate; when humours passe their stint, the body sickens; when passions, the minde . . . This is the center, wherein all both divine, and morall philosophy meet; the rule of life, the governesse of manners, the silken string that runs through the pearl-chain of all vertues, the very Ecliptick line, under which reason and religion moves without any deviation.[94]

So it was that while he upheld the Calvinist position at the Synod of Dort (1618), Hall soon after composed his famous *Via Media. The Way of Peace* in a vain attempt to bring the two sides together. 'I see every Man ready', he declared, 'to ranke himself unto a side, and to draw in the quarrel he affecteth: I see no Man thrusting himself between them, and either holding, or joyning their hands for peace: This good (however thankless) office, I have here boldly undertaken, shewing how unjustly we are divided, and by what means we may be made, and kept entire.'[95]

In many respects Hall was one of the most enlightened churchmen of his day. He is one of the few seventeenth-century clerics who draw their arguments both from Hooker and Calvin.[96] Yet no one fully escapes the prejudices of his own time. In tract after tract Hall reasserts the importance of devotion over controversy and battles bravely towards a generous concept of religious tolerance. Ultimately, however, complete tolerance even among Protestants is beyond his grasp. The reason, I would suggest, is the strong Erastian element in his thought—'No bishop, no King.' When Churches ally themselves too closely with secular authority religious deviance becomes treasonable. This was certainly the case with the Roman Catholics. 'What Client of *Rome*', Hall can ask, 'was ever sentenced to death by the reformed Church, meerely for matter of religion?' 'It is possible', he concedes, 'to see a *Campian* at Tiburne, or a *Garnets* head upon a pole; Treasonable practises, not meere Religion, are guilty of these executions.'[97] His attitude towards Protestant schismatics, or 'sectaries' is no different. Having expressed the wish in *Pax Terris* that all such divisive names as those of Calvinists, Lutherans, Arminians, Episcopalians, Presbyterians, and Independents, may give way to the name of Christians, he goes on to warn of the duty of the secular power to protect the people of God, if necessary by force. He agrees with St Bernard that blasphemous or seditious heretics must be restrained and corrected but adds that should 'the safety of the common-weal be endangered by their doctrines, they are to be destroyed, lest they bring the state to ruin'.[98] *The Peace-Maker* ends in much the same way. The seeds of destruction seem to have been present in even the most moderate spokesmen of the age, although in fairness it must be added that despite these ironies of which he was himself unaware, Hall's desire for peace was entirely sincere. Again and again he bitterly laments the fate of both Church and State and he was certainly not in favour of the so-called Bishops' Wars.[99] For the king to use violent means, he told Laud, 'were no other in so desperate a schism than to reconquer his own with much charge, danger, and blood.'[100]

Translated to Norwich in 1641 in a belated bid to pacify Puritans still smarting from the brusque administrations of Bishops Wren and Montague, Hall witnessed the desecration of the cathedral and suffered the hardships of sequestration. In particular he was hounded by the regicide Miles Corbet.[101]

Such was the 'hard measure' he describes in his second autobiographical tract. Yet he fared better than many of his colleagues. Loyal Anglicans rallied to his support and after his removal to Higham (1644)he spent the last years of his life in relative peace, ordaining, confirming, and preaching as he had always done.[102] He also enjoyed the best of company; his personal friend and physician was Thomas Browne.[103] In such circumstances Hall entered upon one of his most creative periods of literary activity producing over a dozen devotional works of the highest quality, and more surprisingly, of widespread popularity. All were licensed for the press by John Downame, Puritan author of *The Christian Warfare,* who frequently pays tribute both to the excellence of the writing and the sincerity of the author.[104] Some of these works even bear an elegantly engraved portrait of Hall opposite the title-page underneath which appear the lines,

> This Picture represents the *Forme,* where dwells
> A *Mind,* which nothing but that *Mind* excells.
> There's *Wisdome, Learning, Witt*; there *Grace* and *Love*
> Rule over all the rest: enough to prove,
> Against the froward *Conscience* of this *Time,*
> The Reverend Name of *Bishop* is no Crime

In the case of *Resolutions . . . of Divers Practicall Cases of Conscience* (1650) this too was duly licensed by Downame who, however, adds his own far more eloquent tribute:

I Have perused these foure Decades of Practicall Cases of Conscience with much satisfaction and delight, and finde them to be in respect of their subject matter so profitable, necessary and daily usefull; and so piously, learnedly and judiciously discussed and resolved, that they seem unto me best though they come last, (like Wine in the marriage feast made sacred by Christs divine presence and miracle) and therefore doe well deserve (amongst many other the divine dishes and delicacies wherewith this right reverend, pious and learned Authour, hath plentuously furnished a feast for the spirituall nourishment and comfortable refreshing of Gods guests) both the approbation and commendation of all, and my selfe amongst the rest, though unworthy to passe my censure on such a subject.[105]

Since the first publication of his *Meditations and Vowes* in 1605 Hall had remained one of the most popular devotional authors of his time. His *Contemplations* went through edition after edition and his *Occasional Meditations* had a profound influence upon contemporary habits of private devotion. This popularity was unimpaired by the events of the 1640s. Throughout the Interregnum editions of his works continued to pour from the press and it seems that everything he wrote was published and respected. Perhaps it may be said that in devotion he finally united the factions he had previously attempted to bring together in apologies and polemics. Still held in high esteem, he died at Higham on 8 September 1656 at the age of 82—his last published work had appeared only two years previously. No better epitaph has ever been supplied than that of John Whitefoote, who so perceptively captured the very essence of Hall's situation when he wrote, 'all men honoured the *Doctor*, though some loved not the *Bishop*.'[106]

Part I

Satire: 'The World That Did My Thoughts Offend'

1

THE VIRGIDEMIARUM

I. The Nature and Function of Hall's Satires

> I First adventure, with fool-hardie might
> To tread the steps of perilous despight:
> I first adventure: follow me who list,
> And be the second English Satyrist.[1]

The publication of the Martin Marprelate tracts in the late 1580s marked the beginning of a new era in Elizabethan satire. Born of a deeply-rooted dissatisfaction with the Anglican Church, these tracts seriously damaged the fragile 'Elizabethan compromise', and precipitated the censoring of the Puritan press and the famous Star Chamber trials of 1591 to 1592.[2] Their literary consequences were equally striking. Anti-Martinist propaganda appeared almost immediately as savage invectives flowed from the pens of Lyly, Nashe, and Greene and the country was thrown into a state of religious and social turmoil.[3] Late Elizabethan satire had a stormy birth.

The future Archbishop of Canterbury, Richard Bancroft, had uncovered what he claimed to be a vast Presbyterian plot to establish 'presbytery within episcopacy' thereby effectively ending episcopal Church government. As never before, Puritanism became suspect, and the opinions of moderates were discredited by the actions of fanatics. In Cheapside, even as the trials were still in progress, an illiterate simpleton named William Hacket was proclaimed the new Messiah and king of Europe by a pair of zealous gentlemen who had come to identify themselves with the two 'witnesses' of *Revelation*.[4] But London was no Münster, and the Messiah ended up on the scaffold, to be followed soon after by the Separatists Barrow and Greenwood. That same year (1593) a similar fate overtook the Welsh Puritan John Penry. The charge was treason, but many believed him to be Martin Marprelate.[5]

Yet grave though the Marprelate issue undoubtedly was, it was only one of a number of pressing social problems. As the queen approached death without an heir, dangerous factions began to form around the most likely candidates. The Jesuit Robert Parsons, urged the claims of the Spanish Infanta and the threat of invasion was again a reality. Another Armada was prepared after the raid on Cadiz in 1596, and the country was again fortified against the expected invasion.[6] Everything seemed to be going wrong, and unpredictably bad winters and harvests worsened an already dangerous situation. The price of corn soared, and the authorities were forced to take action against illegal enclosures and corn 'engrossings'. Despite their initiative, Oxfordshire was thrown into uproar by the sudden outbreak of a minor uprising late in 1596—just a few months before the publication of Hall's *Virgidemiarum*, the title of which (in the genitive plural governed by *Six Bookes*) means bundle or harvest of rods, apparently with reference to the rods of the Roman lictors, symbols of authority and discipline. Only the first three books comprising the *Tooth-lesse Satyrs: Poeticall, Academicall, Morall* appeared in 1597, the much harder-hitting *Byting Satyres* were published the following year. Both were enthusiastically received, for Hall had assessed the literary climate with remarkable acumen. A classical scholar intimately acquainted with the works of the Roman satirists, he recognized a need he was himself well qualified to satisfy, but soon found he had become the leader of a new fashion—Marston, Guilpin, Tourneur, and Rowlands followed hard in his wake.[7] Moreover, as a fellow of Emmanuel College, the Puritan stronghold of a predominantly Puritan university, he moved close to the fountain-head of popular discontent. The note of challenge in his satire upon Roman ritual (IV.7) is unfeigned,

> Who say's these Romish Pageants bene too hy
> To be the scorne of sportfull Poesy?
> Certes not all the world such matter wist,
> As are the seven hils, for a *Satiryst*. (p. 72)

for given the prevailing circumstances the work could easily be interpreted as an oblique attack upon Anglican ritual also, especially when written by a native of Ashby-de-la-Zouch.

Hall's childhood was passed in an atmosphere of unremitting Puritan complaint. Anthony Gilby, one remembers, was the author of *A Pleasaunt Dialogue betweene a Souldier of Barwicke and an English Chaplaine*, a work which Hall is known to have read and which has been described as a satire 'remarkable for its humour and spirit' belonging 'with the works of Turner, Bale, and Martin Marprelate in the first rank of Puritan controversial productions'.[8] But ecclesiastical controversy formed only one aspect of Puritan complaint. It extended outwards to challenge the whole temper of Elizabethan life, its materialism, its extravagance, its injustice. Not without reason was the term 'Puritan' applied both to a public policy and a private attitude. There were 'Puritans' who were never Presbyterians or Separatists and Hall was of their number. Witness his relentlessly moral interpretation of human experience and his boundless sympathy for all victims of social or economic distress. In his satires and sermons he willingly lent his voice to the popular outcry. Despite what has been said in the past—and indeed what continues to be said by present-day critics—about the 'conventional' nature of his complaints, his *Byting Satyres* are works of uncompromising social criticism and protest.[9] In every sense they represent his reaction against 'the world, that did my thoughts offend' (p. 10).

Despite the provocative tone of the lines placed at the head of this chapter, Hall was well aware that he was not, in any absolute sense, the 'first' English satirist. Even in the *Virgidemiarum* themselves he refers to such predecessors as Chaucer (p. 65), Collingborn (p. 62), and Skelton (p. 89). What he could justly claim, however, was a primacy of form, for no one before him had published a book of short, separate satires so closely modelled upon the works of Horace, Persius, and Juvenal, and no one had pressed the classical form into the service of such pointed social attack. The three rather unexciting satires included in Thomas Lodge's *A Fig for*

Momus (1595) made no impression upon his contemporaries and his plan to produce a whole 'centon of them should the samples 'passe well' was consequently abandoned.[10] As far as the work of Donne is concerned, there is no evidence whatsoever that Hall had any knowledge of the verse satires then circulating in manuscript. As we have seen, the intimacy between the two men dates from a much later period.[11]

Hall's attitude to literature was entirely pervaded by the ideals of Christian morality and didacticism. A candidate for the ministry, he viewed his satires as part of the long homiletic tradition stretching back to the times of the Bible. Perhaps more than anything else it is this attitude of affronted righteousness, this passion to 'bear witness' that constitutes his greatest literary debt to his Puritan background. He remained imbued with the spirit long after he had rejected the polity. For him, as Paul Welsby has put it, 'the Christian preacher is the direct heir of the Hebrew prophet, for the latter, when he declared the Word of God as revealed in the events of his day, passed judgement upon contemporary society.'[12] The relationship between prophets and satirists had been expressly established in 1566 when a godly Puritan named Thomas Drant produced the first English translation of a carefully Christianized Horace. For Drant, as the very title of his work suggests, satire was a valuable weapon in the unending battle against vanity, a battle in which the classical authors take their place alongside the prophets of the *Old Testament: A Medicinable Morall, that is the two Bookes of Horace his Satyres, Englyshed accordying to the prescription of Saint Jerome* ... *Quod Malum est, muta/Quod bonum est, prode. The Wailyngs of the Prophet Hieremiah, done into Englyshe verse, Also Epigrammes.* Drant justifies the association by pointing to what he sees as the complementary nature of the authors thus so boldly juxtaposed. Horace, he informs us, was 'a muche zelous controller of sinne', one that 'with sharpe satyres and cutting quippies, coulde wel displaie and disease a gloser', while Jeremiah 'rufully and waylingly' lamented 'the deepe and massie enormities of his tymes' and foretold divine retribution. It was therefore 'mete' that while the 'man of God' wept for sin, the 'prophane' poet, the decorum of whose work allowed of such humour, should laugh at it.[13] This was also Hall's view of the matter, although he went somewhat further in finding and justifying, 'scornes and taunts' and 'disdainfull scoffes' in the prophets as well.[14] As a result, his adoption of the neoclassical form by no means diminished the moral justification of his satiric attacks, nor in any way isolated them from the Hebrew tradition. Satire was a moral duty, and he spoke. He tells us in one of his sermons that the just man must denounce the sins of God's people and the 'guilt of the great' even though this may imperil his own life.[15] Or, as the satires put it:

> What ever brest doth freeze for such false dread,
> Beshrow his base white liver for his meede.
> Fond were that pitie, and that feare were sin,
> To spare wast leaves that so deserved bin.
>
> (p. 51)

As my discussion of the *Byting Satyres* will demonstrate, the sermons echo, restate, and develop the complaints of the *Virgidemiarum* repeatedly—indeed it would require a whole chapter simply to list the corresponding passages. I mention the matter here because it seems to me to provide the essential context in which to consider Hall's attitude to these apparently very different satires of his early, 'secular' days. Once the relationship between satirist and preacher has been firmly established, it becomes far less surprising—and a good deal more significant—to learn that the *Virgidemiarum* were born of 'Trueth and Holy Rage' (p. 47), or to hear them referred to as 'sacred *Semones*' (satyrs, with a possible pun on Horace's *Sermones*, p. 51) designed to 'check the mis-ordred world, and lawlesse times, (p. 12) by unmasking the 'ugly face of vice' (p. 11). It also becomes easier to appreciate how their frequent bitterness of tone is directly attributable to a sincere sense of moral indignation against the sins of which they treat. As Hall himself put it in his first Paul's Cross sermon (1608): 'These things I vowed in my selfe to reprove, if too bitterly, (as you thinke) pardon (I beseech you) this holy impatience: and blame the foulnesse of these vices, not my just vehemency.'[16] Many years later when the satires became the target of Milton's abuse, one of Hall's supporters (possibly his son Robert) strongly reaffirmed their moral and didactic intention, assigning them a function almost indistinguishable from that of the sermons. The bishop, we are told,

> no sooner came to be capable of the more violent impressions of sin, but his nature and it fell foul; and because he had overcome vices in himself, he took liberty to whip them in others. Which timely zeal, as it did not mis-become his youth, so can it not disparage his Prelacy; no, not as Poesie, not as Satyr.[17]

The passage was written in 1641, but it has become necessary to labour the point just as strongly today when the widely accepted views of Alvin Kernan, as developed in *The Cankered Muse* (1959), have done incalculable damage to the understanding of the *Virgidemiarum*, and, I suspect, to a great many other Renaissance satires as well.

It seems to me that the fundamental error of Kernan's approach lies in assuming that the work of Marston, which is to a large extent *sui generis*, is typical of that of his contemporaries, even of such earlier writers as Lodge and Hall. Furthermore, in seeking to prove that such fictional 'satirists' as Tourneur's Vindice, and Shakespeare's Jacques, are directly descended from the speakers or 'personae' of formal verse satire, he is led to postulate the existence of a completely conventionalized 'satyr persona', at once self-centred, immoral, malcontented, and melancholic. While never to be identified with the author, nor in any way related to his social background, this 'persona' may be regarded as the inevitable product of contemporary attitudes to the satiric genre.[18] Obliged to satisfy extreme expectations of 'savagery, despair, hate, pride, intransigence, prurience, and sadism', the satiric 'persona' becomes of necessity 'strange, twisted, contradictory', and the motivation of his complaints remains at best problematic.[19] In effect, in keeping with the allegedly universal acceptance of the derivation of 'satire' from 'satyr', he was himself a satyr, a shaggy woodland god of ambivalent moral standing. 'Envy, sadism, and discontentedness' subtract from his moral stature, and 'a constant interest in sins of the flesh and near obsession with disease and bodily functions suggest his prurience.' His 'stuttering style' betrays 'an unhealthy state of frenzy'.[20] To its overriding concern with the presentation of such a persona, Kernan traces what he sees as the structural weakness of Renaissance satire. In most cases the satires exist solely to portray the speaker.[21]

The objections to such an approach are many. For a start, the work of Mary Claire Randolph has demonstrated that Renaissance satire is far from lacking in structure—however this may be obscured by Kernan's preoccupation with abstracting 'personae' from poems never intended to bear such analysis.[22] Indeed the very perceptive discussion of the nature of satiric 'plot' with its rejection of the Aristotelian formula of beginning, middle, and end, in his own excellent study, *The Plot of Satire* (1965), seems to me to necessitate a modification of the rather extreme position adopted in his earlier work.[23] Furthermore, to attribute to 'convention' an influence almost totally independent of social background and authorial intention is to render satire completely mechanical and, what is worse, completely predictable. The successful satirist moulds and adapts the more traditional devices of his genre to suit his own particular requirements. As Gilbert Highet remarks, 'in the work of the finest satirists there is the minimum of convention, the maximum of reality.'[24] That he has chosen to write in what may at first appear a purely 'conventional' manner cannot absolve us from the duty of examining how he has used it, and why he adopted it in the first place. In Hall's case, it is quite clear that, all theories of 'satyrs' notwithstanding, the work is modelled squarely upon the *example* of the classical satirists, and Ariosto, in whom the satyr notion is completely unheard of (p. 99). In point of fact, there seems little evidence to suggest that his contemporaries had any universally accepted view of satire at all.

The etymology of the Latin word 'satura' had become confused as early as the fourth century AD when the grammarian Diomedes was reduced to listing several conflicting derivations.[25] The matter was still unresolved in the sixteenth century when Drant offered four possible etymologies none of which could apparently be preferred before any other.[26] This being the case, we can be quite sure that all educated people were well aware of the contentious nature of the issue, and when the 'satyr' hypothesis was finally exploded by Isaac Casaubon in 1605 the effect must have been a good deal less surprising than we have often been led to imagine.[27] It is well to remember too that even Donatus, one of the most ardent spokesmen for the 'satyr' school, was forced to admit that his ideas were *not* universally received.[28] Nor did he ever assert that satyrs 'spoke' in classical satire, only that such writings were descended, as was New Comedy, from the Greek satyr play; Lucilius, he points out, wrote in a new form ('novo conscripsit modo').[29] Among Renaissance critics there is no suggestion that ambivalence of moral stance was considered a hallmark of the satiric genre. Sidney strongly defended the moral purpose of satire, while Webbe, following Horace, banished lasciviousness even from the original satyr plays. Similarly Puttenham, who himself supported the satyr derivation, pointed to the relationship between satire and preaching, while Harington found satire 'free' from wantonness and 'wholly occupied in mannerly and covertly reproving of all vices'.[30] Even William Rankins, the only contemporary satirist actually to assign all his complaints to the mouths of satyrs, represents them as idyllic examples of unspoilt nature whose attacks are directed solely against the evil, and Drant, one of whose four possible etymologies includes the satyr suggestion, explains in conclusion that whatever his origin,

> The Satyrist loves Truthe, none more then he,
> An utter foe to fraude in eache degree.[32]

Hall, of course, was in complete agreement: 'Truth be thy speed, and Truth thy Patron bee' (p. 11). The furthest influence of the 'satyr' derivation upon his own work was its suggestion of three witty puns whose effect, as in all such cases, depends on the reader's ability to distinguish between the terms humorously confused.[33] This is pointed out fully by the author of *A Modest Confutation* in his reply to Milton's quibble against 'toothlesse' satyrs. 'Satyra', he explains,

signified anciently any kind of miscellaneous writing, which we now term *Essayes*; whence *Varro* entituled many of his books of divers subjects, *Satyras suas*: Whence there was also a Law called metaphorically *Lex Satyra*, when by one and the same Vote, divers things were enacted. Last of all, it came to be restrained to such kind of writings, as contained the vices of the times, whether in verse or prose; more commonly now of later terms in verse.[34]

When Hall spoke of 'tooth-lesse' and 'byting' satires he used the terms metaphorically to signify various degrees of strength. He had no intention of applying them 'as we say it of a child, after its teeth are grown, or before'. Had Milton but 'so much life or quicknesse' in his 'pallade' as to have 'tasted an Epigram' he would have found his own ridiculously literal interpretation wittily pre-empted by Hall himself in the lines:

> Euge novam Satyram, Satyrum sine cornibus euge!
> Monstra, novi monstri, haec; et Satyri et Satyrae![35]

For Hall, the 'satyr' derivation is a joke.

Perhaps more important than any of this is Kernan's misrepresentation of the problem of envy—ironically one of the oldest 'conventions' of the genre. As Horace pointed out, far from being motivated by envy, the satirist is its victim. Reviled for speaking the truth, he finds his writings attributed by the guilty to malice and sadism: 'laedere gaudes'/inquit, 'et hoc studio pravus facis' ('You like to give pain', says one, 'and you do so with spiteful intent').[36] In exactly the same way Hall is assailed by an imaginary interlocutor seeking to cast grave doubt on his moral integrity:

> Envie belike incites his pining heart,
> And bids it sate it selfe with others smart.
>
> (p. 21)

As in Horace, the suggestion is immediately denied:

> Nay, no dispight: but angry *Nemesis*,
> Whose scourge doth follow all that done amisse.   (p. 21)

Such conjuring up of an imaginary opponent is one of the satirist's most time-honoured devices of self-defence, yet Kernan represents the passage as an open confession of perversion![37]

The point is made even more explicitly in the introduction to the *Byting Satyres* where Hall recognizes that his work can achieve only a posthumous fame,

> For when I die, shall Envie die with mee
> And lye deepe smothered with my Marble-stone,
> Which while I live cannot be done to die.
>
> (p. 47)

What he hopes future generations will particularly remember
is the moral foundation of all he has written, as important in
its own way as an act of overt devotion:

> sufficeth mee, the world may say
> That I these vices loath'd another day,
> Which I have done with as devout a cheere
> As he that rounds Poules pillers in the eare,
> Or bends his ham downe in the naked Queare.
>
> (p. 84)

The evidence for the opposing viewpoint rests upon a case of
textual misinterpretation. Hall, says Kernan, 'describes his
satiric efforts in this way':[38]

> Envie waits on my backe, Truth on my side:
> Envie will be my Page, and Truth my Guide:
> Envie the margent holds, and Truth the line:
> Truth doth approve, but Envy doth repine.
>
> (p. 11)

As must by now be apparent, envy waits on the poet's back
because he will always have detractors. Hence the image of the
'page' who will trail him until death. Truth, on the other hand,
is his 'guide' because it shows him the way ahead.[39] Envy holds
the margin since it is here that his detractors will place their
black marks to indicate his alleged faults. Labeo is shown in
the act in the final book:

> *Labeo* reserves a long nayle for the nonce
> To would my Margent through ten leaves at once
>
> (p. 87)

Truth holds the 'line' for the obvious reason that the message
of Hall's 'lines' is itself true. The result, quite naturally, is that
while envy repines at his effort, truth applauds it. Quite
appropriately, therefore, Hall opens the *Virgidemiarum* with a
long poem entitled 'His Defiance to Envie'. The matter could
scarcely be more clear.

The treatment of envy was a satiric convention fulfilling the
essential function of keeping the audience on the complain-
ant's side—a need Hall felt keenly throughout his long career
as a satirist, both poet and preacher. Just as in the second

prologue he attempts to defend himself against a possible charge of envious cynicism, in his sermons he is constantly alert lest anyone 'miscontrue' him 'as if in a *Timon*-like, or Cynick humor, I were fallen out with our creation'.[40] Complacency was never to become the note of his attacks, for his sense of 'elect' isolation in a world of vice and folly alerted him to the need to defend his methods. Like Hamlet he was at pains to show that it was the world's trespass and not his madness that spoke. In *The Character of Man*, a court sermon of 1634, for example, he launches into a full-scale defence of his satiric practices in the light of their moral and didactic purpose. This I shall examine in the appropriate chapter. Here we must concentrate on the equally forthright 'Post-script to the Reader' appended to the *Byting Satyres*.

The 'Post-script' takes the form of a frank discussion of the manner and matter appropriate to satire with particular reference, of course, to Hall's own compositions (pp. 97–9). Concerning the manner, we hear first of all of the impossibility of suiting all points of view—a good indication of the confusion surrounding the theoretical issues involved. Far from submitting to the allegedly universal view that satire should be abrupt and obscure, however, Hall points out that the combination of rhyme (absent from Latin but required in the vernacular) and abrupt syntax can only produce a 'loathsome kinde of harshnes and discordance' (p. 99). Let those who doubt this attempt a verse translation of Persius and then decide. His own practice has been to avoid the abruptness and difficulty advocated by such authorities as Julius Caesar Scaliger. In one satire only (IV.1) has he attempted to reproduce the 'soure and crabbed face of Iuvenals', an attempt 'determinately' omitted in the rest (p. 99). His theories are amply supported by his practice, for while making the traditional admission in 'His Defiance to *Envie*' that satire tends to be more pedestrian than other forms of poetry (p. 9), he soon makes it clear that his own satires may well breach this decorum. If his muse cannot sufficiently 'remit' her 'high flight' in order to suit 'a lowly Satyre', then 'lowly Satyres' must 'rise aloft' to her (p. 11). Hence such features as the sophisticated use of the Virgilian half-line usually associated with epic,[41] the moving elegiac pathos of the deserted village

sections (p. 78), and the smooth, sonorous description of the
Golden Age:

> Time was, and that was term'd the time of Gold,
> When world and time were young, that now are old.
> (When quiet *Saturne* swaid the mace of lead,
> And *Pride* was yet unborne, and yet unbred.)
> Time was, that whiles the Autumne fall did last,
> Our hungry sires gap't for the falling mast
>   of the *Dodonian* okes.
> Could no unhusked Akorne Leave the tree,
> But there was chalenge made whose it might bee.
>
>   (p. 33)

Roughness of metre and abrupt riddling couplets are reserved
for special effect. For example, the deliberately 'crabbed' style
and rhythms of IV.1 may be contrasted with the easy, flowing
eloquence of VI.1. Special effects in IV.1 include the highly
appropriate disruption of the decasyllabic metre in a line such
as 'While now my rimes relish of the Ferule still' (p. 54). Yet
this is the exception not the rule; in the eyes of many, Hall
reminds us, his satires 'over-loosely flow' (p. 33).[42] For this,
however, he will make no apology, for such stylistic criticisms
are easily silenced by far weightier considerations.

The 'Post-script' is not merely a personal statement of
artistic intentions, but an apology for satire itself. Since Hall
will admit of no purely aesthetic approach to literature his
choice of style is inextricably connected with what he
conceives to be the moral purpose of his writings. From this
point of view the cultivation of deliberate obscurity would of
necessity diminish their moral impact: 'that which is unseene
is almost undone'. 'The end of this paines', he declares, 'was a
Satyre, but the end of my Satyre [was] a further good, which
whether I attaine or no I know not, but let me be plaine, with a
hope of profit, rather than purposely obscure onely for a bare
names sake' (p. 99). Much affected by the Genevan ideal of
'fraternal' castigation—such mutual examinations formed part
of Gilby's 'prophesyings' at Ashby—Hall could scarcely
conceive of justified satire as other than a moral duty.[43] As he
wrote in a letter of 1608 to an unidentified correspondent:

Whiles I accused the Times, you undertook their patronage. I commend your charity, not your cause. It is true: There was never any Age not complained of; never any that was not censured, as worst... But loe, that Ancient of dayes, to whom all times are present, hath told us, that these last shall be worst: Our experience justifies him, with all but the wilfull.[44]

His complaints, he contends, were fully justified, and were principally aimed at the conscience of the individual: 'Redresse stands not in words. Let every man pull but one brand out of this fire, and the flame will goe out alone. What is a multitude, but an heap of unities?' Yet, although the duty of setting one's own house in order naturally takes precedence, 'who but a *Caine* is not his brothers keeper?', secular authority must uphold moral standards and preachers must vociferously 'cry downe sinne in earnest', but by no means 'may the common Christian sit still and look on in silence'. In this work God will allow no man to be 'private'; 'discreet admonitions' and 'seasonable reproofes' are the duty of all.[45] 'Fraternal' castigation was a Christian duty. Yet at the same time Hall was careful to dissociate himself from such malcontents as spoke '*nothing but* Satyrs and Libels' (my emphasis).[46] 'It is the peevish humour of a factious eloquence', he told Parliament,

to aggravate the evills of the times; which, were they better then they are, would be therefore cryed downe in the ordinary language of malecontented spirits, because present; But it is the warrantable and necessary duty of S. *Peter,* and all his true Evangelicall successors, when they meet with a froward generation to call it so... Who should tell the times of their sinnes, if we be silent? Pardon me, I beseech you ... necessity is laid upon me ... I may not be as a man in whose mouth is no reproofes.[47]

Much of the fascination of the *Virgidemiarum* is born of its author's struggle with these same problems of moral complaint and audience reaction. But here the solution was far more difficult, for if the work was to be anything more than a diatribe after Philip Stubbes's fashion, the moral dilemma had to find an aesthetic solution. Much of the strenuousness and tension of these satires derives, I believe, from the unremitting attempt to woo the reader to the satirist's side by rendering the complaints aesthetically pleasing. Denied the

licence of the preacher, Hall aims at the neoclassical goal of
'utile dulce'. Hence his complete break with English satiric
tradition and the adoption of the classical form.

In the *Tooth-lesse Satyrs*, where the models are normally
Horace and Persius, direct borrowing plays little part. The
significance of the influence lies in tone and treatment. Hall's
attitude to literature, for example, in the first book of
'Poeticall' satires is entirely informed by the standards of
neoclassical criticism, though this is combined, as it was in
most contemporary critics, with strict standards of Christian
propriety. His attack upon contemporary religious verse (p.
19), for instance, is motivated both by its flagrant breach of
decorum, and the indecency of mingling human fictions with
sacred truths. In effect the two become one, for if Solomon is
to sound like 'a newfound Sonetist', the lady of Canticles, 'the
holy spouse of Christ', must necessarily be reduced, if only by
implication, to the level of common 'light-skirts'. Yet the poem
ends not in thundering imprecation, but with a witty, scornful
pun wishing that such authors may be 'transported from
Ierusalem,/Unto the holy house of *Betleem'* (Bedlam).[48]

Whenever Hall feels the need to make his condemnation
more forceful he tends to promote a sharp, fable-style break
between his satiric description and his 'moral'. The irony and
sense of paradox in the satire on costly funerals, for example,
leads suddenly to an outspoken denunciation of vanity complete
with ponderous biblical allusions to the fate of Jezebel:

> Greet *Osmond* knows not how he shalbe knowne
> When once great *Osmond* shalbe dead and gone:
> Unlesse he reare up some ritch monument,
> Ten furlongs neerer to the firmament.
> Some stately tombe he builds, Egyptian wise,
> *Rex Regum* written on the *Pyramis*...
> Deserv'dst thou ill? well were thy name and thee
> Wert thou inditched in great secrecie,
> Where as no passenger might curse thy dust,
> Nor dogs sepulchrall sate their gnawing lust.
>
> (p. 36)

A similar method is employed in the homilies. In *The
Righteous Mammon* (1618), for instance, an excellent, and in

its own time famous, satiric passage on female vanity is quickly
followed by a fiery address to all such 'plaister-faced *Iezabels'*.[49]
But in the *Tooth-lesse Satyrs* this is not the general note. More
typical is the amused ridicule of the newest manifestation of
vanity, the periwig. As the false hair blows off in a gust of ill-
timed wind the satirist can only stand and laugh:

> He lights, and runs, and quickly hath him sped,
> To overtake his overruning hed.
> The sportfull wind, to mocke the *Headlesse* man,
> Tosses apace his pitch'd *Gregorian*:
> And straight it to a deeper ditch hath blowne:
> There must my yonker fetch his waxen crowne.
> I lookt, and laught, whiles in his raging minde,
> *He curst all courtesie, and unrulie winde.*
> I lookt, and laught, and much I marvailed,
> To see so large a *Caus-way* in his head.
>
> (p. 39)

The anecdote is so ridiculous, and the speaker, like Horace, so
genial that the reader has little choice but to support his
conclusion that 'waxen crowns well gree with borrowed
haires.'

But perhaps the happiest device Hall hit upon was that of
the dramatic monologue. In *Virgidemiarum* II.2, for example,
the case of the universities is put best, if unwittingly, by a
wealthy, boorish squire in one superb speech encapsulating
the dangerous prejudices of a whole class, and the myriad of
social problems which stem from them:

> What needs me care for any bookish skill,
> To blot white papers with my restlesse quill ...
> Let them that meane by bookish businesse
> To earne their bread: or hopen to professe
> Their hard got skill: let them alone for mee,
> Busie their braines with deeper bookerie ...
> Have not I lands of faire inheritance,
> Deriv'd by right of long continuance,
> To first-borne males, so list the law to grace,
> Natures first fruits in eviternall race?
> Let second brothers, and poore nestlings,

> Whom more iniurious Nature later brings
> Into the naked world: let them assaine
> To get hard peny-worths with bootlesse paine.
> Tush? what care I to be *Arcesilas,*
> Or some sowre *Solon* ...   (pp. 24–5)

There is nothing obscure or Scaliger-like here. The irony is
sharp; clear, and cutting, the versification smooth. One
wonders whether Jonson had the passage in mind in compos-
ing the very similar lines in 'A speech according to Horace'.[50]
Without realizing it, the speaker engages in an exercise of
complete self-betrayal. His emphasis on 'need' bespeaks his
narrow, mercenary outlook—'allow not nature more than
nature needs', argues King Lear, 'Man's life is cheap as
beast's.' Too ignorant himself to recognize the intrinsic worth
of learning, he regards scholarship as a lower-class trade.
Possessing 'lands of faire inheritance' he 'needs' not 'busie his
braine' in such a fashion. He is a gentleman, and gentility
means wealth. All sense of inner cultivation is foreign to his
social outlook. 'Nature' and 'law' confer gentility quite
gratuitously from without. Why then need he distract himself
with the 'brain-sicke Paradoxes' of *'Parmenides,* or of darke
Heraclite'?,

> Long would it be, ere thou had'st purchase bought
> Or wealthier wexen by such idle thought.   (p. 25)

A telling point is scored by the clever use of classical allusion,
for 'Arcesilas' and 'Solon' are obviously intended as mnemonic
links to the source of the passage immediately following: the
speech of an uncouth, shaggy ('hircosa') centurion in the
third satire of Persius (ll. 77–87). The easy adaptability of his
views to those of the English squire puts the finishing touches
to an already embarrassing portrait. The voice of the satirist is
submerged in that of his 'victim', all of whose normally
unspoken, but guiding, prejudices are brought into clear focus
in a monologue of arrogant self-betrayal. By so dramatizing
the causes of the decline in scholarly patronage, Hall invites
his readers to see in the contemporary social situation as great
a self-betrayal on the part of the squirearchy as is evident in
the opinions of their loquacious representative. In effect, the

situation is the embodiment of those opinions. They are made to satirize themselves.

Always aware of a possible reaction against his complaints, Hall is constantly experimenting with subtle, rhetorical devices designed to involve the reader directly in the act of moral condemnation. In the satire against physicians (II.4), for example, the point hinges upon the interpretation of the ambiguous word 'leech' ('Were I a leech, as who knowes what may bee') and the reader is invited to 'discover' the ironies of the monologue for himself. Almost imperceptibly, of course, this act of 'discovery' becomes an act of moral criticism. As he watches the progress from apparently justified, professional complaint to the worst excesses of charlatan and mountebank, the reader himself takes on the role of probing satirist.

> Fees never lesse, never so little gaine,
> Men give a groat, and aske the rest againe.
> *Groats-worth of health,* can any leech allot?
> Yet should he have no more that gives a grote.
> Should I on each sicke pillow leane my brest,
> And grope the pulse of everie mangie wrest ...
> All for so leane reward of Art and mee?
> No Hors-leach but will looke for larger fee ...
> Were I a leech, as who knowes what may bee,
> The liberall man should live, and carle should die.
> The sickly *Ladie,* and the goutie *Peere*
> Still would I haunt, that love their life so deere ...
> Or would coniure the *Chymick Mercurie,*
> Rise from his hors-dung bed, and upwards flie ...
> And bring *Quintessence* of *Elixir* pale,
> Out of sublimed spirits minerall.
> Each poudred graine ransometh captive Kings,
> Purchaseth Realmes, and life prolonged brings.
>
> (pp. 27–8)

Similarly in II.7 the bogus art of astrology is disposed of not through headlong moral denunciation but through the creation of an elaborate, amusing travesty, modelled on a passage in Rabelais, which efficiently reduces it to the level of the trivial and absurd. Milton criticized the work for declining from the majesty of the 'heavens universall Alphabet' to the 'wretched pooreness and frigidity as to talke of *Bridge street in heav'n, and the Ostler of heav'n*', but in this case Hall was the surer satirist.[51] Like Juvenal he realized that such declension was the very stuff of successful satire.

In the *Byting Satyres* such methods become far more sophisticated. Here, intent upon dealing with pressing social problems, Hall shrewdly abandons Horace for Juvenal. The distinction between their respective styles is a commonplace of classical criticism. They stand at opposite ends of the satiric spectrum, and Hall's division of the *Virgidemiarum* into 'tooth-lesse' and 'byting' satires was obviously intended to reflect this dichotomy. Consequently, his shift to new models is accompanied not only by a change in subject matter, but also by a change in style. Under the Juvenalian influence he begins to work on an increasingly crowded canvas, thronging, like those of Bosch or Bruegel, with scores upon scores of vicious little men acting out their sinful obsessions in a distorted, unnatural landscape. The extreme example of this is *Virgidemiarum* IV.1 with its panoramic sweep of seedy iniquity after the fashion of Juvenal I, III, and VI. But even outside this deliberately imitative exercise the same effect is ensured by the plentiful use of the characteristically Juvenalian device of 'incidental' satire, in which even the illustrations and similes are themselves satiric.[52] The world has become so corrupt that vice can be described only in its own terms. Seeking the 'norm' for comparison, we find ourselves gazing down endless vistas of unrelieved lewdness. In IV.5, for example, the blushing of an usurer, is illustrated with reference to sodomy and extortion:

> So *Cyned*'s dusky cheeke and fiery eye,
> And hayre-les brow, tels where he last did lye;
> So *Matho* doth bewray his guilty thought,
> While his pale face doth say, his cause is nought.
>
> (p. 67)

The device is taken almost as far as it can go in IV. 4 where the supposed 'principal' subject, the effeminate Gallio, is little more than a peg upon which Hall hangs a loose general satire the objects of which, though introduced as contrasts or comparisons, are only tangentially related to the original theme. As well as this, the *Byting Satyres* are full of the imagery of disease and corruption. We hear, for instance, of 'morphew'd skin', 'thick vomiture', 'poysonous fire', 'steaming stewes', and 'dung-clad skin'. We sense a determination to meet vice on its own terms:

> The close adultresse, where her name is red
> Coms crauling from her husbands lukewarme bed,
> Her carrion skin bedaub'd with odours sweete,
> Groping the postern with her bared feet.
>
> (p. 53)

But it was exactly such material that called the whole nature of satire into question, and it is therefore significant that it is at this stage that Hall introduces the subject of satire itself as a major theme into his poems. He shows himself fully aware of the objection, soon to be raised in the *Whipper Pamphlets*, that,

> Silence is safe, when saying stirreth sore
> And makes the stirred puddle stinke the more.
>
> (p. 92)[53]

There is at least as much discussion of the genre in the last three books as there is in the 'Post-script', and it covers all aspects of the problem we have been discussing. In particular, we are constantly reminded of the difficulty of the satirist's position.

In *Virgidemiarum* IV.1, the most difficult Juvenalian satire he ever wrote—in order he says to 'stoppe the mouth of every accuser'—Hall professes himself opposed to obscurity on the grounds that it diminishes a satire's didactic effect. As a result the laboured perplexities of the opening sections, which have caused commentators such difficulty, and which have as their theme the effect of over-obscure satires on unprepared readers, constitute a sharp rebuff to the school of Scaliger whose 'rough-hew'ne *Teretismes*' were 'writ in th'antique vain' (p. 49). Hall is replying to those who considered the *Tooth-lesse Satyrs* too simple, while at the same time cleverly retreating from his promise—having apparently made the attempt to fulfil it—to write henceforth in 'crabbed oke-tree rinde' (p. 43). In order to demonstrate its futility, he turns the art of contrived obscurity against itself. Satire, he asserts, should affect the conscience thereby producing a moral reaction, but this is possible only if it can be clearly understood.

One of the most interesting features of Hall's self-defence is the flat denial that he is too young to write, or that his complaints are born of the immature idealism of a young zealot:

> So let them taxe mee for my hote-bloodes rage,
> Rather than say I doted in my age. (p. 54)

The point is timely. Hall was only twenty-four, and despite the supposed anonymity of the collections his identity was well known.[54] It has been the trend of even twentieth-century criticism to seek explanations for the alleged 'excesses' of Renaissance satire (Hall's included) in the youthfulness of its authors.[55] All in all, therefore, the poem is as much concerned with the writing of satire as with anything else. It serves as a vindication of such brilliantly effective, but 'simple' passages as the portrait of the foppish Gallio, a portrait which points forward to Hall's adoption of the character genre:

> *Gallio* may pull me roses ere they fall,
> Or in his net entrap the Tennis-ball:
> Or tend his Spar-hauke mantling in her mew,
> Or yelping Begles busy heeles persue,
> Or watch a sinking corke upon the shore,
> Or halter Finches through a privie doore . . .
>
> (p. 64)

Experimentation with 'personae' continues throughout Book IV. In IV.5, for example, the position of satirist is offered to a corrupt lawyer named Matho. His major qualifications are his knowledge of usury and his ability to make the guilty pay for their sins in a very literal sense. Again in IV.7, Roman Catholic ritual, one of the most dangerous subjects of all, is seen through the eyes of a resurrected Juvenal, and the personal voice discreetly vanishes. Its disappearance is all the more striking following the highly personal ending of the preceding satire where Hall suddenly steps back from his global survey of human vanity to speak *in propria persona* of his own outlook:

Mong'st all these sturs of discontented strife,
Oh let me lead an Academicke life,
To know much, and to thinke we nothing know;
Nothing to have, yet thinke we have enough,
In skill to want, and wanting seeke for more,
In weale nor want, nor wish for greater store;
Envye ye Monarchs with your proud excesse
At our low Sayle, and our hye Happinesse.

(pp. 71–2)

There is a simplicity and calmness about the lines which indicate that we have reached the eye of the storm. The language is plain and forthright, the balance of the clauses ('know much...nothing know'; 'skill to want...wanting seeke' etc.) suggesting the equanimity of the contented mind. The cacophonous 'sturs of discontented strife' with their harsh 's', 't', and 'r' sounds give way to the soft, euphonic alliteration of the personal message: 'skill to want, and wanting seeke'; 'weale nor want, nor wish'. Although fully aware of the usefulness of fictional 'personae', Hall was not one to forget the potent force of occasional personal statement. He heightens its effectiveness by using it so sparingly.

Despite Hall's tongue-in-cheek promise in IV.4 to tone down the acerbity of his attacks in view of the dangers he may incur, he opens Book V with a renewed avowal of allegiance to Juvenal. Indeed he intends to surpass his mentor by attacking the living instead of the dead. Commentators disagree as to the presence of specific, personal allusions, but there can be no doubt that contemporary issues are the subject of attack.[56] A major concern of these satires, for example, is the enclosure movement, about which Hall would speak even should his mouth be 'enclosed' with 'brazen wals' as thick as 'wealthy *Scrobioes* quicke-set rowes/In the wide Common' (p. 75). What follows is indeed, in Shakespeare's words, 'keen and critical', but Hall constantly retreats behind declarations of feigned inability. According to himself he is far too mild. Satire should be,

like the *Porcupine*,
That shoots sharpe quils out in each angry line,
And wounds the blushing cheeke, and fiery eye,
Of him that heares, and readeth guiltily.

(p. 83)

Needless to remark, the lines serve merely as the prologue to
one of the most scathing attacks of the whole series; the satirist
is playing hide-and-seek.

A striking feature of these poems is their use of shifting
perspectives, aided by a new awareness of the importance of
form. Being upon average three times as long as their
counterparts, the *Byting Satyres* admit of a sense of movement
absent from the earlier work. In the satire upon the decline of
hospitality (V.2), for example, we approach the great inhospitable house in the company of the parasite Saturio (from the
Persa of Plautus). Allured by the grand exterior, he eagerly
responds to the speaker's invitation to approach. Yet 'all is not
so that seemes':

> Beat the broad gates, a goodly hollow sound
> With doubled Ecchoes doth againe rebound,
> But not a Dog doth barke to welcome thee,
> Nor churlish Porter canst thou chafing see.
>
> (p. 80)

As the befooled scavenger walks sadly away, the perspective
suddenly shifts to something less amusing. At least he *can* walk
away, the poverty-stricken tenants cannot. Denied the charity
which it is traditionally the function of the great house to
provide, they are abandoned to despair. The 'humour' has
grown grim and black:

> Grim *Famine* sits in their forepined face
> All full of angles of unequall space,
> Like to the plaine of many-sided squares,
> That wont bee drawne out by Geometars.
>
> (p. 81)

Then, just as the satire seems on the point of ending with the
conventional note of moral exhortation, the scene shifts again
to the house of Virro, and the experiences of another hungry
guest, Trebius (from Juvenal V). Here is charity with a
vengeance—though not at Christmas or 'the wakeday-feast'
(p. 82). Juvenal's celebrated banquet scene is borrowed to
provide the substructure for the portrait of a contemporary
social tyrant, an arrogant, haughty skinflint who makes the
little charity he gives the occasion for emphasizing the social
inferiority of its recipients:

Hold thy knife uprights in thy griped fist,
Or sittest double on thy back-ward seat,
Or with thine elbow shad'st thy shared meat;
Hee laughs thee in his fellowes eare to scorne,
And asks aloud, where *Trebius* was borne . . .
What of all this? Is't not inough to say,
I din'd at *Virro* his owne boord to day?

(p. 83)

We begin and end with a 'great' house. Crushed between the two are the poor and indigent; the structure bespeaks the theme.[57]

The deepening sense of irony reaches its fullest development in the elaborate and long-promised retraction of the single three hundred-line satire of Book VI. This provided the perfect answer to the problem of the satiric 'persona', and won the appreciation of no less a connoisseur than Alexander Pope who termed it 'optima satira'. Apparently he intended to produce an updated version of it himself and even went so far as to annotate its margin with projected modernizations.[58] Augustan satire is usually held to have had little in common with the 'rough', 'unstable' satire of the 1590s, but Pope's recognition of a kindred spirit in Joseph Hall should serve as a reminder that the work of this period cannot easily be so dismissed. Hall's recantation is a model of satiric irony and structure which more than justifies Pope's praise.[59] Surprise is the keynote of its opening. Some fifteen lines have passed before there is any hint of retraction. Then suddenly the satirist confesses:

let me now repent mee of my rage,
For writing *Satyres* in so righteous age:
Whereas I should have strok't her towardly head,
And cry'd *Evaee* in my *Satyres* stead,
Sith now not one of thousand does amisse,
Was never age I weene so pure as this.   (p. 87)

In this way the attack upon satire is itself rendered ridiculous. Whereas the satirist suffers from the charge of seeing only the bad side of life, his opponents are now presented as either naïve innocents or hypocrites. The age is excellent; social development has reached its zenith; man's progress is upwards and onwards to perfection. The great panoramic sweep of Juvenal X ('Omnibus in terris, quae sunt a Gadibus usque/Auroram') is totally reversed:

> Seeke over all the world, and tell mee where
> Thou find'st a proud man, or a flatterer:
> A thiefe, a drunkard, or a parricide,
> A lechor, lyer, or what vice beside?
> Merchants are no whit covetous of late,
> Nor make no mart of Time, gaine of Deceipt.
>
> (p. 88)

As for Hall's previous criticisms, they are simply outdated. They might have 'fitted former times/And shouldred angry *Skeltons* breath-lesse rimes' (p. 89). It is amazing that he did not see this before, but now the 'wrong' is done:

> I would repent mee were it not too late,
> Were not the angry world preiudicate:
> If all the sevens penitentiall
> Or thousand white wands might me ought availe,
> If *Trent* or *Thames* could scoure my foule offence
> And set me in my former innocence,
> I would at last repent me of my rage:
>
> (pp. 90–1)

It was this superb control of irony, this creation of a 'world turned upside down' which was to produce the *Mundus Alter et Idem.* Everything is seen at a second remove. Even the anti-satiric attacks which were soon to follow upon the Bishops' Ban of 1599 are cleverly forestalled by their attribution to the archetypal bad poet, Labeo (p. 92). And should Labeo take the ultimate revenge of denying Hall a poet's status, what of it? Circumstances being what they are, poets either starve or write sloppy love poetry: 'Who would not but wed Poets now a daies!' (p. 96).

Structurally too the satire is quite excellent, for in order to render the 'retraction' complete, Hall traverses the entire range of his former complaints: moral and social (ll. 25–128), academic (ll. 129–62), and poetic (ll. 163–305). The neat reverse order lends to the exercise an air of urbane detachment. Wrapping himself round in layers of irony the satirist at last becomes impenetrable: 'if the iniurious Reader shall wrest [my satires] to his owne spight, and disparraging of others, it is a short answere: Art thou guiltie? complaine not, thou art not wronged: art thou guiltles? complaine not, thou art not touched' (p. 98).

In order to understand who was 'touched' and why, we must examine the themes of the *Byting Satyres*. The discussion, I believe, will totally dispel the widely held belief that the *Virgidemiarum* 'exhibit an experience of a wholly bookish kind',[60] and that Marston's *Scourge of Villanie* was 'the first verse that was obviously written to reach the public as serious, castigating satire, the first verse satire of the times not wholly the vehicle of youthful self-exhibition'.[61]

II. The Social Concerns of the Byting Satyres

Despite the assertion in James Sutherland's *English Satire* that during the sixteenth century 'the fresh air of an essentially rural economy still kept the moral atmosphere clean', it was this same economy which provided Joseph Hall with the principal theme of the *Byting Satyres*.[62] Unlike Marston and Guilpin who concerned themselves almost exclusively with the problems of the city, he turned to examine the question of enclosure with a thoroughness and depth of compassion unequalled in the satirists of the day. Evident also was a large measure of courage, for the issue was as dangerous as it was topical.

In 1593, as a result of the then abundance of corn, the laws prohibiting enclosure of arable land for conversion to pasturage were rescinded. There followed the immediate increase in the rate of enclosures commented upon in the second emergency statute of 1597: 'since whiche time there have growen manie more depopulacions, by turning Tillage into Pasture, then at anie time for the like number of yeares heretofore.'[63] This situation, bad enough in itself, was aggravated by an untimely decline in the corn supply caused by the unpredictably disastrous weather of 1594 and 1595. As a result, the public grew increasingly uneasy and suspicious; the weather might be an act of God but not so the enclosures.

They were definitely attributable to man and soon became a
focal point of popular discontent.[64] To make matters worse,
there were repeated allegations that the dearth of corn was to a
large extent artificial, since supplies were being held back
deliberately in an attempt to inflate prices. Or, as Hall put it:

> Ech Muck-worme will be rich with lawlesse gaine,
> Altho he smother up mowes of seven yeares graine,
> And hang'd himself when corne grows cheap again.
>
> (p. 70)

Similarly in his *Contemplations* he tells us that 'the rurall
Tyrants of our time, doe not more lay up corne than curses:
hee that with-draweth corne, the people will curse him; yea,
God will curse him, with them, and for them.[65]

In December 1596 a minor uprising broke out in Oxfordshire when armed gangs gathered together under the leader-
ship of one Bartholomew Steer with the avowed intention of
pulling down the 'hedges'—the same hedges so scathingly
attacked in *Virgidemiarum* V.3. Under examination Steer
stated that, although far from destitute himself at the time of
the outbreak, he had intended 'to have risen to help his poor
friends, and other poor people who lived in misery'. All other
methods, he declared, had failed, for 'divers people did go to
his Lordship [Lord Norris], and petitioned for some corn to
relieve their distress, and for putting down enclosures.'[66]
Further inquiries revealed that one of the principal causes of
discontent in the county was that 'Mr. Power has enclosed
much; Mr. Frere has destroyed the whole town of Water-
Eaton; Sir Wm. Spencer has enclosed common fields, and
many about Banbury and other places have done the same.'[67]
Just how widespread this discontent actually was can be
inferred from the assertion of Roger Symonds of Hampton
Gay, a leading witness for the Crown, that he had attributed
no importance whatsoever to the initial approaches of the
insurgents because 'he commonly heard the poor people say
that they were ready to famish for want of corn, and thought
they should be forced by hunger to take it out of men's
houses.'[68]

In the official investigation which followed upon the
suppression of the 'rebellious conspiracie', the Attorney-

General was instructed to make particular inquiries 'towching the disorders of their enclosures' from many Oxfordshire landowners called to London for that purpose.[69] In other words, although forced to deal harshly with the 'lewd persons' who had led the outbreak, the government knew only too well where to lay the ultimate blame, and 1597 saw the enactment of two statutes designed not only to stem, but even to undo, the damage already done by the enclosure movement. Under the terms of the first (39 Eliz. c.i), it was ordered that one half of all 'houses of husbandry' which had been 'decayed' for more than seven years were to be rebuilt and apportioned forty acres of land apiece. Furthermore the total number of all those destroyed within the previous seven years was to be restored.[70] The second statute (39 Eliz. c.2), directed that all lands converted from tillage to pasture since the first year of the reign of Elizabeth I were to be made arable again, and that all lands then presently under tillage were to be maintained indefinitely.[71]

Such was the general decision, but the government also made its feelings known in more specific ways. Writing to a landlord named William Harmon in May 1597, for example, the Privy Council let it be understood quite clearly that they were not in favour of his enclosing the common pasture, declaring 'wee...do wishe you rather to consider what is agreable in this case to the use of this State and for the good of the comon wealthe, then to seeke the uttermost advantage that a landlord for his particular profitt maie take amonge his tenaunts.'[72] While not prohibiting him from pursuing his case at law, they gave strict orders that the disputed land should remain open pending the decision of the courts.

The source of the blame was no less apparent to Hall than to the authorities. In *The True Peace-Maker* (1624), for example, he launched a scathing attack upon the 'moral' outrage aroused against local resistance by such worthy citizens as the wealthy enclosers. Who disturbs the state?, he asks, surely not,

the oppressing Gentleman, that tyrannizes over his cottagers, incroches upon his neighbours inheritance, incloses commons, depopulates villages, scruzes his Tenants to death, but the poore soules that when they are crushed, yeeld the juyce of teares, exhibit bils of complaint, throw open the new thornes, maintain the old mounds, would these men be content to be quietly racked and spoiled, there would be peace.[73]

Such then was the general background to the *Byting Satyres,* a background topical enough to have assured their success when they first appeared. But there were even more potent reasons for Hall's opposition to the enclosure movement, reasons which touched closely upon his personal experience and in the light of which his attack can best be understood.
A native of Leicestershire, Hall grew up in one of the counties most badly affected by the enclosures of the sixteenth century. Describing the effect of the movement on that county, Dr W. G. Hoskins writes that,

Between 1540 and 1600 tens of thousands of acres of land passed into the hands of the yeoman families by purchase, at first in parcels of two or three farms and then, by the 1560's especially, in whole manors. By the end of the century the greater yeomen had risen to the rank of gentry, many to that of esquire, owning the manors on which their fathers and grandfathers had been tenants half a century earlier.[74]

Although Ashby-de-la-Zouch, Hall's birthplace, was in one of the fortunate areas least affected by the movement, he must nevertheless have witnessed the distress of many hundreds of people from neighbouring localities. The problem of enclosure had become part of the Leicestershire heritage and grew progressively worse as the century moved to its close.[75] Hall could lay no claim to gentle ancestry. His father, as he tells us himself, was an officer under the Earl of Huntingdon and had the 'government' of Ashby, but as this was probably the highest office he ever held, the origins of the family were undoubtedly quite humble. Only the charity of his relatives enabled Hall to resume his education in Emmanuel College, Cambridge after he had been called home through lack of money.[76] Socially speaking his family was not far removed from those whose distresses he so compassionately observed. Yet their temporary security could not blind him to the sufferings of others. His sermons resound with accounts of their experiences:

What grinding of faces, what racking of Rents, what detention of wages, what inclosing of Commons, what ingrossing of Commodities, what griping exactions, what straining the advantages of greatnesse, what unequall levies of Legall payments, what spightfull Sutes, what Depopulations, what Usuries, what violences abound every where? The sighes, the teares, the bloud of the poore pierce the Heavens, and call for a fearefull retribution.[77]

It has been estimated that roughly fifteen per cent of the rural population owned fifty per cent of the country's personal estate. The average area of a Leicestershire farm was sixty acres, but many, of course, were far smaller than average. As Dr Hoskins puts it:

Between one-third and one-half of the farms (probably a half) were, however, smaller than average: in the second half of the century, at least, 16 per cent. of the Leicestershire farms had less than fifteen acres of arable (total area less than thirty acres) and 48 per cent. had less than thirty acres of arable (total area less than sixty acres).[78]

These would be the farms of the husbandmen, distinguished from the yeomen by achieving subsistence rather than profit. Below them again were the labourers, cottagers, and tenants-at-will, those whose future livelihood depended entirely on the terms which their landlord would offer for their next lease:

> Will one from *Scots-banke* bid but one grote more,
> My old Tenant may be turned out of doore,
> Tho much he spent in th'rotten roofes repayre,
> In hope to have it left unto his heyre;
> Tho many a loade of Marle and Manure led,
> Reviv'd his barren leas, that earst lay dead.
>
> (p. 78)

The conditions under which such people lived are excellently described in *Virgidemiarum* V.1:

> Of one bayes breadth, God wot, a silly cote,
> Whose thatched spars are furr'd with sluttish soote
> A whole inch thick, shining like Black-moors brows
> Through smok that down the head-les barrel blows.
> At his beds-feete feeden his stalled teme,
> His swine beneath, his pullen ore the beame:
> A starved Tenement ... (p. 77)

Poor and therefore vulnerable, the inhabitants of a dwelling such as this would be the first to feel the effects of enclosure.[79] So strongly did their plight affect Hall that he frequently employed it as a metaphor for the uncertainty of life itself. 'We are all Tenants at will', he reminds us, 'and (for ought we know) may be turned out of these clay cottages at an hours warning.'[80] For those who were turned out, there was no hope. The statute concerning rebuilding tells us that, 'there have sundrie Townes Parishes and Howses of Husbandrie bene distroyed and become desolate, by meanes whereof a great number of poore People are become Wanderers, idle and loose, whiche is the cause of infinite Inconveniences.'[81] Writing to Burghley in connection with a possible amendment designed to increase the effectiveness of this statute, Sir Anthony Cope refers to 'the poore, who beinge dryven out of their owne habitacions are enforced into the greate Townes, where beinge verie burthensome, they shutt upp theire dores against them, sufferinge them to die in the streetes and highe wayes for wante of soccour'.[82] It was of such people that Hall was thinking when he wrote his grim account of famine in *Virgidemiarum* V.2. These are the 'hunger-starv'd Appurtenance' who 'must bide the brunt, what ever ill mischance' (p. 81)—the cold connotations of 'appurtenance' accurately reflecting the views of the absentee landlords. Although the satire from which these quotations are taken is directed primarily against the contemporary decline in 'hospitality', this issue was directly associated with the problem of enclosure. In times of hardship, when the great house lay empty, the local people, having nowhere to turn, were rendered completely destitute:

> Looke to the towred chymneis which should bee
> The wind-pipes of good hospitalitie,
> Through which it breatheth to the open ayre,
> Betokening life and liberall welfare,
> Lo, there th'unthankfull swallow takes her rest,
> And fils the Tonuell with her circled nest.

(p. 81)

The irony of the situation was that many such houses had been either bought or built with the profits accrued from enclosure or the shrewd and timely purchase of impoverished holdings[83]. In Ashby under the Hastings family the situation had been far different. A ballad commemorating Hall's late patron, Henry Hastings, third Earl of Huntingdon (died 1595), declares that he 'built up no palace, nor purchased no town':

> His tenants that daily repaired to his house,
> Was fed with his bacon, his beef and his souse;
> Their rents were not raised, their fines were but small
> And many poor tenants paid nothing at all.[84]

This, however, was exceptional. Complaints about the prevailing state of affairs had reached the ears of the Queen, and the Privy Council took action on her behalf when her original rulings seemed to have been neglected. An act of 1596 declares that 'there are more country gentlemen within and about the citty of London then have byn here at any tyme theis many yeares past.'[85]

But if the sons of the gentry were anxious to escape the 'provincial' associations of the countryside, Hall was equally anxious to assert its importance and defend its values. His writings are filled with a love for the open countryside, the wide 'champion' which recalled the days of merry England when 'nothing was in pale or hedge ypent'. And this was exactly what the enclosures threatened: traditions of agriculture reaching back over hundreds of years, the very look and feel of the landscape—this was what he wanted to preserve:

> As Nature made the earth, so did it lie,
> Save for the furrows of their husbandrie;
> When as the neighbour-lands so couched layne,
> That all bore show of one fayre Champian:
> Some head-lesse crosse they digged on their lea,
> Or rol'd some marked Meare-stone in the way.
>
> (p. 84)

Such sentiments, however, had little effect upon contemporary entrepreneurs. The irreversible movement of economics, 'progress' in fact, had its way:

> Then rayse we muddie bul-warkes on our bankes,
> Beset around with treble quic-set rankes,
> Or if those walles be over weake a ward,
> The squared Bricke may be a better gard.
>
> (p. 85)

According to Mr L. A. Parker, enclosure or severance occurred in seventy-one villages or hamlets in Leicestershire between 1578 and 1607. What this means in effect is that during these years a total of 8,245 acres were converted from tillage to pasture, and this figure, it must be remembered, includes only the arable land involved; the amount of extra pastureland and common waste connected with this arable area, and therefore enclosed along with it, is unknown.[86]

Whenever the commons were enclosed the poorest tenants were the hardest hit. Usually they had few sheep, but what they did have depended almost totally on common pasturage. Enclosure meant restriction of space and fewer sheep, or perhaps no sheep at all. Thus Robert Cecil in proposing the statutes of 1597 speaks of 'swarms of poor loose and wandering people bred by these decays, miserable to themselves, dangerous to the state'.[87] Although this particular form of enclosing —of commons—was seen by E. C. K. Gonner as the principal grievance of the time, the problem lay really in the combination of both types, i.e. diminution of commons coupled with conversion to pasturage.[88] Hall attacks along both lines. On the one hand, he complains that land 'which was wont yeeld Usurie of graine' is now condemned to lie fallow, while on the other hand he deplores the land-grabbing of the commons enclosers:

> But when I see thy pitched stakes do stand
> On thy incroched peece of common land,
> Whiles thou discommonest thy neighbours keyne,
> And warn'st that none feed on thy field save thine;
> Brag no more *Scrobius* of thy mudded bankes...
>
> (p. 85)

Nowhere was the consequent desolation of the countryside more evident than in the ruins of the derelict towns and villages deliberately 'decayed' to make way for the great estates. Of such sites Leicestershire in particular offered plentiful examples, for between 1450 and 1600 nearly fifty villages were completely wiped out. That this trend had become extremely acute in Hall's own lifetime is clear from the previously quoted statute of 1597. In 1599, for example, the whole village of Carlton Curlieu was effectively enclosed by the wealthy Bale family, while in 1601, due to the enclosure at Scraptoft, eight farm houses were 'decayed' and forty people displaced—despite the orders of the Privy Council.[89] Our knowledge of such matters, of course, is incomplete. Yet however it may disturb the historian to discover that the exact number of the evicted remains both unknown and unknowable, to the literary critic such considerations are of secondary importance. Behind all the statistics and figures, behind the historical processes of agricultural and economic development, lies the tragedy of human suffering, and it was there that Hall's interests centred. In the final analysis the success of his *Byting Satyres* is attributable not to the amount of social history which may be extracted from them, but to the astonishing power with which they evoke the sorrow and bitterness of the dispossessed. They lent a voice to the inarticulate thereby achieving an elegiac pathos unrivalled in contemporary satire:

> Would it not vexe thee where thy syres did keepe,
> To see the dunged foldes of dag-tayled sheepe,
> And ruined house where holy things were said,
> Whose free-stone wals the thatched roofe upbraid,
> Whose shril Saints-bell hangs on his loverie,
> While the rest are damned to the *Plumbery*?
> Yet pure devotion lets the steeple stand,
> And ydle battlements on eyther hand;
> Least that perhaps, were all those reliques gone,
> *Furious* his Sacriledge could not be knowne.
>
> (p. 78)[90]

What makes the passage so effective is the intense feeling of betrayal and desolation which rises through the studied simplicity of the language. 'Keepe', for example, was a homely,

colloquial word common in the East Anglian region and one
which survives around Cambridge to this day. It is the word
the tenants themselves might have used, and is particularly
appropriate here because of its obvious connotations of
ownership and possession. The places where their sires 'did
keepe' are their ancestral homes, the humble cottages which
generation upon generation had tended as their own, but
which were now thrown open to the elements and defiled by
wandering herds of 'dag-tayled' sheep. The latter detail brings
the picture before us in vivid, concrete terms. These are not
the idyllic sheep of Spenser's pastoral landscape, but the same
foul-smelling, matted creatures with which country dwellers
are so familiar. What has happened in effect, is that people
have been dispossessed by animals. But people are not the only
victims. The fine, 'free-stone' church was also inhabited. Quite
appropriately, therefore, it is remembered not as a 'church',
but as a '*house* where holy things were said'. The statement is
double-edged. The villagers prayed in this house and meant
what they said, but the gentry also prayed there. This was the
place where 'holy things' were only 'said'. Now it stands as
empty as the cottages surrounding it, a testimony to the
hypocrisy of the words spoken inside. As if in protest, the place
itself seems to put forth a voice of its own. Its 'free-stone wals'
'upbraid' the cheap thatch which has replaced the pillaged
lead roof. Paradoxically too the Sanctus bell has now grown
shrill. In former times it was used to summon the congregation
to service, but there is no one left to hear it or to ring it, except
perhaps the wind. Yet it is 'shril' in silence: its discordant,
cracked notes sound in the conscience. All the rest of the
valuables have been melted down, '*damned* to the Plumbery' as
Hall puts it, and his choice of words is significant: more has
been lost than some unimportant ornaments. And yet, we
encounter a strange contradiction. The roof has indeed been
thatched and the bell left hanging in its place. Why? 'Pure
devotion' supplies the answer. The landlord is far too
committed a Christian to desecrate the 'house' of God. Having
driven away the congregation, stripped the roof, and melted
down the valuable metals, he 'lets the steeple stand' with its
supporting 'battlements'—an unusual but strikingly apposite
word in the circumstances—as 'reliques' of the place's sanctity.

There is surely something peculiarly Puritan in this note of protest—the hatred of the reformer for the insignificant externals of religious worship, for 'reliques'. As Hall sees it, there is something extremely un-Protestant about the desecration. The shell of the chapel stands but no more than the shell. The substance of religion has been drained away, and only the empty form remains as an emblem of the landlord's faith. Unwittingly he has bequeathed to posterity a constant reminder of his sacrilege. And all these aspects of his crime—his cruelty, his meanness, his shabby attempt at making amends—are viewed through the eyes of the departing villagers (for such is the context of the passage I have quoted) as they look back on the desolation they are leaving behind. For us, the result of surveying the scene through their eyes is that we identify with their feelings. With deliberate understatement the satirist asks, 'would it not vexe thee?', and the question applies itself equally to victim and reader. The strength of the sympathy is the mark of the satire's success. Hall wants us not *merely* to condemn the outrage—though, of course, he wants this—but to feel the outrage. Having lent the villagers his own voice, he is attempting to give them ours.

The open vexation of the frustrated victims of enclosure appeared in 1607 when what amounted to a minor rebellion broke out in the counties of Leicestershire, Warwickshire, and Northamptonshire. In their *Petition* to all other insurgents the Diggers of Warwick complained of 'incroaching Tirants' who desired to 'grinde our flesh upon the whetstone of poverty ... so that they may dwell by themselves in the midst of theyr heards of fatt weathers'. 'They have depopulated and overthrown whole townes', they continue, 'and made thereof sheep pastures.'[91] Discussing the outbreak in an addition to Stow's *Annales*, Edmund Howes says of the rebels that 'it had beene credible [sic] reported unto them by many that of very late yeeres, there were three hundred and forty Townes decayed and depopulated'.[92] Hall, one remembers, anticipated the Diggers' complaint (even to the use of the term 'tyrant') by nine years:

Oh happy daies of olde *Deucalion,*
When one was Land-lord of the world alone!
But now whose choler would not rise to yeeld
A pesant halfe-stakes of his new-mowne field
Whiles yet he may not for the treble price
Buy out the remnant of his royalties?
Go on and thrive my pety Tyrants pride
Scorne thou to live, if others live beside.

(p. 85–6)

The theme is continued in a sermon of 1637 delivered at a time of renewed enclosing. 'The earth', says Hall,

is the Lords as the possessor, and he hath conveyed it by deed or gift to the children of men: So that by due right of inheritance, or purchase it is lawfully devolved to us. This is no warrant for excesse; *Wo to them that joyn house to house, and land to land, till there be no more place.* Devouring depopulators of whole countries, such men purchase with a vengeance. Let it be our care so to purchase a share on earth, that we loose not our mansion in heaven.[93]

The blame, as Hall saw it, lay squarely with the wealthy landowners, in particular with the squirearchy. Indeed it is remarkable how viciously this class is attacked throughout both *Tooth-lesse* and *Byting* satires. In *Virgidemiarum* II. 2, for example, the scholars of the University are urged to,

scorne contempt it selfe, that doth incite
Each single-sold squire to set you at so light.

(p. 24)

As we have seen, the speaker of the boorish monologue which follows is a pompous ignorant squire to whom money and land mean everything. But the passage simply dramatizes the point made in one of Hall's *Epistles* (1608). 'Our Land hath no blemish', he writes,

comparable to the mis-education of our Gentry... they so live, as if they had forgotten that there were books: Learning is for Priests, and Pedants; for Gentlemen, pleasure. Oh! that either wealth or wit should be cast away thus basely: That ever reason should grow so debauched, as to think any thing more worthy than knowledge.[94]

Again, the offspring of the parsimonious Lolio will, in the fullness of time, become a squire, and subject his tenants to rack-rents and enclosures:

> And well done *Lolio*, like a thriftie syre,
> T'were pitty but thy sonne should proove a squire.
> How I fore-see in many ages past,
> When *Lolioes* caytive name is quite defa'st,
> Thine heire, thine heyres heyre, and his heyre againe
> From out the loynes of carefull *Lolian*,
> Shall climbe up to the Chancell pewes on hie,
> And rule and raigne in their rich Tenancie;
> When pearch't aloft to perfect their estate
> They racke their rents unto a treble rate;
> And hedge in all the neighbour common-lands ...
>
> (p. 58)

The persistence of the attack is properly explicable not as a personal vendetta, but as a reaction to an established social truth. To a considerable extent enclosure was the work of the landed gentry and in Leicestershire in particular the upper classes had much to answer for.[95] Of the 8,245 acres involved, 5,431 are accounted for by nobles, knights, esquires, and gentlemen. Twenty-four squires enclosed 2,479 acres. In forty-five out of the sixty areas listed in the depopulation returns of 1607 the lord of the manor was shown to be implicated in the offending enclosures.[96] But in interpreting this figure we must be careful to remember the mobility of Elizabethan society. Sixteenth-century Leicestershire was in social as well as economic turmoil: Lolio's son, educated at the Inns of Court and destined to inherit all the wealth his miserly father has so ruthlessly accumulated, is in the process of rising above his station.[97] And this, of course, is what the satire is all about:

> Old driveling *Lolio* drudges all he can,
> To make his eldest sonne a Gentleman.
>
> (p. 54)

Unlike Jonson's Fungoso, Lolio's son is completely unper-
turbed 'to see his yeomanly father cut his neighbours throats,
to make his sonne a gentleman'.[98] The consequence of this
gentility we have already noted, but in order to appreciate the
satire correctly it must be understood that the prophecy stems
neither from poetic licence nor irresponsible exaggeration.
The vast majority of Leicestershire squires were actually of
yeoman descent or lower. Dependent as was their rise upon
financial success, such people were naturally attracted by the
profits of enclosure. Lord Burghley defined gentility as
'ancient riches', but in practice quantity often outdid anti-
quity.[99] Mr Parker points out that of the forty-five manorial
lords involved in the enclosures, only eleven came from
families long established in their localities. The others had
acquired their estates within the previous sixty or seventy
years, the great majority by purchase rather than marriage
alliance. In many cases the rapidity of the rise was astonishing.
The Bales who enclosed Carlton Curlieu rose from yeoman to
baronet within the space of a hundred years. Similarly when
William Hawford bought the estates of John Asshe, esquire, in
1551 he was a yeoman. But his grandson who began enclosing
in 1597 was styled gentleman, and by 1614 had become
'esquire'.[100] The position can best be summed up by quoting
Mr Parker's conclusions:

Although enclosure in Leicestershire in the later Tudor period, as
reflected in the depopulation returns of 1607, was largely the work of
the gentlemen, the squires and the knights, it did not take place
within a static society. The old manorial families played their part;
but the majority of the lords, all of whom enclosed on a considerable
scale, were new-comers to the manors.[101]

To a county like Leicestershire with a strong tradition of
free peasant holdings this was a highly unpleasant turn of
events, and goes far, I would suggest, to explain much of the
bitterness which we sense in the *Virgidemiarum*—not only
were the enclosers thieves, they were parvenu thieves, and as
Aristotle points out, nothing gives rise to 'virtuous indignation' so fast as the unmerited success of the *nouveaux riches*
(*Rhetoric*, II.9). The pride of such 'brasse gentlemen' (p. 59),
was one of Hall's principal targets:

His father dead, tush, no it was not hee,
His findes recordes of his great pedigree,
And tels how first his famous Ancestor
Did come in long since with the Conquerour.
Nor hath some bribed Herald first assign'd
His quartered Armes and crest of gentle kinde,
The Scottish Barnacle (if I might choose)
That of a worme doth waxe a winged goose.

(p. 58)

Despite Lord Burghley, once 'riches' were great enough they could always pretend to be 'ancient' as well.

Hall was well aware that the beginnings of many a fortune dated only from the suppression of the monasteries. The Dissolution had thrown a vast amount of land on the market for secular ownership, and was attended by many abuses. Keeping that in mind, the son who dines in 'silken cote' should pause to recall the 'poore hungry swayne', his grandfather, who 'beg'd some cast Abby in the Churches wane',

And but for that, what ever he may vaunt,
Who now's a Monke, had beene a *Mendicant*.

(p. 76)

In this position were the Bales, who had come to own much of the property originally held by Ulverscroft Priory. Indeed twelve of the Twenty-seven enclosing manor lords who had gained their lands by purchase were the possessors of former monastic holdings.[102] Bad enough as it was to beg a 'cast abby', however, it was worse to steal it. It was an open secret that due to illegal 'concealment' at the time of Dissolution many such holdings had never been paid for:

What, did he counterfait his Princes hand,
For some streave Lord-ship of concealed land?

(p. 76)

Hall's readership would recognize the point as topical, for 1597 saw the setting up of a commission to investigate the issue.[103]

Yet enclosure, of course, was not wholly the work of the gentry, nor did Hall represent it as such. The wealthy yeoman in particular could be a 'cormorant' of the first order.[104] Choosing to employ their profits more gainfully, many shunned the expense of gentility. As a result, by systematically purchasing adjoining holdings as their neighbours were driven off, they were enabled to create extensive estates with large annual turnovers:

> *Villius* the welthy farmer left his heire,
> Twise twenty sterling pounds to spend by yeare.
>
> (p. 86)

Although this satire deals with the squandering of his inheritance by a young son who does desire the trappings of gentility, all were not so foolish, and in financial terms many of the wealthier yeomen were often better off than their local gentry. To such men enclosure presented itself as a sound economic policy:

> Go to my thriftie Yeoman, and upreare
> A brazen wall to shend thy land from feare,
> Do so; and I shall praise thee all the while,
> So be, thou stake not up the common stile;
> So be thou hedge in nought, but what's thine owne,
> So be thou pay what tithes thy neighbours done,
> So be thou let not lye in fallowed plaine,
> That which was wont yeeld Usurie of graine.
>
> (p. 85)[105]

The keyword here, of course, is 'thriftie' for the very practices Hall had chosen to satirize had long been thus sanctified in the vocabulary of godly self-interest. Upon such hypocrisy he pours the utmost scorn. After all, he remarks, one would need to be mad to uphold the ideals of common ownership. Such opinions are for jesting Platonists, and whores. And yet, 'our Grandsires... in ages past' were all of the Platonic school and let their lands,

> lye all so widely wast,
> That nothing was in pale or hedge ypent
> Within some province or whole shires extent...
> Some head-lesse crosse they digged on their lea,
> Or rol'd some marked Meare-stone in the way.
> Poore simple men! For what moght that avayle
> That my field might not fill my neighbours payle...
> If they were thriftlesse, mote not we amend,
> And with more care our dangered fields defend?
>
> (pp. 84–5)

Still more damaging was the explicit comparison between the methods of the enclosers and those of Philip II, the *bête noire* of Protestant Europe:

> Go on and thrive my pety Tyrants pride
> Scorne thou to live, if others live beside,
> And trace proud *Castile* that aspires to be
> In his old age a yoong fift Monarchie.
>
> (p. 86)

The great inhospitable house of V. 2, one remembers, is compared to the Escorial, that 'vaine bubble of Iberian pride' which,

> nought within, but louzy coul's doth hold,
> Like a scab'd Cuckow in a cage of gold.
>
> (p. 80)

It is the nature of tyranny, whether political or social, to deny to its victims even such feeble satisfaction as protest may afford. Completely dependent, therefore, on the whims of their landlord, his impoverished tenants must pocket their pride and court his favour. Human dignity does not long survive social justice:

> Yet must he haunt his greedy Land-lords hall,
> With often presents at ech Festivall;
> With crammed Capons every New-yeares morne,
> Or with greene-cheeses when his sheep are shorne
> Or many Maunds-full of his mellow fruite,
> To make some way to win his waighty suite.
> Whom cannot gifts at last cause to relent...?
>
> (p. 77)

Such obsequiousness, however, was generally to little avail. Few recognized the financial advantages of enclosure better than the landlords, and when leases expired they used the new rents to drive their poorer tenants from their former holdings.[106] As Sir Anthony Cope put it when complaining about the limitations of the depopulation bill in 1597, 'yet is there noe lymitacion sett downe eyther for ffyne or Rente. But the poore that owe to be restorred are in both leafte to the will and harde Conscience of him that hath destroyed the Towne, or of him that hath unconsionablye purchassed the Towne so destroyed.'[107]

If there was any hope, it lay, as far as Hall was concerned at least, with the nobility and gentry. Closely linked with his disgust at the dealings of the 'brasse gentlemen' was his desire that these classes should maintain their traditional hold on rural society. Pontice must preserve his inheritance, and the 'ding-thrift heire' must shun usurers; otherwise the land will fall into the hands of unscrupulous upstarts:

> it shall grind thy grating gall for shame,
> To see the lands that beare thy Grandsires name,
> Become a dunghill peasants sommer-hall,
> Or lonely *Hermits* cage inhospitall.   (p. 68)

Once again hospitality is a key issue. It was the need for money, one remembers, that induced the established squire to form a marriage alliance with Lolio's family.

Not surprisingly such attitudes encountered swift reaction. Seizing upon the Lolio satire, for example, Marston completely denied the justice of Hall's attack. Why should he 'snarle at Lollios [*sic*] sonne?'

> That with industrious paines hath harder wonne
> His true got worship, and his gentries name
> Then any Swine-heards brat, that lousie came
> To luskish *Athens*, and with farming pots,
> *Compiling* bedds, and scouring greazie spots,
> By chance (when he can like taught Parrat cry
> *Dearely belov'd*, with simpering gravitie)
> Hath got the Farme of some gelt Vicary...[108]

In Marston's opinion Hall was attacking the very freedom of social mobility by which (albeit by a different route) he himself aspired to rise. Yet as *The Righteous Mammon* (1618) makes clear, it was not the ideal of social mobility to which Hall objected, but the false pride it generated and the methods which commonly promoted it.[109] A firm believer in the benevolent paternalism of a hierarchical society, he demanded that social rank should never be divorced from a sense of social duty. It was far more than just a question of 'ancient riches'. As portrayed in his 'Character of True Nobility' (1608), the good lord:

doth not so use his followers, as if he thought they were made for nothing but his servitude; whose felicity were only to be commanded and please... His wealth stands in receiving, his honor in giving... None can be more pitifull to the distressed, or more prone to succour; and then most, where is least meanes to sollicite, least possibility of requitall.[110]

Having experienced the ruthlessness of the Leicestershire parvenus on the one hand, and the charity of the Huntingdon's on the other, Hall had good reason to put his trust in the old-established families. From those whose rise was attributable almost wholly to a complete lack of social conscience, from those whose sole motivation was profit, there was nothing to be hoped; the leopard would not change his spots. Yet there was nothing naïve about his expectations. He realized only too well how corrupt the nobility itself could become. His views on gentility were perfectly balanced. Just as he rejected the pretensions of money without virtue, he was equally unwilling to award the palm to 'birth' alone. The truly noble man 'stands not upon what he borrowed of his Ancestors, but thinkes he must work out his owne honour'.[111] Hall's attitude is perfectly summed up in his advice to Pontice:

> And were thy fathers gentle? that's their praise,
> No thanke to thee by whom their name decays;
> By vertue got they it, and valourous deed,
> Do thou so *Pontice,* and be honoured.   (p. 60)

In June 1599 satire was officially banned, and the *Virgidemiarum* headed the list of objectionable books. Satire had gone too far, for the ban was directed, as I have shown elsewhere, not against pornography, but against effective, and possibly disruptive, social criticism.[112] Hall's work, however, was not burned along with the others, but confiscated, apparently pending further investigation. Significantly the *Tooth-lesse Satyrs* reappeared in 1602, but the *Byting Satyres* were not to be republished until the eighteenth century. In many respects the ban constitutes the most perceptive criticism passed upon them in their own time. They had set out to 'bite' and the wound rankled. Had they been the 'bookish' compositions of Sutherland's description they would never have appeared on the list at all. In the very act of suppressing them, the ban bore witness to their true nature. But, of course, neither 'truth' nor 'holy rage' could be silenced for long. In the *Virgidemiarum* Hall had groped towards a suitable satiric 'persona', but in his ministry he discovered a far more powerful one than he could ever have invented. The pulpit offered him what he wanted most: an audience convinced of his moral integrity. We shall see how he used this advantage in Chapter 6.

2.

MUNDUS ALTER ET IDEM

I. Genre, Style, and Method

Mundus Alter et Idem was a production of Hall's early years, an exercise in 'university' wit apparently never intended for general publication.[1] When it first appeared in 1605 it did so without its author's consent and probably against his express wishes.[2] Responsibility for its publication was accepted by William Knight, a close friend who promoted the venture in the belief that the work could never prejudice its author's reputation even though he had now abandoned secular letters and betaken himself to the study of 'Theologiae sacra'.[3] Events, however, were to prove Knight wrong, for none of Hall's works caused him so much embarrassment as this: one of its most attentive and critical readers was that redoubtable enemy of episcopacy, John Milton.[4]

Initially the work more than justified Knight's confidence. Besides its great popularity on the Continent it enjoyed the favour of an early English translation by John Healey (first translator of St. Augustine's *City of God*) whose version entitled *The Discovery of a New World* appeared in 1609.[5] This is the version with which English readers are most familiar and upon which critical accounts are usually based in the absence of a good modern edition of the *Mundus* itself. Yet to call Healey's work a 'translation' is to use the term rather loosely, and judging from the apologetic tone of its prefaces it can hardly have commended itself to Hall, then chaplain to the future Earl of Norwich, Sir Edward Denny.[6] Nor is his reaction difficult to understand, for *The Discovery*—apparently produced under the aegis of John Florio—is in many respects a new creation, and no one who has read it can justly claim to have read the *Mundus*.[7]. In view of this the following discussion will concern itself wholly with the original Latin text, but an examination of the relationship between the two versions will be found in Appendix A.

The first problem presented by the *Mundus* is that of genre. How are we to classify the work, and what is its purpose? The most obvious answer is that the *Mundus* is an account of a journey to the Antipodes undertaken by one Mercurius Britannicus in the good ship Phantasia, and his discovery there of the four suspiciously familiar nations of Crapulia (gluttony), Viraginia (women), Moronia (folly), and Lavernia (deceit). Unlike More's *Utopia* which presents an account of a perfect society, the *Mundus* paints a picture of unrelieved depravity and degradation designed to satirize the failings of contemporary Europe. In this respect it may be seen as a continuation of the *Virgidemiarum* in a new form and a new medium. It presents what modern critics term a 'dystopia', a more recent example being Huxley's *Brave New World*. It is an important early ancestor of the more famous imaginary journeys of Butler and Swift, written in what Ellen Douglas Leyburn describes as the ancient tradition of 'satiric allegory'.[8] In so far as allegory may be defined as 'the particular method of saying one thing in terms of another in which the two levels of meaning are sustained and in which the two levels correspond in pattern of relationship among details',[9] the *Mundus* is an allegorical 'dystopia' primarily concerned with satirizing the vices. Mercurius' journey through Moronia, for example, is actually a journey through the various follies and absurdities of seventeenth-century society, each province, city, and university representing a different aspect of that folly. The exact significance of any area is generally clear from the elaborate system of macaronic place-names to which is appended an exhaustive explanatory index. Hence 'Lyperia', glossed 'Greek tristis, tristitia' (sad, sadness) is the land of melancholy, and 'Lisonica', glossed 'Spanish Adulatio' (praise), is the land of flattery (p. 220). As Knight remarked, Hall's Terra Australis is a land of Platonic forms embodying the true and living idea of the world in which we live ('veram ac vivam huius, in quo degimus, mundi ideam').[10] As we shall see, even the positioning of the regions is significant, for the geography of Terra Australis is intended to reflect the interrelationship of the various vices and the sinner's easy progress from one to another. It is by clever design that the city of fools (from the Italian for the same) is followed by Spesius Tractus, the land of wanton extravagance (from the Italian 'spesa', expense) which in turn leads to Lisonica, the land of flattery (pp. 157–65). This is the point of Healey's remark that the work must be read three times, once for Socrates (allegory), once for Strabo (geography), and once for Merlin Coccaius, author of the *Macaronicon*.[11]

Having said all this, however, we have still not answered the question of genre in seventeenth-century terms. The word 'dystopia' was unknown to Hall, and 'allegoria', as George Puttenham declares, was not a form but a figure. What is 'allegorie', he asks, but an 'inversion of sence' by 'a duplicitie of meaning or dissimulation under covert and darke intendments' employing riddles, proverbs, scoffs, taunts, circumlocution, and hyperbole?[12] All such devices are found in plenty throughout the *Mundus* and it is primarily in this sense, rather than that of 'continued metaphor', that the work may be termed allegorical. As in *Hudibras*, however, allegoric consistency is often sacrificed to the demands of satiric attack.[13] Mercurius openly ridicules many of the things he sees and occasionally relates them explicitly to former experience. For Hall, therefore, the genre of the *Mundus* was clearly that of the Menippean Satire, the genre of Petronius' *Satyricon*, Seneca's *Apocolocyntosis*, the lost satires of Varro, and, closer to Hall's own time, Rabelais's *Gargantua and Pantagruel*, a work of which he makes occasional use.[14]

Varro, as Cicero reminds us, wrote in direct imitation of Menippus, mingling 'much that was drawn from the inmost recesses of philosophy' with 'a kind of mirthfulness' in the hope that his readers would be enticed to the matter by the 'pleasantry' of the style.[15] This, of course, was the principal attraction of the form for Hall. For the overlaid device of the imaginary journey he had not far to seek. He had read the *Utopia* (p. 124), and was well acquainted with both Rabelais and Lucian, whose *True History* was the most famous classical account of a trip from one world to another. As well as this he was astonishingly familiar with the whole spectrum of contemporary travel literature ranging from the 'whet-stone leasings of old *Maundevile*' to the most sober productions of Mercator and Ortelius.[16] Nor did Hall's interest in such writings, by which, as we shall see, he was both attracted and repelled, cease with the composition of the *Mundus*—he read Blount's *Voyage into the Levant* soon after it appeared in 1636.[17] Such interests must have made him popular at the court of Prince Henry. Its governor was the much-travelled Sir Thomas Chaloner, to whom he sent a fascinating account of his own first continental voyage of 1605.[18]

To attempt a definition, therefore, we may say that the *Mundus* is a Menippean satire upon the vices of Europe written in the guise of an allegorical travelogue recounting a fantastic journey to the great Southern Continent, 'Terra Australis non adhuc satis cognita'. That the account is also something of a burlesque of Hakluyt by no means detracts from its moral force. In Hall's eyes the wanderlust of his contemporaries was indicative of their vanity, idleness, and greed. Their desire for the marvellous—whether marvellous wealth or marvellous experiences—was a symptom of their moral decline. His verse satire upon the vanity of human wishes concludes with the portrait of a 'brainsicke youth' fed with 'the sweet sauc'd lies of some false *Traveiler*' who forsakes his own peaceful, prosperous way of life in pursuit of fantasies. Only too late does he discover his mistake:

> The brainsicke youth that feeds his tickled eare
> With sweet-sauc'd lies of some false *Traveiler*,
> Which hath the Spanish Decades red a while;
> Or whet-stone leasings of old *Maundevile*,
> Now with discourses breakes his mid-night sleepe,
> Of his adventures through the *Indian* deepe,
> Of all their massy heapes of golden mines,
> Or of the antique Toombs of *Palestine*;
> Or of *Damascus* Magike wall of Glasse,
> Of *Salomon* his sweating piles of Brasse,
> Of the Bird *Ruc* that beares an Elephant:
> Of Mer-maids that the Southerne seas do haunt;
> Of head-lesse men, of savage *Cannibals*;

The fashions of their lives and Governals:
What monstrous Cities there erected bee,
Cayro, or the Citie of the Trinitie ...
His land morgag'd, He sea-beat in the way
Wishes for home a thousand sithes a day:
And now he deemes his home-bred fare as leefe
As his parch't Bisket, or his barreld Beefe.[19]

The learned authorities upon which the *Mundus* draws are far too numerous to cite, but the very fact that the work itself draws our attention to them through the device of authorial annotations tells us a great deal about the type of audience for whom Hall was writing. At the time of composition 'Hall of Imanuel Colledge in Cambridge' was one of the leading satirists of the day.[20] The *Virgidemiarum* had attracted widespread attention, as had the notorious quarrel with Marston, a quarrel unhappily prolonged by other hands in the Cambridge *Parnassus Plays* with dozens of unmistakable verbal echoes.[21] *The Mundus* was undoubtedly a university work intended for the same sort of closed academic circle as these plays. Certainly it was written exclusively for the learned. Much of its humour, depending as it does on scholarly allusion and complicated philology, is quite unsuited to anyone unfamiliar with contemporary academic studies. The humour of the footnote appeals to relatively few. Indeed the very fact that the work was written in Latin rather than the vernacular argues its exclusiveness. Hence the many changes forced upon a translator seeking a wider, more popular audience.

The original text is completely uncompromising. From the outset the 'Itineris Occasio' roots us firmly in the world of the universities. The setting is either Oxford or Cambridge (most probably the latter) and the ethos is that of the informal scholarly debate. Mercurius himself is a young don whose partiality for travellers is notorious in academic circles (pp. 1, 5). While expressing his gratitude to both Oxford and Cambridge he betrays his true allegiance by alluding most frequently to the latter[22]. Like his creator he is obviously a Cambridge man. Throughout his narration he is careful to explain the numerous educational systems he encounters in

the southern lands. His description of the Pamphagonian
school of gluttony, for example, is an elaborate burlesque, after
the fashion of Rabelais, upon the contemporary system of
classical education (pp. 37–8). In Pamphagonia the various
grades of Greek and Latin authors are replaced by various
sizes of bowls, goblets, and dinner portions, and the instruc-
tors read out 'fragmina quaedam Apiciana', fragments from
the writings of Apicius, the celebrated classical gourmand. An
authorial gloss refers the more inquiring to the account of this
worthy's life in the encyclopaedia of Suidas. Yet it is essential
to realize that this attractive piece of burlesque by no means
constitutes an attack upon contemporary education. Rather, it
serves as an appropriately witty device for attacking the vice of
gluttony, and the pretensions of intemperate gourmets who
attempt to make it an art.

Again, in Variana, the land of inconstancy, Mecurius
discovers 'imaginem Academiae, *Dudosam* vocant sui; in qua
occurrebant mihi umbrae philosophorum' (p. 130. 'Something
resembling an university which its scholars called "Dudosa",
in which I encountered the semblance of philosophers'). Here
are two colleges, one of sceptics, the other of innovators. The
former deny the validity of sense-impressions, and consequently the value of human knowledge, thereby reflecting the
forceful revival of Pyrrhonism in contemporary scholarship.
Hall's method is that of *reductio ad absurdum:*

Surripe cuiquam istorum nummum, aut panem, aut pannum (quod
Lacidae cuidam istorum contigit) statim ambigit, num tale quid
unquam habuerit prius...Alloquere, adsta, tange; audit, videt,
sentit, dubius tamen interea ne fallaces sensus mentiantur.   (p.
131)

Snatch from any one of them a coin, a crust, or a coat, and instantly
(as once happened to a certain Lacydas, one of their number) he
begins to doubt whether he ever possessed such a thing ... Speak to
him, stand by him, touch him; he hears, he sees, he feels, yet
doubtfully the while, for his senses may deceive him.

The innovators, on the other hand, seek the startling and
novel, and are much in demand in Moronia Felix, the dwelling
of the Antipodean Pope. This is hardly surprising since the
description follows hard upon the discovery of a coin bearing

the telling motto 'Pour Bon' (Sorbonne, p. 130). The language of Dudosa, as yet current only amongst its originators, is a travesty of Paracelsian terminology intended to debunk both Paracelsus himself and, by carefully contrived implication, the 'new' scholasticism of the Tridentine fathers, and the Jesuits. Not far off shore, as the map of Crapulia shows, lies Sorbonia Insula. As in Rabelais, under the apparent frivolity of the laughter, and the occasionally strained academic wit, lurk real contemporary problems. That they are presented in such an effective manner is largely due to Hall's rapport with his audience. The question of 'persona' with which he grappled in the satires did not arise, for he was addressing himself solely to a sophisticated, learned readership accustomed to the tongue-in-cheek enormities of Erasmus and More. Perhaps this is one of the reasons why the work fared so badly with Milton; its effect upon a serious-minded, radical non-conformist was never considered.

The character of Mercurius, the narrator, is in the nature of a joke. Even the name is double-edged, for while Mercury is undoubtedly the patron of travellers, he is also the patron of thieves, and the principal deity of Lavernia, the land of sharp practice and deceit. But it was here, we are told, that the *Mundus* was written, in Plagiana Provincia, the abode of plagiarists and cribbers—and the work, of course, is full of easily recognizable 'borrowings' (pp. 212–13). In the same bantering vein our guide expresses the desire to be buried in Credulia (land of Catholics, p. 184), subscribes to the laws of the Viraginians (pp. 95–6), and takes up residence in the loins of Pazzivilla, a city shaped like a human body (p. 157). After all, he *is* a traveller, and as Samuel Rowlands pointed out, 'travellers may lie: who knows not that?'[23] If we find it difficult to believe in his Pamphagonian poultry we need only consider the fully authenticated case of the 'Barnacle geese' and 'Samarcandean lambs'. For the latter we have such authorities as J. C. Scaliger and Baron von Herberstein.[24] For the purposes of the allegorical 'dystopia' therefore the 'persona' is perfect. There is no reason to fight it. Rather, the impulse is to enter thoroughly into the joke by accepting it on its own terms, by reading the notes, following up the allusions, detecting the irony, and applauding the witty morality. Although he often

becomes humorously entangled with the characters he encounters, Mercurius remains morally detached. At the end,
having viewed the whole world of Terra Australis, he returns
home laughing:

Hos ego homines, has mores, hos urbes vidi, stupui, risi; annoque
demum tricesimo, itineris tanti laboribus fractus in patriam redii
(p. 214)
These men, these manners, these cities, I saw, wondered at, laughed
at, until finally in the thirtieth year, worn out by the strains of such a
long journey, I returned to my homeland.

The effect, of course, is immensely heightened through the
creation of two very distinct voices. Throughout the narration
itself we are in the presence of our witty, inquiring traveller,
but in the copious and meticulous annotations we are in the
presence of a supposedly detached, scholarly commentator
who goes to work with the thoroughness of a Scaliger or
Casaubon. In other words, whereas Rabelais had allowed his
'extractor of the quintessence' to incorporate his lists of
authorities and allusions into the main body of the text, Hall
went further by turning the work into a burlesque not merely
of the travelogue, but of the contemporary academic textbook
as well. To my knowledge this was the first full-scale use of
this effective device by an English author. With its annotations, scholarly references, maps, illustrations, and explanatory
index, the work stands as the comic counterpart of any of the
masterpieces of classical scholarship being produced at the
same time. As we shall see later on, at least one of their
producers was not allowed to pass unmentioned.

The style of the *Mundus,* also, is appropriate to its scholarly
pretensions. The language in which Mercurius expresses
himself is directly in keeping with his fictional background,
for among the leading lights of Hall's generation—the
generation of Francis Bacon—Ciceronianism had gone out of
fashion. Under the influence of Muret and Lipsius, Latin
prose had begun to seek new models in Seneca, Sallust, and
Tacitus.[25] In itself there was nothing new about this. Politian
had attacked the cult of Ciceronianism in the mid-fifteenth
century; Erasmus had written his scathing *Ciceronianus* in
1528; and Gabriel Harvey had produced a work of the same

name and intention in 1577.[26] The 'new' Senecanism of the
1590s, therefore, was simply the culmination of a movement
which had been gathering force for some time. In adopting the
new clipped style for the *Mundus*—though perhaps as much
under the influence of Plautus and Terence as of Seneca—Hall
set his narrator squarely in the ranks of the most fashionable
literary authorities. Mercurius and his friends are men of their
time.

Generally speaking (and excluding such special effects as
those of burlesqued orations and so forth) the *Mundus* is
composed of short, linear (as opposed to 'periodic') sentences,
making a series of clear, separate points. Few words are wasted
and connective particles are kept to a minimum. In the passage
on the sceptics we have already seen an example of this style at
its most concise: 'Alloquere, adsta, tange; audit, videt, sentit,
dubius tamen interea ne fallaces sensus mentiantur.' (p. 131)
Yet despite their apparent simplicity, such sentences admit of
a high degree of sophistication. Indeed it is one of the ironies
of the 'new' style that it often became as 'artificial' as the style
against which it supposedly represented a reaction. In the
passage above, for example, we find two exactly corresponding
tricola: *alloquere–audit, adsta–videt, tange–sentit.* Hall delighted
in this sort of stylistic poise and was soon to introduce it to
English prose in his *Meditations and Vowes* (1605). Everywhere in the *Mundus* we sense a desire to achieve the effects of
order, arrangement, and patterning. Within single clauses this
is achieved by a careful and precise positioning of words, while
over a wider area the same effect is gained by constructing
whole sentences in the form of balancing (or sometimes
antithetical) clauses accompanied if possible by correspondence of case-ending, form, or sound:

Imaginando, et fingendo nunquam facta, nunquam futura, credendo
quae finxerint, prosequendo quae crediderint.   (p. 137)
In imagining and devising what never was, nor ever will be, in
believing what they have devised, and in pursuing their beliefs.

This particular example displays a number of interesting
features. While the verbal force is borne by the ablative
gerunds, and the asyndeton produces brevity, the sequence of
three balancing pairs takes the account forward in the logical

order of the life-styles in question. The pattern of the sentence
reflects the pattern of its subjects' existences. The awful
inevitability of their fate is hammered home by the sound
effects: the insistence upon the internal rhyme (and asso-
nance) of the ablative endings (*nando/gendo/dendo/quendo*);
the constant repetitions (*nunquam... nunquam... credendo
quae... quae crediderint*); and the elaborate initial alliteration.
The use of such a carefully controlled, if sometimes apparently
artless, style lends to the words of the narrator that sense of
sophistication and easy grace held to be the hallmark of polite
learning. Similar effects are achieved by the employment of
such devices as Senecan antithesis and paronomasia:

praeire volunt omnes, nemo cedere meliori   (p. 174)
non tam portam, quam foramen   (p. 176)
non pedibus... sed manibus genubusque.   (p. 175)
vilissimo ac villosissimo sagulo   (p. 82)
induunt endromida, et superinduunt pallium   (p. 116)
vel natanti nutantique ligno   (p. 119)

   The break with Ciceronianism led not merely to changes in
syntax, but also, as Morris Croll has pointed out, to a new
freedom of expression in terms of vocabulary.[27] Not surprisingly, therefore, the *Mundus* is full of words and expressions
drawn from the comic poets, the satirists, and the late Latin
authors. As in Roman comedy, for example, superlatives and
diminutives abound. Indeed there are over three hundred
superlatives throughout the work, many of which call attention to themselves by appearing in doublets or triplets. The
land of Moronia, for instance, is 'incultissima, vastissima,
populosissima' (p. 113), and its inhabitants, 'frequentissimo
populo', inhabit a climate 'frigore intensissimo' (p. 114). It
would be quite wrong, however, to regard such forms as
merely ornamental. On the contrary, they are extremely
functional, for if the *Mundus* is indeed, as Knight claimed it
was, a land of Platonic forms, everything must be extreme,
either the biggest or smallest of its kind in existence. If we are
dealing with universals, there can be no 'in betweens'.
Moreover, as everyone knows, understatement has never been
characteristic of travellers, and we are in the presence of a
witty, well-travelled scholar entertaining his friends.

Familiar exclamations such as 'pol', 'hercule', 'apage', and 'mi homo' abound, and there is some dialogue and a good many reported or viva voce speeches. Just as Roman comedy is supposed to approximate to the Latin of daily life, it is probably equally true that conversations such as the one with which the work opens reflect the informal Latin debates of the author's university circle. Such language required a subtle blending of the learned and the familiar. Though apparently speaking off the cuff, our narrator frequently draws attention to the appropriateness of his words with such phrases as 'ut cum Apuleio loquar' (p. 25) or 'Apuleiano sensu' (p. 44). His friend Beroaldus is an impassioned storehouse of encyclopaedic knowledge. He can cite authorities at will (pp. 12–13), and quashes interruptions with quick, witty rejoinders. To Mercurius' objection that he may fall into the hands of the Patagonian giants, for example, he replies that opposite Terra Australis lies the Cape of *Good Hope* ('at tu nescis... ex adverso meae terrae incognitae iacere Promontorium *Bonae spei*', p. 10). His whole argument is an academic *tour de force* designed, among other things, to overthrow completely the universally received opinion that the great new world foretold by Seneca—the one discussed in Bacon's essay 'Of Prophecies'—was the Americas (p. 11). Plunging with relish into the vexed question of the position of Solomon's Ophir, he bullies his way through all objections, dismissing them in anticipation:

Quae hic analogia temporis? quae species aequalitatis? Quid pro se heic Varerius?... Increduli mihi iam plane videmini ac pertinaces. (pp. 13–14)
What correspondence of time is here? What sort of equality? What does Varerius say for himself on the issue?... You seem to me clearly incredulous and stubborn.

All the tricks of classical rhetoric are at his fingertips. Blurring reason with emotion, he rails, taunts, asserts, and exhorts. Overwhelmed by the arrogance of his learning and the force of his oratory, opposition collapses: 'vicisti... Beroalde' concedes Mercurius (p. 14)—'you have won'. In effect the whole thing is an elaborate parody of the scholarly disputation. For Hall's contemporaries it reverberates with wryly familiar echoes.

Everywhere too, as in Erasmus' *Encomium Moriae*, sentences
and passages from the great Latin authors are woven
unobtrusively into the text. For example, such an apparently
mundane phrase as 'ut perhibent qui de magnis maiora
loquuntur' (p. 114) is lifted straight from Juvenal (IV.17),
while on a larger scale a good many passages are indebted for
both vocabulary and ideas to similar sources. To mention but
two examples, the description of the life-style in Ucalegon
(pp. 44–5) is heavily indebted to one of Martial's epigrams
(III.82), while the account of the fools' paradise of Moronia
Felix (p. 179) draws upon Cicero's relation of the Endymion
myth in the *Tusculan Disputations* (I. xxxviii, 92). The fact
that such borrowings are difficult for modern readers to spot
should not blind us to their contemporary effect. Commentaries upon the *Encomium Moriae* were produced during
Erasmus' own lifetime, and his mingling of the original and
traditional (in both language and thought) was duly noted.[28]
The annotations to the *Mundus* were intended to ape such
commentaries.

For Hall, Latin was still to a large extent a spoken language.
It had been the normal medium of communication in the
Grammar School at Ashby-de-la-Zouch, and was still the
international language of scholars and diplomats, of the Synod
of Dort, and Convocation, in which it was imperative for a
man such as himself to remain proficient.[29] Hence his concern
for the sound of what he writes. The *Mundus* was designed to
be read aloud, and the new curt style, as Morris Croll points
out, was supposed to approximate more closely than its
predecessor to the rhythms of thought, to the utterances of a
mind thinking aloud.[30] The language of the *Mundus* was very
much a living language, and the voice of Mercurius a living
voice.

Yet perhaps the most striking feature of the style is its
amazing, if deceptive, clarity. 'Acutely clear' was how Peter
Heylyn described it.[31] This clarity, however, is essentially a
device of the ironic satire. On the primary level the narrator is
attacking no one, only relating his own experiences and
commenting upon the manners of his Antipodean hosts. But as
in *Gulliver's Travels,* the apparent simplicity of the account is
contradicted by the plethora of meanings and allusions

lurking just below the surface. The final effect is so far from
simple that both of the work's prospective Victorian translators abandoned it in despair.[32] When we come to examine the
description of the cave of melancholy, we shall have occasion
to see just how deceptive the narrative 'simplicity' actually is.
Indeed in this respect the work is closely related to Rabelaisian
allegory.

In order to appreciate this aspect of the *Mundus* better it is
necessary, however, to proceed beyond considerations of
setting and style to the control with which Hall handles the
levels of primary and secondary (allegoric) narration. Here we
must recognize from the beginning that the Antipodes are not
his creation in the sense that Utopia is the creation of More.
Rather, he anticipated the achievements of modern science-
fiction by basing his imaginary voyage squarely upon universally received scientific and cartographical opinions. If the
whereabouts of Utopia remain undisclosed, the location of
Terra Australis is revealed even to the details of latitude and
longitude. In the five maps which accompany the narration,
fact and fantasy jostle in the same perplexing combinations as
they do in the most scholarly productions of Mercator and
Ortelius. The whole thing is highly suggestive of *Gulliver's
Travels*, and Swift may well have been directly influenced since
a translation of the first new chapters of 'Crapulia' was made
by his good friend Dr William King.[33]

The existence of the great southern continent was a
commonplace of contemporary thought. Much scepticism had
been dispelled by the discovery of the Americas, and in this
case there certainly appeared to be quite an amount of
corroborative evidence. When Magellan saw fires burning on
Tierra del Fuego, he had no way of knowing that the island
was no more than a continuation of the South American land
mass. As well as this, early sightings of Australia only served to
convince the authorities of the time—notably Quiros and
Hakluyt—of the authenticity of the original legends.[34] Discovery seemed imminent.

Just how closely Hall followed contemporary ideas can be
judged from the accompanying illustrations. His Terra Australis is essentially the Australis of Abraham Ortelius and
Gerard Mercator. Since the size and position of their

respective continents are almost identical, their conception of the landscape is also similar. In some areas, as Cornelius Wytfliet pointed out, the projected southern continent came to within a few degrees of the equator, and an extensive portion of its land mass lay well within the temperate zone—it was a land of milk and honey.[35] In the strict sense, therefore, Pamphagonia is not entirely fantastic. Its lush, prolific landscape where birds are too fat to fly corresponds quite closely to what the foremost authorities expected to find. Indeed a particularly zealous Jesuit emphasized the need to gain control of the region before the Protestants for,

from the discoveries and investigations which have been already made in this southern hemisphere, there has been found such fertility, so great plenty and abundance of animals, swine, oxen, and other beasts of different kinds fit for the sustenance of man as has never been seen in our Europe.[36]

Just eleven degrees distant from the Cape of Good Hope, with its headland forty-two degrees from the equator at the exact latitude settled upon by both Mercator and Ortelius, Crapulia is an elaborate travesty of such expectations. Furthermore, as we move along the coastline of the two great continents, 'real' and imaginary, even the same place names recur. In Ortelius's *Epitome of the Theater of the Worlde* (1603), for example, 'Promontorium Terrae Australis', a vast headland jutting far out into the Atlantic, lies close to Tierra del Fuego. As the map of Crapulia makes clear, its resemblance to 'nigellum Crapuliae caput' is far from coincidental, for under the words 'promontorium nigrum' appears the explanation 'olim promontorium Terra Australis'.[37] Moving eastwards along the Ortelian coastline we meet many more familar names, the first being 'Psittacorum Regio' (Land of Parrots), a staple feature of all such maps displaying only minor variations in positioning. Following close upon the parrots comes 'Nova Guinea' usually continued on the extreme left to suggest the rotundity of the globe. To Hall, always alert to the possibility of puns, 'Guinea' suggested the Greek word for 'woman', and the occurrence of parrots in the same area seemed to settle the question. Hence, 'Viraginia' and 'Guinea' are one and the same:

Terra Australis Incognita from *Mundus Alter et Idem* (1605?)

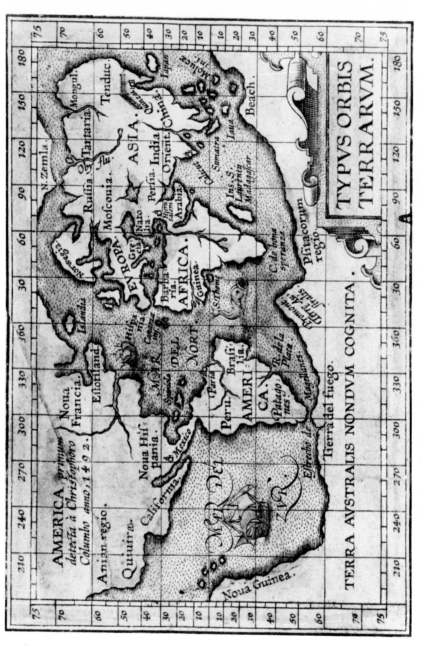

Abraham Ortelius, *Epitome of the Theater of the Worlde* (1603), Map One

Gynia nova, quam alii corrupta voce, *Guineam* appellant; ego vero
Viraginiam, illic sita est, ubi Geographi Europaei *Psittacorum terram*
depingunt. (p. 91)
'Gynia Nova' which some mispronounce as 'Guinea', but which I,
however, call 'Viraginia', is located exactly where European geogra-
phers place Psittacorum Terra.

A marginal note presses the relationship even further:

Guinea nova describi solet extrema pars orientalis terrae Australis
incognitae, proxima regno *Maletur* et *Beach.* hic nos et *Guyniam*
finximus. (p. 91)
'Guinea Nova' is usually described as the extreme easterly area of
Terra Australis Incognita, close to the land of Maletur and Beach.
Here I have placed Guynia.

Both Ortelius and Mercator agree in placing Maletur and
Beach on the promontory of Nova Guinea just below Java and
the Moluccae Insulae, the same Moluccae, of course, alluded
to in Hall's account of 'Insula Hermaphroditica', itself
conveniently positioned between Hermosa and Beach (p.
102).
   Recognizing the satiric potential of Terra Australis was a
master–stroke of invention. A satirist in search of a satiric
landscape could hardly have found better. As it stood in
contemporary maps the continent was the very stuff of satire.
In this respect the comments of Beroaldus must closely echo
those of his creator:

Aegre me semper habuit quod in tabulis Geographicis usque mihi
occurrit; *Terra Australis incognita:* et sane quis haec non plane excors,
sine tacita indignatione legat? nam si *Terram* esse norunt, si
Australem, quomodo tandem incognitam asserunt; et, si incognita sit,
quid mihi illius formam, quid situm unanimes Geographi depinxe-
runt? (p. 8)
It has always annoyed me to find that maps invariably carry the
legend 'The Unknown Southern Land'. And indeed who could be so
soulless as to read it without silent indignation? For if they know it
to be a land, and a southern land, how can they assert that it is
unknown? And if it *is* unknown, whence comes that shape and
position which the cartographers agree unanimously in depicting?[38]

Nothing Hall might write could surpass the fables of serious
scholars. Mercator's marvellous continent of giants and

pygmies, complete with a detailed account of the life-styles of both, rivals even the most fantastic passages of the *Mundus*. Similarly when Mercurius warns Beroaldus of the danger of Patagonian giants (p. 10), he is merely remembering the Ortelian description of the Pampas as 'Patagonum Regio ubi incolae sunt gigantes'.[39] Hall's task was simply to exploit the self-indulgent licence of contemporary cartographers. From Ortelius's non-existent, yet firmly drawn coastline, he led his readers inland to an equally non-existent, yet meticulously detailed interior. Amid so much confusion the road to the hinterland remained open to anyone with an imagination. As Hall himself put it,

What hath any eye seene, or imagination devised, which the pen hath not dared to write? Out of our books we can tell the stories of the *Monocelli*, who lying upon their backs; shelter themselves from the Sunne with the shaddow of their one onely foot. Wee can tell of those cheape-dieted men, that live about the head of Ganges, without meat, without mouthes, feeding only upon aire at their nosthrils: Or those headlesse Easterne people, that have their eyes in their breasts (a mis-conceit arising from their fashion of attire, which I have sometimes seene:) Or of those *Coromandae*, of whom *Pliny* speakes, that cover their whole body with their eares... Or of *Amazons*, or *Pigmees*, or Satyres, or the *Samarcaudean Lambe*, which growing out of the earth by the navell, grazeth so farre as that naturall tether will reach: Or of the Bird *Ruc*, or ten thousand such miracles whether of nature, or event.[40]

Of such material was the *Mundus* born.

The success of the *Mundus* as an imaginary voyage, and an important precursor of *Gulliver's Travels*, rests upon the skill with which Hall brought his Antipodean world to life. With Lucian, Herodotus, and Rabelais before him there could be no shortage of material, yet despite all the undoubted borrowings and allusions the most striking feature of the new continent is its originality. Hall's contemporaries had not been in *this* land before. In Pamphagonia civil honours are proportionate to personal obesity, life centres upon the dinner table, and the chief deity is not Jove, whose thundering sours wine, but insatiable Time, 'edax rerum' as Ovid described him. In Variana the capital city, Farfellia (Butterfly), goes about on wheels, alters its shape in accordance with the whims of its inhabitants, and is entirely composed of collapsible, and therefore mobile, houses. The natives of Lavernia lay magnets along the coast to attract passing ships, while the Yvronians deem it unlawful to rise sober from a meal—and seldom do. The lord of Orgilia controls popular discontent by insisting that all dwellings except his own be constructed of timber. At the first sign of trouble he simply burns the opposition. Everywhere Hall's method is to posit an absurd impossibility, and then to examine the likely probabilities within it. For example, given that choler is hot and dry, and that national characteristics are determined by climatic conditions, how can the choleric Orgilians exist below the Antarctic Circle where Hall has placed them? As Mercurius points out, some explanation is necessary lest the readers should grow incredulous. A flash of academic inspiration saves the day. As it transpires the Orgilians could scarcely live elsewhere:

At novimus, sat bene philosophi, eo verisimilius hoc ex *antiperistasis* posse fieri, quo caelum frigidius; neque illud quisquam stupere poterit, qui noverit Africam regionum torridissimam gelidissimas serpentes generare, et in fornacibus Cypriis vulgo creari muscas, quae sua frigiditate ignem extinguant. E media regione aeris fulgura torqueri ac tonitrua; hanc denique terrae molem ex igne subterraneo; aucto quidem ex ambientis corporis frigiditate quassari hac illac, penitusque commoveri. Nunc ergo suffragante philosophia fidem et spero mihi, et arrogo. (pp. 143–4)

Yet we, clever philosophers that we are, of course realise that such an event is all the more likely to occur through *antiperistasis* the colder the weather becomes. Nor can it be a source of wonder to anyone who knows that the scorching terrain of Africa brings forth the most cold-blooded snakes, or that the fires of Cyprian furnaces are quenched by frosty flies born inside them. Thunder and lightning are hurled from the midst of the heavens, and this great mass of earth is tossed to and fro, and shaken to its very foundations by the force of subterranean fires stirred to action by the coldness of the encircling earth. Now, therefore, with philosophy on my side, I desire, nay demand, your credence.

And so we pass on, our doubts resolved. Elsewhere similar qualms are set at ease by appeals to such unshakeable authorities as Mandeville and Munster, a device common in Rabelais.[41] But just as in Rabelais also, there is a serious side to even the most apparently abandoned laughter.

In the account of Lyperia, for example, there occurs the following description of Antrum Maninconicum (the cave of melancholy):

Vestibulo quidem angusto, et caerulea glacie concreto, intus vero, ut ex sono licet coniectari, tractu valde spatioso. A limine pendent stiriae grandiores, quae velut dentes totidem in horridissimis speluncae faucibus videntur induruisse: Hic fama est raptas melancholicorum animas, intensissimo frigore torqueri: Quisquis ori appropinquaverit introspecturus... sternitur exanimis... sed qui aurem admoverit terrae vel aliquantulum remotiori, quae suspiria, et sive catenarum sive stiriarum decidentium clangorem inaudire sibi videbitur? (pp. 141–2)

The entrance is narrow and thick with bluish ice, but the hollow sound suggests a large open space within. Huge icicles hang from the threshold like so many teeth growing in the horrid jaws of the cave. As legend has it this is where the lost souls of the melancholy are racked in the most intense cold. Anyone who approaches the mouth of the cavern to look inside... falls to the ground lifeless... but should someone put his ear to the ground even a little further off, what sighs of anguish, what crashing of falling chains or icicles will he not seem to hear?

Whereas at first this might seem a purely 'fabulous' product of Hall's fertile imagination, examination proves otherwise. The source of the passage, though hitherto unnoticed, was undoubtedly a paragraph in Richard Eden's *Decades of the New World,* a book which Hall had certainly read and the obvious choice for a writer intending to describe the South Pole. It is one of the works which influenced the 'brainsicke youth' of the *Virgidemiarum.*[42] The passage in question concerns the subterranean caverns of Mount Hecla:

Nere unto these mountaynes are three chynkes or open places in the earthe of houge byggenesse and suche depth (especially at the mounte Hecla) that no syght can attayne thereto. But to such as looke into them, there fyrst appeare men as thowgh they were drowned and yet breathyng furth theyr sowles... Ise floweth abowt the Ilande for the space of seven or eyght moonethes, makynge by runnynge togyther a certeyne miserable waylinge and gronynge noyse not unlyke the voyce of man.[43]

Significantly the account adds that in the opinion of the natives these are the places 'where the evyll soules of theyr people are tormented'. The margin bears the word 'Purgatory'. Similarly, while on their way to visit the Sacred Wineskin of Yvronia, Mercurius and his fellow pilgrim pass Glacialis Insula (Iceland) upon which the narrator notices a snow-capped volcano the nature of which causes him no small amusement:

Mons, inquit, *sacer Dionysii*...Hic scilicet poenas dant infelices umbrae, assidueque cruciantur, donec quis amicorum superstitum, Capellam ardentem inviserit...Subrisi ego, iam mihi visus cantatis-simi illius Purgatorij originem explorasse. (p. 88).
'It is the sacred mountain of Dionysius', he said...'here the unfortunate souls pay for their crimes and are continually tortured until one of their survivors makes a pilgrimage to the Fiery Chapel'...I smiled to myself at having discovered the origin of the much lauded Purgatory.

This was the attraction of the passage in Eden. This was the point of locating the melancholic mountain in a section which concentrates upon the intensely melancholic manners of the three most Catholic nations of Europe, France, Spain, and Italy. Here is no fantasy for its own sake, the intention is pointedly satiric. Some six hundred years previously, we are informed, Odilo, the Abbot of Cluny, had himself in all seriousness located Purgatory under Mount Etna (pp. 88–9). Such gross superstition seemed to Hall to typify the worst aspects of Roman Catholicism. Its 'fables of Purgatory' he thought 'not unworthy of a Satyre',[44] so in terms of contemporary religious controversy the discovery of the Eden passage provided him with the perfect means of reducing the whole doctrine to absurdity. It was exactly what was required to answer the powerful images of Dante's *Purgatorio*, images which in times of peril possessed the minds of even the most resolute Protestants. Perhaps it is no coincidence that Swift also locates Purgatory in Terra Australis Incognita.[45] From the beginning Hall realized that fantasy was a two-edged sword, at once the great flaw and great strength of Roman Catholic dogma. In using fantasy against fantasy he was bravely trying to turn the tables for the last time. Drawing upon the accounts of Homer, Virgil, and the Alcoran, medieval Catholicism had created a terrifying underworld of torture and punishment which the Catholics of his own day had pressed unscrupulously into the service of the Papacy, and its trade in indulgences.[46] In reply he determined first to reduce Purgatory itself to the level of the *absurdly* fantastic, to a symptom of the mental disturbance called melancholy, and then to create another world for the Pope and his minions, the grotesque world of Moronia Pia (land of devout inanity) in which they appear so dwarfish and fatuous as to seem more worthy of pity than scorn. Divine comedy becomes divine farce. Such techniques are typical of the *Mundus*. The satirist is seldom lost in the story-teller. The work is rigidly didactic, and we must now examine its themes more closely.

II. Themes

According to Milton, the fatal flaw of *Mundus Alter et Idem* was its complete lack of moral purpose. In his opinion the work was no more than a bawdy perversion of the 'grave and noble invention which the greatest and sublimest wits in sundry ages. *Plato in Critias,* and our two famous countreymen, the one in his *Utopia,* the other in his *new Atlantis* chose ... to display the largenesse of their spirits by teaching this our world better and exacter things, then were yet known, or us'd.'[47] Just two years after these words were written, however, the *Mundus* was republished in Germany together with Bacon's *New Atlantis* and Tommaso Campanella's *City of the Sun* 'propter affinitatem materiae' (due to the closeness of subject matter).[48] It is therefore of considerable importance that we assess the true relationship of the 'dystopia' to what was, in Milton's eyes at least, the more respectable and dignified 'invention' of the ideal commonwealth. Why, for example, did Hall not compose a new *Utopia* upon solidly Christian lines? Why did he not anticipate the *Christianopolis* of Johann Andreae with whom he had much in common, including a deep respect for Calvin's Geneva? The answer to such questions, I believe, takes us straight to the heart of Hall's conception of human nature.

It is clear from his homilies and devotional tracts that one of Hall's most fundamental tenets was a firm belief in the innate degeneracy of the human race. A Calvinist, he regarded sin, suffering, and ignorance as the inevitable effects of the Fall from which it was impossible for either individuals or communities to escape. While divine grace might help man attain the glory of salvation in some future state, here he could never hope to transcend the conditions of his own mortality. Imperfection was his inalienable inheritance. Doctrines such as those of the Antinomians and Separatists resulted from interpreting a spiritual promise in a worldly sense. But the kingdom of Christ was not of this world. The New Jerusalem was a spiritual state, and could not be erected by politicians and churchmen, let alone by carpenters and masons. Attempts to establish exclusive congregations of the regenerate in the midst of 'Babylon' were completely misguided; until the last harvest the chaff was destined to grow with the grain. Whenever Hall uses the expression 'Utopian', therefore, he does so in the context of an attack upon the unreal expectations of fanatical separatists. Discussing the spiritual beauty of the Church, for example, he writes:

But let no idle Donatist of Amsterdam dreame hence of an Utopicall perfection . . . The rifenesse of their familiar excommunications may have taught them to seek for a spotlesnesse above; And if their furious censures had left but one man in their Church, yet that one man, would have need to excommunicate the greater halfe of himselfe, the old man in his owne bosome.[49]

Similarly in connection with the subject of Christian liberty, he refers to such 'rebellious spirits' for whom 'there is no freedom . . . but in the bold censures of authority, in the seditious calumniations of superiours, and in their own utopical prescriptions.'[50] In the *Mundus* itself he suggests that the Brownists and members of the Family of Love may well divert their attention from the Americas to the Antipodes— perhaps allured by the attractions of his own account. Their holy city may now rise in Moronia Pia (land of devout inanity, p. 189). In other words, Hall could not countenance the Utopian ideal either theologically or scientifically: theologically, because the earthly Paradise had already been irretrievably lost; scientifically, because, as he never tired of explaining, the advancement of learning was no substitute for the natural righteousness which was the first casualty of the Fall. Between

Hall and the Utopians, therefore, there gaped the same ideological chasm as had previously separated the Humanists from the early Reformers.[51] The scholars cherished a hope of human perfection, the divines pronounced such hopes vain.

In Hall's opinion the world was in moral and physical decline. While still at university he became celebrated for his defence of the proposition 'Mundus senescit', 'the earth is growing old.'[52] Seen in this light, his use of the myth of the Golden Age in the *Virgidemiarum* is more than just a skilful redaction of a conventional classical motif. For him, the legend symbolized man's inevitable decline following the loss of his original perfection:

> Then crept in *Pride*, and peevish Covetise:
> And men grew greedy, discordous and nice.[53]

He warns in his *Epistles* that the world must degenerate before the Second Coming. Already 'three great Idols, Honour, Pleasure, Gaine' have 'shared the earth amongst them' and common experience justifies the prophecy that 'these last [days] shall be worst.'[54] It is hardly surprising, therefore, to find him launching a full-scale attack in 1650 upon the millenarian expectations of the fifth monarchist John Archer. His views remained unchanged to the end. In *The Revelation Unrevealed* (1650) he insists that the innate imperfections of human nature will always render even the best-led, best-planned Utopias completely unworkable. Here below, we can be free of neither sin nor bodily affliction 'since both these are, and ever will be the unavoidable companions of frail humanity; and the miserable symptomes of our fleshly nature'.[55]

The *Mundus* is essentially a satire upon human imperfection, one of the foremost manifestations of which is, of course, the vanity of human wishes. In many respects, the very decision to write a 'dystopia' itself constitutes a sharp comment upon delusive worldly expectations. As has often been pointed out, the discovery of the New World lent a new impetus to Utopian aspirations.[56] Hand in hand with the ideal of the noble savage went the hope of re-establishing the Eden of primitive Christianity on the other side of the Atlantic. 'The discovery and colonization of the New World', we have been reminded, 'took place under the sign of eschatology.' Columbus wrote his *Book of Prophecies*, and the transatlantic voyaging of the more religious was commonly represented as a return 'to Christ, to Nature, to Paradise'.[57] Little less was expected of the lush, temperate lands of the Antipodes. According to Richard Eden, for example, 'yf there bee any earthely Paradyse in the worlde, it can not bee farre from these regions of the south.'[58] We may take Hall's reply from *The Remedy of Prophanenesse* (1637). There, commenting upon the legend that St. Brendan 'upon long and wearisome travell, at last went so farre, as to come to the sight of the earthly Paradise', he declares,

They may, that list, believe it, but sure I am; Never any mortall eye (since the Angell brandished his sword there) could find ought worthy the name of a *Paradise*, in this inferiour world; here is Purgatory enough, and perhaps, some hell above ground: But if, as *Ortelius* of late held, that all the whole earth was, at the first, *Paradise*, any man shall now think that any part of it is so still, I shall pitty him; and think him worthy the pleasure of these earthly torments.[59]

With the publication of his *Quo Vadis?* in 1617, Hall entered the great debate on the grand tour taking a firm stand against the wanderlust of some of his contemporaries. Central to his argument was the contention that idle travelling partook of the fruitless but age-old quest for some form of earthly Paradise, some ultimate sensual pleasure—an idea perhaps implicit in the legend of Brendan, itself a late Christianization of older pagan myths concerning the fabled 'western paradise'.[60] In striking contrast, when Hall himself first journeyed abroad in 1605 it was to witness at first hand the depravity of Roman Catholicism. He was indignant that man should become 'the drudge or Lacquay of his owne imagination'. What mattered was peace of mind:

The private contentment of a mans owne hart in the view of forraine things, is but a better name of an humorous curiosity. If a man yeeld to run after his appetite and his eye, he shall never know where to rest, and after many idle excursions, should lie downe, weary, but unsatisfied. For, give me a man that hath seen *Iudasses* Lanthorne at Saint *Dennises*, the Ephesian *Diana* in the Louvre, the great vessell at

Heidelberg... what peace hath his heart, above those that sit at home, and contemne these toies? And what if that mans fancy shall call him to the stables of the great *Mogol*, or to the solemnities of *Mecha*, or to the Library of the Mountaine of the Moone, will he be so far the drudge or Lacquay of his owne imagination, as to undertake this pilgrimage?[61]

When Mercurius sets forth in the good ship Phantasia, he does so under the influence of Peter Beroaldus, an insuppressible dreamer in love with fame, and longing for the title 'Inventor orbis novi' (p. 11). But his dreams of a new world have served merely to increase his dissatisfaction with the world he inhabits, and while promising to his companions a life of wondrous adventure, he is forced to admit that hitherto his own adventures have been a series of disappointments (pp. 2–4). Yet instead of drawing the conclusion that his aspirations may be inherently deceptive, he merely concludes that he has not as yet travelled far enough. Hence the projected journey to the Antipodes. He is like Tennyson's Ulysses who 'cannot rest from travel' and for whom all experience is an arch 'wherethro/gleams that untravelled world, whose margin fades/For ever and for ever when I move'. Totally committed to the world and its vanities, he is exactly the sort of person of whom Hall entirely disapproves. In the event, however, and quite fittingly, he gets no further than Montauban, and Mercurius is forced to sail on alone towards the 'black headland of Crapulia' thereby fulfilling the great expectations ('tantam expectationem') of the voyage (p. 18).

Taken at face value, what he discovers is indeed an earthly Paradise, a land flowing with milk and honey after the fashion of the medieval Land of Cokaygne. The inhabitants do no work, yet have everything. There are mountains of butter and rivers of wine, and the abundance of the earth comes forth of its own accord. Yet despite it all, the life-style of the inhabitants is one of complete moral, and even physical, degradation. Having made gods of food and drink, they wallow in their own unhealthy obesity. Though seen in comic perspective, they are clearly those of whom St. Paul has written 'the belly is their god.' Perhaps intentionally, they are the equivalent of Rabelais's 'Gastrolaters'.[62] When not simply grotesque, they are completely revolting:

(quod vix prae nautea memorare possum) caseum vulgo tam diu
servent, dum totus in vermiculos resolvatur, et tum demum viva
animalcula ipsam putidissimi cibi putredinem, paulo sacchari
adspersa, nimis avide vorant delicatissimi Epulones. (p. 40)
And something so disgusting I can scarcely bring myself to recall it:
these fastidious diners are in the habit of preserving cheese so long
that the whole thing dissolves into a mass of maggots, at which point,
sprinkling a little sugar on top, they eagerly devour the worms live,
the very rottenness of the rotting food.

This is Cokaygne gone wrong, the earthly Paradise after the
Fall:

Iure quidem avito Frugiona, terra nunc paulo remotior, hanc sibi
regionem vendicat: Ferunt enim Saturni aevo, Principes Frugionios
toti huic orbi dedisse iura, et istic regiam suam posuisse. (p. 23)
By virtue of ancient law, Frugiona [land of the good life], a land
now lying a little further off, claims this region as its own. The story
goes that in the age of Saturn [the Golden Age] the rulers of
Frugiona held sway over all this domain, and had their palace there.

Frugiona has now moved further off not because of any
essential change in the land, but because of the marked change
in its inhabitants ('moribus prorsus immutatis') who have
become increasingly vain and foolish: '*Moronia* sola interponi-
tur Crapuliae et Frugionae' ('only the land of folly separates
gluttony from the good life', p. 23). The earthly Paradise is
destroyed by, and helps to destroy, its inhabitants. What Hall
seems to be saying is that a return to Eden in our present state
is impossible, Eden would destroy us. 'By the sweat of thy
brow' is a prescription for health:

Exulant lege Sybaritica, non modo Galli omnes, sed et omne genus
artificum; Agricolas enim soli hic agunt porci, quod antiquitus
factum Aegyptiis; nec reliquis est opus: sunt tamen ditioribus
ministri; quorum alter expergiscentis oculos aperit lenta manu; alter
edenti ventulum facit flabello, alter frusta hiantis ori immitit; excipit
alter urinam, alter cingulum solvit nectitque; domino sat est
ingestum ori cibum mansitare, digerere, egerere. (p. 44)
The Sybaritic law has driven not merely all cocks [possibly
eunuchs], but also all sorts of artisans into exile. As in ancient Egypt,
their only farmers are pigs, they need no others. The wealthy,
however, are attended by servants: one opens the eyes of his
wakening master with a gentle touch; another raises a delicate wind

with a fan as he eats; another places morsels of food in his gaping mouth; another collects his urine; and another looses and ties his girdle. Their master need only chew, digest, and void the food put into his mouth.

To the extreme left of the maps of the Antipodes (an area never visited by Mercurius) lies Terra Sancta, 'ignota etiam adhuc', the Holy Land as yet unknown—and destined to remain unknown as long as the traveller, like Bunyan's pilgrims, wanders through 'vanity fair'. 'Ignota etiam adhuc' or some such phrase was, of course, the common way of referring to Terra Australis in contemporary maps, and it is therefore the irony of Mercurius' journey that in seeking to chart the unknown he discovers that the world is the same everywhere. The same vices and follies plague both hemispheres, but the spiritual world, the holy land, remains an uncharted mystery. Yet here all the really important discoveries await their Columbus; here lies the real Paradise. The 'dystopia' of the *Mundus* presents a purposely distorted view of worldly contentments in order to encourage the prospective 'traveller' to undertake the spiritual journey into the unknown. Paradoxically, of course, the physical distortion presents an accurate image of the spiritual state of the present world. Seen from the Christian point of view this *is* how it appears for in this sort of satire 'social rituals are seen from the outside, not to make them more consistent but simply to demonstrate their inconsistency, their hypocrisy, or their unreality.'[63] Hall's *Heaven upon Earth* (1606), one remembers, presents not a blueprint for the perfect society, but a personal religious philosophy. Its Paradise is a state of mind. To have 'heaven upon earth' is to believe in the heaven to come.

Seen in this perspective the central section of the *Mundus*, the description of Moroniae Felicis Paradisium, Fool's Paradise, takes on a new significance. The 'Paradise' is the focal point of all Moronia (land of fools) and is visited at least once by everyone, both Antipodeans and Northerners alike: 'semel insanivimus omnes' (p. 173). It consists of a golden mountain on top of which is a resplendent crystal palace, an archetypal feature of 'the earthly paradise in all mythologies'.[64] Here is the dwelling of the goddess Fortuna, the dispenser of worldly goods, who, according to the old proverb, invariably favours fools ('favet fatuis', p. 173). Impressive as her establishment at first appears, however, it is not what it seems. For a start the 'golden' mountain is not really made of gold at all, only of alchemists' gold, or 'fools' gold': 'qui tamen si lubet ferro metalli robur experiri, in pulverem illico evanescit; si flamma, in fumum' (p. 172: 'Should anyone seek to assay the firmness of the metal with iron, it vanishes instantly into dust, with fire, into smoke'). In the valley below gather thousands of suppliants in the hope that whatever they pray for in a spirit of belief ('credula mente'), and are prepared to wait for long enough, must eventually be forthcoming. Desire attracts them, and hope detains them. In effect the scene is a powerful dramatization of Juvenal's famous tenth satire:

Notavi hic alium negatos precaturum amores, alium pacem modo domesticam, alium honores, divitias alium...Sedebat hic prope portam superciliosus quidam rerum Dominus, novissimae proximam, uti ferunt, monarchiam petiturus: Heic deformes quaedam virgunculae, formae gratiam; illic anus rugosae redivivam sperabant adolescentiam; hic sterilis liberos, illic serva libertatem; omnes aliquid, singuli aliud meditabantur. (pp. 174–5)

Here I saw one about to beg the fulfilment of unrequited love; another who sought only a peaceful household; another who sought honours and another still wealth...Here beside the gate sat an haughty lord of public affairs whose suit, it was said, was the next available monarchy. Here some ugly young girls sought beauty; there wrinkled old women sought the restoration of youth. Here a barren matron sought children; there a maidservant sought her liberty. All desired something, but each one something different.

Upon a given signal the suppliants crawl frantically up the mountain on hands and knees, pushing one another aside, cruelly mocking those behind, and bitterly envying those ahead (p. 174)—yet all in vain. The suppliants are gulls, and find many only too ready to take advantage of their stupidity. The goddess is surrounded by a swarm of avaricious priests who embezzle and pilfer the possessions of her clients, for on the level of religious allegory—and we are still in the papal regions of the Antipodes—she is also the Madonna of Loreto, and Erasmus's Madonna Parathalassia.[65] Such overlapping gives rise to no inconsistency, for in Hall's eyes it was to

worldly vanity that the baroque Catholicism of the Counter-
Reformation made its strongest appeal. The splendours of the
papal court, the dazzling attractions of ornate basilicas, and
the breath-taking pageantry of Catholic ritual, smacked of a
kingdom very much of this world.[66] Hence his objections to
the grand tour, and the dangerous exposure of the young to
the strangely compelling Madonna before whose numerous
shrines thousands of suppliants prostrated themselves each
year. Standing between Rome and the advance of the
Reformation, she offered to her clients indulgences, blessings,
and miracles. To her enemies she was worse than Fortuna: she
made 'vanity' respectable.

That this passage prompts such specific applications cannot
in any way detract from its more general significance.
Essentially Hall is concerned with the human condition: *Spera,
Crede, Expecta* (p. 176) are the bywords of more than the
superstitious. What he is saying is that the cult of the
Madonna partakes of the vanity of human wishes which is his
major theme. The wild scramble up the hill of Fortune to the
glittering, but insubstantial, crystal palace at the top symbolizes the futility of all worldly aspirations. Fortuna, goddess of
the world rejected by the heavens, is the arch cony-catcher
whose victims are the worldly. The fate of the one pilgrim
whose progress we are privileged to follow is indicative of the
fate of them all. For one fleeting day he attains the glory and
pomp of a non-existent crown, only to be cast headlong down
in the midst of his celebrations as a spectacle of folly. Yet his
fall impairs neither his own faith nor that of the onlookers.
Not Fortune but his own inadequacy takes the blame, and
others are far too intent upon their own progress up the gilded
hill to pause long over his calamity (pp. 178–81). The point, of
course, is not merely that the pleasures of this life are
ultimately as unreal as the pilgrim's non-existent crown, but
also that man seldom learns from his own mistakes. For the
majority the attractions of the earthly Paradise are too great.

The more we examine the *Mundus* the more apparent
becomes its moral purpose, a purpose to which even its
subversion of the 'noble invention' adopted by so many of
Milton's worthies directly contributes. Hall was suspicious of
Utopias, and Campanella's fanatical and disastrous attempts to

realize the plans of *The City of the Sun* (with which the *Mundus* was republished in 1643) can only have served to justify his own choice of 'dystopian' satire.[67] If the views of Frances Yates are correct, even Andreae's *Christianopolis* and Bacon's *New Atlantis* were associated with such suspect philosophies as those of the shadowy Rosicrucian brotherhood from which Hall, an extremely orthodox Christian, would quite naturally wish to dissociate himself.[68] Therefore, although Milton's strictures provide us with an excellent approach to Hall's work, we must always remember that he was anything but an unprejudiced reader. Actually the didactic intention of the *Mundus* is clear from the outset, for, as I explain in Appendix A, the earliest annotations serve as instructions on how the work should be read, as does the explanatory index to the place-names. The moral teaching which Milton found wanting in the satire—or pretended to find wanting for polemic purposes—is actually omnipresent, since the very realization that the work *is* a 'dystopia' posits the existence of an accepted norm.[69] Terra Sancta adjoins Terra Australis.

Though fundamentally an attack upon vice, the *Mundus* makes no attempt to follow the age-old and somewhat exhausted pattern of the seven deadly sins. Nevertheless it does display a highly intelligible plan of 'travel'. With Pamphagonia and Yvronia, the two provinces of Crapulia, we begin with what are predominantly sins of the flesh: gluttony, drunkenness, and sloth. From the land of wine (Yvronia) we then pass appropriately to the land of women, Viraginia, and onwards to the various sexual enormities of Aphrodysia and Insula Hermaphroditica. Having now witnessed the sins of the body, we proceed to the sins of the mind, and it soon becomes apparent that these are the more harmful and serious of the two. In Moronia (land of folly) we encounter the Paradise of Fortuna, the Catholic powers of the continent, the Antipodean Pope, and a great variety of assorted heretics: these destroy both body and soul. There follows Lavernia (land of deceit), the place where the intellect is pressed into the service of unrighteous Mammon. Here, in the province of Codicia (from the Spanish for avarice), the journey concludes with an image of complete bestiality, of men turned into swine. It is Hall's equivalent of Swift's Yahoo:

Quadrupedum more prona semper facie incedunt, ne quid inter
eundum surreptione dignum praetermittant; neque caelum unquam
suspiciunt: quod ad vocem, grunniunt illi quidem, non loquuntur.
(p. 213)
They go about like four-legged beasts with their face to the ground
lest they miss anything worth snapping up; they never look up at the
sky. As far as speech is concerned, they grunt rather than talk.

Refusing to traverse the various 'pigsties' yet remaining, the
narrator suddenly breaks off bringing his account to an abrupt
end (p. 214). The conclusion is certainly unexpected, but
perhaps in terms of the allegory the narrative could have gone
no further. The image of the unclean swine is traditionally the
ultimate in human degradation.[70] The fact that the Codicians
never look at the sky is extremely significant since man's
upright stature has long been used as a symbol of his higher
intellectual nature. 'Other Creatures', Hall tells us, 'grovell
downe to their earth, and have all their senses intent upon it;
this [man] is reared up towards Heaven, and hath no more
power to looke beside Heaven, then to tread beside the
Earth.'[71] Ideally man looks beyond the world to God. But this,
of course, is true only when he exercises the gift of reason, the
determining factor in the distinction between man and beast.
Hence the centrality of the description of Moronia, by far the
longest and most elaborate section of the work.

The heartland of Moronia is Moronia Fatua (land of
unreason) from whence springs the entire race. The Fatuans
are of two sorts, Scioccians (from the Italian for fatuous) and
Bavarians (from the French for nonsense). Having chosen to
ignore nature's gift of reason, the former live like animals. The
closest analogy Mercurius can suggest is a herd of human
'sheep' apparently oblivious of their relationship to the rest of
homo sapiens. In other words they represent man's rejection of
the distinction between himself and lower life-forms. They
serve to remind us how easily he can slip from his station in the
chain of being through 'Arcadian' apathy (pp. 150–2).

More interesting, however, are the Bavarians, who use
reason with a vengeance. Discontented with ordinary affairs
they busy themselves *de natura rerum*. Among their number
are the tribe of Alchemists who cannot realize that the easiest
way to make gold is, as the oracle tells them, to work for it (p.

153). The greatest folly of the Bavarians is their intellectual presumption. Noticing, for example, that we commonly shut one eye in order to focus the other, they save their children the bother by plucking out one eye at birth (p. 152). They are those who, in biblical terms, as Hall declares elsewhere, 'blind the right eye of [their] understanding' through pride.[72] Like Swift's Laputans they discover folly in their quest for singularity and profundity. On the comic level this is excellently demonstrated in the account of the debates in the senate of Pazzivilla, city of fools and mother city of all Moronia. The question before the house at the time of Mercurius' visit is that of the improvement of the metropolis, and the suggestions range from the construction of a mountain to the conversion of the completely land-locked city into a seaport. But since mountains are dangerous and seas hazardous, a new suggestion wins the day:

ut unaquaeque domus pro mole sua pyramidem sibi altiorem erigeret, cuius apici summo gallus aeneus argenteusve, aurea crista insignis, quavis aura versatilis insideret; in unaquaque pyramide horologium collocaret; singulis horologiis campanulam adiungeret; nec dici posse, quam elegans ac iucundum spectaculum, tam frequens excelsarum pyramidum series adventantibus peregrinis videretur, quamque per horas aurem deliniret tot tintinnabulorum iugiter sonantium harmonia. (p. 160)

(I suggest) that each house, in proportion to its size, should erect upon its roof a lofty pyramid, on whose summit shall perch a golden or silver cock adorned with a golden comb and free to twirl in every breeze. Each pyramid must have its clock, and every clock its bell. This being effected, words cannot express how charming and delightful a spectacle such a cluttered array of lofty spires must present to the eyes of [approaching] travellers, nor indeed how melodious a harmony must hourly strike the ear from the concerted jangling of so many bells.

The speaker's victory is entirely appropriate. Weathercocks are symbols of all that is fickle and arbitrary, bells are the traditional trappings of fools, and the discordant jangling aptly suggests the disruption of Elizabethan ideals of social 'harmony'. Since reason has been ousted by illusions of grandeur, the passage forms an excellent link between Moronia Fatua and Moronia Felix, the abode of Fortuna who favours fools.

And fortune, one remembers, is the principal enemy of the
Stoic *sapiens.* Hence the dramatization of Juvenal's vanity of
wishes theme. Hall is saying that neither appearance nor
fortune have any more significance than we are pleased to
attribute to them, and that at the heart of all human
imperfection lies the misdirection or perversion of human
reason.[73]

It is this persistent emphasis on rationality, even in
theological matters, which makes the *Mundus* such a characteristically Protestant satire: all the lands of Moronia acknowledge the Antipodean Pope, *Il Buffonio Ottimo Massimo* (p.
190). This aspect of the work becomes clearest in the
treatment of Moronia Pia (land of devout inanity) which
follows hard upon the description of Moronia Felix. Pia is
composed of two provinces, Credulia, the land of superstitious
Catholics, and Doxia, the abode of separatists and schismatics.
The one trait which unites them is the abandonment of reason,
whether it be to tradition, superstition, or pride. Yet, as in the
case of Crapulia, the land itself is essentially good, since
devotion and religion are essentially good. The fault lies solely
with the inhabitants. The Credulians are the most pious
people on earth. When they walk they put one foot before the
other transversely thereby making the sign of the cross at
every step (p. 183). They exorcize and bless a wide range of
inanimate objects, and create hundreds of new 'gods' (saints)
each year (p. 184). Yet who their chief deity actually is, or
what they believe of him, they hold it unfit to inquire: 'sat illis
est maiorum vestigia sequi, et sanctorum olim sedes occupare'
(p. 183. 'It is sufficient for them to follow in the footsteps of
their ancestors, and in time take possession of the dwellings of
the saints'). Luther or Calvin could have said no more.

The Doxians, on the other hand, inquire far too much.
Rejecting the fundamentals of Christianity they substitute
their own fantasies instead. The result is the nightmare of
schism and fragmentation which had already overtaken
Holland and was now threatening England: the account ends
with the Brownists and the Family of Love (p. 189). In Hall's
opinion all such heretics were labouring under a self-induced
illness. Doxia is the spiritual 'Bedlam' of which he warned in
his meditations.[74] Nor does he view the confusion with any

feeling of pity; his attitude is totally uncompromising. In so far as they have rejected the dictates of enlightened reason, both heretics and Catholics are ultimately responsible for their own folly. In *The Peace-Maker* (1645), a book concerned with this very problem, he writes, 'They are much mistaken that sleight the mistakings of the understanding, as no sinnes; rather, as that faculty hath more of the man then the other inferiour; so the aberrations of that must be more haynous.'[75] Anyone, he held, who listened to enlightened reason in a spirit of sincerity would be convinced. Hence the emphasis upon reason in his own sermons and religious tracts. For him, enlightened reason is reason directed towards man's ultimate good, both physical and spiritual. As such it is the 'norm' in the *Mundus* which must be grasped and held. However, in Variana, the land of mutability, nobody has the power to decide upon anything. Here are the twin colleges of sceptics and innovators, and here also is the sometime Calvinist, sometime Lutheran, sometime Catholic Justus Lipsius, the notoriously inconstant expounder of the virtues of 'constancy'. Holding a half-open book, with one hand resting upon his beloved dog (his customary pose), he appears as 'Const. Lip.' (constant Lipsius) on one side of an old coin recovered in an archaeological dig—a glance, of course, at his interest in Roman antiquities (p. 129). On the reverse side is a multicoloured chameleon, and all around lies the restless, shifting landscape suggestive of the many striking passages in the famous *De Constantia* (1584) which depict so powerfully the mutability of earthly things.[76] Here, a faded memory on an old coin, their author has himself become a part of that mutability. He symbolizes the seduction of spiritual constancy by the vagaries of the physical world. In the *Mundus* even the most apparently specific allusions make points of universal significance.

Below the surface of the narration the *Mundus* is deeply concerned with central human problems, and just as Hall followed the science of the day in establishing the position of his southern world, he did the same on a more serious level in endeavouring to depict the workings of the human psyche. Lyperia and Orgilia (the two provinces of Moronia Aspera), the most apparently fantastic of all the Moronian landscapes, are none other than allegoric depictions of the theory of the

humours, and the received views upon the nature of melancholy and imagination.

The world of Moronia Aspera represents an attempt to
portray mental disturbance in concrete terms. In keeping with
Hall's usual practice it is a world of extremes excluding all
elements except those which take their being from itself. As
one might expect, the details of the depiction are neither
original nor peculiar to Hall, occurring previously in such
authorities as Montaigne or Timothy Bright, and recurring
afterwards in Burton.[77] Indeed Hall has built up his picture in
much the same way as a modern author might set about the
creation of an 'Oedipus castle' in which every element of the
description represented some feature or other of the Oedipus
complex. In such a case only the objective reality of the castle
would be considered fictional. So it is with Moronia Aspera, or
rather, so it was for Hall's contemporaries.

Since melancholy was caused by an excess of black bile, for
instance, the castle of 'Le Grand Chagrin', the ruler of
Lyperia, is made of jet (p. 136). Since melancholy is also cold
and dry, Lyperia (land of solitary melancholics) is situated
'sub ipso polo...gelu perpetuo constricta...caelo fruitur
sicco, et frigidissimo' (p. 135: 'beneath the pole itself...per-
petually locked in ice...having an intensely cold, dry
climate'). Its inhabitants are the casebook examples of the
melancholic temperament:

Incolae plerique hispidi, macilenti, inculti, colore fusco, crine nigro,
cute dura et aspera, fronte torva, neglecta veste, vultu tristi, oculis
cum stupore quodam fixis, nec se facile moventibus, introrsum vero
demissis, ac veluti in cavis maxillarum tumulis iam diu sepultis.   (p.
136)
The inhabitants for the most part are shaggy, lean, and uncouth, of
dark complection, with black hair, coarse rough skin, savage brow,
negligent attire, and sombre face. Their eyes, fixed in a sort of daze
and moving only with great effort, are cast far back as if long since
buried away in the cavernous tombs of their jaws.

Preferring to live alone like hares ('leporum more') they
anxiously shun all society, for as Burton explains 'the
Egyptians...in their hieroglyphics expressed a melancholy
man by a hare sitting in her form.'[78] Speaking of the sorrows of

the melancholic, the same author refers to their 'cordolium' or heart-break.[79] The palace of the Lyperian duke, one remembers, is aptly named Cordolium (p. 136).

This is typical of Hall's method. Even the list of wild imaginings attributed to his Lyperians is not, except in the way he handles it, original. As a comparison with Burton shows, they are the usual delusions popularly associated with melancholy: one man thinks he is dead, another that he is made of glass, another still that he supports the burden of Atlas.[80] In some cases we are even provided with annotations directing us to the source of the information. For an account of men who think themselves dead, for example, we are referred to Tommaso Garzoni's *L'hospidale de' pazzi incurabili* (1586), a work with which Hall seems to have been well acquainted (p. 137).[81]

Belief in the power of the imagination and its connection with melancholia and mental disturbance was the orthodoxy of the day. Montaigne notes the theory (to which he partly subscribes) that the imagination can alter even the physical world.[82] Hence it was fashionable to attribute various aspects of 'magic' and witchcraft to the same faculty. Burton's discussion of the power of the imagination, for example, relates witchcraft to fantasy and illusion.[83] In this connection Hall allows Mercurius a cynical aside at the expense of decrepit 'sagae' (witches) who claim astonishing supernatural powers, yet commonly die of such mundane complaints as hunger and poverty (p. 140). At this point, to a modern reader, the narration seems to have gone off at a tangent, but contemporary audiences would certainly have appreciated the logic of the progression.[84] Within the superstructure of the travelogue Hall was recreating the world of diabolic illusion into which the melancholic was in danger of plunging himself. Hamlet alludes to the same belief when he voices the fear that the devil may, out of his 'weakness' and his 'melancholy' abuse him to damn him. Contemporary society believed in witchcraft, and Hall himself explained the phenomenon as a dual illusion practised by Satan: 'Hee both deludes the Witches conceit, and the beholders eyes.'[85] As he also extended the explanation to werewolves, it is not surprising to find 'lycanthropici' prowling about in the same melancholic

landscape as the witches (p. 141). The world of Lyperia, like
that of Macbeth—and Burton mentions ambition as a cause of
melancholy—is a world of delusions, sleeplessness, and traffic
with the forces of Hell; for those trapped inside 'nothing is but
what is not':

Quaeris quid agant, vel quo tandem modo aetatem terant? Sane,
imaginando, et fingendo nunquam facta, nunquam futura, credendo
quae finxerint, prosequendo quae crediderint.   (p. 137)
You ask what they do, or how they spend their time? In imagining
and devising what never was nor ever will be, in believing what they
have devised, and pursuing their beliefs.

Unless we set Hall's account in historical perspective we are in
danger of missing the whole point, for as we proceed from
Lyperia to Orgilia the connection with medicine becomes even
more exact. Orgilia is the domain of choleric melancholy, one
of the traditional divisions of the malady established by
Galen.[86] Consequently the division of the dukedom into the
four provinces of Lechitia, Prasinia, Iodia, and Glastia, each
with suitably coloured inhabitants, is based upon the common
resolution of 'unnatural choler' into four distinct kinds
designated by colour (p. 144). Such an account is to be found,
for example, in Thomas Elyot's standard work, *The Castel of
Helth.*[87]
    These are among the most difficult and complex sections of
the *Mundus,* and my analysis has necessarily involved some
over-simplification. As almost everywhere else in the work, the
satire is functioning on a number of complementary levels
woven together by the elements I have emphasized. Owing to
the abundance of French, Spanish, and Italian place-names,
for example, (as opposed to the German, Dutch, and English
names in Crapulia), it is obvious that this is also an attack
upon the Catholic nations of the Continent. The seat of the
Duke of Orgilia is called the Tarocchium (from the Italian
'taroccare', to become angry). Here he lives upon a hill of
skulls (p. 145), devours all who come within the sphere of his
influence, and maintains within his palace the sacred chapel of
the Inquisition, Saint Shambles ('Sacellum Inquisitorium,
ipsis *Sancta Carniceria',* p. 147). Its horrific description needs
no explanatory gloss. The presence of such elements, however,

is by no means inconsistent with the treatment of the humours. As we have seen, the contradiction between the heat of the Orgilians and the coldness of their climate (for they are choleric melancholics) is wittily explained away with reference to *antiperistasis*. But more importantly, melancholy and choler in their various manifestations were commonly held to be primary ingredients of the Spanish and Italian temperaments, in keeping with the theory of national characteristics to which Beroaldus alludes at the outset of the journey (pp. 4–5). [88] In this way the different levels of the satire are made to cohere. The tyranny of the Inquisition, and the belligerence of the Catholic powers are satirized as symptoms of mental disturbance. Their appearance in the Antipodes justifies Drogius's warning about the Patagonian giants, for they are described as being more bloodthirsty than the Patagonians themselves (p. 143). In this way too all the references to cannibalism, particularly in Orgilia, are made to reflect darkly upon the doctrine of Transubstantiation while at the same time remaining consistent with the primary level of the travelogue.[89] The work, in effect, is a subtle blending within the superstructure of the fantasy of the various levels of national, personal, and religious satire. This, of course, lays it open to the sort of moral attack with Milton so unscrupulously exploited for his own purposes. Now that the controversies of their age are over, however, we can assess both authors more accurately than circumstances allowed them to assess one another. Even in such exalted company the 'first' English satirist holds his own.

3.

CHARACTERS AND CONTROVERSIES

I. Characters of Vertues and Vices

While Hall's claim to be the first English satirist has often been disputed, his position as the first of the seventeenth-century Character–writers has won widespread acceptance. Indeed, as a result of the revival of interest in the genre, the *Characters* have attracted more attention than most of his other literary writings. Ironically, however, they were quickly overshadowed in his own lifetime by the works of Overbury and Earle.[1] Nevertheless, it seems indisputable, that the credit for introducing the new genre to English letters must go to Hall.[2]

The *Characters of Vertues and Vices* appeared in 1608 with a dual dedication to Lord Denny and Lord Hay, Hall's new patron and his son-in-law. Originally the work comprised eight sketches of virtuous types as opposed to fifteen of the vicious sort, but in 1614 two new portraits ('The Penitent' and 'He is a Happy Man') were added to the *Vertues,* thereby bringing the final total to twenty-five. Hall's declared model throughout was Theophrastus, the Greek character-writer whose works had been popularized comparatively recently in a new edition of the Greek text meticulously edited and translated by Isaac Casaubon. This work first appeared in 1592, but it now seems clear that it was the slightly enlarged edition of 1599 with which Hall was familiar.[3]

Essentially the Theophrastan character presents a portrait of a moral or social type written in a pithy, concise style and preserving throughout an attitude of amused ironic detachment.[4] Structurally the form is extremely simple: the nature of each vice is first defined and then illustrated in a series of striking cameos intended to bring it to life in concrete, contemporary terms. For our purposes, however, the strictly classical attitude to the genre is of far less importance than what the Renaissance made of it. As we shall see, failure to appreciate this has led to many misunderstandings. Casaubon's Theophrastus was the text read by Hall and the scholarly preface had almost as great an effect on the new English Characters as had the Theophrastan portraits themselves. Certainly there are many indications that Hall's attitude to the genre derives almost totally from that of Casaubon. For a start he approaches the work from a purely moralistic point of view in the belief that the Characters were originally composed with a clear didactic purpose. 'The Divines of the old Heathens', we are told, 'were their Morall Philosophers', and the purpose of Theophrastus, 'that ancient Master of Morality', was the creation of 'so many speaking pictures, or living images, whereby the ruder multitude might even by their sense learne to know vertue, and discerne what to detest'.[5] Herein lay the principal attraction of the new genre, an attraction perhaps more easily derived from the opinions of the Renaissance editor than from a close reading of the text. In point of fact it is quite unclear from the Characters themselves whether they ever formed part of a moral treatise at all. It is at least equally possible that they were primarily designed to illustrate the rhetorical device of *descriptio*, although we must, of course, be wary of drawing too sharp a distinction between rhetoric and ethics. The Characters in the second book of Aristotle's *Rhetoric*, for example, cannot easily be assigned exclusively to either.[6] Casaubon, however, had no such doubts:

Argumentum autem et subiectum scripti istius philosophicum plane est: de moribus enim hominum hic agitur, et ad bene honesteque vitam degendam nobis hoc scripto praeire Theophrastus voluit: quo nihil est φιλοσοφικώτερον, nihil philosopho dignius.[7]

This was the Theophrastus in whose path Hall set out to follow albeit 'with an higher and wider step' as one 'that in worthy examples hold imitation better than invention' (p. 151). Yet had he adhered strictly to the 'examples' of his

model his work would have been entirely different from what
it is, for there appear no virtuous types among the Greek
Characters at all. Basing his opinions on a spurious preface,
however, Casaubon held that the extant work was incomplete,
and that the better part of it ('melior pars') consisting of the
portraits of the virtues had been lost.[8] Consequently, despite
Hall's assertion that he has drawn portraits of 'both sorts' from
the 'Tablets' of the ancients, he had no classical models for the
first section of his work. What he did have were Casaubon's
speculations on the nature of the lost Characters.

As well as accepting the spurious preface, Casaubon also
accepted the somewhat moralizing conclusions which had
become attached to eight of the Characters.[9] These he
published as integral parts of the original work. As a result the
Characters concerned lost much of their native classical
detachment thereby paving the way for the ever-present
authorial comment and analysis in Hall's *Virtues*. In short,
Casaubon's work had the effect of transforming the Greek
Characters into a moral tract, and to a large extent Hall simply
followed in his wake:

Mores igitur hominum ita hic olim erant descripti, ut liceret
tanquam in speculo hinc virtutis splendorem et pulcherrimam
intueri faciem: illinc vero vitiorum turpitudinem et dedecus animad-
vertere... Erat namque hoc tanquam exemplar et speculum quod-
dam morum, ubi virtutis et vitij cuiusque expressae notae cerneban-
tur.[10]
Vertue is not loved enough, because shee is not seene; and Vice
loseth much detestation, because her uglinesse is secret. Certainly,
my Lords, there are so many beauties, and so many graces in the face
of Goodnesse, that no eye can possibly see it without affection,
without ravishment: and the visage of Evill is so monstrous through
loathsome deformities, that if her lovers were not ignorant, they
would bee mad with disdaine and astonishment... Loe here then
Vertue and Vice stript naked to the open view, and despoiled, one of
her rags, the other of her ornaments, and nothing left them but bare
presence to plead for affection.   (p. 154)

Encouraged by Casaubon, Hall approached the Characters
in much the same way as he approached illustrative sermon
material. 'This worke', he says, 'shall save the labour of
exhorting, and disswasion.' Such attitudes go far towards

explaining, and indeed vindicating, the often criticized 'gravity' of the *Vertues*. it is due to the failure to recognize the influence of Casaubon that they have tended to fare so badly at the hands of their commentators. According to Wendell Clausen, for instance,

Hall did not write a true English Character. His *Vertues* for which he had no Theophrastian model, are mere moral exhortations. They are couched in Character form, but their sole aim, as Hall admitted in his *Proem*, is 'to discover these two virtue and vice to the world'.[11]

By way of a footnote he adds that 'a good portion of the subject matter in Hall's *Vertues* may be found, though in less developed form, in his earlier *Meditations and Vowes.*' As I shall demonstrate later on, this allusion to meditation is even more apt than Mr Clausen imagined—a similar parallel was drawn by Casaubon.[12] Here it is sufficient to remark that Clausen's summary of Hall's achievement sets him squarely in the tradition of Theophrastan Character-writing as the best contemporary scholars understood it.

It is true, of course, that there is a marked difference in tone between the *Vertues* and the *Vices*, but this too, I believe, is explicable in terms of Hall's conception of the genre. Whereas the *Vertues* are generally grave, admonitory, and abstract, the *Vices* tend to be humorous, satiric, and concrete. According to Rudolf Kirk, this 'shift' in style is evidence of a major advancement in Hall's literary technique, and can be taken as a sound indication of his order of composition.[13] According to Hall, on the other hand, the change was necessitated by the nature of the subject-matter; it was a question of decorum rather than development:

Perhaps in some of these (which thing I doe at once feare, and hate) my stile shall seeme to some lesse grave, more Satyricall: if you find me not without cause jealous, let it please you to impute it to the nature of those *Vices*, which will not be otherwise handled. The fashions of some evils are besides the odiousnesse, ridiculous; which to repeat, is to seeme bitterly merry. I abhorre to make sport with wickednesse, and forbid any laughter here, but of disdaine. (p. 167)

Similar ideals of decorum had produced the satires and were to produce the great satiric onslaughts of the sermons.

Such a procedure was by no means alien to the Character form as it was then understood. Standing midway between philosophy and poetry, the Characters had a particular affinity ('affinitas') with the works of the comic poets, especially the dramatists 'quos esse optimos exprimendorum morum artifices scimus'.[14] Traditionally Menander was the pupil of Theophrastus. Closely allied also was the world of the satirist. Horace's famous encounter with a bore, for instance, was none other than an exercise in the art of 'charactery' (p. 151), and duly appears as such in an appendix to Casaubon's edition.[15] But whereas Hall's *Vices* afforded plentiful opportunities for exploiting such associations, the *Vertues*, of course, did not. The example of Theophrastus was sufficient warrant for the keen style of the vicious types, and as a result these portraits are full of Theophrastan echoes and allusions of a highly satiric or humorous nature.[16] As we have just seen, Hall was fully aware of the stylistic differences between his two sets of Characters. He intended them to function as part of the overall moral contrast upon which the entire work is based. Deprived of any ancient models for his gallery of *Vertues* he adopted a style suitable to what both he and Casaubon believed the originals must have been like. Hence the grave dignity of the language and the frequent passages of moral analysis.

The adoption of such an attitude towards the Greek Characters was facilitated not only by the opinions of their editor, but also by the influence of the Bible. As Benjamin Boyce has pointed out, the moral 'characters' of Proverbs and Ecclesiastes were among the strongest 'native' influences upon the development of the new genre.[17] In Hall's case they would seem to have been of especial importance, for scarcely a year after the publication of the *Characters* he issued *Salomons Divine Arts,* a methodical collection under various convenient headings of the 'ethical', 'political', and 'economic' lore of Proverbs and Ecclesiastes.[18] This work is full of 'characters' many of which recur in Hall's formal collection: to name but some, the slothful, covetous, prodigal, humble, and patient men are common to both. Whereas a few of these Characters are drawn almost directly from the biblical texts, the majority are of a composite nature, composed of scattered allusions and references. In other words Hall is going out of his way to attribute the composition of Characters to the great philosopher of the Old Testament, to make of Solomon the biblical Theophrastus. The texts offered little resistance: the 'he that doth . . .' construction abounds everywhere. Solomon's slothful man, for example, displays nearly all the features which have come to be generally associated with the Character form as developed by Hall. Even the pithy, proverbial quality of the language is very similar. This is hardly surprising in view of the influence of Proverbs on the *Holy Observations,* for although Hall was certainly a 'Senecan', he recognized distinct resemblances between the two styles.[19] In one of his sermons he speaks in highly Senecan terms of the 'antitheticall' 'propositions' of a verse from Proberbs 'wherein pride is opposed to humility, honor to ruine'.[20] Solomon's style reinforces his use of Senecan syntax:

The slothfull, *is he that* foldeth his hands, and eateth up his owne flesh; That hideth his hand in his bosome, and will not pull it out againe to his mouth; That turneth on his bed, as a doore turneth on the hinges, *and saith,* Yet a little sleepe, a little slumber, a little folding of the hands to sleepe. *Every thing that he ought to doe is troublesome:* The way of the slothfull man is an hedge of thornes, (*which he is loth to set foot in*) There is a Lion without (*saith he*) I shall be slaine in the street: *who although herein* he be wiser in his owne conceit, than seven men that can render a reason: Yet (*the truth is*) he that (*so much as*) followes the idle, is destitute of understanding . . . The very desire of the slothfull slayeth him, for his hands refuse to worke . . . He that will not plough because of Winter, shall beg in Summer, and have nothing.[21]

He is a religious man, and weares the time in his Cloister; and as the cloke of his doing nothing, pleads contemplation; yet is he no whit the leaner for his thoughts, no whit learneder . . . and when businesse importunes him, (he) is more troubled to fore-think what he must doe, than another to effect it . . . He loves still to have the Sunne witnesse of his rising; and lies long, more for lothnesse to dresse him, than will to sleep . . . when Winter is come, after some sharpe visitations, he looks on his pile of wood, and askes how much was cropped the last Spring . . . He is wittie in nothing but framing excuses to sit still, which if the occasion yeeld not, he coyneth with ease . . . This man is a standing Poole, and cannot chuse but gather corruption. (pp. 174–5)

As one might expect, Hall's technique is more taut and uniform, but the basic similarities are none the less clear. The use of irony, imagery, and well-chosen illustrative detail is common to both passages, as is the unmistakable tone of moral denunciation. What was acceptable to Solomon could not be inappropriate for Hall. Similarly, as a comparison of the two patient men would show, there are equally strong correspondences between the lofty approbative tones adopted towards the virtues. Hall's 'gravity' finds ample support here, as also in the 'character' of the happy man which opens the Book of Psalms. No less grave is Herbert's verse imitation 'Constancy', nor Hall's own verse translation:

> 1   Who hath not walkt astray,
> In wicked mens advise,
> Nor stood in sinners way;
> Nor in their companyes
>   That scorners are,
>   As their fit mate,
>   In scoffing chayre,
>   Hath ever sate;

> 2   But in thy lawes divine,
> O Lord set his delight,
> And in those lawes of thine
> Studies all day and night;
>   Oh, how that man
>   Thrise blessed is!
>   And sure shall gaine
>   Eternall blisse.

> 3   He shall be like the tree,
> Set by the water-springs,
> Which when his seasons be
> Most pleasant fruite forth-brings:
>   Whose boughes so greene
>   Shall never fade,
>   But covered bene
>   With comely shade.[22]

It might, of course, be objected that Hall's composition of the *Characters* influenced his compilation of the biblical material and not vice versa, but it would surely be absurd to suggest that Hall had not noticed Solomon's 'characters' before 1609. The passages concerned were very popular, and semi-characters, or near-characters, were common in both religious and secular literature.[23] It seems clear, therefore, that Hall's awareness of the biblical passages encouraged his acceptance of Casaubon's view of the genre, and influenced his decision to follow his Greek models 'with an higher and wider step'. Regarded in this light his opening remarks take on an added significance:

The Divines of the old Heathens were their Morall Philosophers: These received the Acts of an inbred law, in the *Sinai* of Nature, and delivered them with many expositions to the multitude: These were the Overseers of manners, Correctors of vices, Directors of lives, Doctors of vertue... (p. 151)

What Hall intended to add to Theophrastus, in the light of Casaubon's theories and his own biblical reading, was the concept of divine law and sin drawn from a spiritual Sinai by a Christian divine. The most striking feature of his portraits, both *Vertues* and *Vices* alike, is that they are all pervaded by Christian values. Recent critical attempts to relate Hall's characters too exclusively to the classical and 'Neo-Stoic' traditions upon which they are supposed to have been based have made it doubly important to emphasize this central aspect of their make-up, for until it is understood their relationship to the rest of Hall's work must remain unclear.[24]

'The Patient Man' provides perhaps the best indication of how far the process of Christianization has gone, for this, is the virtue which should be most Stoical. The inculcation of patience derived from a correct understanding of the natural law was one of the distinguishing marks of that great ancient philosophy, but Hall's patience is of a very different nature:

The patient man is made of a metall, not so hard as flexible: his shoulders are large, fit for a load of injuries; which hee beares not out of basenesse and cowardlinesse, because he dare not revenge, but out of Christian fortitude, because he may not... He is above nature, while he seemes below himselfe... He is Gods best witnesse, and when he stands before the barre for truth, his tongue is calmely free, his fore-head firme, and he with erect and setled countenance heares his just sentence, and rejoyces in it . . . Contrariety of events doth but exercise, not dismay him; and when crosses afflict him, he sees a divine hand invisibly striking with these sensible scourges: against which he dares not rebell or murmure. (p. 159)

Similarly, in a late Character entitled *The Christian*, the same 'Christian courage' is opposed to the 'naturall fortitude' or 'ambition of fame' which may 'set a face upon a patient enduring of losse, or pain'. 'Herein', says Hall, 'the Christian goes beyond the Pagans, not practise onely, but admiration . . . Lo here a point transcending all the affectation of Heathenism.'[25]

Often too, as in the case of 'the Faithfull Man (pp. 156–7), the Characters are enriched by plentiful biblical allusion, and some of the virtues chosen are themselves wholly Christian possessing no real classical or Stoic counterpart. Such, for example, is the portrait of penitence:

Hee hath lookt into the depth of the bottomlesse pit, and hath seene his owne offence tormented in others, and the same brands shaken at him. He hath seene the change of faces in that evill one, as a tempter as a tormentor; and hath heard the noise of a conscience, and is so frighted with all these, that he can never have rest, till he have run out of himselfe, to God . . . He bleeds first from the hand that heales him. The Law of God hath made worke for mercy; which he hath no sooner apprehended; than he forgets his wounds, and looks carelessly upon all these terrors of guiltinesse . . . Nothing but an out-side is the same as it was, and that altred more with Regeneration, than with age. None but he can relish the promises of the Gospell . . . and now that he hath found his Saviour he hugs him so fast, and holds him so deare, that he feeles not when his life is fetcht away from him, for his martyrdome. (pp. 162–3)

In the enlarged and final version of the *Characters*, one remembers, the progress is towards spiritual happiness. 'The Penitent' is followed immediately by 'He is a Happy Man', essentially a portrait of one of the elect: 'God himselfe takes pleasure to converse with him, and hath Sainted him afore his death, and in his death crowned him.' Living a life full of 'heavenly contentments' he 'sees with *Steven*, and heares with *Paul*, and enjoyes with *Lazarus*, the glory that hee shall have' (p. 164). As had been explained some years previously in *Heaven upon Earth* (1606), such happiness was obtainable only through grace: 'No marvell then if all the Heathen have diligently sought after it, many wrote of it, none attained it. Not *Athens* must teach this lesson, but *Ierusalem.*'[26]

At the opposite extreme among the *Vices*, 'The Profane' is a portrait of one of the damned, one of the non-elect whom neither preacher nor Character-writer can ever hope to reach:

His conscience would faine speake with him, but he will not heare it ... He never names God, but in his oathes ... He quarrels for the hard conditions of his pleasure, for his future damnation; and from himselfe laies all the fault upon his Maker ... The inevitable necessity of Gods counsell makes him desperately carelesse: so with good food he poysons himselfe ... He cannot thinke of death with patience, without terrour, which he therefore feares worse than hell, because this he is sure of, the other he but doubts of. He comes to Church as to the Theater, saving that not so willingly ... He loves none but himselfe, and that not enough to seeke his true good ... He is hated of God, as much as he hateth goodnesse, and differs little from a Devill, but that he hath a body.   (pp. 171–2)

All of these Characters are pervaded by the concept of sin. 'The Flatterer', for example, is 'a factor for the Devil'; 'the Superstitious', a misguided Catholic; 'the Covetous', a usurer breeding money 'to the third generation'; 'the Presumptious', a theological overreacher; and 'the Envious', a 'leane and pale carcase quickened with a Fiend'. Even such apparently comic figures as 'The Busie-bodie' have their dark side, for in Hall's account he emerges as an agent of social disruption:

His tongue, like the taile of *Sampsons* Foxes, carries fire-brands, and is enough to set the whole field of the world on a flame. Himselfe begins table-talke of his neighbour at anothers boord; to whom he beares the first newes, and adjures him to conceale the reporter: whose cholirick answer he returnes to his first Oast, inlarged with a second edition; so, as it uses to be done in the fight of unwilling Mastives, he claps each on the side apart, and provokes them to an eager conflict.   (p. 170)

In almost every case the evil in Hall's types is of a threefold nature. Personally they torment and delude themselves; socially they cause dissension and enmity; and theologically they oppose themselves to the saving grace of God. 'The Distrustfull Man', for instance, lives a life of self-imposed

misery, alienates his neighbours through his suspicions, and
refuses to credit the promise of salvation (pp. 177–8). Such
humour as enters into these portraits is of a rather grim
variety. As Hall put it in one of his sermons, godless men
dance 'a Galliard over the mouth of hell'.[27]

Whatever other elements they may or may not incorporate,
it seems quite clear that both *Vertues* and *Vices* are thoroughly
pervaded by Christian attitudes and standards. Indeed, even
their very differences in technique were designed to function
as part of the over-all moral contrast upon which the entire
work was based and to which Hall himself drew his readers'
attention in his 'Prooeme' to the *Vices*. 'I have', he says,

shewed you many faire Vertues: I speak not for them; if their sight
cannot command affection, let them lose it. They shall please yet
better, after you have troubled your eyes a little with the view of
deformities; and by how much more they please, so much more
odious, and like themselves, shall these deformities appeare. This
light, contraries give to each other, in the midst of their enmity, that
one makes the other seeme more good, or ill.   (p. 167)

The practice of illustrating either vices or virtues by the
depiction of their opposites was well established by the early
seventeenth century. Indeed there were few more universally
recognized literary devices.[28] In choosing to structure his work
as he did, Hall was not merely following the advice of
Casaubon, but setting himself squarely within one of the most
time-honoured didactic traditions of both literature and
iconography. Indeed Casaubon's own views may well have
been moulded by such traditions. In any case Hall had read
Chaucer, and was probably acquainted with a considerable
range of medieval allegory.[29] His depiction of the 'Good
Magistrate' guiding the ship of state and dispensing justice
amid a host of personifications might well have been drawn
from some such source:

Hee sits quietly at the sterne, and commands one to the top-saile,
another to the main, a third to the plummet, a fourth to the anchor,
as he sees the need of their course and weather requires ... Displeasure, Revenge, Recompence, stand on both sides of the Bench,
but hee scornes to turne his eye towards them; looking onely right
forward at Equity, which stands full before him.   (p. 161)

This passage might equally well have been suggested by some
emblematic depiction of the same scene, for Hall was fully
aware of the relationship between 'charactery' and the visual
arts. His classification of the Greek Characters as 'so many
speaking pictures, or living images' is immediately followed by
a direct, if brusque, allusion to such works: 'if pictures have
beene accounted the books of Idiots, behold here the benefit of
an image without the offence' (p. 151). Teaching through
emblems was to become ever more important as the century
wore on.[30]

Even without Hall's allusion, however, contemporary readers must have been stuck by the correspondences between the
two genres. Contrasting galleries of moral types had become a
staple of Western art and inform even the *Meditations and
Vowes* in which the customs of worldlings are continually
offset by those of the devout.[31] In the *Characters* such contrasts
are worked out not simply on a thematic level, but also in
terms of the variations in tone and technique encountered as
we move from one series to the next. It is quite misleading to
speak of either development or disunity. The principle of
contrast is central to the work.

The *Vertues* are informed by the theme of self-knowledge
and self–contentment.[32] Of the wise man, for instance, we
learn that, 'There is nothing that he desires not to know, but
most and first himselfe: and not so much his owne strength, as
his weaknesses; neither is his knowledge reduced to discourse,
but practice.' (p. 155.) Here, however, the style is as important
as the matter. Indeed in some sense the style *is* the matter in so
far as the careful patterning of the clauses is designed to mirror
the movements of the wise mind itself. Hall is fascinated by
the workings of enlightened reason, by the 'premisses',
'syllogismes', and 'conclusions' of his 'skilfull Logician'. Not
only does he tell us what the wise man thinks, he helps us to
experience the thought–process itself. Beginning with a broad
generalization we proceed through three important qualifications ('but most ... and not ... neither') to an ever clearer
image of the essential characteristics of our subject's knowledge. We are following in his footsteps to reach his conclusions. Later the same qualities of strength and self-reliance are
conveyed by the imagery: 'He confineth himselfe in the circle

of his owne affaires, and lists not to thrust his finger into a needlesse fire. He stands like a center unmoved, while the circumference of his estate is drawne above, beneath, about him' (pp. 155–6.) In this respect the wise man resembles his God whose perfections are likewise traditionally associated with the symbol of the circle. Indeed there is a circular quality to the whole portrait, for just as we begin by exploring the wise man's attempts to know himself, we end with a statement of his success: 'blind in no mans cause, best sighted in his owne'. Throughout the whole Character the stately progress of the Senecan prose suggests the dignity and poise of the mind with which we are dealing. It is methodical, intelligent, and self-reliant, and the language and syntax reflect all these qualities:

The best is first regarded; and vaine is that regard which endeth not in security. Every care hath his just order; neither is there any one either neglected or misplaced. He is seldome over-seene with credulity; for knowing the falsenesse of the world, he hath learn'd to trust himselfe alwayes; others so farre, as he may not be dammaged by their disappointment. (p. 155)

As there can be no ambiguity, the language is simple, forthright, and clear: 'The best is first regarded'. The wise man's approach is methodical, but his method is based on a predetermined scale of moral values—he knows what the 'best' is. Yet the first clause has a false finality; 'regarding' is a continuous activity, not an end in itself. Its position at the end of its clause is therefore qualified by its recurrence in mid-sentence: 'vaine is that regard . . .'. The wise man is suspicious of aimless speculation. As in divine meditation it must come to some 'issue' or result. In this case the 'issue' is 'security'. 'Regarding' is only an intermediate activity; even by position 'best' and 'security' stand out as the keywords. 'Every care', we are now informed, 'hath his just order.' Having considered the 'best', the wise man can move on to lesser priorities. Once again the initial statement is clear and concise, and the logical method is informed by moral terminology, 'just order'. This 'order' reflects that of the Elizabethan chain of being no link of which can be either 'neglected' or 'misplaced', and the unexpected way in which the sentence turns back upon itself adds to the impression of completeness and precision. Viewed from both positive and negative standpoints, the system is unassailably 'secure'. Yet suddenly there occurs a suggestion of limitations: 'He is seldome over-seene', 'seldome' not 'never'. We are surprised by the admission, for it seems to damage the sage's 'security'. As the sentence proceeds, however, our reactions alter yet again. Expecting to hear why the wise man is 'seldome', but sometimes, deceived, we discover instead why he is never 'dammaged' despite occasional deception. Yet once more it is a question of 'order'. He knows both himself ('nosce teipsum') and the 'falsenesse' of the world, and apportions his trust accordingly. All dealings with the world are in the nature of a gamble, but his stake is never more than he can easily afford to lose. Such 'deception' as occurs reflects on 'others' not himself. They 'disappoint' his trust, but the real loss is their own. The unexpected twists of the sentence suggest both the *apparent* vulnerability of the wise man, and his actual 'security'. 'Seldome' serves merely to lead to a more convincing 'never'.

As the above quotation might suggest, most of the discussion of the *Vertues* is carried out on a rather lofty, abstract plane. Here there are but few of the illustrative 'character-in-action' incidents so beloved of Theophrastus, but this too is in keeping with Hall's views on the nature of good and evil. As Seneca had argued in an epistle (XCV, 65–7) dealing briefly with the Character form and quoted in part by Casuabon, virtue far more than vice is of a private, hidden nature. It is the mark of Hall's wise man to 'see the world unseene' (p. 155), and his humble man lives a life far removed from 'the stages of common resorts' (p. 158). Even the valiant man 'lies ever close within himselfe, armed with wise resolution, and will not be discovered but by death or danger' (p. 158). The more abstracted the concept of virtue becomes, the more difficult it is to depict it in action. If virtue is essentially an inner quality it must be expressed in terms appropriate to itself. Once again it is a question of decorum. Despite a recent attempt to prove that 'observation and verisimilitude are obviously the principles to which Hall adheres', in the *Vertues* the opposite is true.[33] That Hall was well aware of this is demonstrated by the opening remarks of 'A decription of a good and faithful Courtier', a character reserved for publication among the *Epistles*. 'I desire not to describe a Courtier', he tells us,

How should I, that have but seene and saluted the seat of Princes? Or why should I, whose thoughts are sequestred to the Court of heaven? But if I would decypher a good Courtier, who can herein controll my endevour? Goodnesse in all formes is but the just subject of our profession: what my observation could not, no lesse certaine rule shall afford me. Our discourse hath this freedome, that it may reach beyond our eyes with beleefe.[34]

In the *Vertues* there is a great deal of this 'reaching beyond our eyes with beleefe'. It is indicative of Hall's attitude that in both the 1608 and 1614 editions of the *Characters* the names of the virtuous types alternate between the abstract and the concrete. 'The Patient Man' and 'The True Friend' appear in the list of contents as 'Of Patience' and 'Of True-Friendship'.

As it is the nature of hypocrisy to appear virtuous, the integrity of the truly virtuous is a matter between themselves and God. Hence Hall's rejection of the impossible ideals of the Separatists. In this world the 'godly' can never properly be distinguished, for whereas man must judge by appearance, virtue resides in sincerity of motivation.[35] Hence too all the analysis and explanation. Since Hall was a moralist not a psychologist, the actions of the vicious could be left to speak for themselves. To explain why a miser hoarded money was unnecessary; to explain why a valiant man might refuse to fight was essential:

He is the master of himselfe, and subdues his passions to reason; and by his inward victory workes his owne peace . . . The sword is to him the last of all trials, which he drawes forth still as Defendant, not as Challenger, with a willing kind of unwillingnesse . . . The height of his spirits over-lookes all casualties, and his boldnesse proceeds neither from ignorance nor senselesnesse: but first he values evils, and then despises them: he is so ballaced with wisdome, that hee floats steddily in the midst of all tempests. (p. 158)

That the valiant man should be 'ballaced with *wisdome*' is characteristic of the way in which the virtues blend together thereby losing the sense of distinctness some commentators seem to demand.[36] But the criticism is quite unfounded for Hall's procedure is directly in keeping with his understanding of the moral qualities involved. A major problem of adapting the Theophrastan genre to virtuous subjects was the necessity of dealing separately with what were essentially different aspects of a single outlook. As Hall had explained only a year before, the possession of one virtue argued that of others. According to one of his *Holy Observations* 'spiritual gifts' are so 'chained together, that who excels in one, hath some eminency in more, yea, in all.' While it was true that 'vices are seldome single', 'virtues goe ever in troups: they goe so thick, that sometimes some are hid in the crowd; which yet are, but appear not. They may be shut out from sight; they cannot be severed.'[37] This, combined with the plentiful use of distinctive illustrative detail, is why the *Vices* appear more clear-cut and 'individual' when in fact they are simply more limited. The effect of the *Vertues* is intentionally cumulative. As we read through the series surveying the same basic problems from different points of view, the underlying unity becomes increasingly clear. The happy man with whom we end is a composite figure. The others are to him what various shades and nuances of colour are to a completed portrait. On the other hand, for the vices to combine is either impossible or unnecessary. Almost all are so obsessive as to leave little room for anything else, while many are diametrically opposed. Any one of them can lead to damnation; together they can do no more.

In many respects the *Vices* presented far fewer problems than their opposites. In their case Hall had excellent models, and his work as a satirist fitted him eminently for the task of composition: the vices are the very stuff of satiric attack. Whereas all the virtuous types know both who and what they are, the vicious ones are marked by a distinct lack of self-knowledge. They neither meditate nor analyse, at their most profound they simply scheme. In sharp contrast to the wise man, the inconstant man 'treads upon a mooving earth, and keepes no pase. His proceedings are ever heady and peremptory; for hee hath not the patience to consult with reason, but determines meerly upon fancie' (p. 173).

The vicious have no inner spiritual life, nor is there any depth to their actions; for them everything lies upon the surface. Whereas the *Vertues* cultivate real values in retire-

ment, the *Vices* have neither real values nor real identities—
they merely act a part. The hypocrite, we are informed, is 'the
worst kinde of Player, by so much as he acts the better part'
(p. 169). The inconstant is 'so transformable into all opinions,
manners, qualities, that he seemes rather made immediately of
the first matter, than of well tempered elements; and therefore
is in possibilitie any thing, or every thing; nothing in present
substance' (p. 173). Best of all, perhaps, is the description of
the vainglorious, 'a Spanish Souldier on an Italian Theater' (p.
176). Such remarkable theatricality makes description easy.
We simply watch and criticize the act. Hence all the concrete
details so reminiscent of the *Virgidemiarum*. The secret of
Hall's success lies in skilful selection. Here, for example, is one
of the stratagems of the 'Spanish Souldier':

Under pretence of seeking for a scrol of newes, he drawes out an
handful of letters indorsed with his owne stile, to the height: and
halfe reading every title, passes over the latter part with a murmur;
not without signifying, what Lord sent this, what great Lady the
other; and for what sutes; the last paper (as it happens) is his newes
from his honourable friend in the French Court. (p. 176)[38]

The appearance of the virtuous types was hardly ever (and
then only marginally) of any importance, not so that of their
opposites. The slothful man, for example, is 'descried amongst
a thousand neighbours by a dry and nasty hand, that still
savours of the sheet, a beard uncut, unkembed; an eye and eare
yellow, with their excretions; a coat shaken on, ragged,
unbrusht; by linnen and face striving whether shall excell in
uncleannesse' (p. 175). The portraits of such types are full of
the imagery of disease and self-destruction. Ambition, we
learn, is 'a dry thirst of honour, the longing disease of reason,
an aspiring and gallant madnesse' (p. 178). Envy 'feeds on
others evils, and hath no disease but his neighbours welfare'
(p. 180). Sloth is 'a standing Poole, and cannot chuse but
gather corruption' (p. 175). The malcontent can most aptly be
likened to 'the wheele of a well-couched fire-worke; that flies
out on all sides, not without scorching it selfe' (p. 173).

In these portraits Hall remains close to the methods of his
Greek model. In Theophrastus, as in Chaucer, the use of well-
selected detail gives the illusion of individuality while at the

same time preserving the universality of the type. In order to make his Characters all the more convincing, therefore, Hall supplies occasional allusions to well-known contemporary events and practices.[39] Also like his mentor, he adopts an ironic mocking tone—though allowing no laughter, but laughter 'of disdaine'. Wit is ever-present. When we read, for example, of how the covetous man 'would dispatch himselfe when corne falls, but that he is loth to cast away money on a cord' (p. 176), we can understand why it occurred to Nahum Tate to produce a version of the *Characters* in heroic couplets.[40]

Whereas in the *Vertues* the language and syntax served to confirm the high moral values of the characters they described, here they have the opposite effect. The balanced clauses now tend completely to debunk the pretences of their subjects:

He can command teares when hee speaks of his youth; indeed because it is past, not because it was sinfull.   (p. 169)
Hee comes to the sicke bed of his stepmother, and weeps, when he secretly feares her recovery.   (p. 169)

Similarly the intellectual activity of the superstitious man is a parody of that of the Christian sage:

'One event is enough to make a rule; out of these he concludes fashions proper to himselfe, and nothing can turne him out of his owne course. If he have done his taske, he is safe, it matters not with what affection' (p. 171).

The language and syntax are similar to what we have encountered before, but the effect is totally different. The bold assertiveness of the opening clause, for example, is all the more striking for being wrong; 'one event' and 'rule' are contradictions. Immediately we are confronted not merely by the character's stupidity, but also by his infuriating stubbornness. Having established his premises, however, he proceeds 'logically' to his conclusions. No less than the wise man, he knows what is his due, although here is a neat, undercutting irony in the assertion that he develops 'fashions *proper to himselfe*'. Next, of course, comes his security: 'nothing can turne him'—except, perhaps, another 'event' which may well produce a conflicting 'rule'. If the wise man was a circle, this gentleman is a set of wild tangents. Yet 'he is safe', he assures

himself, 'if he have done his taske.' To hedge his assertions
with such conditionals displays his wisdom. For him, religion
is a set of extrinsic, ritual 'tasks' directed by 'rules' similar to
those which he himself propounds. Strictly speaking, perhaps,
the phrase 'it matters not with what affection' should come
before 'he is safe', that is where it logically belongs. But the
displacement is indicative of the mental process we are
following. 'Events' and 'taskes' come first, and lead to the
'safety' and security from which the superstitious mind cannot
be 'turned'; its thoughts never wander beyond them. In the
Vertues theme and syntax combine to promote agreement with
the characters' conclusions, but here what happens is the
complete reverse. For the superstitious man, all after 'safe' is
insignificant; his interest stops at the second comma. But the
reader, by now accustomed to Hall's satiric style, reads on in
the knowledge that the real point is yet to come. The style
undermines its subject and condemns him. The reader is
invited to react against the vice—and this, of course, is the
point of the work.

In so far as they reflect the nature of their subjects,
therefore, the stylistic and tonal differences between the two
sets of Characters are intended to suggest the central moral
contrast about which the entire work is constructed. Ideally
neither should be read in isolation for they are designed as
complementary halves of a single unified work with a clear
didactic purpose. Hall was uninterested in simple description.
This is why it was left to Overbury and Earle to develop the
purely social Character. Among Hall's portraits only 'The
Good Magistrate' approaches the social type, but even here his
real concern is how social justice should be made to pervade
the entire spectrum of Christian life. In much the same way,
'Of the Truly-Noble' is more concerned with defining the
essence of real 'nobility' than with presenting accurate cameos
of various social ranks. With Hall the moral purpose remains
dominant. He is dealing with virtue and vice, and here, if
anywhere, he answers the objection so often levelled against
the satirist, of seeing only a distorted view of human life.
Presenting both good and evil, he can justly claim in an epistle
of the same year (1608) that he has 'both censured and
directed'.[41]

But are we to conclude, therefore, that Mr Clausen's suggestions are substantially correct, that Overbury and Earle were influenced solely by Jonson, and that Hall never wrote a 'true English character'? I think not. In the first place, however suggestive the portraits of *Everyman Out of his Humour* and *Cynthia's Revels* may be, they are not as close to the Theophrastan manner as Hall's *Vices*, nor do they stand alone as a separate genre. This is a vital point, for the history of the form in the seventeenth century is that of a distinctly new genre, and this is precisely what Hall offered. Moreover, not merely do his *Vices* resemble the Theophrastan portraits, they borrow from them, and the debt to Theophrastus is openly and clearly acknowledged. Secondly it is completely wrong to suggest that Hall's virtuous characters find no equivalent in those of Overbury and his circle. In attempting to depict virtuous types Overbury encountered exactly the same sort of problems, and solved them in exactly the same way. His 'Noble Spirit', for example, is stylistically indistinguishable from Hall's 'Wise Man'. He too is one who, 'Hath surveyed and fortified his disposition, and converts all occurrents into experience, between which experience and his reason, there is a mariage: the issue are his actions. He circuits his intents, and seeth the end before he shoot.'[42]

In his portrait of 'A Good Woman' Overbury himself recognizes why this must be so. The lady, he tells us, is 'much within, and frames outward things to her minde, not her minde to them'. As a result, she is 'indeed most, but not much to [*sic*] description, for shee is direct and one, and hath not the varietie of ill'.[43] Thirdly, Hall's enduring influence on the English Character can be gauged from the way in which his Senecan style became a hallmark of the genre to the end of the century. To give but one example, we find Richard Flecknoe informing us in 1658 that the Character is of its nature, 'more *Senica* [*sic*] than *Cicero*, and speaks rather the language of *Oracles* than *Orators*: every line a *sentence*, and every two a *period*'.[44]

Finally I find the term '*true* English character' entirely subjective. As Mr Clausen employs it, it necessitates the rejection not merely of Hall but of Adams, Breton, Cleveland, Fuller, Halifax, Addison, and, I suspect, the vast majority of the items listed in Chester Greenough's *Bibliography of the Theophrastan Character in England*. Even many of Butler's Characters fail to qualify. To my mind a definition which excludes so much is far too narrow. The English Character developed in several directions, and Hall's *Vertues* and *Vices* stand at the head of two distinct but equally legitimate varieties. Those who desired the pure Theophrastan form could look to his *Vices*, while those interested in exploiting the relationship with the essay and sermon could take the *Vertues* as their model. In *The Holy State; the Profane State* Fuller did the latter with excellent results. It is well to remember that Bacon was the first to sound the call to Character-writing in 1605 in *The Advancement of Learning* when he asserted the need for 'sound and true distributions and descriptions of the several characters and tempers of men's natures and disposi- tions'.[45] From the beginning, therefore, the English Character was likely to contain a discursive element. Hall's legacy to his successors is twofold. Not only did he introduce the pure Theophrastan form into English literature, but he freed the new genre from servility to Theophrastus by suggesting alternative modes of development.

In the *Virgidemiarum* Hall dealt at first hand with some of the most pressing problems of contemporary society. In the *Mundus* he widened the scope of his satire to embrace almost the whole of Europe while at the same time distancing his comments through the device of allegory and paying particular attention, underneath all the more specific allusions, to the nature of vice itself especially in relation to the perversion of enlightened reason. In effect he created a vast 'dystopia' in which personifications of vice and folly could be manipulated in appropriately ridiculous settings. Unfortunately, however, the 'persona' of neither work suited the image of the preacher Hall was destined to become, and neither was ever deemed worthy of inclusion in the sober canon of the collected works. For satirist and minister to come together something new was required, something of a fresh, imaginative nature which was still obviously a work of sound moral didacticism. As presented by Casaubon, the Theophrastan Character was just this.

Casaubon made Theophrastus morally respectable. Henceforth what Seneca was to the epistle, Theophrastus was to the Character. In both cases the process of Christianization was extremely simple. At the same time, from a purely literary point of view, the new genre fulfilled the neoclassical requirements of being at once both old and 'new'. While the *Vertues,* for which he had no classical model, allowed Hall to set forth his meditations on the nature of election in a style determined by the demands of decorum, the *Vices* encouraged the development of his pungent satiric wit. The resulting contrast only served to strengthen the moral point. It was Hall's first approach towards the integration of the two most prevalent modes of his thought, meditation and satire. Although an even closer integration remained to be achieved in the *Sermons,* the *Characters* were deemed successful enough to be included in every edition of the collected works published during Hall's lifetime. Indeed, as we shall see, they formed an integral part of his total devotional output, for they are closely related to the meditative works to be examined in the following chapter and like them bear strongly upon the problems of grace and election. They may be regarded as manuals for the direction of self-examination. Their presentation of the various marks of virtue and vice was supposed to prompt a private analysis of the reader's own spiritual state. What the wise man desires to know, one remembers, is 'most and first himselfe'. Hence the complete rejection of any purely aesthetic standard by which the *Characters* might be judged, and the repeated insistence upon their devotional nature:

If thou doe but read or like these, I have spent good houres ill; but if thou shalt hence abjure those Vices; which before thou thoughtest not ill-favoured, or fall in love with any of these goodly faces of Vertue; or shalt hence find where thou hast any little touch of these evils, to cleare thy selfe or where any defect in these graces to supply it, neither of us shall need to repent of our labour.   (p. 151)

II. Controversy

He that hath a satirical vein as he maketh others afraid of his wit, so he hath need be afraid of others memory—Bacon.

Just a few months after the publication of Milton's *Animadversions upon the Remonstrants Defence against Smectymnuus* (July 1641), an anonymous assailant launched a vicious attack upon his character in *A Modest Confutation of A Slanderous and Scurrilous Libell, Entituled, Animadversions upon the Remonstrants Defence against Smectymnuus* (February 1642). Since the *Animadversions* appeared anonymously, the evidence for the Confuter's attack was supposedly inferred from the style and tone of the work itself.[46] Not surprisingly, Milton regarded the pamphlet as a deliberate exercise in libel. His opponent, he claimed, knew him well, but finding his reputation so impervious to attack he 'thought it his likeliest course under a pretended ignorance to let drive at randome, lest he should lose his odde ends which from some penurious Book of Characters he had been culling out and would faine apply'.[47] Since it was Milton's belief that Hall had either written the *Confutation* himself or had encouraged one of his sons to do so, the allusion is clearly to the *Characters of Vertues and Vices*.[48] Disregarding for the moment the undoubted scurrility of Milton's own controversial style, the implication of his remarks is of some importance. Whereas the moral intention of the original *Characters* was unquestionable, the position was certainly less clear when the 'characters' concerned were real individuals, and the satire an instrument of polemic controversy. During the period of the civil wars both sides were quick to realize the pamphleteering potential of the Character genre. Scores of Characters such as 'The True Character of an Untrue Bishop' and 'The Noble Cavalier' poured from the presses and some earlier collections were polemically adapted to suit the needs of the times.[49] The *Confutation* is certainly related to such literature. In places it does read more like a 'character' than a credible account of a real individual, but as Milton well knew, the effect is quite deliberate. Both sides were interested in type-casting their opponents, and neither ever suggests that the rights and wrongs of the episcopal debate are any less plain than the clear-cut distinctions between virtue and vice. In such circumstances moral issues become blurred, and the contemporary 'success' or 'failure' of any particular satirist depends on the nature of the dominant viewpoint. During the Smectymnuan debate, perhaps for the first time in his life, Hall found himself in a 'moral' minority—at least so far as the world of pamphlets was concerned. Yet even though his standards were no longer 'universal', he sought the same measure of acceptance for his satire.

Hall had begun his *Humble Remonstrance to the High Court of Parliament* (January 1641), with a complaint about the scurrility of the Puritan press;[50] 'You love toothlesse Satyrs', replied Milton, 'let me informe you, a toothlesse Satyr is as improper as a toothed sleekstone, and as bullish.'[51] If the retorts seem trivial, the issues were not. What was in question was no less than the freedom of the press, for despite his own early sufferings at the hands of the State censors, Hall's subsequent experience had led him to believe very strongly in the need for a rigid censorship. As set out in *The Peace-Maker*, his views on the press are diametrically opposed to those of Milton's *Areopagitica*.[52] Effectively, through upholding the licensing laws, they limited the scope of human expression to received, establishment views, and the scope of satire to attacks upon the government's enemies. It seemed to many Puritans, therefore, that the political and ecclesiastical authorities were attempting to establish a monopoly of satiric forms, for whereas anti-Puritan propaganda was apparently being licensed quite freely, their own presses were continually harassed. Anti-episcopal views such as those expressed in Smectymnuus' *Answer to . . . An Humble Remonstrance* were branded as defamatory, libellous, and unchristian, yet who could define such words in an age when their very use was itself an act of polemic debate?: 'The rest of our Answer (you say) is but a *meere declamation*. And good Sir, what was your whole Remonstrance but a *declamation*? And what is your *Defence* but a Satyre?'[53]

Once all common ground between the two factions had been lost, arguments as to the moral justifications of their respective attacks were destined to be futile. After the appearance of the *Animadversions*, for example, the Confuter rushed to Hall's aid with a moral apology for the *Virgidemiarum*, while at the same time branding Milton as one of those who, in Bacon's words, 'turn Religion into a Comedy or *Satyr*' (my emphasis) through the composition of 'scurrilous mimes'.[54] The response, of course, was predictable. Seizing upon the word 'mime' and the notion that an author's character can be deduced from his writings, Milton turned his attention to the *Mundus*:

Could he not beware, could he not bethink him, was he so uncircumspect, as not to forsee, that no sooner would that word *Mime* be set eye on in the paper, but it would bring to minde that wretched pilgrimage over *Minshews* Dictionary call'd *Mundus alter et idem*, the idlest and the paltriest Mime that ever mounted upon banke. Let him ask *the Author of those toothlesse Satyrs* who was the maker, or rather the anticreator of that universall foolery . . . Certainly he that could indure with a sober pen to sit and devise laws for drunkards to carouse by, I doubt me whether the very sobernesse of such a one, like an unlicour'd *Silenus*, were not stark drunk . . . And let him advise againe with Sir *Francis Bacon* whom he cites to confute others, what it is to *turn the sinnes of Christendome into a mimicall mockery, to rip up the saddest vices with a laughing countenance*, especially where neither reproofe nor better teaching is adjoynd.[55]

And so the recriminations go on. The debate had reached the stage where neither side was prepared to recognize the moral integrity of the other, and its continuance—particularly its satiric continuance—could only drive them further apart.

Ironically, before the outbreak of the Smectymnuan troubles, Hall had laboured might and main to exclude satire from inter-Protestant debate. At the Synod of Dort he had even gone so far as to argue for the expurgation of all such matter from the works of the early Reformers.[56] The proper object of satiric attack, he insisted, was Rome. His own reputation in this field was international, and it remained his most cherished hope that anti-Catholicism would act as the focal point for a realignment of the Reformed Churches, that involved theological disputes would be pushed aside in the face of the common enemy. Similar hopes had inspired his famed moderation towards the various interests within the Anglican Church, and for a time the policy worked quite well. With the advent of Laud and the 'Arminian faction', however, the position altered. For many thousands of articulate Protestants episcopacy now became synonymous with Papacy. That the Archbishop had reputedly refused a red hat mattered less than that the Pope had offered one.[57] As a member of the episcopal bench serving under Laud, Hall suddenly found himself identified with the very forces against which he had sought to direct Reformed anger—and satire. His hitherto respected works of controversy were swept aside as so much 'thundering upon the steele cap of *Baronius* or *Bellarmine'.*[58] Such was the quality of Hall's writing, however, that despite these complaints he remained one of the most popular devotional authors of his age. After it had first appeared in 1649 his *Resolutions and Decisions of Divers Practicall Cases of Conscience* went through five editions in ten years. Understandably this popularity proved a great embarrassment to his enemies, so in order to employ it to their own advantage the Smectymnuans exploited the 'Remonstrant's' supposed anonymity by deviously confronting him with his own works. The device, of course, was intentionally transparent: the identity of their opponent was, as he himself pointed out, an open secret.[59] In *An Answer to ... An Humble Remonstrance* (1641), for example, the Smectymnuans find that they must apply to the excesses of the liturgy what 'Dr. *Hall* spake once of the pride of *England'*. They then proceed to quote from the celebrated attack on female vanity which forms part of a sermon entitled *The Righteous Mammon* (1618).[60] This is but one example among dozens; everywhere Hall the devotionalist is opposed to Hall the controversialist. It was as if his opponents had set out to exploit the tensions in his own mind:

For though we acknowledge the Defence, for the substance of it wholly, and for the phrase of it in a great part, borrowed from episcopacie by Divine Right, yet the extream disdainfulnesse that breaths in every page and line pleads with us, to thinke that it is not his [Hall's] ... if to be scornfull and insolent be to be unlike Doctor *Hall,* you have done the Doctor exceeding wrong to say the Remonstrant looks like him.[61]

The truth of the matter, of course, was that there were limits to Hall's moderation. By very definition it involved the exclusion of all extremes. For him this was a matter of principle, to others it seemed a policy of compromise. But with the Smectymnuans even compromise was impossible. They would accept no less than all, and the adoption of their proposals would have destroyed the church as the Anglicans

understood it. To Hall, they represented the fanatical fringe of
English Puritanism, and he addressed them accordingly. The
scorn once reserved for enclosers and corn engrossers now
turned upon them. The satirist entered the lists against yet
another form of extremism.

Hall's moderate tone is in evidence at the beginning of
Episcopacie by Divine Right (1640) in his address to ex-Bishop
Graham, but thereafter the work modulates into a scathing
anti-popularist attack. He had seldom written better satire:

Can it therefore be possible...for every Parish, to furnish an
Ecclesiasticall Consistory, consisting of one, or more Pastors, a
Doctor, Elders, Deacons...And if this were faisible, what stuffe
would there be? Perhaps a young indiscreet giddy Pastour; and for a
Doctor, who, and where, and what? *Iohn a Nokes,* and *Iohn a Stiles,*
the Elders; *Smug the Smith,* a Deacon; and whom, or what should
these rule, but themselves, and their ploughshares? And what
censures, trow we, would this grave Consistory inflict? What
decisions would they make of the doubts, and controversies of their
Parish? What orders of government? For, even this Parochiall
Church hath the soveraignty of Ecclesiasticall jurisdiction...and
what a mad world would it be, that the Ecclesiasticall Lawes of such
a company should be like those of the Medes and Persians,
irrevocable...And if a King should, by occasion of his Court fixed
in some such obscure Parish, fall into the Censure, even of such a
Consistory or Presbytery, where is he? Excommunicable he is with
them, and what then may follow, let a *Buchanan* speake.[62]

The allusion to Buchanan is an interesting indication of the
tradition in which Hall felt himself to be writing. Yet
engaging as such passages may appear in retrospect or from a
purely literary point of view, at the time they enabled Hall's
opponents to pose as the defenders of popular liberty (and
democracy) against the encroachments of arrogant privilege.[63]
The witty sallies intended to illustrate the absurdity of the
Smectymnuan position were calculated to inflame any popular
support such people might hope to capture. In fact, in almost
everything he said, Hall proved remarkably inept at conciliat-
ing his opponents. He used all the wrong terms in the worst
possible way. His constant appeals to history and tradition, for
example, encouraged already deep-seated suspicions of episcopalian 'popery', and were rejected as quite frankly 'un-

Protestant' by Milton.[64] His insistence upon the authority of Mother Church smacked equally, it was held, of Rome, and was at total variance with the fiery new individualism now representing itself as the true spirit of the Reformation.[65]

In many respects Hall was the survivor of a former age, the last of the Elizabethans, equally unsuited to radical Puritanism and Laudian Anglicanism. The political and ecclesiastical order he so revered was on the point of disintegrating; much of it had already vanished. Approaching seventy, oppressed by fears of a popular uprising, of the *'Jack Straws,* and *Cades,* and *Watt Tylers'* of the rabble, he was quite unable to recognize the vast social and political forces at work behind contemporary unrest.[66] Without the benefit of our historical hindsight he saw only divine portents of the approaching dissolution of creation. Often, through his satiric thrusts, he succeeded merely in inflaming an already critical situation, but even at his best, as Don Wolfe has said, he 'futilely opposed the tactics of restraint to the disturbing genius of Protestant individualism, a force divisive and unpredictable, full of creative aberrations, with each man finally his own church, pregnant with ideas, but questing in vain for the ultimate assurance'.[67] In such circumstances satire had a way of recoiling upon itself.

Some thirty years previously in his *Apologie* for the Church against the Brownists, Hall made the supposedly satiric suggestion that the new Israelites of the Separatist congregations in Amsterdam would soon make the ocean their 'red Sea' and Virginia their 'wildernesse'.[68] Similar jibes had been made five years before in the *Mundus.*[69] When the *Mayflower* set sail in 1620, however, it went with the blessing of one of the recipients of the *Apologie,* and indeed of the epistle which gave rise to it.[70] His name was John Robinson, pastor to the Pilgrim Fathers and spiritual counsellor of the famous congregation at Plymouth, a source of inspiration to Puritans everywhere. Fortified by the new-found freedom many were soon to make the journey back. Even while the Smectymnuan debate was still in progress, radical preachers such as Roger Williams were recrossing the 'Red Sea' to lend their support against the episcopal order that had driven them into the 'wilderness'. Satire has seldom proved more double-edged, or history more relentless.

Part II

Meditation: 'A bending of the mind upon some spirituall object'

4

THE MEDITATIONS

I. The Satirist as Divine Meditator

The transition we now make is far less violent than might at first appear to be the case, for incompatible as the worlds of satire and meditation may seem to us, to a mind such as Hall's they are closely, perhaps even necessarily, related. He emphasizes their relationship himself in an epistle of 1608 upon 'the pleasure of study and contemplation' when he writes that,

Study it selfe, is our life; from which wee would not be barred for a world. How much sweeter then is the fruit of study, the conscience of knowledge? In comparison whereof, the soule that hath once tasted it, easily contemnes all humane comforts. Goe now yee worldlings, and insult over our palenesse, our needinesse, our neglect. Yee could not be so jocund, if you were not ignorant . . . I had as leive be a bruit beast, as an ignorant rich man. How is it then that those Gallants which have privilege of bloud and birth, and better education, doe so scornfully turne off these most manly, reasonable, noble exercises of scholarship? . . . the minde onely, that honourable and divine part, is fittest to be imployed of those which would reach to the highest perfection of men, and would be more than the most.[1]

Immediately one thinks of the wealthy but ignorant squire of *Virgidemiarum* II.2 ('What needs me care for any bookish skill'), and the expression of contented detachment with which the 'vanity of human wishes' satire so surprisingly concludes ('Mong'st all these sturs of discontented strife,/Oh let me lead an Academicke life').[2]

In the first chapter we have already examined how, under the influence of Geneva, Hall came to regard the castigation of vice and folly as a fraternal duty, and how he laboured both in the *Characters* and *Epistles* to combine positive teaching with satiric attack, in his own words 'to both censure and direct'. In some senses this was to make the 'norm' of the satires explicit. For example, one of the earliest meditative tracts, *Heaven upon Earth: Or, Of True Peace and Tranquillitie of Minde* (1606) ends on exactly the same note as the satire on the vanity of human wishes:

Goe now, yee vaine and idle worldlings, and please your selves in the large extent of your rich Mannors, or in the homage of those whom basenesse of mind hath made slaves to your greatnesse, or in the price and fashions of your full ward-robe, or in the wanton varieties of your delicate Gardens, or in your coffers full of red and white earth; or if there be any other earthly thing, more alluring, more precious, enjoy it, possesse it, and let it possesse you: Let me have only my Peace; and let me never want it, till I envy you.[3]

The correspondence should not surprise us; the theme of the two works is one and the same: the attainment of true happiness, or in Senecan terms 'tranquillity', through a resigned detachment from the vanity of worldly desires. *Heaven upon Earth* is itself enlivened by numerous satiric attacks on the sort of people who provide material for the satire, just as the *Meditations and Vowes* (1605) frequently assail vices familiar from the *Virgidemiarum*. *Meditations and Vowes* I.70, for instance, is almost a prose version of *Virgidemiarum* III.2, 'Greet *Osmond* knows not how he shalbe knowne/When once great *Osmond* shalbe dead and gone':

A mans best monument is his vertuous actions. Foolish is the hope of immortality, and future praise, by the cost of senselesse stone; when the Passenger shall only say, Here lyes a faire stone, and a filthy carkasse. That only can report thee rich: but for other praises, thy selfe must build thy monument alive; and write thy owne Epitaph in honest and honourable actions. Which are so much more noble than the other, as living men are better than dead stones: Nay, I know not if the other be not the way to worke a perpetuall succession of infamie, whiles the censorious Reader, upon occasion thereof, shall comment upon thy bad life: whereas in this, every mans heart is a Tombe, and every mans tongue writeth an Epitaph upon the well-behaved. Either I will procure me such a monument, to be remembered by; or else it is better to be inglorious, than infamous.[4]

The moral in each case is the same: 'a mans best monument is his vertuous actions.' The real difference is that the satire turns outwards to assail the follies of the world directly, while the meditation contrives to include its moral criticism within the pattern of its own private speculations thereby arriving at a personal moral resolution. Given the demands of their separate genres the passages are extremely close, and the more we read of Hall the clearer it becomes that some element of satire was essential to his meditative art. It is not merely that his satiric attacks derive strength from the convictions born in those precious contemplative hours when the mind 'easily contemnes all humane comforts' and disorders, but also that satire functions perfectly as a vehicle for the rejection of the material world in favour of what lies beyond. Satire in other words is the medium of the 'contemptus mundi'. Its 'distorted' vision of worldly affairs facilitates the attainment of meditative detachment. Only as the earth becomes small and insignificant in his sight does Chaucer's Troilus reconcile himself to spiritual love. Similarly it is only as the liberated soul rises through the spheres in *The Soules Farewell to Earth, and Approaches to Heaven* (1651), that worldly vanities are seen in proper perspective.[5] But such ascents can only be imagined. Satire, however, achieves comparable effects of diminution for those who find themselves earth-bound. Not without good reason did Augustine and Bernard know and practise the arts of invective, and for Hall too satire became an instrument of spiritual detachment, a step on the ladder of spiritual ascent. Commenting upon Psalm 144: 3 in *The Character of Man*, for example, he explains that there are,

but two lessons that we need to take out here, in the world, God and man; and here they are both: Man in the notion of his wretchednesse; God in the notion of his bounty: Let us (if you please) take a short view of both, and in the one see cause of our humiliation, of our joy and thankfulnesse in the other, and if in the former there bé a said Lent of mortification, there is in the latter, a cheerfull Easter of our raising and exaltation.[6]

This twofold pattern pervades almost all his religious tracts both meditative and devotional. Its recurrence, however, need not surprise us when we remember that Calvin's *Institutes* begin with the assertion that 'nearly all the wisdom we possess, that is to say, true and sound wisdom, consists of two parts: the knowledge of God and of ourselves.'[7] For him, knowledge of ourselves automatically involves an acknowledgement of man's innate depravity. He directs our attention to what he regards as two basic truths. First that 'we are so vitiated and perverted in every part of our nature that by this great corruption we stand justly condemned and convicted before God', and secondly 'that this perversity never ceases in us, but continually bears new fruits'.[8] Merciless with human pride, dismissive of human achievement, Calvin paints a picture of unrelieved depravity not from any perverse satisfaction in destruction but in order to heighten the blessings of grace and redemption, in order to emphasize the difference between the elect and the damned. He assails man in order to elevate him by raising the knowledge of God on the bitter knowledge of human debasement. And so it is in Hall. Even in his most lofty meditative tracts the voice of the satirist is clearly audible.

Among his contemporaries the justice of John Whitefoote's claim that Hall was 'one of the first that taught this Church the Art of *Divine Meditation*' was universally recognized.[9] His influence remained dominant for the first three quarters of the century. Among the more devout the practice of private contemplation became under his guidance one of the distinguishing features of the godly. It has recently been shown that the private meditations of Mary Rich, Countess of Warwick, are deeply indebted to his influence, while more surprisingly, Edmund Calamy, the 'ec' of Smectymnuus, based his *Art of Divine Meditation* on Hall's work of the same name—perhaps the most striking indication one could have that 'all men honoured the *Doctor,* though some loved not the *Bishop.*'[10] Indeed so prevalent was Hall's influence that when Robert Boyle came to write his own volume of meditations in 1665 he felt the need to apologize for 'deviating . . . from *Bishop Hall's* way of writing *Occasional Meditations*'. In order not to 'prepossess or byas' his 'fancy' he explains, he had 'purposely (till of late) forbad my self, the perusing of that Eloquent Praelates devout Reflections'.[11] In order to understand Hall's popularity we must examine his theory of meditation in relation to its source and intentions, and it is to this subject I now turn.

II. Sources and Theory

Hall defined meditation clearly and succinctly as early as 1606 when he asserted that,

Divine Meditation is nothing else but a bending of the mind upon some spirituall object, through divers formes of discourse, untill our thoughts come to an issue: and this must needs bee either Extemporall, and occasioned by outward occurrences offered to the mind; or deliberate, and wrought out of our owne heart.[12]

The allusion to 'divers formes of discourse' is of some importance for at the time Hall was writing the devotional practices being advocated were far from popular. Indeed *The Arte of Divine Meditation* from which the quotation is drawn was itself the first such work to appear in post-Reformation England, and 'diversity' or variety of form was to play a large part in Hall's strategy of wooing his countrymen back to the meditative tradition. Before the religions upheaval of the 1530s divine meditation had become firmly established as a highly respected element of English devotional life through the labours of such figures as Dame Julian of Norwich, Richard Rolle, Walter Hilton, Richard Methley, John Norton, and the anonymous author of *The Cloud of Unknowing*. Among Roman Catholics this tradition continued well into the sixteenth century though even here new influences began to take precedence. With the coming of the Counter-Reformation the practice of meditation underwent a great revival on the still predominantly Catholic Continent. Ignatius of Loyola, St. John of the Cross, François de Sales, Luis de Granada, and a host of others produced devotional works of intensely aesthetic appeal—a combination characteristic of the Baroque style—none of which, however, were ever deemed suitable for Protestant audiences. Such works as did make their appearance were either smuggled in by recusant priests or carefully censored by Protestant editors. The same fate befell even the works of St. Augustine and Thomas à Kempis—the whole fourth book of *The Imitation of Christ* was deleted—at the hands of Thomas Rogers.[13] More and more the practice of meditation became associated with Roman Catholicism while at the same time the growing influence of Luther and Calvin served to render native English mystics and contemplatives even less appealing.[14] In fact the only form of meditation still popular was that of self-analysis, intimately related as it was to the whole question of personal salvation. William Perkins and Richard Rogers, for example, were fascinated by the psychology of election, and devoted much of their time to examining the various 'motions' of the Holy Spirit. Beyond this the only other acceptable subject of contemplation centred upon Bible reading.

Matters took a step forward, however, with the publication of Richard Greenham's *Grave Counsels and Godly Observations* in the collected works of 1599 for which Hall wrote two dedicatory poems. They appear on the page directly facing the *Grave Counsels* themselves.[15] As a personal friend, Greenham must have exercised a powerful formative influence on the development of Hall's ideas. He was one of the pioneering expounders of methodical meditation in the late Elizabethan era, and his definition of the subject is close to Hall's own. 'Meditation', he writes, 'is that exercise of the minde, whereby we calling to our remembrance that which wee knowe, doe further debate of it, and applie it to our selves, that wee might have some use of it in our practice.'[16] This emphasis on 'use' and 'practice' is something we shall meet again and again in Hall, and Greenham goes on to say that meditation is 'the very life and strength of reading, hearing, prayer, and the Sacraments, without which they are made weake and unprofitable unto us'.[17] Towards the end of his career, Hall was to write a tract entitled *The Devout Soul* (1644) proving this to be the case. Both authors conceived of meditation as a form of preaching to the self, and both saw its pattern as that of a movement from reason to emotion. Yet although his eleven 'rules' form an art of divine meditation in miniature, Greenham was insistent that 'the word bee the object, and beware of mingling it with mens devises'.[18] Hall was to promote a far more liberal view although his own biblical contemplations became quite renowned. The *Grave Counsels* purport to comprise a posthumous collection of Greenham's personal meditations some of which were left imperfect on his death (1594) and some of which have been supplied from memory by his literary executors. The result is a series of curt, pithy observations arranged alphabetically which may well have provided the inspiration for Hall's *Meditations and Vowes* (1605). It must be stressed, however, that important as it undoubtedly is, Greenham's work leaves much room for development; the *Grave Counsels* bear all the signs of hasty compilation.

The subject of divine meditation was again explored in 1603 in Richard Rogers's *Seven Treatises*. Rogers admits that meditation is now little practised, though profitable for the laity and essential for the ministry. In order rectify this situation he deals at some length with what he considers to be the principal difficulties or 'lets' that the godly may encounter, and supplies quite a comprehensive set of rules designed to direct their choice of subject matter. Most of these, however, revert to the relentless insistence of Psalm 119 on the 'statutes' and 'precepts' of the Word. Rogers's margins abound in biblical references and he displays something of the typical Puritan horror of human authority. Like Greenham he effectively confines meditation to self-examination and Bible reading. Just two years later Hall produced his *Meditations and Vowes*.[19]

From the beginning Hall committed himself to the ideal of 'practical' Christianity, of Christianity not as a set of theoretical speculations, but a code of living. 'Christianitie', he tells us, 'is nothing but a divine and better Philosophy', but by 'philosophy' he means master-plan for life.[20] His *Meditations and Vowes* were produced in direct reaction to the barren religious controversies then raging. 'The world', they complain, 'is furnished with other writings, even to satietie and surfet, yet of those which reduce Christianity to practice, there is (at least) scarce enough.'[21] Yet laudable as was the wish to redress the balance of an age 'more brain then heart', the hope of relegating religious disputes to 'the Schooles and Masters of Controversies' was doomed to disappointment.[22] The love of theology left little room for Christian charity. Hall was soon to be swept into the war of the pamphlets himself, yet perhaps more than anyone else he repeatedly insisted on the need for private devotion. The inextricable nature of the problem is demonstrated by *The Remedy of Prophanenesse* (1637), one of his most eloquent statements on the importance of meditation.

The immediate purpose of the work was to counteract the Puritan attack on ceremonies and ritual—this is the 'prophanenesse' of the title—but the first book is actually an elaborate treatise on the art of divine meditation, on 'the true sight and feare of the Almighty' as the subtitle puts it. In other words, the purely devotional part of the work is intended as the basis of an appeal for 'holy decency' in liturgical and ceremonial matters. Hall the devotionalist and Hall the prelate are desperately attempting to come together with the result that the two halves of *The Remedy* complement each other in their author's eyes in a way wholly unacceptable to many of his readers, particularly to those whose 'prophanenesse' is under discussion. This was something he never quite appreciated.

Overlooking such ironies, however, *The Remedy of Prophanenesse* is a highly important meditative tract presenting a clear statement of Hall's views on the nature and function of divine contemplation. As usual we are presented with two subjects, God and man, and the essential problem of Christian life is seen as the struggle to remain aware of the presence of God in a world in which the perpetual maintenance of a high level of spiritual intensity is beyond our ability. 'We cannot hope', we are told, 'in this life (through our manifold weaknesses, and distractions) to attaine unto the steddy continuance of the actuall view of him that is invisible, yet, to the habituall, and virtuall power of apprehending him, wee may, (through the goodnesse of him, whom we strive to see) happily aspire.'[23] Meditation is therefore designed to cultivate such habits of mind as may empower the Christian to keep the idea of God as vividly before him as is humanly possible:

as in a pilgrim towards the holy Land, there are not alwaies actual thoughts concerning his way, or end; yet there is still, an habituall resolution, to begin and compasse that journey; and a secret power of his continuall will, to put forward his steps to that purpose; there being a certaine impression remaining in the motive faculty, which still insensibly stirres him towards the place desired.   (p. 52)

Moses saw God two ways, 'first, by viewing the visible signes, and sensible representations of Gods presence; as in the Bush of *Horeb* (the hill of visions;) in the Fire and Cloud in the Mount of Sinai; Secondly, by his owne spirituall apprehen-sion' (p. 14). We share only in this second way. To see God face to face is impossible for 'mortall eyes' (p. 27) and was denied even to Moses himself. This is what distinguishes Hall's methods from those of the great mystics of the Counter-Reformation. He does not entertain the notion of ecstasy, that supreme achievement of the unitive life enjoyed by Teresa of Avila and Philip Neri.[24] Instead what he envisages is a difficult daily 'renovation' of the 'awfull apprehensions' (p. 55) of God effected through tough intellectual disciplines. We see God, he explains, only in his works and in his words, but going far beyond Greenham and Rogers he interprets 'works' in the widest possible sense. God is reflected in his numerous acts of creation:

there is nothing that we can see, which doth not put us in mind of God; what creature is there, wherein we do not espy some footsteps of a Deity? every herb, flower, leafe, in our garden; every Bird, and Fly in the aire; every Ant and Worme in the ground; every Spider in our window, speakes the omnipotence, and infinite wisedom of their Creator: None of these may passe us without some fruitfull monition of acknowledging a divine hand. (pp. 54–5)

This is *what* we see; meditation is the faculty of seeing, a system of 'divine Opticks' (p. 47). 'The carnall eye looks through God, at the world; The spirituall eye lookes through the world, at God.' It glimpses the one through the other 'as thorow a prospective glasse, we can see a remote mark; or thorow a thin cloud wee can see heaven' (p. 48). For Hall sight became a major symbol. 'There is a threefold world', he declares, 'objected to humane apprehension; A sensible world, an intelligible, spirituall or divine; and accordingly man hath three sorts of eyes, exercised about them; The eye of sense, for this outward and materiall world; of reason, for the intelligi-ble; of faith, for the spirituall' (pp. 12–13). The passage is in some ways reminiscent of Loyola's appeal to the three powers of the mind, memory, understanding, and will, but here, as in Calvin, the emphasis falls entirely on faith.[25] While acknowl-edging the reflection of God in his works, the *Institutes* locate the basis of Christianity solely in faith in the revealed Word.

Reason alone cannot guide us. 'It is all one', remarks Hall, 'for a beast to take upon him to judge of matter of discourse; and for a Philosopher to determine of matters of faith' (p. 23). Immediately he proceeds to give an example from Jean Gerson, 'a great Master of Contemplation', of whom we shall have much to say later on. Gerson professes,

that he knew one, (which is, in Saint *Pauls* phrase, himselfe) who after many temptations of doubt, concerning a maine article of faith, was suddenly brought into so cleere a light of truth, and certitude; that there remained no reliques at all of dubitation; nothing but confidence, and serenity, which (saith hee) was wrought by an hearty humiliation, and captivation of the understanding to the obedience of faith; neither could any reason bee given of that quiet, and firme peace in beleeving, but his owne feeling and experience.   (pp. 24–5)

As the *Meditations and Vowes* make clear it is faith that opens the third eye of the mind:

A faithfull man hath three eyes: The first of sense, common to him with bruit creatures: the second of reason, common to all men: the third of faith, proper to his profession: whereof each looketh beyond other; and none of them medleth with others objects... What a thick mist, yea what a palpable, and more than Aegyptian darknesse, doth the naturall man live in! what a world is there that he doth not see at all! and how little doth he see in this, which is his proper element!... No, not so much, as what is in his owne bosome; what it is where it is, or whence it is that gives Being to himselfe... Hee sees no whit into the great and awfull Maiestie of God. He discernes him not in all his creatures, filling the world with his infinite and glorious presence. He sees not his wise providence, overruling all things, disposing all casuall events, ordering all sinfull actions of men to his owne glory... Though my insight into matters of the world be so shallow, that my simplicitie moveth pitie, or maketh sport unto others; it shall be my contentment and happinesse, that I see further into better matters. That which I see not, is worthlesse, and deserveth little better then contempt: that which I see, is unspeakable, inestimable, for comfort, for glory.[26]

Not surprisingly Hall's meditations turn away from any attempt to understand God in a purely academic or scholastic way, to an intensely devotional acceptance of the divine will which Evelyn Underhill quite appropriately relates to the long tradition of European mysticism: 'the stronger our faith is, the clearer is our sight; and the clearer our sight is, the greater is our measure of blessedness' (p. 77).[27] More important still, because of its close relationship with grace and faith the inclination towards this sort of contemplative devotion can easily be interpreted as a sign of election. Judging well the Calvinist temper of the English Church, Hall labours this point assiduously:

such a powerfull, and glorious influence there is of God into our spirituall senses, that we cannot see him by the eye of our faith here, and not be the happier; we cannot see him above by the eye of our separated soules, and not be perfectly glorious; and the one of these doth necessarily make way for the other: for, what is grace here but glory begun? And what is glory above, but grace perfected? (pp. 79–80)

One word stands out from the rest, 'necessarily'. It was the purpose of meditation to provide that sense of assured inevitability which alone could satisfy the Calvinist mind. It promoted faith in one's own election. By thus relating hitherto suspected devotional practices so closely to the doctrines of saving faith and divine grace, Hall helped to effect a remarkable change in outlook. Greenham and Rogers had complained of the decline in divine meditation, but by 1650 it was one of the most popular forms of private devotion and Hall himself was universally recognized as one of its first 'great masters'. By so vigorously attempting to reconcile Calvinism to the meditative tradition disrupted during the previous century he greatly enriched the literary potential of his own age. Meditation was no longer a Catholic monopoly.

III. 'A metaphoricall God': Extemporal Meditation

Extemporal meditation is meditation 'occasioned by outward occurrences offered to the mind'. It was one of Hall's favourite devotional forms. Between the years 1605 and 1651 he published no less than six short collections of such works beginning with the first 'century' of *Meditations and Vowes, Divine and Morall*. This little volume proved so successful that two further 'centuries' appeared soon after (1606). The *Holy*

Observations followed in 1607 and the *Occasional Meditations* in 1630. The latter received almost instant recognition as one of Hall's most outstanding contributions to literature and devotion. A greatly enlarged edition, the third, appeared in 1633, and a Latin translation by Hall himself in 1635. Thirteen years later appeared *The Breathings of the Devout Soul* and *Select Thoughts... A century of Divine Breathings for a ravished Soul.* The final collection, *Susurrium cum Deo: or Holy Self-Conferences of the Devout Soul,* was published in 1651 five years before Hall's death. Generally speaking these meditations are of two basic kinds. First of all there are meditations on some chance thought, axiom, proverb, or biblical phrase the significance of which is suddenly rediscovered in a moment of meditative illumination. This is what extemporal meditation is all about. It is the art of rediscovering the significance of experience, of making our normally random and distracted thoughts 'come to an issue':

I will use my friend as *Moses* did his rod: While it was a rod, he held it familiarly in his hand: when once a Serpent, he ran away from it.
    Every sicknesse is a litle death. I will be content to die oft, that I may die once well.[28]

Although their length varies from one or two clauses to many long sentences, most of the *Meditations and Vowes* and the *Holy Observations* are essentially of this nature, but in the later collections the form develops into something approaching the late Baconian essay. One can, of course, trace a similar development from aphorism to expansive discourse in Bacon himself.

    The second type of extemporal meditation is the 'occasional' meditation proper, the form developed by Robert Boyle and travestied by Swift in *Meditations upon a Broomstick.* Milton too allows himself a snide glance at it in his *Animadversions upon The Remonstrants Defence against Smectymnuus.*[29] Occasional meditation is characterized by taking as its object not some phrase or idea but some facet of creation, some lesson from 'this great volume of the creatures'.[30] Its scope is unlimited. Anything that may be apprehended by the senses serves its purpose. As Hall himself puts it, 'God hath not straited us for matter, having given us the scope of the whole world.' 'Thoughts of this nature', he tells us, 'are not only lawfull, but so behovefull, that wee cannot omit them, without neglect of God, his creatures, our selves. The creatures are halfe lost, if we onely employ them, not learne something of them.'[31] He is very careful to link such practices with the Puritan tradition of private devotion, and especially with his own personal experience of that tradition. We hear, for instance, how,

that learned and heavenly soule of our late *Estye, when we sate together* [my emphasis], and heard a sweet consort of Musicke, seemed upon this occasion carried up for the time before-hand to the place of his rest, saying, not without some passion, What Musicke may we think there is in heaven? Thus . . . that faithfull and reverend *Deering*, when the Sun shined on his face now lying on his death-bed, fell into a sweet Meditation of the glory of God, and his approaching joy.[32]

It is in tones suggestive of Bunyan and Puritan literature in general that we are urged towards such forms of devotion: 'Thou idle Truant, doest thou learne nothing of so many masters? Hast thou so long read these capitall letters of Gods great Booke, and canst thou not yet spell one word of them?'[33]

Although technically distinct, the two forms of extemporal meditation I have described have a great deal in common. Ideas, proverbs, and aphorisms are as much a part of God's creation as are natural phenomena and are so regarded: there is no 'creature, event, action, speech' that does not provide us with suitable subject-matter. Moreover, as Hall employs them, the two forms share the same basic tripartite structure, each level of which corresponds to one of the three 'eyes' of Christian vision: sense, reason, and faith. Whatever is apprehended by the eye of sense, is examined by reason, and applied by faith. In the *Meditations and Vowes* where the initial stage of the exercise comprises some thought or idea, the process corresponds quite closely, as I have mentioned, to the Ignatian pattern of memory, understanding, and will. In practice, however, there is little difference between the two varieties except that one is less regular than the other. In the *Meditations and Vowes* it is quite common for one or even two stages to be deleted, and for the meditation to collapse into a fervent ejaculation addressed to the deity.

On their first appearance in 1605 the *Meditations and Vowes* made a powerful impact and gained Hall admittance to the court of Prince Henry.[34] What captured the popular imagination was the novelty of form. To some extent, of course, the way had been prepared by the widespread popularity of the meditations attributed to St. Augustine, particularly as translated by Thomas Rogers, and by the publication of Greenham's *Grave Counsels.*[35] Another important factor was the relatively recent focusing of attention upon the *Meditations* of Marcus Aurelius, a work which Hall certainly knew later on and must have encountered as a lecturer in rhetoric at Cambridge. Xylander's *editio princeps* dates only from 1558 although the work was known in manuscript much earlier. In the background also was the enormous literature of the emblem and device of which we shall have much to say, not to mention the innumerable commonplace-books, anthologies, and compilations of all sorts stretching from Erasmus to Francis Meres. Despite the undoubted novelty of Hall's meditations, therefore, it would be quite misleading to separate them from the mainstream of English devotional literature where they undoubtedly belong.

Although Louis Martz has convincingly demonstrated the influence of Hall's theoretical works upon the tradition of English meditative poetry, the collections of extemporal meditations are still to a large extent ignored.[37] Yet in many respects the extemporal meditation is the prose equivalent of the 'metaphysical' poem. Take, for example, the following passage from the *Meditations and Vowes*:

(I)   The World is a stage; every man an actor, and plaies his part, here, either in a Comedie, or Tragedie, (II) The good man is a Comedian; which (how-ever he begins) ends merrily: but the wicked man acts a Tragedie; and therefore ever ends in horrour. Thou seest a wicked man vaunt himselfe on this stage: stay till the last act, and looke to his end (as *David* did) and see whether that be peace. Thou wouldest make strange Tragedies, if thou wouldest have but one Act. Who sees an Oxe, grazing in a fat and ranke pasture, and thinkes not that he is neere to the slaughter? whereas the leane beast, that toiles under the yoke, is farre enough from the shambles.

(III) The best wicked man cannot be so envied in his first shewes, as he is pitiable in the conclusion.
(Numerals are mine.)[38]

Here the tripartite structure is very clear. The image presented in section I is examined in all its ramifications in section II, thereby allowing us to arrive at a resolution or 'issue' in section III. It is an essay in 'justifying the ways of God to men'. The metaphor of the stage with its comedies and tragedies is used to resign us to the apparent contradictions in the moral order. Life is a 'play' whose last act is performed on a higher level of existence, but a play in which the actors become identified with their dramatic parts. For the elect, life is a divine comedy. An occasional meditation—that of the grazing ox—serves to illustrate the analysis of the dramatic imagery. We have the perfect form of beginning (image), middle (analysis and illustration), and end (resolution) so insisted upon in the very first meditation of the collection, itself an excellent example of what it advocates:

In Meditation, those, which begin heavenly thoughts, and prosecute them not, are like those which kindle a fire under greene wood, and leave it, so soone as it but begins to flame; leesing the hope of a good beginning, for want of seconding it with a sutable proceeding: when I set my selfe to meditate, I will not give over, till I come to an issue. It hath beene said by some, that the beginning is as much as the middest; yea, more than all: but I say, the ending is more than the beginning.[39]

Such a movement is by no means unique. Discussing the structure of the sonnet 'This is my playes last scene', for example, Joan Bennett writes that, 'Donne's pattern is the pattern of thought, of a mind moving from the contemplation of a fact to deduction from a fact and thence to a conclusion. The framework of the poem is logical.'[40] The similarity in imagery is equally obvious. It is not by chance that the *Holy Sonnets* were subtitled *Divine Meditations*. Essentially Hall and Donne are doing the same thing. Martz has no difficulty in demonstrating the similar tripartite structure of such sonnets as 'Why are wee by all creatures waited on?' while further pointing out that even sonnets which do not display the full threefold pattern nevertheless qualify as curtal meditations in the Ignatian tradition.[41] As we have observed, not even all of

Hall's meditations are strictly regular. That the vast majority are, is attributable to the greater ease with which the rigid structure may be preserved in prose. The arrangement of Donne's *Devotions upon Emergent Occasions* is a case in point. Its recurrent order of meditation, expostulation, and prayer has obvious affinities with the regular movement of Hall's meditative works. The term 'emergent occasions' is itself of some significance, for no less than Hall's *Occasional Meditations*, Donne's work is born of direct personal experience. For both men, as Donne put it, the Christian God is 'a metaphoricall God'.[42]

Donne was much influenced by the notion that the world was God's great 'book',[43] an idea which springs from what we might call a sacramental view of experience dating well back into the Middle Ages and beyond. Deeply influenced by Platonic philosophy, St Augustine came to inhabit an intensely symbolic universe every facet of which afforded further evidence of a higher level of reality beyond the material. In order to use the world correctly one had to become aware of its true spiritual significance. Hence Hall remarks how 'holy and sweet *Augustine*, from occasion of the watercourse neere to his lodging, running among the pebbles, sometimes more silently, sometimes in a baser murmure, and sometimes in a shriller note, entred into the thought and discourse of that excellent order which God hath setled in all these inferiour things.'[44] In part, at least, the Elizabethan 'chain of being' was the product of such an outlook and once established, did much to promote the development of related systems of thought. In many respects the Elizabethan world-picture is the medieval world-picture slightly adapted to Elizabethan needs. For them, as for Alanus ab Insulis,

> Omnis mundi creatura
> quasi liber et pictura
>   nobis est et speculum:
> nostrae vitae, nostrae mortis,
> nostri status, nostrae sortis
>   fidele signaculum.[45]

This is certainly what Hall has in mind in recommending extemporal meditation. He is fascinated by the age-old concept of the world as a theatre, the great *Theatrum Mundi* image of John of Salisbury.[46] 'Man is placed in this Stage of the world', he tells us, 'to view the severall natures and actions of the creature; to view them, not idly, without his use, as they doe him ... Whence it is, that wise *Salomon* putteth the sluggard to schoole unto the Ant; and our Saviour sendeth the distrustfull to the Lilly of the field.'[47] Again, in describing the act of creation itself, he writes that, 'the stage was first fully prepared, then was man brought forth thither, as an Actor or Spectator: that he might neither be idle nor discontent: behold, thou [God] hadst addressed an earth for use, and Heaven for contemplation.'[48] Just as for Luther all of profane history was merely God's 'puppet play', for Hall the profane themselves are like 'fond spectators, that when they see the puppets acting upon the ledge, think they move alone not knowing that there is an hand behind the curtain that stirs all their wires'.[49] To adopt such a view is to reject the very purpose of man's being, for he alone of all the creatures is capable of responding to the work of creation: 'none but he can see what thou hast done; none but he can admire, and adore thee in what he seeth; how had he need to do nothing but this, since he alone must doe it?'[50] Such ideas were also growing in popularity upon the Catholic Continent. A sign of the times was the publication in 1615 of Cardinal Bellarmine's *De Ascensione Mentis in Deum per Scalas Rerum Creaturum*, an English version of which appeared the following year.[51] More important, however, this mode of thinking pervades the whole tradition of English meditative poetry. As Herbert puts it,

> O Sacred Providence, who from end to end
> Strongly and sweetly movest, shall I write,
> And not of thee ...
> Of all the creatures both in sea and land
> Onely to Man thou hast made known thy wayes.
> And put the penne alone into his hand,
> And made him Secretarie of thy praise.
> Beasts fain would sing; birds dittie to their notes;
> Trees would be tuning on their native lute
> To thy renown: but all their hands and throats
> Are brought to Man, while they are lame and mute.[52]

In order to exploit the lessons of creation to the full, meditative writers developed elaborate analytical techniques for uncovering the spiritual message of the material world. Grammatical *claves* or keys, rules of etymology, logical categories, and rhetorical topics were all pressed into the service of interpretation. As one medieval authority put it, 'as many properties as a thing has, it has as many tongues telling us of something spiritual and invisible.'[53] Hence all the lapidaries, bestiaries, and encyclopaedic compilations of 'unnatural natural history'. Like Donne, Hall is very much a part of this ancient tradition. His analysis of the motion of the heavens, for example, is directly in line with the methods of his medieval ancestors:

The motion of this thy Heaven is perpetuall, so let me ever be acting somewhat of thy will; the motion of thine Heaven is regular, never swarving from the due points; so let mee ever walke steddily in the wayes of thy will; without all diversions; or variations from the line of thy Law; In the motion of thine Heaven, though some Starres have their own peculiar, and contrary courses, yet all yeeld themselves to the sway of the main circumvolution of that first mover; so, though I have a will of mine owne, yet let mee give my selfe over to bee ruled, and ordered by thy Spirit in all my wayes. Man is a little world; my Soule is heaven, my Body is earth; if this earth bee dull and fixed, yet O God, let my heaven (like unto thine) move perpetually, regularly, and in a constant subjection to thine holy Ghost.[54]

Similarly the *Meditations and Vowes* abound in all sorts of time-honoured animal lore from the pelican sacrificing herself for her young (II.52)—a favourite subject of the emblem books—to the elephant shunning its own reflection (II.4). Since such *exempla* may be developed either *in bonam partem* or *in malam partem* it is not unusual for the same creature to point either a cautionary or encouraging moral. The bee, for instance, 'though in all other things commendable' is yet the 'patterne of fond spightfulnesse' in its willingness to maim itself in the pursuit of revenge.[55] The point of such applications is made clear towards the end of the second century where we learn that,

there is no beast upon Earth, which hath not his like in the Sea, and which (perhaps) is not in some sort paralelled in the Plants of the earth: so there is no bestiall disposition, which is not answerably found in some men. Mankind therefore hath within it selfe his Goats, Chameleons, Salamanders, Camels, Wolves, Dogs, Swine, Moles, and what ever sorts of beasts: there are but a few men amongst men: to a wise man the shape is not so much as the qualities.[56]

One could not ask for a clearer statement of the correspondences between different levels of the hierarchical system of being. Hall is deeply imbued with all such lore. His sermon on *The Beautie and Unitie of the Church* (1626?) introduces a long list of emblematic birds the 'qualities' of only one of which, the dove, are shown to correspond to those of the subject under discussion. Hence the biblical reference to 'my dove my undefiled one' (Canticles 6: 9). As always the bestiary supports biblical exegesis, and the dove emerges as a perfect 'hieroglyphick of simplicity . . . Neither did the holy Virgin offer any other, at her purifying, than this embleme of her selfe, and her blessed Babe.'[57] Obviously emblem and hieroglyphic are keywords. Living in such a spiritually significant universe Hall could not but be drawn to the literature of the emblem, the visual equivalent of his own meditative exercises. As Francis Quarles put it, 'an Embleme is but a silent Parable . . . before the knowledge of letters, God was knowne by *Hierogliphicks;* And, indeed, what are the Heavens, the Earth, nay every Creature, but *Hierogliphicks* and *Emblemes* of His Glory?'[58] But the art of the emblem is itself intimately related to that of the 'metaphysical' image. The work of Mario Praz in *Seventeenth-Century Imagery* has made it virtually impossible to approach the subject without reference to the literature of the emblem and device. Similarly Rosemary Freeman has demonstrated the effect of these genres on the poetry of Spenser and Herbert, while more recently Martz has brought the same discoveries to bear on the poetry of Vaughan and Traherne.[59] More important still, in *Protestant Poetics and the Seventeenth-Century Religious Lyric,* Barbara Lewalski has convincingly, and I think definitively, demonstrated the centrality of Protestant emblematics to the work of all the major religious poets of the time. The correspondences she finds between emblematics and imagery are completely convincing and one can only assent to her conclusion that

'Protestant formulations of emblem theory and Protestant varieties of sacred emblem books contributed significantly to the poetics shaping the dominant strain of religious lyric poetry in seventeenth-century England.'[60] More specifically the influence of emblems on the poetry of Donne has been examined by Josef Lederer,[61] while Joseph Summers has suggested how Herbert's 'Altar' and 'Easter Wings' attempt to become visual as well as verbal 'hieroglyphics' while at the same time remaining closely allied to contemporary trends in religious meditation, for it was open to the religious lyric poet to 'make his poem a meditation on one of the innumerable hieroglyphs in nature, art, or the Church, or he could use the hieroglyph as the central image in a meditation on some doctrine or experience'.[62]

That meditation and emblem are almost inextricably related is indicated by the way in which unmistakably emblematic 'visions' appear to Spenser in *Visions of the Worlds Vanitie* just as he begins to 'enter into meditation deepe'.[63] It is all the more understandable, therefore, that Hall's interest in the emblem should be inseparable from his pursuit of divine meditation. It should come as no surprise to find the *Occasional Meditations* referring to themselves so frequently as emblems. In the absence of illustrations their visual element is supplied by vivid descriptive detail.[64] For Hall the book of the creatures is a book of divine emblems unlocked or 'read' by the faculties of sense, reason, and faith. Hall and Quarles shared much the same audience, and it is highly probable that the *Emblemes* (1635) themselves were influenced by the *Occasional Meditations*.[65] Certainly Quarles's *Enchyridion* (1639) and *Observations concerning Princes and States, upon Peace and Warre* (1641) bear a marked resemblance to Hall's early meditations. The first is comprised of four 'centuries' of 'rules' for the Christian life and bears an obvious similarity to the *Meditations and Vowes* while both adopt the curt, clipped Senecan style of which Hall was one of the foremost pioneers. Just as Hall frequently refers to his meditations as emblems, Quarles refers to his emblems as meditations: the two genres draw strength and inspiration from one another. That this should have been the case was virtually inevitable. In my discussion of the *Characters,* I have shown how Hall skirts the realm of 'pictures' in attempting to supply 'the benefit of an image without the offence'.[66] His meditations merely take the process one stage further. The influence was inescapable. Emblems or emblematic decorations were omnipresent in Elizabethan domestic art. In his patron's house at Hawstead, for example, Hall would have seen an emblematic screen displaying forty-one illustrations and mottoes at least one of which occurs also (probably quite independently) in the *Mundus*.[67] His more original emblem from the same work of a round rolling stone on a smooth surface reappears much later in a sermon dealing with the instability of worldly things, and is highly reminiscent of one of the plates from Quarles's *Emblemes*.[68]

The influence of the emblem is also unmistakable upon Hall's early poetry. His epitaph on Richard Greenham is really a description of the emblematic tombstone he would like to see erected over his friend's grave:

> Some skilfull Carver helpe me to endorse
> The blessed stone that hideth GREENHAMS corse,
> Make me a tree whose branches withered beene,
> And yet the leaves and fruit are ever greene.
> The more the stock dyes let them flourish more,
> And grow more kindly greene then earst before.
> Set Time and Envy gazing at the roote,
> Cursing their bootlesse hand, and sliding foote.
> Let all the Graces sit them in the shade,
> And pull those leaves whose beautie cannot fade.[69]

Similar in effect, if far more difficult to unravel, is his employment of a mixture of heraldic and astrological imagery in the witty emblematic poem addressed to James I entitled 'Ad Leonem Anglo-Scoticum'.[70]

A preacher constantly called upon to expound difficult texts before courtly audiences, Hall became fascinated with the imagery of the Bible for here he found emblems and symbols chosen or inspired by God himself. Perhaps more than anything else it was the example of Christ that sanctified extemporal meditation in his eyes. 'Our Saviour', he writes, 'tooke occasion of the water fetcht up solemnly to the Altar, from the Well of *Shilo*, on the day of the great *Hosannah*, to meditate and discourse of the Water of life.'[71] Similarly in

Christ Mysticall (1647) he expends many chapters exploring the implications of the similes in which God has chosen to suggest the nature of the mystical union between his Church and his Son. These chapters are essays in what one might now term literary analysis, but an analysis undertaken with a very different end in view. What is at stake is not aesthetic evaluation, but insight into the divine mind. In the case of the 'branch and stock' analogy, for example, immediate appeal is made to our own experience in an attempt to understand what Christ meant by the phrase, 'I am the vine, ye are the branches':

Look but into thy Garden, or Orchard; and see the Vine, or any other fruit-bearing tree how it grows, and fructifies; The branches are loaden with increase; whence is this, but that they are one with the stock; and the stock one with the root? were either of these severed, the plant were barren and dead: The branch hath not sap enough to maintain life in it self, unlesse it receive it from the body of the tree; nor that, unlesse it derived it from the root; nor that, unlesse it were cherished by the earth.[72]

However, should the 'analogie seem not to be so full, for that the branch issues naturally from the tree, and the fruit from the branch' we are invited to consider 'that clearer resemblance which the Apostle fetches from the stock and the griffe, or cion':

The branches of the wilde olive are cut off; and are graffed with choice cions of the good olive; those impes grow, and are now, by this insition, no lesse embodyed in that stock then if they had sprouted out by a natural propagation: neither can be any more separated from it then the strongest bough that nature puts forth: In the mean time that cion alters the nature of that stock; and whiles the root gives fatnesse to the stock, and the stocke yeelds juice to the cion, the cion gives goodnesse to the plant, and a specification to the fruit: so as whiles the impe is now the same thing with the stock, the tree is different from it was; So it is betwixt Christ and the beleeving soul.[73]

Such analyses are by no means restricted to what are obviously similes or analogies. Biblical events are also made to bear the same type of interpretation. The lifting of Moses from the Nile, for instance, is seen as 'a true embleme of a regenerate soule'.[74]

Not surprisingly, Hall was much affected by the poetry of the Bible and in particular by the Psalms. Their connection with divine meditation has been examined by Louis Martz who has pointed out that the word 'meditation' occurs here no less than six times in the King James version though nowhere else to be found. A number of recent critics have corroborated Martz's findings and the present study has emphasized how Richard Rogers bases his appeal for renewed meditation on Psalm 119. The conclusion seems inescapable, therefore, that 'in the Psalms lay the prime models for the soul in meditation.'[75] Martz supported his claims with reference to François de Sales, but he might just as well have used Hall who, in the first meditative tract of its kind to be published in post-Reformation England, makes the association explicitly:

we cannot goe amisse, so long as we keepe our selves in the tracke of Divinitie; while the soule is taken up with the thoughts either of the Deity in his essence, and persons . . . or of his attributes, his Iustice, Power, Wisdome, Mercy, Truth: or of his workes, in the creation, preservation, government of all things; according to the Psalmist, *I will meditate of the beautie of thy glorious Majestie, and thy wonderfull workes.*[76]

Hall, one remembers, began a verse translation of the Psalms in 1607, or rather, he began to publish it then. The plan was to produce a complete translation, but only the first ten Psalms ever appeared. Even so, the translation of the eighth underlines the connection with meditation:

> But when I see thine heavens bright
> The Moon and glittering stars of night,
>   By thine almighty hand addrest;
> Oh! what is man, poore silly man,
> That thou so mind'st him, and dost daine
>   To look at his unworthy seed![77]

Once more we return to the basic contrast between the human and the divine. The 'beautie' of God's 'wonderfull workes' leads David to realize both his own vileness and his creator's mercy. He ends in adoration: 'How noble each-where is thy name.' Hall calls the passage to our attention again in *The Arte of Divine Meditation* when, among other examples of the extemporal form, he mentions, 'that Meditation of the divine Psalmist, which upon the view of the glorious frame of the Heavens, was led to wonder at the mercifull respect God hath to so poore a creature as man.'[78] It is no coincidence, therefore, that the *Meditations and Vowes, The Arte,* and the translation of the Psalms follow one another so rapidly.

Hall was fascinated not merely by the practice but equally by the theory of Protestant emblematics of which English authorities such as Samuel Daniel, Abraham Fraunce, and Andrew Willet supplied a great deal.[79] Take, for example, his lengthy discussion of the nature of the heraldic device in the two sermons entitled *The Imprese of God* (the title itself is significant) delivered at court in 1610 and 1611. Their theme is the explication of the rather difficult divine emblem or 'impres' with which the Book of Zachariah concludes: 'In that day shall be written upon the bridles (or, bels) of the Horses, Holinesse unto the Lord: and the pots of the Lords house, shall be like the bowles before the Altar.' In strict accordance with contemporary practice the discussion is divided into a consideration of the 'body' or image of the emblem and its 'soule' or motto, and the ancestry of the form is traced back in the received fashion through *The Testament of the Twelve Patriarchs* and the early books of the Bible to the 'Aegyptian Hieroglyphicks' supposedly invented by Horus Apollo. The conclusion can only be that 'God himselfe was the first Herald, and shall be the last.'[80] This was the generally accepted notion and Hall's discussion represents a convenient epitome of contemporary theory. He is aware of every aspect of the subject, and his sympathies are wide. He recognizes the fundamental generic connection between hieroglyphics, emblems, impresses, devices, coats of arms, and inn signs. The resulting sermons are 'metaphysical' in the fullest sense in that every aspect of Zachariah's emblem is subjected to intense intellectual examination so that its true meaning may be fully uncovered. They must have proved highly congenial to an audience accustomed to unravelling the significance of the characters, actions, and devices, of court masques. Hall is exploiting secular tastes in an effort to arouse the same level of interest in the word of God. 'What now is more fit for Courtiers to heare of', he asks, 'than an Imprese of honour?

What more fit for kings and Princes than the Imprese of the God of heaven?' We are reminded of the *imprese* of 'the witty *Alphonsus* King of *Arragon* (to whom we are beholden for so many *Apothegmes*)' consisting of 'a Pellican striking her selfe in the brest, and feeding her young with the bloud; with a word, *Pro lege, et grege*'. On a less elevated level Hall cannot resist a satiric swipe at the Anabaptists: 'their king *Becold* ... carries a Globe of Gold, with two swords acrosse. His pressing iron and sheeres would have become him better.'[81] In much the same manner in *The Fashions of the World* (1626?) what 'was wont to be upbraided as a scorne to the English' is interpreted as 'the Embleme of a *Man*; whom ye may imagine standing naked before you with a paire of sheeres in his hand ready to cut out his owne fashion. In this deliberation, the world offers it selfe to him, with many a gay, mishapen, fantasticall dresse: God offers himselfe to him, with one onely fashion, but a new one, but a good one.'[82] In the case of *The Imprese of God*, one might say that the sermon, though long, serves as the 'soule' of the emblem, the 'body' of which is supplied by the biblical text under discussion. This is certainly the way things developed on the Continent where 'the prose commentary ... becomes ever more voluminous, stuffed with quotations, a sermon in the full sense of the word, to which the emblem offers but the starting-point, the *concetto predicabile.*'[83]

In order to illustrate just how widespread the contemporary interest in emblems was, in order, that is, to place Hall in the tradition in which he belongs, it will be instructive to compare him briefly with his friend John Donne. As is now generally well known, Donne's famous compass image appears at the end of one of Hall's *Epistles* where it serves to crystallize and encapsulate the argument in much the same way as it does in the 'Valediction forbidding mourning'.[84] Yet there is no need to argue influence in either direction since not only is there a possible Italian source, but the compass was a popular contemporary emblem used as the impress of the famous Plantin printing house. Other correspondences between the two writers can best be explained in the same way. Interesting comparisons can be drawn, for example, between the imagery of *Holy Sonnet* I and that of *Occasional Meditation* 43 'Upon the loadstone and the jet':

> And thou like Adamant draw mine yron heart.
> I am thine yron, O Lord, be thou my Loadstone.

Hall explains his imagery thus:

Me thinks, I see in these two [iron and jet] a meere embleme of the
hearts of men, and their *spirituall* attractives; The grace of Gods
spirit, like the true Loadstone, or Adamant, drawes up the yron heart
of man to it, and holds it in a constant fixednesse of holy purposes,
and good actions.[85]

Donne's interest in emblems has received a good deal of
critical attention, and it now seems clear that he consciously
introduced emblematic imagery into his poetry. He even
devised his own emblematic seal (a cross upon an anchor),
copies of which were distributed to a chosen circle of friends
(including Herbert and Hall) after his death. Indeed in
having himself depicted apparently rising from his burial urn
in his shroud, he all but made an emblem of himself.[86]
Emblematic imagery pervades his sermons also, for just as Hall
found in the dove a hieroglyphic of simplicity, Donne finds in
the circle one of the most 'convenient Hieroglyphicks of
God'.[87] Furthermore, whether or not Hall's meditations refer
to their 'occasions' as emblems, and many do, the function of
the image remains highly similar to that of the more overtly
emblematic passages in Donne's poetry. One comparison must
suffice:

> But must we say she's dead? may't not be said
> That as a sundred clocke is peecemeale laid,
> Not to be lost, but by the makers hand
> Repollish'd, without errour then to stand....
> May't not be said, that her grave shall restore
> Her, greater, purer, firmer, then before?

When I saw my precious watch (now through an unhappy fall
grown irregular) taken asunder, and lying scattered upon the
workmans shop-board; so as here lay a wheel, there the balance, here
one gimmer, there another, straight my ignorance was ready to
think, when and how will all these ever peece together again in their
former order? But when the skilful *Artisan* had taken it a while in
hand, and curiously pined the joynts, it now began to return to its

wonted shape, and constant motion, as if it had never been disordered.[88]

In this case Hall proceeds to discover in his 'occasion' 'the just embleme of a distempered Church and State' under the hand of God.

If his contribution to English literature is to be properly assessed, Hall must be seen as a central figure of the 'metaphysical' or meditative movement of the first half of the seventeenth century. In many respects his natural successor is Traherne, and not merely in prose. The quiet simplicity of his *Anthemes* bears witness to a considerable talent in the field of the religious lyric:

> Lord what am I? A worm, dust, vapor, nothing!
> What is my life? A dream, a daily dying!
> What is my flesh? My souls uneasie clothing!
> What is my time? A minute every flying:
>   My time, my flesh, my life, and I;
>   What are we Lord but vanity?
> Where am I Lord? downe in a vale of death:
> What is my trade? sin, my dear God offending;
> My sport sin too, my stay a puffe of breath:
> What end of sin? hells horrour never ending:
>   My way, my trade, sport, stay, and place
>   Help to make up my dolefull case.
> Lord what art thou? pure life, power, beauty, bliss:
> Where dwell'st thou? up above in perfect light:
> What is thy time? eternity it is:
> What state? attendance of each glorious sp'rit:
>   Thy self, thy place, thy dayes, thy state
>   Pass all the thoughts of powers create.
> How shall I reach thee, Lord? Oh soar above,
> Ambitious soul: but which way should I flie?
> Thou, Lord, art way and end: what wings have I?
> Aspiring thoughts, of faith, of hope, of love:
>   Oh let these wings, that way alone
>   Present me to thy blissfull throne.[89]

The tradition of which Hall formed a part was born of the interaction of a number of forces. During the sixteenth century the discovery of emblems coincided with a great revival of meditative devotion and a renewed concern for biblical exegesis. On the Protestant side this came to concentrate more and more on the language and imagery of the Bible in an attempt to unlock the literal sense which most of the Reformers considered vital. It was essential to realize, for example, that Christ spoke figuratively when he said 'this is my body', that he intended the Eucharist as a sign or emblem of the spiritual nourishment derived from a mystical union with God.[90] Meanwhile the astonishing survival of the medieval world-view with its various ladders of physical and spiritual hierarchies into an age when the 'new philosophy' had supposedly 'called all in doubt' assured the continuity of older traditions. The 'Book of the creatures' was read even more avidly during the first half of the seventeenth century than during preceding years. Such tensions as were felt seem only to have strengthened the meditators' determination. Hall wrote in direct and conscious reaction to what he himself recognized as distinct advances in the state of human knowledge: 'Nothing is more evident', he conceded, 'then that there have been further discoveries made of the visible and materiall heavens . . . but into the spirituall Heaven, in vaine shall we expect any further insight, then the already-revealed will of the Father hath vouchsafed to open to us.'[91] His world-view stands forth not naïvely, but in bold challenge to the beginnings of modern science. He refused to allow the secularization of the universe. Like poets such as Vaughan, with whom he has so much in common, he aspired to a higher level of reality than telescopes could attain. As the *Occasional Meditations* put it:

It is a good thing to see this materiall World; but it is a better thing to thinke of the intelligible World; this thought is the sight of the Soule, whereby it discerneth things, like it selfe, Spirituall, and Immortall; which are so much beyond the worth of these sensible objects, as a Spirit is beyond a body, a pure substance beyond a corruptible, an infinite God above a finite Creature.[92]

Vaughan's 'Providence' and 'I walkt the other day (to spend my hour)'—the hour of meditation—eloquently bespeak Hall's world-view. In the latter the poet upon missing a 'gallant flowre' delves down into the earth to find 'the warm

Recluse' hidden comfortably away from the winter cold. Quite unexpectedly he has found an emblem of the resurrection:

> Many a question Intricate and rare
>   Did I there strow,
> But all I could extort was, that he now
>   Did there repair
> Such losses as befel him in this air
>   And would e'r long
> Come forth most faire and young.

Yet realizing 'how few believe such doctrine springs/From a poor root' he celebrates the 'Book of the creatures' and prays,

> That in these Masques and shadows I may see
>   Thy sacred way,
> And by those hid ascents climb to that day
>   Which breaks from thee
> Who art in all things, though invisibly.[93]

Vaughan was, of course, much influenced by the poetry of Herbert, and the poem just quoted bears an obvious resemblance to 'The Flower'. Moreover, in *The Mount of Olives*, a work in which he expressly recommends the practice of occasional meditation, Vaughan quotes Herbert's 'Life' as an example of what he intends. The choice is an excellent one.[94] The first stanza of the poem describes the flowers and their fate; the second explores the meaning of these observations; and the third, in the form of an address to the flowers, comes to a moral resolution: 'if my sent be good, I care not if/It be as short as yours.' This is the pattern of countless *Occasional Meditations*. Not surprisingly, similar patterns are to be found everywhere in Vaughan's own poetry. One might compare 'The Timber', for example, with *Occasional Meditation* 133 'Upon the shining of a peece of rotten wood'. The first six verses of the poem focus upon the wood in its present 'dead' state, but notice nevertheless, how it seems to sense the approaching storm as if remembering its own fall or 'murder'. The following four verses concern themselves with the spiritual meaning of this observation—'And is there any murth'rer worse then sin?' —applying it ultimately to the remorse of the regenerate. In the last three verses the speaker resolves to lament past failings, and dwells on the value of repentance. All three meditative stages are therefore quite clear, and become even more so by comparison with Hall's prose.[95] In the meditation the strange shining of the rotten timber is first described and revealed as an 'embleme' of man's future state. Immediately this emblem is examined for its spiritual significance: 'Thus it is with us: whiles wee live here...' The meditation then ends with a rhetorical question, or self-questioning which strongly implies a spiritual resolution: 'why are wee so over-desirous of our growth, when wee may bee thus advantaged by our rottennesse?'[96] Whether they wrote in prose or verse, the meditators regarded the world as a book of divine emblems or hieroglyphics detected by the senses, understood by the reason, and applied to spiritual matters by faith.

One further point: since Ignatius of Loyola identifies memory as one of the three principal faculties of the mind actively involved in the meditative process, it may well be asked how Hall's art of meditation relates to the art of memory in which his contemporaries appear to have shown such an interest. Even if not conversant with the rather esoteric body of material recently examined by Frances Yates, Hall would still know of the art from Quintilian and other classical sources. In *The Devout Soul* he describes how a godly man listens to a sermon,

like a practiser of the art of memory, referring every thing to its proper place; If it be matter of comfort, There is for my sick-bed, There is for my outward losses, There for my drooping under afflictions, There for the sense of my spiritual desertions; If matter of doctrine, There is for my settlement in such a truth... Thus in all the variety of the holy passages of the Sermon, the devout minde is taken up with digesting what it hears; and working it self to a secret improvement of all the good counsell that is delivered, neither is ever more busie than when it sits still at the feet of Christ.[97]

There are undoubtedly many distinct points of contact between the two exercises. In particular, as developed by the medieval memory treatises and Guilio Camillo, the art of memory is, or can be, closely related to the art of the emblem and device. Francis Yates reminds us that 'the *impresa*... is the attempt to remember a spiritual intention through a similitude.'[98] Yet Hall does not readily seem to relate to this tradition, a tradition which under the influence of Bruno and his circle tended to attribute to symbols an importance and potency abhorrent to the Protestant mind. Melanchthon, Ramus, and the Reformers reacted strongly against it, or rather against what it had become by their time. Yates writes that 'in the Elizabethan world of 1583, the Protestant educational authorities, and probably public opinion generally, were against the art of memory.'[99] Educated in Cambridge, Hall was far more likely to absorb Ramist teachings on the natural progression of logical argument, on memory as an ordered system of logical conclusions. His friend William Perkins is thought to have been responsible for one of the most outspoken attacks on the new systems.[100] Moreover, his own 'practiser of the art of memory' is not represented as attempting to associate moral *dicta* with any sort of visual imagery. Instead, what he envisages is a commonplace-book method of categorization whereby particularly notable 'sententiae' are set down under the appropriate headings: 'sick-bed', 'outward losses', 'afflictions', 'spiritual desertions', 'matter of doctrine', and so on. His devout man 'reducts all things to a saving use; bringing all hee hears, home to his heart, by a self-reflecting application'. This is what we should expect from a writer such as Hall. His *Salomons Divine Arts*, for example, is really a sophisticated commonplace-book reducing to order and therefore to 'use' the various scattered *dicta* of the great philosopher-king. Similarly *The Balme of Gilead: or, Comforts for the Distressed, Both Morall and Divine* (1646) arranges its counsels under a series of headings denoting the most common human afflictions such as those of the sick-bed, loss of friends, blindness, deafness, and old age. This procedure is characteristic of Hall's consolatory writings, and of his rhetorical methods in general. In *Ludus Literarius* his brother-in-law John Brinsley recommends 'that little booke called the Art of Meditation' as a help towards teaching 'invention of matter'.[101] The comment is valuable in illuminating Hall's intentions. What he wanted to teach were the methods of clear, analytic thinking. If at all interested in the construction of a 'memory theatre', it was only in the sense of appreciating how the various 'props' of the *theatrum mundi* can serve to remind us of their creator. As Robert Boyle puts it, those diligent in the arts of divine meditation may attain the ultimate satisfaction 'of making almost the whole World a great *Conclave Mnemonicum*, and a well furnished *Promptuary*, for the service of Piety and Vertue, and may almost under every Creature and Occurrence lay an *Ambuscade* against Sin and Idleness'.[102]

For Hall what is important is not the image, whether it be a stage or a piece of rotting timber, but the 'issue'. In the proem to the *Occasional Meditations* he speaks of preserving his thoughts in order to share them with mankind: 'would wee but keepe our wholsome notions together, Mankind would bee too rich.' Yet what matters most is not the preservation of particular thoughts, but of the meditative way of thinking. His 'example' may 'perhaps be more usefull' than his 'matter'. He desires 'to teach weake mindes, how to improve their thoughts upon all like occasions . . . how to read Gods great Booke, by mine'. 'Our active Soule', he tells us, 'can no more forbeare to thinke, then the eye can choose but see, when it is open . . . For mee, I would not wish to live longer, then I shall bee better for my eyes.'[103] He wants his readers not merely to remember his meditations, but to experience them emotionally, to have their lives changed by them in a way they can never forget: 'Let these good Meditations not rest in the eye, but descend into the Bosome of the Perusers: and effectually work in their Hearts, that warmth of pious Affections, which I have here presumed to exemplifie in mine.'[104] In the end he finds 'one dram of faith more precious then a pound of knowledge'.[105]

IV. Methodology: The Arte of Divine Meditation

In 1606, less than a year after the first appearance of his *Meditations and Vowes*, Hall produced his most important and influential meditative tract, *The Arte of Divine Meditation: Exemplified with two Large Patterns Of Meditation: The one of eternall life, as the end: The other of Death, as the way.*[106] This work was the first of its kind in post-Reformation England, and served as the basis for most other seventeenth-century discussions of the same topic.[107] It also appears to have influenced a number of contemporary metaphysical poets, notably Crashaw.[108]

When John Whitefoote spoke of Hall as 'one of the first that taught this Church the Art of *Divine Meditation'* he chose his words very carefully. Hall's claim to primacy was that he was one of the first English Protestants to concentrate on meditation as an 'art' or system. He was one of the first to attempt to allay the suspicion that all such practices were tainted by the influence of Rome, but he was not the first Reformed minister to advocate meditation as a private devotional exercise. Among others, Greenham and Rogers had espoused this cause very strongly. But Rogers displays the typical Puritan reaction when he complains that once custom makes meditation a 'ceremonie' (the word is noteworthy) its inner meaning is immediately lost.[109] As both he and Hall were well aware, contemporary interest in systematizing various methods of divine meditation partook of a wider European movement which began in the early Renaissance but reached its fullest development in the works of Garcia Ximenes de Cisneros and Ignatius of Loyola.[110] Hence the dread of 'popish' influence. But Hall was far less of a fanatic than many of his contemporaries. Though equally opposed to Rome, he refused to destroy what he saw as part of the Christian heritage simply because it happened to be in use amongst his opponents. This explains his attitude to religious ceremony and episcopacy. Anyway, as he frequently reminds us, his own system of meditation is not intended in any sense as a rigidly prescriptive rule for all such exercises. It is merely an aid to private devotion. 'Divers paths', he writes,

lead oft-times to the same end, and every man aboundeth in his owne sense. If experience and custome hath made another forme familiar to any man, I forbid it not ... If any man be to chuse, and begin, let him practice mine, till he meet with a better Master: If another course may be better, I am sure this is good.[111]

Despite his upbringing, Hall never came to share the Puritan horror of the liturgy or 'prescribed' prayer. Nor did he ever adopt the practice of spontaneous preaching. On the contrary, he was one of its sternest opponents. Towards the end of the 1640s when the Puritan attack was at its height he came to the defence of the Anglican liturgy in a manner which was also, of necessity, a defence of his own devotional writings.

He rose to their challenge with a brilliantly apposite analysis of the Lord's Prayer:

He, whose Spirit helps us to pray, and whose lips taught us how to pray, is an all-sufficient example for us: all the skill of men, and Angels, cannot afford a more exquisite modell of supplicatory Devotion, than that blessed Saviour of ours gave us in the mount; led in by a divine, and heart-raising preface, carried out with a strong and heavenly enforcement; wherein an awfull compellation makes way for petition; and petition makes way for thanksgiving; the petitions marshalled in a most exact order, for spirituall blessings, which have an immediate concernment of God, in the first place; then for temporall favours, which concern our selves, in the second; so punctuall a method had not been observed by him that heareth prayers, if it had been all one to him, to have had our Devotions confused, and tumultuary.[112]

That Christ should have set such a premium upon the decency of his services was all the defence the meditations needed. Such works as the extemporal meditations and *The Arte of Divine Meditation* could now be represented, *because* of their careful patterning and structure, as the natural development of the sort of devotion advocated by Christ himself. Hence too could be deduced the need for the elaborate rhetorical skills we shall shortly examine.

Seen in the perspective of Hall's other works *The Arte of Divine Meditation* represents the logical extension of his interest in short 'extemporall' meditations. Whereas these were almost totally dependent upon some external 'occasion', 'deliberate' meditation was a process 'wrought out of our owne heart' not 'occasioned by outward occurrences offered to the mind' (p. 96). It was a carefully structured, devotional exercise consciously undertaken at a specific time, for a particular reason, in a pre-arranged manner. In any given case its exact purpose was determined exclusively by the spiritual requirements of the meditator at the time of the exercise. But as far as Hall is concerned it is purely and solely an instrument of Christian devotion. Of the two sorts of deliberate meditation possible he completely rejects 'matter of Knowledge, for the finding out of some hidden truth, and convincing of an heresie by profound traversing of reason' (p. 96). The rejection is characteristic. 'Matter of knowledge' would have taken him far into the realm of religious controversy. Instead his choice falls upon 'matter of Affection, for the enkindling of our love to God' (p. 96). Indeed, *The Arte* was produced in reaction to the dominant trends in contemporary religious composition. The number of polemical books Hall found 'rather to breed than end strifes', and the multitude of doctrinal works 'rather to opresse than satisfie the Reader' (p. 91). Meditation, however, is 'the very end God hath given us our soules for' (p. 113); 'it is not more impossible to live without an heart', he assures us, 'than to bee devout without Meditation' (p. 114).

Ideally the effect of such devotion is threefold. First of all it involves the practice of self-analysis and self-questioning which animates the soul towards the devout life: it begins in repentance. Secondly it quickens the spirit of formal rituals and ceremonies by rendering them spiritually meaningful, a feature with obvious appeal to the sort of audience Hall was attempting to reach. Finally, it is the pathway towards a form of devotional 'mysticism' and other-worldliness whereby we become 'strangers upon earth'. 'By this', we are told, 'we see our Saviour with *Steven*, we talk with God as *Moses*, and by this we are ravished with blessed *Paul* into Paradise, and see that Heaven which we are loth to leave, which we cannot utter.' (p. 95.) As we shall see, Hall's later meditations strongly develop these mystical tendencies.

Essentially *The Arte of Divine Meditation* is a highly practical didactic tract designed to introduce to English readers meditative techniques already well established on the Continent. As befits a work addressed to the novice, not the expert, its style and arrangement are eminently simple and clear. Everything is discussed as 'order requires' (p. 97). 'Our Meditation', we learn, 'must *proceed* in due order, not troubledly, not preposterously... Not suddenly, but by cer-taine staires and degrees, till we come to the highest (p. 103). On the question of subject-matter, for example, Hall first acknowledges that all thought involves meditation. The worldling, the scientist, and the politician all meditate after their own fashion and yet, 'the God that made them, the vilenesse of their nature, the danger of their sinnes, the multitude of their imperfections, the Saviour that bought

them, the Heaven that he bought for them, are in the meane
time as unknowne, as unregarded, as if they were not' (p.
101). The essence of religious meditation is that it should be
devotional; it is a 'bending of the mind upon some spirituall
object'. Its 'issue' is a change of values (p. 95).

The most striking feature of Hall's meditative technique is
undoubtedly its division into two halves, one rational, the
other affective: 'It begins in the understanding, endeth in the
affection; It begins in the braine, descends to the heart; Begins
on earth, ascends to Heaven' (p. 103). In other words, in
keeping with Hall's view of the process of salvation, enlightened reason serves as the basis for all acceptable religious
emotion. To carry the meditation through the various 'heads
of reason' is not merely to perfect the 'understanding' but to
lay 'grounds of matter for our affection'. The blind, tradition-
alist devotion which characterizes the 'Credulians' of 'Moronia
Pia' he finds abhorrent, and he is equally suspicious of
'ecstasy'.[113] His emphasis upon the importance of the reason
(though not, as we shall see, upon its over-importance)
pervades not only *The Arte of Divine Meditation,* but all his
devotional works and is closely related to his insistence upon
the need for order and method.[114] Elsewhere, for example, he
speaks of the '*Art* of Christianity' and the 'divine *art* of
Contentation'.[115] It is important at this stage to appreciate the
significance of this approach.

Since Hall was educated at Emmanuel College, a noted
centre of Ramist logic, it is tempting to trace such attitudes
back to his university days. Theoretically it is quite possible to
attribute the antithetical divisions of a work such as *Heaven
upon Earth* to the influence of the disjunctive syllogism, or to
analyse some of the sermons in the same manner.[116] It seems to
me, however, that far too much has been made of this
influence. If Hall owes any debt to Ramus, whom he mentions
only once in the entire body of his work, it is surely in his
insistence upon proceeding argumentatively in a 'natural'
order, that is, in presenting his arguments in a 'natural' order
of priorities, or as a 'natural' progression.[117] Such notions are
particularly important in the work under discussion, a didactic
tract on a meditative 'method' addressed to the layman. As we
have already noticed, circumstances, qualities, and matter are

discussed as 'order requires', and the rest of the tract follows in the same methodical fashion. Indeed the whole first half of the 'art' is basically a convenient system of definition, division, and analysis, broadly corresponding to the 'topics' of *inventio* as commonly employed in contemporary rhetoric: description, division, causes, effects, location, qualities, contraries, comparisons, similitudes, names, testimonies of scripture (pp. 105–10).[118] This procedure is designed to reflect the patterns of inquiry and logic allegedly innate in the human brain. These are the 'heads of reason, which nature hath taught every man' (p. 105). We must pursue our theme 'through all, or the principall of those places which naturall reason doth afford us: wherein, let no man pleade ignorance, or feare difficultie: we are all thus farre borne Logicians' (p. 104).

Yet this logical 'system', important though it is, serves simply as a devotional tool. Not all of the categories need be employed in every case, nor is it necessary to expend much labour on difficult points, 'which were to strive more for Logique, than devotion (p. 104). While appending the elaborate meditational scheme of Johan Wessel Gansfort in the margin, therefore, Hall simultaneously rejects it is a model on the grounds of 'darknesse' and 'coincidence' (pp. 103–4). In other words, it obscures the 'natural' order by a failure to distinguish clearly between the different stages. The meditator becomes entangled in the system, and forgets its purpose: 'for as the mind, if it goe loose and without rule, roves to no purpose; so if it be too much fettered, with the gieves of strict regularitie, moveth nothing at all.' In Hall's alternative method the divisions are clear and the progression orderly. At each stage the mind turns outward from the system to the subject, just as in continental meditations colloquies may occur at any point.[119] The structure remains logical and analytic, but the spirit of the language suggests other values:

What dost thou here then, O my soule? What dost thou here groveling upon earth? where the best things are vanitie, the rest no better than vexation. Looke round about thee, and see whether thine eies can meet with any thing but either sinnes or miseries... (p. 107)

To teach the art of meditation is in once sense to teach the art of divine rhetoric. The meditator must become his own preacher, hence the constant element of self-address. The composition of *The Arte* may therefore be seen as an extension of Hall's work as a university rhetorician. Here he is engaged in teaching the methods employed in his own meditations and sermons, in teaching his readers to preach to themselves.

As it will become a matter of some importance in the next chapter, it is perhaps well to emphasize here that even in this very early work Hall's view of meditation is by no means as contrary to the imaginative flights of the Ignatian system as critics have recently suggested. U. Milo Kaufmann, for example, sees Hall as beginning a strain of Protestant meditation almost hostile to the Ignatian tradition in its insistence on strict adherence to the all-sufficient 'Word' of Scripture. The imagination is simply not required.[120] How this agrees with the composition of the *Meditations and Vowes* is difficult to see, but certainly it receives little support here. Of *The Arte's* ten rational stages only one, that concerning 'testimonies of Scripture', ties itself to the biblical text. On the other hand, five bear distinct resemblances to the various stages of the *Spiritual Exercises*. I must emphasize, however, that when I speak of 'distinct resemblances' I imply no direct influence of any kind. I am simply attempting to set Hall's work in the contemplative tradition to which it rightly belongs. To recognize only his divergence from the continental system is to neglect the evidence afforded by the texts themselves. For example, the chapter dealing with 'the Subject wherein or whereabout' has obvious affinities with the famous Ignatian 'composition of place' which exercised such a profound effect on Metaphysical poetry. In his *Spiritual Exercises* Ignatius explains that,

in the contemplation or meditation of a visible object, as in contemplating Christ our Lord, Who is visible, the composition will be to see with the eye of the imagination the corporeal place where the object I wish to contemplate is found. I say the corporeal place, such as the Temple or the mountain where Jesus Christ is found, or our Lady, according to that which I desire to contemplate.[121]

As we shall see, such 'composition' is to be found everywhere throughout Hall's *Contemplations,* and his sensitivity to the importance of place in meditative exercises is clear from his assertion in *Christian Moderation* that,

it was good counsell that *Bernard* gave to his novice, that he should put himselfe (for his meditations) into the place where the dead bodyes were wont to be washt, and to settle himselfe upon the beare, whereon they were wont to be carryed forth: so feeling and frequent remembrances could not but make death familiar; and who can startle at the sight of a familiar acquaintance?[122]

What is commonly overlooked in this regard is that Ignatius intended his composition of place for both 'visible' and 'invisible' subjects. Hall's two examples of the 'deliberate' art are of the latter type: 'eternall life, as the end' and 'death, as the way'. Of this variety Ignatius tells us that,

in a meditation on an invisible thing, such as the present meditation on sins, the composition will be to see with the eyes of the imagination and to consider that my soul is imprisoned in this corruptible body, and my whole compound self in this vale [of misery] as in exile amongst brute beasts; I say my whole self, composed of soul and body.[123]

He would certainly have approved of the way in which Hall handles the question of eternal life:

what lesse happinesse doth the very place promise, wherein this glory is exhibited? which is no other than the Paradise of God. Here below we dwell, or rather we wander in a continued wildernes, there we shall rest us in the true Eden: *I am come into my Garden, my Sister, my Spouse*... the great City, *Holy Jerusalem,* the Palace of the Highest, hath her walls of Iasper, her building of gold, her foundation of precious stones, her gates of pearle.   (p. 106)

The process of imaginative anticipation goes even further in the chapter dealing with 'Appendances and Qualities' where the meditator takes the allowable liberty of placing himself in the company of the blessed. There he shall meet with his 'deare Parents and friends' and there too he shall see and converse with 'those ancient Worthies of the former World; the blessed Patriarkes and Prophets, with the crowned Martyrs and Confessors... shining each one according to the measure of his blessed labours' (pp. 106–7). Under the heading of 'that which is *divers*... or *contrary*' Ignatius's 'vale of misery' where we live 'in exile amongst brute beasts' is also powerfully evoked in a series of curt, graphic vignettes:

This man layeth his hand upon his consuming lungs, and complaineth of short wind: that other, upon his rising spleene: a third shaketh his painefull head: another roares out for the torment of his reines or bladder... one grovels and fometh with the falling sicknesse; another lyeth bed-rid, halfe senselesse with a dead Palsie... There, thou hearest another lament his losse: either his estate is impaired by suretiship, or stealth, or shipwracke, or oppression; or his child is unruly, or miscarried; or his wife dead, or disloyall... thine eies see nothing but pride, filthinesse, profanenesse, bloud, excesse, and whatsoever else might vex a righteous soule: and if all the world besides were innocent, thou findest enough within, thy selfe to make thy selfe weary, and thy life loathsome. (p. 107)

There follows a vivid depiction of Hell where the damned 'ever boyling never consumed; ever dying never dead; ever complaining, never pitied' suffer their various torments. After this comes a chapter of 'comparisons and similitudes' in which the mind makes 'comparison of the matter meditated, with what may neerest resemble it' and 'illustrates' it with the 'fittest similitudes, which give no small light to the understanding, not lesse force to the affection'. This procedure is so close to the Ignatian method that it requires little comment. As chance would have it even the particular images correspond, for just as Ignatius employs the similitude of an earthly king in attempting to illustrate the majesty of Christ, Hall uses the 'sumptuous buildings of Kings' to suggest the glory of Heaven.[124] The method is also much used by Donne in *The Second Anniversarie.*

By concentrating in the chapter immediately following upon the 'Titles and Names of the thing considered' the meditation might at first seem to be reverting to a Puritan insistence on the importance of the Word—if such terms are in any sense still applicable to Hall's work—but the practice can easily be related with equal justice to the medieval method, repeated by Ignatius, of dwelling on every word of a prayer or sacred text until it yields its inmost meaning.[125] The belief that the name of a thing in some way encapsulates its nature is as old as Adam's naming of the animals. In no sense has Hall here cut himself off from the imaginative, contemplative tradition.

The ten rational stages of deliberate meditation are immediately complemented by seven stages of affection: taste, complaint, desire, confession, petition, enforcement, and confidence. The conclusion consists of thanksgiving and recommendation of the soul to God. These, we are informed, comprise 'the very soule of Meditation, whereto all that is past serveth but as an instrument. A man is a man by his understanding part: but he is a Christian by his will and affections' (p. 110). Once again order and method are of supreme importance, but in a different way. Now we are following not the workings of reason, but the natural sequence of emotions as the enlightened mind approaches God. Like Perkins, Hall is fascinated by the psychology of salvation. It is clear, for example, why desire should follow complaint 'for, that which a man hath found sweet, and comfortable, and complaines that he still wanteth, hee cannot but wish to enjoy' (p. 111). 'After this *Wishing*', we read, 'shall follow humble *Confession*, by just order of nature: for, having bemoaned our want, and wished supply, not finding this hope in our selves, we must needs acknowledge it to him, of whom only we may both seeke and find.' We then pause to observe how the mind is 'by turnes depressed, and lifted up: being lifted up with our estate of joy, it is cast downe with *Complaint*: lift up with *Wishes*, it is cast downe with *Confession*' (p. 111). This, of course, is the sort of predictable pattern from which religious allegory can easily arise, and sometimes it is difficult not to think of Spenser or Bunyan:

After this *Enforcement*, doth follow *Confidence*; wherein the soule, after many doubtfull and unquiet bickerings, gathereth up her forces, and cheerefully rowzeth up it selfe; and like one of *Davids* Worthies, breaketh thorow a whole Armie of doubts, and fetcheth comfort from the Well of Life, which, though in some latter, yet in all is a sure reward from God of sincere Meditation.   (p. 112)

The importance of such presentation can be fully appreciated only when we remember that Hall was fighting an uphill battle to have his ideas accepted.[126] For reasons already discussed, English Protestants were highly suspicious of the meditative art. Recognizing this, Hall endeavoured to put his message across in a manner they would find attractive, and with reference to authors of whom they would approve.

Martz has demonstrated that the rejected 'table' quoted in the margin of the sixteenth chapter is drawn from the 'Scala Meditatoria' of Mauburnus's *Rosetum,* which in turn derives from the *Scala Meditationis* of Wessel Gansfort. He further points out that while Hall professes to have abandoned the intricacies of the system in favour of a simpler method, he returns to it again at the end, structuring his seven stages of affection about the 'Gradus Processorii amoris voluntatis et affectus' sections of the same work.[127] This theory seems correct, for an abridged version of the same system occurs in one of the *Epistles* (1608) with an acknowledgement of indebtedness to the 'Table of an unknowne Author, at *Antwerp*'.[128] The allusion corresponds to the mentioning of an 'obscure namelesse Monke' in the dedication to *The Arte*—originally, of course, the *Rosetum* was published anonymously. It seems likely, therefore, that Hall became acquainted with the work while travelling on the Continent with Sir Edmund Bacon in 1605. He is known to have stayed at Antwerp, and was likely to have been in pursuit of such material at the time, being already engaged upon the composition of the *Meditations and Vowes.*

Important as the *Rosetum* undoubtedly was, however, the fact remains that Hall rejected large sections of it in favour of a 'great Master of Meditation' whose influence has passed almost completely unnoticed.[129] This was Jean Gerson (1363–1429), at one time Chancellor of the University of Paris, whose *La Montaigne de Contemplation* appeared in 1397.[130] Although directly referred to only three times throughout *The Arte of Divine Meditation,* Gerson's influence on the work is quite pervasive, particularly in the earlier sections, and with good reason. Not only had he written exactly the sort of treatise at which Hall was aiming, but he was also rapidly coming into favour among Protestants as his popularity with Rome declined. Quite recently Cardinal Bellarmine had launched an attack on the famous *De Excommunicationis Valore,* one of his most outspoken statements on the limits of papal power. A reply by Fr. Paulo Sarpi appeared in an English translation in 1607.[131] The original was in circulation while *The Arte* was being written. Hence Hall can refer to Gerson 'whose authority I rather use, because our adversaries, disclaime him for theirs' (p. 99).[132] The discovery was extremely happy. Such an authority was desperately needed in order to allay Protestant fears. Here was an author cried down by the foremost supporter of papal power, who had written one of the most outstanding works on deliberate meditation ever published; Bellarmine's enemy was the Reformers' friend.

Gerson's *La Montaigne de Contemplation* was written in French rather than Latin in an attempt to bring meditation out of the cloisters. Intended principally for women, its appeal to laymen in general had always been strong. Far from addressing himself to the learned, Gerson complains bitterly of 'profound' theologians who lose the spirit of Christianity in pursuit of scholarship; it is better to taste honey, he asserts, than to hold an opinion of its sweetness.[133] As we have seen, almost identical attitudes motivated Hall, the extent of whose reliance upon Gerson may be judged from the following brief summary.

Although Hall often refers to the 'ladder' of contemplation (Gansfort's 'scala'), it is clear that Gerson's image of the mountain remained very much at the centre of his thoughts. The 'hill of Meditation', he tells us, 'may not be climbed with a profane foot . . . no beast may touch Gods hill, lest he die' (p. 97). Furthermore, 'it must be a free and a light mind that can ascend this Mount of Contemplation, overcomming this height, this steepnesse' (p. 98). Surprisingly in Chapter 5, the image of the 'ladder' is itself attributed not to Gansfort or Mauburnus but to 'that worthy Chancellour of *Paris*' who made repentance 'the first staire of his Ladder of Contemplation' (p. 97). As might also be expected, Hall's attitude towards language and method strongly reflects that of Gerson. They share the same emphasis on clarity and simplicity in the interests of the layman. To descend to particulars, however, the distinction between 'matter of knowledge' and 'matter of affection' is drawn straight from the pages of *La Montaigne,* as is the even more basic and important distinction between reason and affection ('taste').[134] The image of the worldly soul as a bird 'whose feathers are limed' is found in exactly the same context in Gerson, as is the analogy between a sinner's reluctance to repent and a cold man's irrational fear of fire.[135] Hall's preference for monks who blended contemplation with a life of physical exertion recalls Gerson's similar attitudes, and the passage ends with a direct quotation from *La Montaigne*.[136] Almost the whole of Chapter 9 is derivative, being little more than a skilful adaptation of ideas and phrases from the French. The anecdotes about St. Jerome and St. Chrysostom, the insistence upon forming the meditative habit, the need for internal as well as external solitude, and indeed even the quotation of St. Bernard's 'wittie and divine speech' are all borrowings.[137] So also is the citation of William of Paris in the next chapter but one, and much of the discussion regarding the position of the body during the contemplative exercise.[138]

This account is by no means exhaustive; only the most salient features of Gerson's influence have been mentioned. However, since the majority of these occur in that section of *The Arte* in which the influence of Gansfort has been openly rejected, they serve to clarify Hall's intentions. He has rejected scholarly complexity for the simplicity of an author writing for the layman. He draws upon a popular tract for the sort of tone, imagery, and anecdote required to render his message both interesting and unambiguous. As well as this, he gains the added advantage of allaying Protestant suspicions by the skilful introduction of an author who was becoming increasingly unpopular on the Catholic Continent.

V. Style: Theory and Practice

That Hall was a 'Senecan' was the agreed belief of his contemporaries, that he was also the leading 'Neo-Stoic' of his age is the contention of modern criticism. The two issues, of course, are intimately linked, but not in the way most people seem to imagine. Hall's present-day reputation for Stoicism has grown from his contemporary reputation for Senecanism, yet 'Senecan' was primarily a stylistic term, not a description of subject-matter. Thomas Fuller tells us that Hall was 'commonly called our English Seneca, for the purenesse, plainesse, and fulnesse *of his style*' (my emphasis).[139] Despite this, by stressing what he sees as the ethical correspondences between

Stoicism and Protestantism, and by associating these with stylistic considerations, Philip Smith has argued that Hall was in fact 'the leading Neo-Stoic of the seventeenth century'.[140] Similarly Rudolf Kirk believes that both *Heaven upon Earth* and the *Characters* are so pervaded by Stoic thought that 'the two strands' of Stoicism and Christianity have become 'inextricable'.[141] Certain ironies underlie both arguments, for Kirk cites Cicero (against whom Seneca reacted stylistically) as a major source of Stoic thought, and Lactantius, one of Smith's 'Stoic' Church Fathers, was himself known to Hall as 'the Christian Cicero'.[142] Furthermore, as has often been noticed, on the question of rhetorical ornament Seneca himself was frequently at odds with received Stoic opinion.[143] This being the case, the connection between style and philosophy cannot possibly be as absolute as has been suggested: Hall may well have been a 'Senecan' without adopting Seneca's Stoicism. Indeed in the opening sections of *Heaven upon Earth* he employs an undoubtedly Senecan style to describe the limitations of Senecan philosophy, and his equally Senecan remarks upon Stoicism in the *Meditations and Vowes* are often less than favourable: 'To show no passion, is too Stoicall; to shew all, is impotent; to shew other than we feele, hypocriti-call.'[144] It is therefore quite unnecessary to adopt Harold Fisch's rather extreme suggestion that Hall is not a real Neo-Stoic because his style is not truly 'Senecan'.[145] The two are not inseparable, and there is no need to do violence to the texts in attempting to dissociate them.

The more closely we examine Hall's alleged innovations, the less new they begin to appear. The connection between Seneca and Christianity was legendary. As Hall himself points out, the philosopher is reputed to have corresponded with St. Paul—his supposed letters to the apostle were edited by Erasmus.[146] The matter was a commonplace of Christian thought dating from the days of the early Church. Indeed there is much to be said for the conclusion that 'if . . . we are to follow Smith in calling Hall "the leading Neo-Stoic of the seventeenth century" we must assume that in seventeenth-century England Neo-Stoicism was no different from the Christian Stoicism which had existed during the Middle Ages.'[147] The major flaw in Kirk's argument, for example, is that the supposed inextricability of the two strands produces results indistinguishable from the most conventional statements of traditional Christianity. In any other context they would pass unnoticed. This is particularly true regarding the sentence from *Heaven upon Earth* from which alone, it has been alleged, 'one can understand now he [Hall] came to be called "the Christian Seneca"':

> Thus then, the mind resolved that these earthly things (*Honour, Wealth, Pleasures*) are casuall, unstable, deceitfull, imperfect, dangerous; must learne to use them without trust, and to want them without griefe; thinking still, If I have them, I have some benefit with a great charge: If I have them not; with little respect of others, I have much security and ease, in my selfe: which once obtained, we cannot fare amisse in either estate; and without which, we cannot but miscarry in both.[148]

As any educated man must, Hall intensely admired the intellectual achievements of the ancients, but his admiration was qualified by his yet more intense awareness of being a Christian, of living in the light of divine revelation. In the dedication to *Heaven upon Earth*, one of the major sources of which is Seneca's *De Tranquillitate*, he tells us in phrases reminiscent of his attitude towards Theophrastus, that:

> I have followed *Seneca*, and gone beyond him; followed him as a Philosopher, gone beyond him as a Christian, as a Divine. Finding it a true censure of the best Moralists, that they were like to goodly Ships, graced with great titles, the *Savegard*, the *Triumph*, the *Goodspeed*, and such like, when yet they have beene both extremely Seabeaten, and at last wracked.[149]

In the third section, having given what he terms an 'abridged' summary of Seneca's 'rules of Tranquillitie', he concludes that,

> All these in their kinds please well, profit much, and are as soveraigne for both these, as they are unable to effect that for which they are propounded. Nature teacheth thee all these should be done, she cannot teach thee to doe them: and yet doe all these and no more, let me never have rest, if thou have it.[150]

While he 'envies' the Stoics their natural 'wit', he 'pities' their lack of grace. They were like hounds 'swift of foot, but not exquisite in sent, which in an hasty pursuit take a wrong way, spending their mouthes, and courses in vaine'. Their 'carefull disquisition of true rest' led them ultimately to 'meere unquietnesse'.[151] As well as this, many of their beliefs were simply wrong. In *Resolutions and Decisions of Divers Practicall Cases of Conscience* (1649), for example, he retreats in horror from their teachings on suicide, Seneca's own manner of death.[152]

Despite all the controversy on this issue, what is perhaps its single most important aspect has been entirely forgotten. One indisputable fact about Hall is that he was a staunch Calvinist, and I would suggest that if we must find a contemporary source for his interest in Senecan philosophy we shall sooner find it here than in Lipsian Neo-Stoicism. Calvin's first work was not a theological treatise but a commentary on Seneca's *De Clementia*, and his attitude towards that philosopher closely resembles that of Hall.[153] This is particularly true regarding the flaws in the Stoic position. Calvin believed, for example, that, due to its failure to appreciate man's real needs, Stoic philosophy was fundamentally alien to human nature, demanding as it did an impossible apathy of the passions. Hall's views were much the same, and in *Heaven upon Earth* he explains at some length that whereas Seneca may well have gained some idea of what real tranquillity was, with only 'nature' to guide him, he could never attain it. This is why the 'rules' of the Stoics often bear such little relationship to the reality of human emotions. 'Reason', he asserts, 'bids the angry man say over his Alphabet ere hee give his answer . . . He was never throughly angry, that can endure the recitall of so many idle letters. Christianity gives not rules, but power to avoid this short madnesse.'[154]

As a result, when he comes to speak of death his discussion, despite any references or allusions to Seneca, is purely Christian—only faith in revealed truth can withstand the terrors of dissolution. On all the most important issues Hall and Calvin are saying exactly the same thing; there is nothing new in Hall's approach:

the mynde of a man being voyed of the very wysedome of the fleshe or natural man, turneth it selfe al together unto the becke and pleasure of Goddes spirite. Of thys transformyng or turning which Paule calleth the renuinge of the mynde, though it be the first enteraunce into life, al the philosophers were ignoraunt, for thei say that reason only ruleth man, onely reason they thynke worthy to be hearde: finally to reason onely, they geve and suffre the government or rule of their dedes. But christian philosophy biddeth reason to geve place, to obey and be in subiection, unto the holy gost that man do not nowe hym selfe lyve, but rather beare Christ lyvinge and reigning in hym.[155]

All our heady and disordered affections, which are the secret factors of sin and Satan, must be restrained by a strong and yet temperate command of Reason and Religion...Reason hath alwayes been busie in undertaking this so necessary a moderation: wherein although shee have prevailed with some of colder temper, yet those which have beene of more stubborne metall...have still despised her weake endevours. Only Christianity hath this power; which with our second birth gives us a new nature: so that now, if excesse of passions bee naturall to us as men, the order of them is naturall to us as Christians.[156]

For both Hall and Calvin man was possessed of a dual nature, the spiritual half of which could only be reached by regenerate reason, reason transformed by faith. Practical as some Stoic suggestions might be, the power to adopt them lay ultimately with the Christian. The keyword for both writers was not 'nature' but 'grace':

If *Seneca* could have had grace to his wit, what wonders would he have done in this kinde? what Divine might not have yeelded him the chaire for precepts of Tranquillity without any disparagement? As he was, this he hath gained: Never any Heathen wrote more divinely: never any Philosopher more probably. Neither would I ever desire better Master, if to this purpose I needed no other Mistris than Nature. But this in truth is a taske, which Nature hath never without presumption undertaken, and never performed without much imperfection... And if she could have truly effected it alone, I know not what employment in this life she should have left for grace...nor what privilege it should have been here below to be a Christian, since this that we seek [true peace of mind] is the noblest worke of the soule, and in which alone consists the only heaven of this world...No marvell then if all the Heathen have diligently sought after it, many wrote of it, none attained it. Not *Athens* must teach this lesson, but *Ierusalem*.[157]

Exactly forty years later in *The Balme of Gilead* Hall was still saying the same thing: in that he was wise after the fashion of natural wit, Seneca could be useful; in that he was not a Christian, he was insufficient.[158] That there are so many allusions to Seneca throughout Hall's works should hardly surprise us. It would not have surprised his contemporaries, nor would it have been interpreted to mean that he was a Stoic. T. H. L. Parker puts the point well in his biography of Calvin when he writes that,

to the sixteenth century Seneca was a Stoic with Christian sympathies. It is to be expected, therefore, that certain of his ideas will bear a strong resemblance to corresponding Christian doctrines. Calvin will sometimes point to the resemblance even if the two concepts also contain a serious difference.[159]

The point of interest for Hall's contemporaries was not that he had become a Stoic, but that the pagan philosopher upon whose writings he had modelled his style could be so astonishingly 'Christian' in outlook. Having thus qualified the nature of Hall's commitment to Stoic philosophy we may proceed to examine his use of the Senecan style.

The English Senecan movement of the 1590s was directly influenced by the changing trends in continental prose style. Lipsius, Muret, and Montaigne were all well known and highly admired, and played a large part in effecting the transition from the majestic, rolling periods of Hooker to the clipped, sententious, and curt style of Bacon and Hall. Bacon was the first to publish in the new manner. His *Essayes* and *Meditations* appeared in 1597, and an English version of the latter was produced the following year.[160] This in itself is of some importance since the influence of Latin on the vernacular is often underestimated. In Hall's case his English is sometimes even more recognizably Senecan (or Lipsian) than his Latin. The *Occasional Meditations* were originally written in English: the Latin version is merely a translation. We must also recognize that although it has become common to speak of the Senecan 'movement', there was really no 'movement' at all in the sense of a group of writers bound together by strongly similar religious, moral, or intellectual ideals. It was far more a question of sympathy in attitude and temperament. Almost all

of the Senecan or 'anti-Ciceronian' writers— that is, all who
rejected the Ciceronian period—reacted not merely against
Ciceronian style but against the attitudes towards learning and
knowledge which it seemed at the time to embody. For many,
Ciceronianism had become the art of speaking majestically
about nothing.[161] Adopting Seneca's avowed preference for
matter over manner, they attempted to shift the emphasis from
style to content. One early symptom of this is Hall's rejection
of the popularly held opinion that satire should be difficult
and obscure after the fashion of Scaliger, a noted Ciceronian.
He will 'say nothing to be untalkt of, or speake with my mouth
open that I may be understood.[162] It is the function of
language, he tells us, 'to cloath the true notions of our hearts'
and truth 'is when we speak as we think, and think as it is'.[163]
'Heedlesse abuses of words' have 'bred confusion of things'
whereas 'the assured sense of words is the safety of propriet-
ies'.[164] Theoretically, at least, the new writers were agreed that
style should remain subordinate to subject-matter. Bacon, one
recalls, opposed a curt, aphoristic style (the 'way of Proba-
tion') to Ciceronian 'methods' (the 'Magistral way') in an
attempt to smash what he termed the 'contract of error'
between teacher and student.[165] Similarly, desiring that his
letters should present an accurate image of his own mind,
Lipsius adopted the clipped, clear, 'hopping' style described in
his famous *Institutio Epistolica* (1591). By applying this advice
to style in general, Ben Jonson helped to establish the Lipsian
manner as one of the foremost modes of seventeenth-century
prose.[166]

Following in this tradition, Hall's *Meditations and Vowes*
were written in direct reaction to what he saw as the barren
intricacies of theological controversy. They were intended to
re-focus public opinion upon essential Christian truths, to
affect 'practice' rather than opinion. Choice of style was
therefore of the utmost importance. Communication was at a
premium: 'it is more behovefull to the common good, for
which (both as men and Christians) we are ordained, that
those thoughts which our experience hath found comfortable
and fruitfull to our selves, should (with neglect of all
censures) be communicated to others.' Such considerations
have led him to 'cloath these naked thoughts in plaine and

simple words'.[167] The advantages are twofold. First of all, by presenting a truthful account of his inmost thoughts, the *Meditations*, like Lipsius's letters, will create an exact image of his own mind whereby the sincerity of his religious professions may be judged by all: 'so many men as I live amongst, so many monitors I shall have.'[168] There is no 'contract of error' here. Hall's readers are invited to be critical, to judge him by the standards he has himself established. It is no coincidence that he should be the one who introduced the familiar epistle to English literature. Secondly, the development of this critical awareness involves the reader more actively with the text. The *Meditations* have been written 'not for the eye, but for the heart'. They are commended not to our 'reading' but our 'practice'. Their process of thought is more important than the individual thoughts themselves. By adopting this the reader becomes not simply 'a meere and ordinary *agent*' (note the word) but 'a patterne propounded unto others imitation'.[169] Everywhere the emphasis falls on awareness and involvement. The *Meditations* are not to be 'read' in a passive sense, but imitated. In each case the reader is expected to involve himself actively in the journey from idea to conviction. The clipped, clear style is the result of a deliberate and conscious choice made in accordance with the 'practical' aims of the composition.

As Morris Croll has pointed out, the Senecan style, like the Baroque movement in the visual arts, is concerned with motion, with capturing the movement of the faculties as they seek an answer to their questioning:

It preferred the forms that express the energy and labour of minds seeking the truth, not without dust and heat, to the forms that express a contented sense of the enjoyment and possession of it. In a single word, the motions of souls, not their states of rest, had become the themes of art.[170]

Written in a clearly Senecan style, Hall's meditations portray the devout mind's ceaseless attempt to ascend from the world of sense to the world of faith. Yet he is not, of course, seeking truth in any absolute sense. For him, truth has already been revealed. What he is seeking are new manifestations of this truth in the world around him. In the *Occasional Meditations* he concentrates on the 'book of the creatures', on seeing God in his creation. In the more pronouncedly Senecan *Meditations and Vowes* his field is human consciousness. Here he records the normally transient thoughts and opinions suggested by ordinary daily experience. The refusal to accept their transience, to allow them to pass without coming to an 'issue', is the hallmark of the mind endowed with grace. As Bacon maintained, the worth of an 'aphorism' lies in its ability to provoke thought.[171] To put the matter in Senecan terms, when not properly investigated, 'sententiae' easily became platitudes. The assertion that 'every worldling is a mad man', for example, is rather striking in itself, but neither its real meaning nor its application to the reader's moral character is clear until he has followed to the end the meditative process it evokes. He must re-explore the experience which made the formula possible before he can fully accept it. Like many of the Metaphysical poets, he ends where he began but with a heightened awareness.[172]

Croll identified two basic types of Senecanism, the curt (*coupé*) and the loose. While both are generally to be found side by side in the pages of most Renaissance authors, it is nevertheless true that the early compositions of both Bacon and Hall are more markedly curt than those of most other writers.[173] Bacon, it is true, thoroughly revised his *Essayes* as the century wore on, and his later style is far more relaxed and loose, but this stylistic shift corresponds to a change in intention. When Bacon became more interested in synthesizing existing knowledge rather than exploring new areas of thought, he naturally returned from 'aphorisms' to 'methods'.[174] As I hope to demonstrate, a similar change occurs in the writings of Hall.

In his *Epistles* (1611), however, Hall declares his allegiance to the curt form of Senecanism. What he particularly admires is its brevity, its readiness for 'use'. Economy of words heightens the impact of the moral message. The 'powers of good advice' gain force from firm, compact expression:

brevity where it is neither obscure, nor defective, is very pleasing, even to the daintiest judgements. No marvell therefore, if most men desire much good counsell in a narrow roome; as some affect to have great personages drawne in little tablets; or, as we see worlds of Countries described in the compasse of small maps: Neither do I unwillingly yeeld to follow them; for both the powers of good advice are the stronger when they are thus united; and brevity makes counsell more portable for memorie, and readier for use.[175]

Not surprisingly the style of the *Meditations and Vowes* is almost the textbook example of what Croll understood by the curt style: short sentences; asyndeton; Lipsian 'hops'; and self-contained, aphoristic openings containing the whole idea of the period. A passage such as the following is typical:

'A Man under Gods affliction, is like a bird in a net; the more he striveth, the more he is intangled. Gods Decree cannot be eluded with impatience. What I cannot avoid, I will learne to beare.'[176]

Here the first dozen words contain the entire message, and little time is wasted in its development. The simile of the bird is expounded clearly and concisely with the minimum of exposition. Generally speaking the style is typical of Seneca; the use of witty analogies, sharp, concise sentences and clauses, and 'balanced' constructions such as 'the more . . . the more' are all characteristic of the *Epistulae Morales*.[177] The Ciceronian period is completely abandoned. Instead the progress is direct and linear, following the development of the thought. There are no connective particles and the meditation moves by means of the famous Lipsian 'hop'. The links depend on the sense and the agility of the reader's mind. After the two balanced clauses we are presented with a bald statement of moral fact representing the judgement of the reason on those who strive in the divine net. Then, completely without warning, we abandon the restrained, distancing mechanism of the general observation for the first person singular. The 'I' comes with a jolt, as we are suddenly made aware that this is not an abstract, philosophic discussion, but a personal consideration affecting our own lives. As we read we are invited to come to the same conclusion as the writer. The groundwork has been laid for us. The propositions are irrefutable; the will follows the reason. The balance of the concluding clauses ('I cannot avoid . . . I will learne to beare') reflects the balance of the speaker's mind. Much has been achieved in a mere 37 words, yet this is by no means the shortest meditation.

To writers attempting to create the illusion of a mind
engaged in thought, the Ciceronian period appeared too pre-
planned and elaborate; one could not imagine a sudden
meditation shaping itself spontaneously in that form. On the
contrary, the mind leaps associatively from notion to notion as
by a series of stepping-stones. Hence the use of the Lipsian
'hop'. In the following passage, for example, the rapid
movement of the curt clauses mirrors the brisk agility of the
mind as it grapples with the various aspects of the problem in
hand:

I can doe nothing without a million of Witnesses: The conscience is
as a thousand witnesses; and God is a thousand consciences: I will
therefore so deale with men, as knowing that God sees me; and so
with God, as if the world saw me; so with my selfe, and both of them,
as knowing that my conscience seeth me: and so with them all, as
knowing I am alwaies over-looked by my accuser, by my Judge.[178]

The ideas seem to tread upon one another's heels, and the
sustained impression of constant self-qualification leading to
the powerful monosyllabic 'judge' creates the atmosphere of
apprehension and circumspection which is the speaker's
theme; the syntax is as circumspect as the ideas, indeed it
embodies those ideas. But, of course, the prose only *seems*
hurried and artless. Actually it is all carefully ordered and
planned. We notice first the patterning of 'witnesses ... conscience ... witnesses ... consciences', and then the clever balancing of the following clauses:

>   deale with men/God sees me
>   with God/world saw me
>   with my selfe and both/conscience seeth me
>   with them all/over-looked by ... my Judge

The effect is designedly incremental; the scope widens with
each addition, and as in any court room we look from the
witnesses to the judge. The minor variations in word
arrangement and phrasing (ending so emphatically on 'judge',
for example, rather than on 'me') exemplify what Croll meant
when he spoke of Senecan 'asymmetry'.[179] Actually, they may
more properly be regarded as highly effective variations on a

fixed pattern—and made possible solely by the establishment of such a pattern—designed to achieve special effects. In this case it is the effect of emphasis: the movement of the piece is from 'I' to 'my Judge'.

Patterning and symmetry are essential elements of Hall's style, serving to reflect his appreciation of the divinely ordered, methodical universe of which he writes. Nor do they impair his carefully sustained illusion of the thinking mind, since his conception of enlightened intelligence is of a mind in which all the faculties know and perform their functions in the orderly threefold fashion of the meditations themselves. Far from losing itself amidst clouds of witness, for example, the mind in the last quotation charts its way through them all, however circumspectly, to its judge. Similarly in the following passage the elaborate poise and balance of the clauses within the sentences, and of the words within the clauses, suggest both the providential order of the natural and spiritual universe and, by implication, man's ability to appreciate that order despite the apparent contradictions:

With God there is no free man, but his servant, though in the Gallies: no slave, but the sinner, though in a Palace: none noble but the vertuous, if never so basely descended: none rich, but hee that possesseth God, even in rags: none wise, but hee that is a foole to himselfe and the world: none happy, but he whom the world pities: Let me be free, noble, rich, wise, happy to God; I passe not what I am to the world.[180]

Just as the apparent dichotomies which seem so significant to worldly eyes are absorbed thematically into the mysterious order of God, they are also absorbed syntactically into the patterning of the sentences which describe it. In other words the syntax reflects the theme. In quite a literal sense the worldly objections become part of the regular order:

no free man/but his servant/*though in the Gallies*
no slave/but the sinner/*though in a Palace*
none noble/but the vertuous/*if never so basely descended*
none rich/but hee that /*even in rags*
possesseth God

In much the same manner the frequent use of antithesis is

designed to underline the fundamental contrast between the Christian and the 'worldling' which pervades so much of the work, while at the same time the equally frequent device of pairs of balanced clauses functions to suggest the workings of a mind endeavouring to establish a *via media* between extremes. Of the various *schemata* Hall might have employed he makes use only 'of those of structure, to set off resemblances or oppositions of thought':

Then onely is the Church most happy, when Truth and Peace kisse each other; and then miserable, when either of them balke the way, or when they meet and kisse not. For truth, without peace, is turbulent: and peace, without truth, is secure injustice. Though I love peace well, yet I love maine truths better. And though I love all truths well, yet I had rather conceale a small truth, than disturbe a common peace.[181]

Here we find clearly expressed his whole attitude towards ecclesiastical controversy, the tension between the claims of truth and peace, and the dangerous, narrow pathway to which he tried to keep. The style is part of the meaning.

As his *Characters* demonstrate, Hall is much concerned with attempting to represent the workings of enlightened reason within the syntax of individual sentences. Of the wise man, for example, we hear that,

Hee is a skilfull Logician, not by nature so much as use; his working mind doth nothing all his time but make syllogismes, and draw out conclusions, every thing that he sees and heares, serves for one of the premisses: with these he cares first to informe himselfe, then to direct others.[182]

In this case the impeccable order and precision of the wise mind is suggested by the controlled, cautious movement of the clauses, always afraid of saying too much, always qualifying and classifying: 'not ... nature as much as ...', 'nothing but ... syllogismes ... and conclusions', 'first himself ... then ... others'. But, of course, the mind for which everything serves as a premise, and every premise leads to a conclusion is best depicted in the *Occasional Meditations* (1630) where the contemplative process invariably originates in some experience in the natural universe, and proceeds step by step through the faculties of sense, reason, and faith. From the point of view of style these meditations stand midway between the earlier and later works, for whereas some are indisputably of the same curt manner I have just been examining, others display a notable shift to a looser style. Sentences begin to be held together by 'loose' connectives ('and', 'as', 'but') while at the same time becoming less taut and epigrammatic:

How goodly a creature is light, how pleasing, how agreeable to the spirits of man? no visible thing comes so neere to the resembling of the nature of the soule yea of the God that made it; As contrarily, what an uncomfortable thing is darknesse; in so much as wee punish the greatest malefactors with obscuritie of Dungeons; as thinking they could not be miserable enough, if they might have the priviledge of beholding the light; yea, hell it selfe can be no more horribly described then by outward darknesse.[183]

The movement away from the quick, pithy points of *Meditation and Vowes* II. 1 has already begun. Now there is less insistence on brevity and concision. The tendency to linger and amplify bespeaks an ever-increasing emphasis on the generation of emotion: 'How goodly . . . how pleasing . . . how agreeable . . . the nature of the soule yea of the God that made it.' Anaphora begins to play an important role and sentences are fitted more smoothly together ('How goodly . . . As contrarily') while at the same time becoming less disjointed within themselves as loose connective particles link clause to clause ('in so much as . . . as . . . yea'). As well as this, the imagery has become more complex: the dungeon, its inmates, and our reaction to them are disconcertingly suggestive of the ultimate prison in which we ourselves may yet be incarcerated. This is more than a witty analogy illustrating a moral precept. It works on a deeper level and elicits a more personal response. Though still based on a single, central antithesis (light/darkness) the meditation is far less sharply handled than it might earlier have been. As always there is much to ponder but perhaps more to feel. Indeed as we read such passages we are constantly reminded that these meditations were written at the same time as the great biblical *Contemplations* in which, as we shall see, the demands of narration and description compelled Hall to develop a far more relaxed and flexible form of Senecanism than he had previously employed. As in Bacon, the change of style reflects a change in intention. That this change should have affected the *Occasional Meditations* is hardly surprising in view of their descriptive bias. Emblems without pictures, they must convey 'the benefit of an image without the offence'.

Amongst the rest, see how cunningly this little Arabian hath spred out his tent, for a prey; how heedfully hee watches for a Passenger; so soon as ever he heares the noyse of a Fly a farre off, how he hastens to his doore, and if that silly heedlesse Traveller doe but touch upon the verge of that unsuspected walk how suddenly doth he seize upon the miserable bootie; and after some strife, binding him fast with those subtile cords, drags the helplesse captive after him into his cave. What is this but an Embleme of those Spiritual free-booters, that lie in waite for our soules.[184]

Here, as so often in these writings, we are close to the art of the fable. The mock-heroic humour of the description leads to a serious moral point. No matter how attractive the emblem's 'body', what matters is its 'soul'.

Thematically Hall's range is very wide. Of the 140 meditations a little less than half are drawn from the world of nature, while thirty are of the 'men and manners' variety introducing such subjects as the carting of a harlot, London street-cries, and the arraignment of a felon. The rest are comprised of perceptive meditations on inanimate objects with a marked preference for the ordinary and mundane such as sundials, candles, guns, globes, and so forth. At their best they achieve a provocative blending of simplicity and wit, sympathy and irony, emotion and reason:

How much am I bound to God that hath given me eyes to see this mans want of eyes: With what suspition and feare he walkes? How doth his hand and staffe examine his way? With what jealousie doth he receive every morsell, every draught, and yet meets with many a post, and stumbles at many a stone, and swallowes many a fly. To him the world is as if it were not, or as if it were all rubbes and snares, and downfalls; and if any man will lend him an hand, he must trust to his (how ever faithles) guide without all comfort save this, that he cannot see himselfe mis-carry.[185]

Transitions from image to analysis are effected, as here, with the minimum of effort: 'Many a one is thus Spiritually blind ...' Otherwise formulas of the 'so have I seen' or 'neither is it otherwise' variety carry us forward with little ceremony. Invariably there follows a meticulous application of the analogy to man's moral and spiritual state, which leads in turn to the resolution or conclusion. As we have seen, the movement of the heavens gave rise to the following elaborate applications:

The motion of this thy Heaven is perpetuall, so let me ever be acting somewhat of thy will; the motion of thine Heaven is regular, never swarving from the due points; so let mee ever walke steddily in the wayes of thy will ... In the motion of thine Heaven, though some Starres have their own peculiar, and contrary courses, yet all yeeld themselves to the sway of the main circumvolution of that first mover; so, though I have a will of mine owne, yet let mee give my selfe over to bee ruled, and ordered by thy Spirit in all my wayes.[186]

The analogy is pressed so far that the distinction between tenor and vehicle breaks down. This is what the speaker wants. In spiritual terms he wishes to become the sky, to be as constant, obedient, and regular as an inanimate 'creature' with no will but God's. His own free will he dismisses almost *en passant*: 'though I have a will ...'. The vigorous application of every aspect of the image to his own situation reflects the degree to which it embodies his spiritual ambitions. This is the meditative art at its best. Though in one sense the meditator himself has created, or, as he would see it, discovered, the image, his desire is to be re-created in its likeness, to discover its harmony within his own soul. The meditative process is the means whereby such re-creation may be effected.

The conclusions to these exercises are generally brief and aphoristic reminding us strongly of the curt effects of the earlier meditations: 'Hee that seekes to win all hearts, hath lost his own.' 'It is a great imperfection to want knowledge, but of the two, it is better to be a child in understanding, then a man in maliciousnesse.'[187] Now, however, they owe their effect less to their concision, striking though it is, than to their positioning. No longer do they stand in isolation in order to shock or surprise us, but serve instead to distil the essence of the meditative experience into a clear, memorable phase. They represent the generalized result of each particular contemplation.

After the appearance of the enlarged edition of the *Occasional Meditations* in 1633, Hall produced nothing in the same genre for another fifteen years. Having completed his *Contemplations* (1634), he turned to lesser works of devotion, and far less willingly, to works of controversy. Soon the Anglican Church as he knew it was swept away in the upheaval of revolution, and he found himself forced into retirement. As a result, when *The Breathings of the Devout Soul* and *Select Thoughts* appeared in 1648 the meditations had undergone a profound change. Although some 'occasional' meditations do occur, they are the exceptions; the *Select Thoughts* are closer to essays, and the *Breathings* are prayers. *Susurrium cum Deo,* the final collection which appeared in 1651, stands midway between both. In all three the curt style has almost vanished. Hall was now in his seventies and the cultivation of the swift, witty 'point' was unsuited to both his message and his character. No longer written from an assured position of episcopal authority, the meditations reflect the more personal and private world of spiritual retirement. This is not to say that they are any less assured than formerly, but rather that their assurance (like Augustine's in *The City of God*) is of a more purely spiritual and other-worldly nature. Perhaps the change can best be described (in the *Breathings* and *Susurrium* at least) as a shift from the Aurelian to the Augustinian manner. Aurelius surveys the universe with informed rationalism, Augustine falls on his knees before its creator.

The Breathings of the Devout Soul in particular introduce us to a more introverted and introspective world. As one critic has put it, 'if the dominant temper of the age was iconoclastic and mechanizing and print-orientated, it was also marked by a growing self-awareness, a sharpening sense of man's interiority.' Significantly he adds: 'Man's interiority resonated with the sound of his own voice.'[188] Immediately one recalls how Baxter, in *The Saints Everlasting Rest*, singles out the 'soliloquy' as perhaps the most important tool of private meditation, analogous to the rigorous sections of 'application' in Puritan sermons.[189] *Susurrium cum Deo,* we recall, was subtitled *Soliloquies.* Indeed, as Hall had pointed out by implication many years before in *The Arte of Divine Medita-*

tion, the meditator was expected to become his own preacher. Hence the elaborate attention to rhetoric, to the art of verbalizing one's thoughts. Hence too his insistence on the element of the colloquy. Whereas *The Arte* pays relatively little attention to the theoretical intricacies of 'meditation' in the abstract, it is almost entirely concerned with equipping its readers to handle any given theme, with teaching them the rhetorical and logical methods of self-persuasion. To some extent this is true of the earlier collections of short meditations as well. The sudden shift from generalized comment to first person singular in *Meditations and Vowes* II.1, for example, sufficiently demonstrates how a personal meditative stance can be used to persuade not only the meditator but also his reader. Even at this early stage Hall knows 'how to address an audience by placing them in a third-person, overhearing relationship while he himself addresses now God, now the divisiveness within his own soul.'[190] But this technique of persuasive 'interiority' is taken much further in the later meditations. As I have suggested, *The Breathings of the Devout Soul* are meditative prayers. The 'soliloquys' or monologues we are allowed to overhear centre on the two poles characterized by the words 'God' and 'I'. Yet although the speaker is always addressing either the deity or his own soul, his constant employment of apostrophes and questions (both rhetorical and otherwise) acts as an externalizing device whereby the reader almost imperceptibly comes to identify with the praying voice. The meditations have such an obvious relevance to his own circumstances that they involve him involuntarily. The soliloquy becomes his:

Whither now, O whither do ye rove O my thoughts? Can ye hope to finde rest in any of these sublunary contentments, Alas? how can they yeeld any stay to you, that have no settlement in themselves? Is there not enough in the infinite good to take you up; but that ye will be wandering after earthly vanities? ... Take thou my heart to thee, it is thine own; keep it with thee, tye it close to thee by the cords of love, that it may not so much as cast down an eye upon this wretched and perishing world.[191]

The dominant mood is one of self-questioning and spiritual aspiration, the tone that of an almost childlike simplicity:

Blessed Lord God; thou callest me to obedience; and fain would I follow thee: but what good can this wretched heart of mine be capable of, except thou put it there? thou know'st I cannot so much as wish to think well without thee; I have strong powers to offend thee; my sins are my own; but whence should I have any inclination to good but from thee, who art only, and all good? Lord, work me to what thou requirest, and then require what thou wilt.[192]

Hitherto the language set a premium on sharpness and clarity, on conveying the impression of a vigorous, active mind systematically and deliberately interpreting God's emblems. But now the timbre is more overtly devotional: 'fain would I follow thee' (Augustine's famous 'late I have loved thee', 'sero te amavi'); 'who art only, and all good'.[193] The clausal balance suggests calm resignation and passivity: 'work me to what thou requirest, and then require what thou wilt.' Here, in the second half of the meditation, 'me' tends to disappear, to blend into the divine will. Once again comparison with Augustine is interesting: 'give me the grace to do as you command, and command me to do what you will.'[194] Such effects are immeasurably strengthened by Hall's new reliance upon biblical materials—many of the most successful of the later meditations deal with biblical themes[195]—and the frequent use of the 'hast' and 'doeth' forms of the verbs in an attempt to suggest the cadences and tone of the Authorized Version, and the Prayer Book: 'there is a peace which thou disclaimest; and there is a sword which thou challengest to bring . . .'.[196]

Susurrium cum Deo and *Select Thoughts* are pervaded by the loose style of Senecanism which Croll, long before the present interest in meditation, singled out as the most perfectly meditative style. Even its characteristic faults and eccentricities are those of the thinking mind: loose illogical connectives, digressive remarks, 'trailing' clauses bringing up the rear.[197] It is a far different sort of mind, of course, from the brisk, agile intelligence revealed in the curt, clipped style of the younger Hall. As he ponders old questions at essay length giving his mature and final considerations, brevity is of less importance than atmosphere. We come away with the impression of a highly experienced, eloquent speaker at leisure to follow the course of his thoughts. We might also remember that one of Hall's closest friends in the days of his retirement was his doctor, Thomas Browne:

I see many eyes have looked curiously upon that glorious frame [the sky], else they should not have made so punctuall observation of the site, and motion of those goodly Globes of light, which thou hast placed there, as to foretel all their Conjunctions, and Oppositions, for many hundred yeares before; but, whiles they look at the Motions, let me look at the Mover; wondering, not without ravishment of spirit, at that infinite Power and Wisedom, which keeps up those numberlesse and immense bodies in so perfect a regularity, that they all keep their just stations, and times, without the least varying from the course which thou settedst them in their first Creation; so whiles their observation makes them the wiser, mine shall make me the holier.[198]

Much could be said of this passage, but for our present purposes the most important feature is undoubtedly the sentence length. Repeatedly, as in Browne's *Religio Medici*, just as the sense seems completed or exhausted, the sentence branches out in a new direction carrying us ever further into the speaker's mind. 'Loose' connective particles ('but', 'that', 'as', 'so') join the clauses together in so suggestively contemplative a way that we are left with the impression of thought in progress, associative thought. Particularly interesting in this respect is the employment of the present participle 'wondering' followed by the almost parenthetic phrase 'not without ravishment of spirit'. Such devices help greatly towards the sense of comprehensive 'fullness' which is the hallmark of this style admitting of amplifications, digressions, and exclamations, in fact of everything that occurs to the mind as the meditation proceeds. In Hall's early years a passage such as this would have been broken up into a series of pithy, sententious observations arranged in a sequence of sharply balanced or contrasted pairs, for, however disguised, we are still dealing in antithesis.

The voice we hear in the later meditations is that of an old man who frequently reminds us of his approaching death. Personal anecdote and reminiscence are plentiful in these later works, and it is clear that Hall was attempting to make his literary and personal image cohere as they had done in his youth. That he was largely successful is evident from John Whitefoote's account of his last years. 'He took good notice', he tells us, of the approach of death, and set his House in order, as *Israel* did, by distributing the blessings that God had left him to his Children. He indeavour'd also to prepare others for that change by his last Books, and last Sermons that he preached, which were all upon the *last things, Death,* and *Judgement, Heaven,* and *Hell.*[199]

In Higham he was regarded as a wise old patriarch awaiting death, and this is the note struck in the sermons of those years. The result for the meditations was a change of perspective. They still deal with the world and its affairs but from a far more other-worldly viewpoint, from the viewpoint of *The Free-Prisoner* (1644) and *The Soules Farewell to Earth, and Approaches to Heaven* (published with *Susurrium* in 1651) in both of which the soul forsakes the body, travels upwards through the spheres, and views the earth from the vantage point of its new spiritual heights. To such a perspective we are indebted for the panoramic widening of the canvas as Hall makes global surveys of men and mores. Repeatedly we plunge into long, exhaustive lists embracing the whole spectrum of human discontent, or folly, or sin, or sadness. We have encountered the device before, but now the effect is very different. These are not the powerful, Juvenalian lists of the satires. Their purpose now is not so much to effect a vituperative *tour de force* as to establish a distancing perspective on the world and its values, the perspective of someone on the point of departing, of an 'old man's eagle eye'.[200] Also, beneath the apprehension of apparent disorder and flux, there is still the insistence on pattern and providence, though evoked in a different manner. The creation of atmosphere and mood has become more important than the cultivation of wit. A good example is the following description of the progress of life:

When we are young the world is but little enough for us; after wee have seene our owne Island, wee affect to crosse the Seas, and to climbe over Alpes, and Pyrennees, and never thinke we have roved farre enough; When we grow ancient, wee begin to bee well-pleased with rest; now long and unnecessary journies are laid aside. If businesse call us forth, wee goe, because wee must; As for the visits of Friendship, one Sunne is enough to measure them, with our returnes; And still, the older we grow, the more wee are devoted to our home; there wee are content to sit still, and enjoy the thoughts of our youth, and former experience, not looking further than a kinde neighbour-hood: But, when Age hath stiffened our joynts, and disabled our Motions, now, our home-pastures, and our Gardens become our utmost boundaries; from thence a few yeares more confine us to our own floor; Soon after that, we are limited to our chamber, and at last to our chaire, then to our bed, and, in fine, to our Coffin.[201]

This is more than a matter of clever phrasing or categorizing. There is a deeper emotional power in the prose as we spiral inwards and downwards to the word 'coffin'. By the time it reaches this point, the account has accumulated layers of feeling and emotion (the interaction, for example, of the fleeting youth and vigour of the first few phrases with the prolonged analysis of the slow, progressive disablement which follows) which were absent from the often more purely intellectual examinations of the *Meditations and Vowes*. Yet the meditative structure is still preserved. We begin with a vividly imagined account of confinement, but immediately afterwards reason explains to the soul that these are merely the confinements of sense, and the passage ends in a moving prayer for spiritual 'dilation'. The subject, of course, had been treated before in the earlier collections, but never in the same way. It is therefore quite pointless to complain of repetitions.[202] As Hall himself explained, repetition is of the very essence of meditation, and each new attempt at deciphering the Book of creation possesses its own individual integrity:

For as there is infinite scope and variety of matter, wherein to employ my meditations, so in each one of them, there is such marvellous depth, that I should in vaine hope, after all my exquisitest search, to reach unto the bottome: Yea the more I look upon the incomprehensible Deity, in any one of his glorious attributes, or any one of his omnipotent works, of creation, government, redemption; the more I long to see, and the less am I satisfied in seeing.[203]

Holy Observation 8, *Occasional Meditation* 13, and *Soliloquy* 71, all deal with the one subject: the tantalizing paradox of unwearied motion and eternal rest in the heavens and its relationship to man's spiritual state. Yet none of them makes the others redundant. Although all three present us with the same basic image or idea, they do so from different points of view and in different moods, thereby inviting different responses. The *Holy Observation* is witty and precise making a clever, intellectual point. The *Occasional Meditation* presents the same idea as the vivid perception of a suddenly revealed message from the 'Book of the Creatures'. The *Soliloquy* offers the mature, considered opinion of an old man 'weary of the day and more weary of the night' addressing his soul on the same topic with a different sort of emotion. The unity of Hall's work is therefore a progressive, cumulative unity; ideas become experiences, and thoughts become feelings.

VI. The Characters, the Epistles, and The Devout Soul

So far my examination of Hall's methods of meditation has confined itself to specifically contemplative genres, but for their full importance to be understood it is essential to recognize that they were never restricted to such forms. Even Hall's earliest definition suggests otherwise when it speaks of the 'divers formes of discourse' through which the mind may be bent upon some spiritual object.[204] Meditation as a habitual process influencing every aspect of a man's thought must be distinguished from artificial systems of meditation intended to guide and direct its use as a devotional exercise. It is hardly surprising, therefore, that almost everything Hall wrote is in some way influenced by his interest in contemplation even when not directly based upon the particular system expounded in *The Arte of Divine Meditation*. As will become apparent later on, its most pervasive influence was, perhaps, upon the sermons, but here, I wish to concentrate upon the *Characters of Vertues and Vices*, the *Epistles*, and *The Devout Soul*.

It has been suggested that Hall's earliest Characters are to be found in *Heaven upon Earth*, but they have their real origins in the *Meditations and Vowes*. Here there appear four or five completely recognizable, if not completely developed, Characters, at least some of which reflect the same conditions of moral contrast as inform the 1608 collection.[205] A particularly good example of this is the portrayal of the wicked man and the godly man in *Meditations and Vowes*, II, 74. Indeed as I have suggested before, Hall's interest in the Character genre was in many respects born of his interest in meditation, and the two remained closely allied thereafter. It can hardly be mere coincidence, for example, that the Character returns to Hall's work after an absence of thirty years at exactly the same period as did the short meditation. The incorporation of the two contrasting Characters of poor affluence and rich poverty into the typically meditative, tripartite structure of *Soliloquy* 52, demonstrates quite strikingly how close the two forms could become. Appropriately enough the meditation opens with a quotation from the Book of Proverbs—the book which had suggested the Christianization of Theophrastus and supplied some of the axioms for the *Meditations and Vowes* and *Holy Observations*: 'There is that maketh himselfe rich, yet hath nothing; There is that maketh himself poor, yet hath great riches' (13.7). In this case the pair of character sketches serves simply as an illustration of the truth of this assertion thereby forming stage two, and the exercise then concludes with an address to the soul and a prayer for humility and grace.[206] Nor must it be thought that this fusion represents a late development. It does not. Similar in almost every respect are the techniques of *Epistles* V.3 (1611) in which a pair of contrasting characters is fitted with equal convenience into a meditation on the distinction between a Christian and a worldling, a recurrent theme of the *Meditations and Vowes*.[207] Setting aside considerations of length, the epistle and soliloquy are structurally identical.

Beyond such purely formal correspondences, however, lie even closer thematic relationships. The 'Premonition' to the *Characters*, one remembers, hints at their association with the practice of spiritual self-analysis, and therefore, by implication, with the doctrine of election:

if thou shalt hence abjure those Vices; which before thou thoughtest not ill-favoured, or fall in love with any of these goodly faces of Vertue; or shalt hence find where thou hast any little touch of these evils, to cleare thy selfe or where any defect in these graces to supply it, neither of us shall need to repent of our labour.[208]

The problem of discovering within oneself the marks of either election or damnation was an almost obsessive preoccupation of the Calvinist mind, and it is in this light that the *Characters* may best be approached. Their simple presentation of the *essential* characteristics of each moral quality, whether virtuous or vicious, was intended as an aid to self-analysis. This purpose is underlined in the preface to *The Christian*, a late Character published in 1647 with *Christ Mysticall* and designated a work of meditation by the then licenser of the press, the celebrated author of *Christian Warfare*, John Downame.[209] *The Christian* is a portrait in unswerving devotion depicted from the twin perspectives of daily living and lifelong commitment. As Hall himself stresses, it was intended primarily as an unashamedly 'practical' work of devotion:

> Having therefore leisure enough to look about me, and finding the world too prone to this worst kind of hypocrisie, I have made this true draught, not more for direction, then for tryall. Let no man view these lines as a stranger; but when he looks in this glasse, let him ask his heart whether this be his own face; yea, rather when he sees this face, let him examine his heart whether both of them agree with their pattern. And where he findes his failings, (as who shall not) let him strive to amend them; and never give over, whiles he is any way lesse fair then his copy.[210]

'Glasse', 'pattern', 'copy': these are the terms in which we are accustomed to discuss the Puritan autobiography, and as we shall see, in his own autobiographical tracts Hall makes much of the providential pattern which he detects in the history of his own life. Drawn not from observation but from private meditation and spiritual precept, *The Christian* was intended as the ideal pattern to which the lives of the godly were expected to conform. In this respect it served exactly the same function as did the numerous semi-characters and archetypes with which the works of the Puritan preachers abound.[211] But the influence worked in both directions. Not long after the publication of Hall's first Characters, Thomas Adams, one of his closest stylistic imitators, began to incorporate whole series of moral Characters into his published sermons.[212] The intention of both Character-writer and preacher, therefore, was clearly the promotion of self-analysis in their audience. But self-analysis 'went hand in hand with the entire process of meditation'.[213] Almost the whole first 'week' of Ignatius of Loyola's *Spiritual Exercises* is devoted to detailed examinations of conscience and intention.[214] Similarly *The Arte of Divine Meditation* begins with repentance, and some of its later stages, notably that of complaint 'wherein the heart bewaileth to it selfe his own poverty, dulnesse, and imperfection', certainly presume some prior examination of conscience, the fruits of which are now to be integrated into the pattern of meditative 'ascent'.[215] Given the disposition of his readers, the relationship was one Hall found it useful to encourage and he succeeds best in doing so in his *Epistles* (1608–1611).

Although this appeal to a genre in which 'we doe but talk with our friends' may seem incongruous in the present context, it is essential to remember that 'familiar' and varied as they may at first appear, Hall's *Epistles* are almost all of a purely devotional or moral nature. What he discusses familiarly with his friends are matters of religion, and while certainly introducing a 'new fashion of discourse' from the point of view of genre, he remains highly traditional thematically.[216] He is neither more nor less familiar than Seneca. Central to the collection, for example, are the letters addressed to close personal relatives and friends. Such epistles as that to his father 'against the feare of death' (I.10) or to his sister 'of the sorrow not to be repented of' (II.4) set the tone of the entire work. The image of the Hall family intended to emerge is that of an extremely 'godly', devout set of people, almost totally preoccupied with the state of their souls—puritans in temperament if not in their attitude to Church government. In such circles meditation and self-analysis had their very roots, and in epistle after epistle they blend inextricably. The godly recipient of *Epistles* IV.6, for instance, has fallen prey to that characteristic malady of the Calvinist outlook, loss of assurance in one's own election. Neglecting true self-analysis, she has allowed herself to be deceived by external appearances; she believes while complaining 'of unbeleefe'. The prescribed remedy—'looke into your owne heart'—is a vigorous renewal of self-examination. To illustrate his point Hall turns to the methods of occasional meditation. The spiritual crisis finds an analogy in nature: 'Take two boughs in the dead of winter; how like is one wood to another? how hardly discerned? Afterwards, *By their fruit you shall know them*. That faith, whose nature was obscure, is evident in his effects. What is faith, but the hand of the soule?' (p. 316.)

What follows is rather like an exercise in courtroom detection. Every facet of the lady's state of mind is subjected to intense spiritual investigation. Her acts, beliefs, and doubts are all probed to the quick. Like Greenham before him, Hall is dealing in the 'experimental' divinity of 'cases of conscience'. Yet despite its undoubtedly personal aspect the process is anything but purely subjective, involving as it does the related attempt to define godliness itself. How else could it proceed? Not until the criteria for the examination have become clear can the spiritual entanglements be resolved. The Puritans saw the process of salvation as following a definite pattern of predictable depressions and elations, in fact as a 'pilgrim's progress'. As a result, much of their work of spiritual consolation lay in persuading the patient that his private tribulations exactly fitted this universal pattern. What we are witnessing in Hall is the fusion of spiritual self-analysis and thematic meditation. In this case the 'issue' towards which both are moving is identical; neither is, nor can be, independent of the other. The spiritual resolution summed up in the famous image of the compass answers both the particular problem with which we began, and all such problems:

Charity and faith make up one perfect paire of Compasses, that can take the true latitude of a Christian heart: Faith is the one foot, pitcht in the centre unmoveably, while Charity walks about in a perfect circle of beneficence: these two never did, neither can goe asunder: Warrant you your love, I dare warrant your faith: What need I say more?   (p. 316)

In the *Epistles* such fusion is the norm. The consideration of divine love in the letter to Sir George Fleetwood, for example, quickly resolves itself into a four-dimensional meditation embracing self-analysis. Indeed without this element the process would be incomplete:

Under this head therefore, there is sure remedy against sinne, by looking upwards, backwards, into our selves, forwards. Upwards, at the glorious Majestie, and infinite goodnesse of that God whom our sinne would offend, and in whose face we sinne . . . Backwards, at the manifold favours, whereby we are obliged to obedience. Into our selves, at that honorable vocation, wherewith he hath graced us, that holy profession we have made of his calling, and grace, that solemne vow and covenant, whereby we have confirmed our profession; the gracious beginnings of that Spirit in us, which is grieved by our sinnes, yea quenched. Forwards, at the joy which will follow upon our forbearance... (pp. 350-1)

On a yet more personal level in *Epistles* II.1, Hall describes the importance of such devotional practices as tactical manœuvres in his own spiritual warfare against moods of worldliness and despair. 'What an heaven doe I feele in my selfe', he declares,

when (after many traverses of meditation) I find in my heart a feeling possession of my God! When I can walke, and converse with the God of heaven, not without an opennesse of heart and familiaritie... When I can looke upon all this inferiour creation, with the eyes of a stranger, and am transported to my home in my thoughts; solacing my selfe in the view and meditation of my future glory, and that present of the Saints... Sometimes I can be thus, and pity the poore and miserable prosperitie of the godlesse... But then againe (for why should I shame to confesse it?) the world thrusts it selfe betwixt me and heaven; and, by his darke and indigested parts, eclipseth that light which shined to my soule... Thus I am, till I single my selfe out alone, to him that alone can revive me: I reason with my selfe, and conferre with him... and after some spirituall speeches interchanged, I renue my familiarity with him... Thus I hold on, rising and falling. (p. 269)

Except in the two autobiographical tracts, such explicitly personal confessions are rare in Hall's writings. Here, however, he is simply taking advantage of the exceptional opportunities afforded by the new genre. The more 'familiar' the letters become, and the more fully the reader finds himself drawn into the intimate circle of devout friends and relations to whom they are addressed, the greater must be their effect upon his own private devotions. Hence, in *Epistles* IV.3 we find a passionately written account of Hall's personal commitment to 'the pleasure of study and contemplation' (including occasional meditation), while the relationship of meditation to his other numerous daily devotions is set forth in meticulous detail in *Epistles* VI.1.

From Hall's point of view, therefore, the great benefit of the epistolary form was that it allowed him to express more

intimately and personally than before what he had been saying
persistently since the publication of the *Meditations and Vowes*
in 1605. Indeed the more one reads the *Epistles* the clearer it
becomes that the influence of various forms of meditation,
whether extemporal, deliberate, or self-analytic, pervades
every decade of the work. Examples are easy to cite. Among
the letters entirely devoted to meditative matters, for instance,
there appear two fully developed Characters (III.8,10), a
fascinating discussion addressed to the actor Edward Alleyn
on how best to 'conceive of God in our devotions and
meditations' (IV.7), and an abridged 'art' of spiritual meditation indebted to the same source as the larger work (III.8). As
well as this, the final epistle of the first decade is actually a
meditation on the coming of death in which the insistent
repetition of the word 'think' recalls the extremely similar
device in Donne's *Anniversaries:*

Think how fondly we feare a vanquisht enemie . . . Think that death
is necessarily annexed to nature . . . Think, there is but one common
rode to all flesh . . . Think not so much what Death is, as from whom
he comes . . . Think of death, and you shall not feare it.   (p. 266)

In both cases the authors are employing variations of what
Martz calls 'the traditional self-address of religious meditation'.[217]

   Again, the second epistle of the same decade is really a
contemplative exercise 'de contemptu mundi' in which the
pleasures of this world are contrasted unfavourably with those
of the next. Somewhat further on one of the most beautifully
written of all the *Epistles* (III.2) declares its own affinity with
the 'ars moriendi', perhaps the oldest and most valued strand
of the Western contemplative tradition. To continue is
unnecessary. Despite the apparent diversity of their themes,
and the very real diversity of their recipients, the message of
the *Epistles* is both clear and simple. Though it may be realized
and evoked in a myriad of imaginative forms and images—and
that is the province of the artist—devotion, they say, is
essentially a private, contemplative matter between the soul
and its God:

All our safety or danger therefore is from within . . . Thinke how
little the World can doe for you, and what it doth, how deceitfully:

what stings there are with this Honey, what Farewell succeeds this
Welcome... Thinke how sincere, how glorious those joyes are,
which abide you elsewhere, and a thousand times more certaine
(though future) than present.
And let not these thoughts be flying, but fixed: In vaine doe we
meditate, if we resolve not: when your heart is once thus setled, it
shall command all things to advantage. (pp. 349–50)

The importance of emphasizing the centrality of such
systems of thought to the *Epistles*, and indeed to the
Characters, is that it helps us to appreciate the underlying
unity and cohesion of all Hall's early writings. What at first
might appear a random movement from form to form emerges
as a series of related attempts to embody the same intellectual
and emotional disciplines in a variety of unusual artistic
modes. It is the old attempt to captivate the conscience
through the imagination, the neoclassic ethic of 'utile dulce'.
Apart from the *Contemplations* which we are soon to consider,
all that remained to be written was a work of synthesis, a
complete manual of Christian living after the fashion of
François de Sales's *Introduction to the Devout Life*. This,
however, was to be the work of later years. Entitled *The
Devout Soul* it appeared in 1644.

Extending across the entire range of Christian devotion
from a 'habitual' apprehension of the omnipresence of God, to
'actual' devotional duties such as reading the Bible and
receiving the sacraments, *The Devout Soul*, tirelessly insists
upon the need within each one of them for the by now
inextricable practices of self-appraisal and divine meditation.
Indeed 'devotion' and 'meditation' seem to have become
synonymous. Without meditation, we are told, there can be
little value in either sermons or religious books.[218] Without
meditation even the sacraments may become meaningless.[219]
And all varieties of meditation are intended. As befits a work
of synthesis, all the familiar forms—occasional meditations,
deliberate meditations, ejaculations, colloquies, soliloquies,
and biblical contemplations—are simply woven together into
the pattern (I choose the word deliberately) of a single devout
life. It is the proof of the earlier assertion that meditation 'is
the very end God hath given us our soules for'. 'Unto this only
neglect', are attributed, 'the commonnesse of that *Laodicean*

temper of men, or (if that be worse) of the dead coldnesse which hath stricken the hearts of many, having left them nothing but the bodies of men, and visors of Christians; to this only, *They have not meditated.*[220]

With the ending of *The Devout Soul* our study comes full circle, for the 'result of all' is the Character of a devout man, a Character appended in the style of the collection published more than thirty years before. Had Hall purposely sought to illustrate the interconnection of the various genres he could have done it no better, for here it is clear that the Character exists for the sole purpose of embodying and encapsulating the preceding arguments and precepts. Easy to remember and imaginatively striking, its pithy phrases and formulas were designed to unlock at a glance memories of the spiritual directions set forth in the body of the work. Its sentences invite us to renewed meditation.

A devout man is he that ever sees the invisible, and ever trembleth before that God he sees; that walks ever, here on earth, with the God of heaven; and still adores that Majesty with whom he converses; That confers hourly with the God of spirits in his own language; yet so, as no familiarity can abate of his aw, nor fear abate ought of his love. To whom the gates of heaven are ever open; that he may go in at pleasure to the throne of grace, and none of the Angelical spirits can offer to challenge him of too much boldness... He accounts all his time lost that falls beside his God; and can be no more weary of good thoughts, than of happinesse.[221]

5.

CONTEMPLATIONS ON THE BIBLE

The *Contemplations upon the Principall Passages of the Holy Storie* were composed over a period of twenty-two years (1612–1634), the work being continually interrupted by Hall's many engagements as representative of Church and State.[1] By the time of their completion he was sixty years old, and consequently regarded them, wrongly as it proved, as his last major work. Owing to ill health he had not thought to see them completed at all, and it was therefore with a sense of extreme satisfaction that he published the final section in 1634.[2] Quite understandably, he had come to regard the *Contemplations* as the most important achievement of his career, for their theme was the vernacular *Bible*, the foundation of all his disagreements with Rome, the corner-stone of Reformed Christianity. In choosing to write such a commentary he was following directly in the tradition of Melanchthon, Bucer, Calvin, and a host of other Reformers who had attempted to guide and discipline the new 'freedom' of interpretation attained through the break with Rome.[3] This was universally held to be a task of great urgency, for although it was one of Luther's most cherished dreams that all men should read and become familiar with the Word of God in their native language, it had become apparent to the civil authorities, both in England and on the Continent, that such reading was not without its dangers. If it was generally agreed that 'In the beginning there was the Word', it had become equally clear that the 'Word' had suffered the curse of Babel; there were potentially as many interpretations as there were readers.

For the Reformers this situation posed a serious problem of authority. On the one hand they had ceaselessly to attack the policy of Rome which forbade all personal interpretation and actively discouraged vernacular translation, while on the other they had to attempt to stem the tide of extreme, radical interpretations fostered by their own insistence upon the need for scriptural knowledge. As a result they were forced to become biblical interpreters themselves, in some cases, rather incongruously, interpreters of near-papal authority—a position quickly assailed by Anabaptists, Antinomians, and Independents of all sorts. The more emphasis one placed on inner revelation or salvation through grace and personal election, the less seemed the need for any commentary at all, and the greater became the likelihood of social disruption.[4]

In England towards the end of the sixteenth century the beginning of the sects was clearly distinguishable. The Brownists, with whom Hall fought a long and embittered pamphlet war, were using sacred Scripture to maintain anti-episcopal and independent views, while more generally, fostered by such events as the Vestiarian Controversy and the formation of the classis movement, the great rift between priest and presbyter was starting to widen. The seventeenth century saw a worsening of divisions with the failure of the Millenary Petition, the strengthening of the High Commission, the plans for alliance with Spain, and, after the death of James I, the encouragement of the 'Arminian faction' at court. As always, the pulpit was at the centre of the debate, and almost every position from the most radically parliamentarian to the most uncompromisingly monarchist was zealously expounded by impassioned preachers (licensed and unlicensed alike) to eager audiences throughout the country. Yet if the preachers had one thing in common, it was undoubtedly their unflagging attempt to root their arguments firmly in the words of Scripture, an attempt which the Bible itself encouraged: the book which upheld the 'powers that be' on pain of damnation, said also 'bind their kings in chains and their nobles with fetters of iron'.[5]

Hence the need to discourage dangerous 'private interpretations', and to reassert the teaching authority of the Church:

There is an audacious and factious liberty of this loose filme [the tongue]; which not only ill-tutor'd Schollers take to themselves under the name of *libertas prophetandi*, pestering both Presses and Pulpits with their bold and brainsick fancies; but unletter'd Tradesmen, and tattling Gossips too; with whom deep questions of Divinity, and censures of their Teachers are grown into common table-talk; and peremptory decisions of Theological problems is as ordinary almost, as backbiting their neighbours.[6]

And this was the remedy:

There are plain Truths, and there are deep mysteries. The bounty of God hath left this Well of Living-water open for all; what runs over is for all commers; but every one hath not wherewith to draw. There is no Christian that may not enjoy Gods Book, but every Christian may not interpret it; those shallow Fords that are in it, may be waded by every Passenger, but there are deeps wherein he that cannot swim, may drown. *How can I without a Guide*, said that Ethopian Eunuch: Wherefore serves the tongue of the Learned, but to direct the Ignorant? Their modesty is of no lesse use than the others skill. It is a woefull condition of a Church when no man will be ignorant.[7]

Unless we read the *Contemplations* against the background of contemporary controversy and debate, and with a vivid recollection of the fate of Charles I and Laud, we are in danger of seriously underestimating their relevance and force by too hastily dismissing as 'conventional' passages of central importance to Hall's contemporaries. The frequent discussions on the sanctity of kings, the duties of subjects, and the relative merits of 'ceremony' and 'substance' may indeed be called forth by the needs of the text, but they are ordered and developed in accordance with the needs of the time. This, as we shall shortly see, was directly in keeping with what had come to be a highly popular branch of exegetical typology. Indeed one cannot read very far in the *Contemplations* without coming face to face with the problems of seventeenth-century England. However, before passing on to discuss the more difficult questions of contemporary allusion it is necessary to understand exactly what sort of biblical commentary Hall set out to produce, and what he meant by the term 'contemplation'. For the answer to the first question we must look to Geneva.

As far as Hall was concerned the basis of all modern biblical commentary was laid by Calvin, 'whose judgement I so much honour, that I reckon him amongst the best Interpreters of Scripture, since the Apostles left the earth.'[8] It follows, therefore, that an understanding of Calvin's methods and those of the Reformers in general helps greatly towards the assessment of Hall's own achievement. Recent studies have shown that the Reformation caused three major shifts in the direction of biblical exegesis.[9] First of all it led to the abandonment of the traditional four levels of interpretation in favour of an insistence upon the literal meaning of the text together with such carefully restrained spiritual meanings as could be gleaned through the methods of typology, a mode of analysis founded upon the belief that the characters and events of the Old Testament prefigured or foreshadowed the characters and events of the New. What distinguishes typology from allegory most clearly is its assertion of the historicity of both sign and signification. Nor is it to be confused with symbolism, for as Erich Auerbach explains, 'what actually makes the two forms completely different is that figural prophecy relates to an interpretation of history—indeed it is by nature a textual interpretation—while the symbol is a direct interpretation of life and originally no doubt for the most part, of nature.'[10] As far as was possible, Protestant exegetes regarded typology not as a separate spiritual level of meaning but as a legitimate extension of the literal level, as evidence within the 'letter' of God's plan for the future, as part of the promise of salvation guaranteed in the covenant with Abraham.

Secondly, and closely associated with the question of typology, there arose a new interest in asserting the spiritual identity of the two testaments. From now on the Old Testament was to be regarded not so much as a history of the Jews, as a history of the Church before Christ. This change in emphasis is crucial. Calvin, for example, comes to the conclusion that 'the covenant made with all the patriarchs is so much like ours in substance and reality that the two are actually one and the same.'[11] The result was that contemporary Protestants could now identify far more easily with the happenings of the pre-Christian era. Once the history of the Jews had become the history of the covenant, their own covenant, it had become their history. The chosen people of the sixteenth and seventeenth centuries could trace their ancestry back to the chosen people of Genesis. They were far more disposed to regard the two Testaments as representing the continuous history of one people rather than two separate histories interrupted by the coming of Christ.

Thirdly, as a direct result of this change in outlook, it became ever more common to interpret the present in the light of the Old Testament past. Again and again we encounter what Barbara Lewalski terms 'the assimilation of the events and circumstances of contemporary history—and even the lives and experiences of individual Christians—to the providential scheme of typological recapitulations and fulfilments throughout history.'[12] In other words, typological correspondences were discovered not merely between the two Testaments but between the Bible and the contemporary Church, between the written word and the story still being written. According to William Perkins, the Reformation itself was the spiritual fulfilment of Israel's escape from Egypt,[13] and elsewhere endless correspondences are drawn between contemporary figures and their supposed biblical prototypes. Depending upon the individual author's stance, typology could become a poweful instrument of either praise or blame. A ruler might be cast as the antitype of a David or a Herod, a minister as a Paul or a Judas. Of this last development I shall have much to say later on, but at present I wish to concentrate on the other two.

In so far as Christ frequently asserts his own fulfilment of various biblical prophecies and signs, the basis of typology is to be found in the Gospels themselves. The Pauline epistles take the issue much further but their terminology is unfortunately imprecise, with the result that throughout the Middle Ages allegory and typology are frequently confused, and even the Reformers themselves sometimes use the words rather loosely. It is therefore essential to be guided by practice rather than terminology. According to Calvin the greatest virtue to which any commentary could aspire was 'perspicua brevitas': that it should be clear and relevant.[14] In order to achieve this goal it should concern itself with the literal meaning of the text, with what the writer has said and not what the commentator might prefer to read. The intricate fourfold system of medieval exegesis must be abandoned. Despite the practice of the early Fathers there was to be no more 'toying' with the text. But this was not to say that Scripture was devoid of spiritual meaning. Quite the contrary, the perception of the spiritual sense was of vital importance, but it was to be found in the text itself and not in the reader's ingenuity. The idea that there could be any secondary sense not directly expressed in the words of the author was completely rejected. In all cases the rule to be observed was as follows: 'eum esse verum Scripturae sensum, qui germanus est ac simplex.'[15] Such an approach fostered Calvin's interest in the historical aspects of the sacred story, and cultivated his concern with the real historical circumstances of both authors and events. As a result there was no need to allegorize the accounts of either Testament after Augustine's manner of dealing with the episode of David and Bathsheba, an interpretation in which Bathsheba comes to represent the Church.[16] For Calvin, the spiritual meaning is the moral meaning inherent in the story itself. When allegory had to be employed it was only in the limited sense of typology obeying 'the rule of the text'. For example, if some incidents in the life of Hezekiah can be seen as representative, or better still as prophetic, of the triumph of Christ, such an interpretation though spiritually useful, is to be accepted only with great caution: 'But lest anyone should think I am following *allegories, a quibus sum alienus,* I do not interpret it *simpliciter* of Christ ... Therefore I would wish to regard it as an *anagoge* from Hezekiah to Christ with all the beauty that shall be his.'[17]

In Galatians 4: 22 St. Paul speaks of the two wives of Abraham as 'allegories' of the two Testaments, but the passage was interpreted by William Whitaker as an exercise in typology. 'There is a certain catachresis in the word *allegoroumena*', he tells us,

for that history is not accomodated by Paul in that place allegorically, but typically; and a type is a different thing from an allegory. The sense, therefore, of that scripture is one only, namely, the literal or grammatical. However, the whole entire sense is not in the words taken strictly, but part in the type, part in the transaction itself ... When we proceed from the sign to the thing signified, we bring no new sense, but only bring out into light what was before concealed in the sign.[18]

Since Hall was a great admirer of Whitaker whom he described as 'that honour of our Schooles, and Angell of our Church . . . than whom our age saw nothing more memorable' it is hardly surprising that his own interpretation of the problem in Galatians is very similar.[19] For him also, the keyword is 'type':

Which things are an allegory . . . Which, as it is a true history, so it is an allegory also of spiritual things: for these two mothers resemble and express the two covenants; Sarah the covenant of grace, and Hagar the covenant of work . . . Which same thing is also typed forth unto us by Sinai and Jerusalem.[20]

Although by no means averse to employing the term 'allegory', Hall invariably intends it in Whitaker's sense. A striking example of this occurs in his treatment of the closing passages of *Deuteronomy*:

And well doth *Joshua* succeed *Moses;* The very acts of God of old were allegories: where the Law ends, there the Saviour begins; we may see the Land of Promise in the Law; Onely Jesus the mediator of the new Testament can bring us into it. So was he a servant of the Law, that he supplies all the defects of the Law to us: Hee hath taken possession of the promised land for us, he shall carry us from this wildernesse, to our rest.[21]

Similarly, when Moses turns his rod into a serpent it is merely God's way of presenting Pharoah with a 'real Embleme' of himself, and the sweetening of the waters of Marah is similarly interpreted as a lesson both to Israel and to us:

God taught his people by actions, as well as words. This entrance shewed them their whole journey; wherein they should taste of much bitternesse: but at last through the mercy of God, sweetned with comfort. Or did it not represent themselves rather, in the journey? in the fountaines of whose hearts, were the bitter waters of manifold corruptions, yet their unsavorie soules are sweetned by the graces of his Spirit. O Blessed Saviour: the Wood of thy Crosse, that is, the application of thy sufferings, is enough to sweeten a whole Sea of bitternesse. I care not how unpleasant a portion I finde in this Wildernesse, if the power and benefit of thy pretious death may season it to my soule.[22]

These examples should make it clear that Hall is using the

term 'allegory' in a very restricted sense. Unlike the interpretations of the early Fathers, all his renderings obey the 'rule' of
the text in the sense that they never offer violence to the
primary level of narration. The first is strictly typological since
Joshua was traditionally held to prefigure Christ. The second
and third are highly orthodox extensions of the 'living parable'
idea of the *New Testament*—the blasting of the barren fig tree,
for example. Furthermore it is very noticeable that none of
these 'allegories' are either speculative or 'mystical'. Instead
they teach a particular moral point. Far from leading the
reader away from the text into the realm of abstruse
theological speculation, they apply it rigorously to his own
situation, very much in the manner of the *Occasional
Meditations* with which, as we shall see, they have a strong
connection. The difficult and perplexing numerology so
beloved of Augustine and Origen is completely absent. It fact
Hall dismisses it out of hand. In *The Revelation Unrevealed*
(1650), for example, Calvin is quoted with approval as saying
that he is no 'Pythagorean' in respect of numerical analysis.[23]
Elsewhere we are informed that, 'religion consisteth not now
in numbers at all.'[24] Everywhere the treatment is cautious and
orthodox. 'I seeke not mystery in the number; These tenne are
met together', is a typical comment.[25] For Hall numerology
smacks strongly of superstition and paganism: 'away with all
niceties of Pythagorean calculations.'[26]

Such differences as arise between Hall and Calvin are best
explained in terms of genre. At most they are differences of
emphasis rather than interpretation. Hall is writing a work of
meditation, Calvin a scholarly commentary. Their respective
treatments of the 'shoes of Moses' incident makes the point
clear. Initially Calvin is literal and cautious: Moses is merely
reminded of the need for reverence when approaching God.
But well aware of the deeper significance apprehended in the
incident by others, he continues, 'if any prefer the deeper
meaning *(anagoge)*, that God cannot be heard until we have
put off our earthly thoughts, I object not to it; only let the
natural sense stand first, that Moses was commanded to put off
his shoes, as a preparation to listen with greater reverence to
God.'[27] In the *Contemplations* Hall seems far more assured of
the deeper meaning from the outset:

This rite was significant. What are the shooes but worldly and carnall affections? If these be not cast off when wee come to the holy place, wee make our selves unholy: how much lesse should we dare to come with resolutions of sinne? This is not only to come with shooes on, but with shooes bemired with wicked filthinesse; the touch whereof profanes the pavement of God, and makes our presence odious.[28]

In this way Hall tends to apply the text more narrowly and exactly to the moral requirements of his reader—a practice which enlivens his best sermons—but basically his approach is that of Calvin. In keeping with his customary meditative techniques, he fills in the details where his mentor is content with more general observations. But his own concern with literal interpretation is demonstrated by his publication in 1632 of an exegetical work clearly intended as a companion to the *Contemplations*. Significantly entitled *A Plaine and Familiar Explication of the Old and New Testament*, it consists quite simply of a straightforward paraphrase of all the passages likely to cause difficulty for the average reader. Here he supplies the plain sense of the Moses passage: 'In token of reverence and respect unto so holy a place, and in token of laying aside all carnal thoughts and affections, put off thy shoes.'[29] In other words, just as he was bringing his more elaborate and literary commentary to a close, Hall was ensuring that the most fundamental level of instruction should not be neglected, that the plain unvarnished meaning of the text should be available to all. He was doing exactly what Calvin had done so often in his lectures when breaking the commentary he would begin to paraphrase the text under discussion with the words 'as if he were to say...' or some such formula. He explains his intentions quite clearly in his preface:

For, since the Scriptures are through the liberal blessing of God promiscuously allowed to all hands, I ask whether it be not much better they should be put into the way of being rightly understood by the simplest, than to lie under the danger of an ignorant misconstruction... The inconveniences that are pretended to have followed upon the open and free permission of Scriptures in vulgar languages have sensibly arisen from the misunderstanding of them.

Remove that peril, and the frequence and universality of them can be no other than a blessing. This service I have here endeavoured to perform.[30]

The attempt to arrive at the 'plaine' sense of any passage is a hallmark of Protestant exegesis, and questions of genre and rhetorical intention figure strongly in all such discussions. Perhaps the most crucial problem of the time, that of the significance of the Eucharist, hinged to a large extent on methods of rhetorical analysis. In practical terms the issue resolved itself into asking, 'what the true and genuine sense of those words of Christ was: "This is my body"; and whether they were to be understood in the letter, or in the figure.'[31] As a former lecturer in rhetoric, Hall was particularly alive to such issues and particularly offended by what he saw as mistaken interpretations. Indeed much of his disagreement with the Smectymnuans centres upon the question of whether certain passages in St. Paul are to be taken 'literally' or 'synecdochically', as 'plaine narrations' or 'emblematicall representations'.[32] On the subject of the Eucharist he has no doubts:

Take, eat; this is my body—Take, eat; this bread is sacramentally my very body: so as, if ye do worthily receive this element, ye do therewith partake of me: while your hand and your mouth take and eat this bread, your souls do truly and really receive me, who am represented, and exhibited, and conveyed into you, by and with this outward sign.[33]

Hall is fascinated by the imagery of the Bible, by God's use of emblem, symbol, and metaphor, and insists that all must be recognized for what they are. In *Episcopacie by Divine Right* he ridicules fanciful allegorical interpretations clumsily pressed into the service of weak theological arguments. 'Thus', he concludes, 'the Bells say what some Hearers think.'[34] Not surprisingly, when he became involved in the millenarian controversy of the 1650s he centred his arguments on exactly the same principles. It is highly instructive to compare his version of Revelation with that of his chief opponent John Archer, whose *Personal Reigne of Christ Upon Earth* explains the work as a prophecy for the 1650s, even supplying timetables for the various events which were, in the author's reckoning, about to occur.

Although fully convinced that the end of the world was imminent, and that the seven-headed dragon and the scarlet woman represented Rome and the Papacy, Hall was content to let God keep his own counsel. His interpretations are guarded. His vocabulary abounds in words such as 'figure', 'signify', and 'import'. For him, *Revelation* is an allegory in the sense that God reveals the history of Christianity to St. John through symbols and images. The angel who stands by his side functions as the interpreter of these devices. He speaks for Hall also when he says, 'I will show thee the true and plain meaning of this vision; and the signification both of the woman and the beast.'[35] Hall's paraphrase is suggestive. What the angel actually says is, 'I will tell thee the mystery of the woman.' Unlike Archer, Hall is uninterested in compounding 'mysteries'; 'true' and 'plain' are his watchwords. In *Revelation* he finds the 'estate of the Church' 'represented' in 'several visions' each one dealing with a different aspect of its development but all quite intimately interrelated.[36] Numerology is not emphasized, and there are no claims to predict the manner of the ultimate fulfilment towards which the course of human history is heading. To Archer's various allegorical predictions the most effective reply is that, 'symbolicall Divinitie is not to be trusted for matter of proofe.'[37] For Hall, as for Calvin, the only sure guide to biblical interpretation is the Bible itself: 'when a strange doctrine is raised out of the construction of a doubtful text, it should be shewed to be seconded by the accordant testimony of other Scriptures.'[38] His historical bias declares itself in his handling of the various calculations from the Book of Daniel which Archer had contrived to introduce into his argument. These are shown to relate solely to the history of Daniel's own time, a history set forth with meticulous accuracy.[39] The procedure is exactly what we should expect since Calvin himself had warned that 'the Spirit must never be isolated from the Word, for this is to fall into the error of the enthusiasts.'[40] Hall's sentiments were identical. For those who had gone so far as 'already to date their Letters from New *Jerusalem*' he had nothing but contempt. 'We must crave pardon to with-hold our assent', he remarks, 'and to leave them to their own imaginations.'[41] His acceptance of the spiritual identity of the two Testaments led

him away from 'symbolicall Divinitie' to what earlier exegetes
would perhaps have recognized as a form of tropology. Like
Calvin before him, he strongly emphasizes the historical books
of the Old Testament. Indeed in the *Contemplations* he limits
himself entirely to historical material. He has 'purposely
omitted those peeces, which consist rather of speech then of
act.'[42] Occasionally he even supplies additional background
information designed to enable his readers to appreciate the
true historical significance of the scriptural account:

Now therefore, during the last yeers of *Cyrus,* and the raigne of his
son *Cambyses,* and the long government of *Darius Histaspides,* and of
his son *Xerxes,* or *Ahasuerus,* and lastly of his son *Artaxerxes;* untill
the dayes of *Darius Nothus,* (which was no lesse than five successions
of Kings, besides Cyrus) do the walls of the Temple stand still.[43]

The result is that for Hall the spiritual meaning is invariably
the moral one, the lesson to be derived from the factual
account of the dealings of God with man. It seems quite clear
that this insistence upon 'moral use' corresponds closely to
Calvin's distinction between 'frigid' and 'solid' interpretations.[44] The account of the surrendering of the rebel Sheba to
the forces of Joab, for example, ends on this note:

Spiritually, the case is ours: Every mans brest is a City inclosed:
Every sin is a Traitor, that lurks within those wals; God cals to us for
Shebaes head; neither had he any quarrell to our person, but for our
sin: If we love the head of our Traytor, above the life of our Soule, we
shal justly perish in the vengeance: we cannot be more willing to part
with our sin, than our mercifull God is to withdraw his judgements.[45]

Similarly 'solid' is the judgement on the conversion of
Manasseh: 'Who can complaine that the way of heaven is
blocked up against him, when he sees such a sinner enter?'[46] In
a sense allegory of the Augustinian type distances the reader
by presenting some lofty meaning for high speculation, but
neither Hall nor Calvin desire their readers to be so distanced.
In their interpretation the story itself has a personal and
individual significance for all. Their readings centre in the
believer's heart.

It might be supposed that the next logical stage in my
argument should be to trace specific sources for some of Hall's

interpretations in the writings of Calvin. This, however, would be quite impractical, for Hall was familiar with almost the entire range of Reformation commentary, and it is well-nigh impossible to establish indebtedness with any degree of certainty. At times even Calvin himself is so close to Luther and other early Reformers that we cannot be sure of his own sources. What is abundantly clear, however, is that Hall's principal debt to Calvin is one of method. As well as this, he prides himself, as always, on the originality of his contribution. The *Contemplations* were not intended as a Joseph's storehouse into which might be gathered the riches of the past, but as a personal contribution to a living tradition:

Yet this let me say (without any vaine boasting) that these thoughts (such as they are) through the blessing of God, I have woven out of my selfe, as holding it (after our Saviours rule) better to give, than to receive. It is easier to heape together large volumes of others labours, then to worke out lesser of our owne: and the suggestion of one new thought, is better then many repeated.[47]

Everywhere Hall's readings and interpretations are pervaded by Calvinist ideas of election and predestination, but the point by point commentary owes little specific debt to Calvin's own writings. If we compare the two accounts of the raising of Lazarus, for example, we find many striking shifts of emphasis. Whereas Calvin is concerned with the great issues of providence and theological truth, Hall pauses to comment in his own meditative way upon such features of the *story* as he finds particularly fascinating. The crowd of sympathizers who follow the weeping Mary, for instance, evokes from Calvin a statement on the hidden policy of God leading men all-unknowingly to a perception of his power. For Hall the event sparks off a series of thoughts on the nature and suffering of the passionate mind.[48] While Calvin delays long over the phrase 'I am the Resurrection', Hall passes it by without even a mention, and as Lazarus emerges in his funeral bands, Calvin gives a lesson on the Jewish method of embalming and attacks the Catholic doctrine of auricular confession, while Hall, alert as ever to minute detail, wonders at the meaning of this lesser miracle:

He that guided the soule of *Lazarus* into the body; guided the body of *Lazarus* without his eyes, moved the feet without the ful liberty of his regular paces; no doubt the same power slackned those swathing bands of death, that the feet might have some little scope to move, though not with that freedome, that followed after.[49]

Similarly the taking away of the stone has a deep spiritual lesson for Hall, while Calvin ignores it. The one is giving a lecture, the other is extending his meditative work from the 'Book of the creatures' to the book of the Word:

There are but two Bookes wherein wee can reade God; The one is his Word, his Works the other: This is the bigger Volume, that the more exquisite. The Characters of this are more large, but dim; of that, smaller, but clearer. Philosophers have turned over this and erred; That, Divines and studious Christians, not without full and certain information. In the Works of God we see the shadow, or footsteps of the Creator, in his Word we see the face of God in a glasse.[50]

Where Calvin must be concise and exact, Hall can afford to attempt something more exciting and suggestive:

He cried with a loud voice. His divine power is the better shown by the fact that He did not touch with the hand but only cried with His voice. At the same time He commends to us the secret and wonderful efficacy of His Word. For how did Christ restore life to the dead by His Word? Therefore, in raising Lazarus He exhibited a visible sign of His spiritual grace which we daily experience by the perception of faith, when He shows that His voice is quickening.[51]

Was it that the strength of the voice might answer to the strength of the affection? since we faintly require what we care not to obtaine, and vehemently utter what wee earnestly desire; Was it that the greatnesse of the voice might answer to the greatnesse of the worke? Was it, that the hearers might be witnesses of what words were used in so miraculous an act; no magicall incantations, but authoritative, and divine commands? Was it to signifie that *Lazarus* his soule was called from farre, the speech must be loud that shall be heard in another world? Was it in relation to the estate of the body of *Lazarus,* whom thou hadst reported to sleep; since those that are in a deep and dead sleep cannot be awaked, without a loud call: Or, was it in a representation of that loud voice of the last trumpet, which shal sound into all graves, and raise all flesh from their dust?[52]

Calvin sums up, but Hall rushes through a series of probing 'meditations' any of which will supply abundant material for the reader who wishes to pursue it. Hall's commentary is written as a series of 'contemplations' designed to open up new avenues of thought rather than answer specific questions. After the fashion of continental meditation, he appeals not merely to the understanding but to the imagination. This afforded him a choice of three principal methods: to visualize the scene as if one were present oneself; to imagine that the biblical figures were present in one's own time; or finally to imagine that all events which formed the matter of the contemplation were taking place in one's own heart.[53] The first procedure, the imaginative reconstruction of the scene, is the one usually adopted by Hall, but we find strong traces of the third mode when biblical events are applied 'spiritually' to the individual soul:

Whiles *Baals* Altar and grove stood in the hill of *Ophrah*, Israel should in vaine hope to prevaile... Wouldest thou faine be rid of any iudgement? Inquire what false Altars and groves thou hast in thy heart! downe with them first.

No lesse than eighteene yeeres did the rod of Moab rest upon the inheritance of God... Wee live in bondage to these Spirituall Moabites, our owne corruptions.[54]

More specifically, however, Hall's methods of visualization are very close to those suggested in the contemplative writers. The Jesuit Richard Gibbons, for example, urges the meditator to call to mind,

the places where the thinges we meditate on were wrought, by imagining our selves to be really present at those places; which we must endeavour to represent so lively, as though we saw them indeed... which to performe well, it will help us much... to have read or heard what good Authors write of those places, and to have noted well the distance from one place to another, the height of the hills, the situation of the towns and villages.[55]

What Gibbons is suggesting is the famous Ignatian 'composition of place' and it is exactly this sort of meticulous reconstruction that renders Hall's accounts so extremely vivid:

The vault, or cave, which *Ioseph* had hewne out of the rock, was large, capable of no lesse then ten persons; upon the mouth of it, Eastward, was that great stone rolled: within it, at the right hand, in the North part of the Cave, was hewne out a receptacle for the body, three handfuls high from the pavement; and a stone was accordingly fitted for the cover of that Grave.

The place, both solitary, and a sepulcher: nature abhorres, as the visage, so the region of death, and corruption. The time, night; Only the Moone gave them some faint glimmering, (for this being the seventeenth day of her age afforded some light to the latter part of the night). The businesse, the visitation of a dead corps.[56]

On other occasions he will note the passions and reactions of the actors as if he were himself an onlooker at the scene:

Me thinks I see the man of God change countenance at this sharpe sauce of his pleasing morsels; his face before-hand is died with the palenes of death: me thinks I heare him urging many unkinde expostulations with his injurious host.
What pity it was to see those goodly Cedars of the Temple flaming up higher than they stood in *Lebanon?* to see those curious marbles, which never felt the dint of the pick-axe, or hammer, in the laying, wounded with mattocks, and wounding the earth in their fall?
Methinks I see this young man who was thus miraculously awaked from his deadly sleepe, wiping and rubbing those eyes that had beene shut up in death; and descending from the Beere, wrapping his winding sheet about his loynes, cast himselfe downe in a passionate thankfulnesse, at the feet of his Almightie restorer.[57]

Nor is he always content to remain a silent spectator, but occasionally 'steps forth' to address the protagonists:

Revell, O *Herod*, and feast, and frolick; and please thy selfe with dances, and triumphs, and pastimes; thy sinne shall be as some fury that shall invisibly follow thee, and scourge thy guilty heart with secret lashes, and upon all occasions, shall begin thine hell within thee.[58]

Passages such as these place Hall firmly in the imaginative tradition descending to his own time through the works of the medieval Church Fathers. The point needs to be made quite strongly as it is diametrically opposed to the prevailing critical view. Hall, we are told, 'skipped over the whole Ignatian tradition to rediscover Mauburnus'.[59] Yet it is easy to detect striking correspondences between Hall's work and that of contemporary Catholic meditators. One has only to compare his account of the Passion with that of Luis de Granada to see that the *Contemplations* were intended as a direct contribution to the highly visual, dramatic tradition of St. Bonaventure to

which the Ignatian meditations themselves clearly belong.[60]
Drawn to a large extent from the writing of Bernard of
Clairvaux, one of Hall's favourite medieval authors, Bonaventure's *Meditations on the Life of Christ* counsel not merely the
visualization but the dramatization of biblical events, advice
Hall proved both eager and able to accept.[61] Repeatedly
throughout the *Contemplations*, he encourages his reader to
view the biblical story from a dramatic point of view either by
establishing his perspective in such a way as to suggest his
presence at a morality play, or by creating an 'audience' within
the scene itself:

A. The stage was first fully prepared, then was man brought forth
    thither, as an Actor or Spectator: that he might neither be idle
    nor discontent.
    As it is in the market, or the stage, so it is in our life; One goes in,
    another comes out, when *David* was withering, *Adonijah* was in
    his blossome.
    He [Elisha] knew that the blessing was at the parting; and if he
    had diligently attended all his life, and now slacked in the last
    act, hee had lost the reward of his service. The evening praises
    the day, and the chiefe grace of the theater is in the last Scene.[62]
B. which of the savagest Heathens that had bin now upon the hill
    of *Moriah*, and had seen (through the bushes) the sword of a
    Father hanging over the throat of such a sonne, would not have
    beene more perplexed in his thoughts, then the unexpected
    sacrifice was in those briers?
    If the parents of *Samson* had now stood behind the hedge and
    seene this incounter, they would have taken no further care of
    matching their sonne with a Philistim.[63]

The power with which Hall evokes the inherent drama of
the biblical narrative, together with his ability to humanize the
situations by psychologically re-creating the minds of the
characters, is seen to its best advantage in his lengthy
treatment of the story of Haman.[64] At first we see Mordecai
absorbed in anxious contemplation at Queen Esther's gate
when 'who should come ruffling by him, but the new-raised
favourite of King *Ahasuerus*... Him had the great King
inexpectedly advanced' (p. 1337). We are then acquainted
with the irrational pangs of ignorant pride as Haman is
spurned by his insignificant inferior:

In what a flame of wrath doth *Haman* live this while? wherewith hee
could not but have consumed his owne heart, had he not given vent
to that rage in his assured purposes of revenge ... *Haman* scorns to
take up with the blood of *Mordecai;* This were but a vulgar
amends ... Millions of throates are few enow to bleed for this
offence.   (pp. 1338–9)

Point by point, we follow the several stages of Machiavellian
logic by which he persuades the king to sanction the genocide
of the Jews, and watch as he squanders his own wealth in an
attempt to put his plans into effect.

From the counsel chamber the scene shifts suddenly to the
wretched Israelite bitterly lamenting the stubbornness of his
soul, and the fate it has brought upon his people:

Wretched man that I am; It is I, that have brought all this calamity
upon my nation; It is I, that have been the ruine of my people: woe is
me that ever I put my selfe into the Court, into the service of a
Pagan; how unhappy was I to cast my selfe into these straits, that I
must either honour an *Agagite,* or draw a vengeance upon
Israel? ... Why did I not hide my selfe rather from the place of that
proud *Amalekite?* Why did I stand out in contestation with so over-
powerfull an enemy? ... Oh, that my zeale should have reserved me
for so heavy a service!   (p. 1341)

But as the positions of the two men suddenly begin to reverse,
we are led further and further into the confused and self-
destroying mind of the great courtier:

How was *Haman* thunder-striken with this killing word, *Do thou so
to Mordecai?* ... Doubtlesse, at first, he distrusts his eare, and then
muses whether the King be in earnest; at last, when he heares the
charge so seriously doubled, and findes himselfe forced to beleeve it,
he begins to thinke, What meanes this unconceiveable alteration? Is
there no man in all the Court of Persia to be pickt out for
extraordinary honour, but *Mordecai?* Is there no man to be pickt out
for the performance of this honour to him, but *Haman?* have I but
one proud enemy in all the world, and am I singled out to grace
him? ... That which he would rather die, and forfeit the life of all his
nation, than do to me, notwithstanding the Kings command; shall I
be forced by the Kings command to do unto him?   (p. 1347)

And so the self-torturing examination continues, twisting
through all the complexities and ironies of his position, until

he finds relief in the hatred and malice which alone can console him: '*Mordecai*, I will honour thee now, that by these steps I may ere long raise thee many cubits higher. I will obey the command of my Soveraigne in observing thee, that he may reward the merit of my loyalty, in thine execution.' (p. 1348)

We follow him the next morning as he rushes to the palace to arrange for the execution of his rival, but 'how little do we know what is towards us? As the fishes that are taken in an evill net, and as the birds that are caught in the snare, so are the sons of men snared in an evill time, when it falleth suddenly upon them.' Esther's banquet quickly turns to tragedy as the revelation of the queen's nationality effectively seals Haman's fate:

In what a passionate distemper doth this banquet shut up? King *Ahasuerus* flyes from the table, as if he had beene hurried away with a tempest. His wrath is too great to come forth at his mouth; only his eyes tels *Haman* that he hates to see him, and vowes to see his dispatch. (p. 1351)

Alone with the queen, the culprit breaks forth into an impassioned plea which must rank as one of the most outstanding examples of Hall's 'dramatic' art:

Wretched man that I am, I am condemned before I speake; and when I have spoken, I am condemned: Upon thy sentence, O Queene, I see death awaits for me, in vaine shall I seeke to avoid it; It is thy will that I should perish; but let that little breath I have left, acquit me so farre with thee, as to call heaven and earth to record, that in regard of thee, I dye innocent: It is true that mine impetuous malice miscarried me against the nation of the Jewes, for the sake of one stubborne offender; but did I know there was the least drop of Isrealitish blood in thy sacred person? could I suspect that *Mordecai*, or that people, did ought concerne thee? Let not one death be enough for me if I would ever have entertained any thought of evill against nation, or man, that should have cost but a frowne from thee: All the court of Persia can sufficiently witnesse how I have magnified and adored thee, ever since the royall crowne was set on thy head; neither did I ever faile to doe thee all good offices unto that my Soveraine Master, whom thou hast now mortally incensed against me. O Queene, no hand can save my life, but thine, that hath as good as bereaved it: show mercy to him, that never meant but loyalty to thee: As ever

thou wouldest oblige an humble and faithfull vassall to thee, as ever
thou wouldst honour thy name, and sexe, with the praise of tender
compassion, take pitty on me, and spare that life which shall be
vowed to thy service: and whereas thy displeasure may justly alleage
against me that rancorous plot for the extirpation of that people,
whom I, too late, know to be thine; let it suffice that I hate, I curse
mine owne cruelty; and only upon that condition shall beg the
reprivall of my life, that I shall worke, and procure by thy gracious
ayd, a full defeazance of that unjust execution. Oh let fall upon thy
despairing servant one word of favour to my displeased Master, that
I may yet live.   (pp. 1351–2)
(*Biblical source:* 'and Haman stood up to make request for his life to
Esther the Queene: for he saw, that there was evill determined
against him by the King.' Esther 7:7.)

Comparison with the biblical account affords striking
evidence of the extent of the dramatization. Far from adopting
the rigidly Puritan position that the *Logos* is sufficient to itself,
Hall has merely used the text as a framework upon which to
build an entirely original, or should I say fictional, reconstruction of the scriptural account. The energy and sweep of
Haman's speech, set as it is at a climactic moment of the
narrative, rivals any of the orations attributed by Livy to his
gallery of Roman generals and statesmen. It is a speech of
frenzy and distraction, the futility of which the speaker
himself acknowledges at the outset: 'in vaine shall I seeke to
avoid it.' But desperation is seldom silent, and as the words
proceed he slips almost imperceptibly from a discussion of his
own guilt to one of sovereign intractability: 'my Soveraine
Master, whom *thou* hast now mortally incensed against me.'
By midway there is far more talk of innocence than of guilt
and the crime dwindles to a side-issue, something that must be
conceded in debate but hardly of the first importance: 'and
whereas thy displeasure may justly alleage ... let it suffice ....'
The word 'despairing' recalls us to reality. As Haman well
knows, a royal decree of Persia can never be revoked; he
cannot undo the 'unjust execution' to which he has persuaded
the king. He may no more hope to escape than the Jews he has
himself condemned. The wheel comes full circle as he ascends
the gibbet erected on his own orders for Mordecai. The proud
courtier once so enamoured of fame regrets having ever been

born: 'Wo is me whose eyes serve me onely to foresee the approach of a dishonorable, and painefull death! what am I the better to have beene great? O that I had never beene, O that I could not be ... Oh that the conscience of mine intended murder could dye with me.' (p. 1352.)

Quite clearly Hall is not one of those for whom 'the Scripture as revealed Word offered no purchase for imagination' and is certainly not to be grouped with Greenham and the other Puritans who opposed the intermingling of the human and the divine.[65] This interpretation cannot survive the experience of the *Contemplations*. The Puritan insistence on the all-sufficient *Logos*, which it has become common to contrast with the acknowledgement of its limitations in Baxter and Sibbes, can hardly be ascribed to the creator of the Haman drama. In fact, there is far more 'sanctified fancy' in Hall than in the authors generally opposed to his 'tradition', for neither Baxter nor Sibbes 'achieve that sharpness of focus which is to be found in the Ignatian tradition'.[66] This could never be said of Hall's account of the death of Jezebel, or of the sons of Ahab pleading with their executioners, or of the high priest stepping forth to restrain the rash Uzziah, or of the wonderful Hamlet-like soliloquy of Jael as she hesitates before killing the sleeping Sisera:

Now, whiles he was dreaming, doubtlesse, of the clashing of armors, ratling of chariots, neighing of horses, the clamor of the conquerd, the furious pursuit of Israel, *Iael* seeing his temples lie so faire, as if they invited the naile and hammer, entred into the thought of this noble execution, certainly not without some checks of doubt, and pleas of feare: What if I strike him? And yet who am I, that I should dare to thinke of such an act? Is not this *Sisera*, the famousest Captaine of the world, whose name hath wont to be fearefull to whole Nations? What if my hand should swarve in the stroke? What if he should awake, whiles I am lifting up this instrument of death: What if I should be surprised by some of his followers whiles the fact is greene, and yet bleeding? ... Did I not invite him to my Tent? ... But what doe these weake feares, these idle fancies of civility? ... Is it for nothing that God hath brought him into my Tent? ... No, *Sisera*, sleepe now thy last, and take here this fatall reward of all thy cruelty and oppression.[67]

It scarcely needs saying that there is nothing like this in

Calvin. The emphasis on history is exactly the same, but the manner in which it is brought to life is quite different. Short of the composition of plays, Hall has taken 'dramatic' meditation as far as it can go. Indeed when we encounter Satan addressing Christ, or the risen Christ addressing his disciples, we may well ask what debt these contemplative methods owe to Hall's youthful experience of the Elizabethan morality drama to which he refers in his sermons.[68] The difference, of course, is that Hall had no stage, and many of his most 'dramatic' effects are due to the often rather colloquial and uninhibited richness of his language. The Haman story begins, when the villain comes 'ruffling by'; Jezebel 'prankes up her old carkasse' to confront Jehu, and Judas goes off to haggle with 'pelting petty chapmen'.[69] As Pilate washes his hands the author's comment is 'Now, all is safe; I wis this is expiation enough', and why should Nehemiah distrust Sanballat? No less a witness than Gashmu has guaranteed his truthfulness, 'aske my fellow else.'[70]

But whereas this accounts for the surface attractiveness of the *Contemplations,* their real strength lies in the interplay between vividly evoked drama and intellectual analysis. As in the Ignatian meditations, imaginative reconstruction of biblical events serves merely to focus the mind more precisely on the spiritual issues underlying the narration. Ignatius's own six-point contemplation on the Last Supper, for example, is designed to lead from the events themselves to a consideration of the nature of Christ's various sufferings as God and man, and finally to an acknowledgement of our own culpability. All three powers of the mind are brought into play: memory, understanding, and will.[71] Perhaps the central difference between the meditative approach of the seventeenth century and that of the medieval era lies in the new intellectual toughness of the later age.[72] In Hall's case this becomes clear the moment we place his account of the Purification beside that of Bonaventure. The latter sees only the general wonder of the occasion: 'O God! what an offering is this; never had such been made from the beginning of time, nor ever shall be again.'[73] But Hall with his taste for emblems and paradoxes takes the matter much further:

It is fit the holy mother should present God with his owne: Her first born was the first born of all creatures; It was he, whose Temple it was, that he was presented in, to whom all the first born of all creatures were consecrated, by whom they were accepted; and now is he brought in his mothers armes to his owne house, and as man is presented to himselfe as God ... There was nothing either placed, or done within those walls, whereby he was not resembled, and now the body of those shadowes is come, and presents himselfe, where he had been ever represented: *Jerusalem* is now every where.[74]

It is the mark of the seventeenth-century mind to emphasize all the paradoxical and ironic aspects of the Scriptures; Hall shares this practice with poets such as Herbert and Donne. The affinity is very noticeable in his handling of symbolism and imagery. The 'wet cloth' with which Hazel murders Benhadad, for example, becomes a symbol of the guilt from which he can never escape: 'I am deceived, if this wet cloth shall not wipe thy lips in thy jolliest feasts, and make thy best morsells unsavory.'[75] As Abimelech watches the slaughter of his brothers he remains 'as senselesse as the stone' upon which they perish. But the imagery is reversed as the fatal millstone, cast from the hands of a weak opponent, crushes him to death.[76] The force of Jael's blow drives Sisera's ear 'so close to the earth, as if the body had beene listening what was become of the soule.'[77]

This intellectual or witty quality of the *Contemplations* is also apparent from the often restless and self-qualifying movement of the prose, drawing its ideas together in thought-provoking combinations:

He that meant to take mans nature without mans corruption, would bee the Sonne of man without mans seed, would bee the seed of the woman without man; and amongst all women, of a pure Virgin; but amongst Virgins, of one espoused.
He that was by signification the strength of God, to her that was by signification exalted by God, to the conceiving of him, that was the God of strength.[78]

Although Hall is undoubtedly fascinated by the biblical story in its own right, much of the over-all tension and force of his work springs, as I have said, from the interaction of narration and analysis. Not actions but motives interest Hall (witness his soliloquies), and not motives only, but the concealed and often scarcely conscious modes of thought that shape motivation itself. In a passage such as the following we sense the rising tide of intellectual excitement as the meditator slowly unravels the mystery of human aspiration and moves ever closer to God. As is often the case, the motion in literary terms is towards an aphorism or 'sententia' which represents the result of the inquiry:

Gideon refused the Kingdome of Israel when it was offered; his seventy sonnes offered not to obtaine that Scepter, which their Fathers victory had deserved to make hereditary: onely *Abimelec,* the concubines sonne, sues and ambitiously plots for it. What could *Abimelec* see in himselfe, that hee should over-looke all his brethren? If hee looke to his Father, they were his equals; if to his mother, they were his betters. Those that are most unworthy of honour, are hottest in the chase of it, whilst the conscience of better deserts bids men sit still, and stay to bee either importuned, or neglected. There can bee no greater signe of unfitnesse, than vehement sute. It is hard to say, whether there be more pride, or ignorance in Ambition. I have noted this difference betwixt Spirituall and earthly honour, and the Clients of both; wee cannot be worthy of the one without earnest prosecution; nor with earnest prosecution worthy of the other: The violent obtaine heaven, onely the meeke are worthy to inherit the earth.[79]

The first sentence presents us with a plain statement of the facts, but then we are immediately confronted with the problem of motivation; why did it happen? Two conditional clauses examine probable answers but find them both inadequate. There was, therefore, no apparent reason why Abimelech should prefer himself to his brothers, yet this is clearly what happened, and the situation is explicable only in terms of one of those unpleasant yet true antitheses drawn from human experience: 'those that are most unworthy of honour, are hottest in the chase of it.' The mind leaps from dilemma to explanation instantaneously without any intermediate stage. With equal celerity, reminding us that Hall is still writing in a basically Senecan as opposed to a Ciceronian mode, the explanation suggests a maxim, a sentence for the common-place-book, to be observed in all our further dealings: 'there can be no greater signe of unfitnesse, than vehement sute.' But

there still remains something unexplained. The root of the evil
has been shown to be the pursuit of honour or 'ambition', but
what is ambition? Was Abimelech proud, or simply ignorant,
or both? In human terms 'it is hard to say'; we can go no
further along the present road of inquiry. Ultimately the
answer lies not in the man but in the goal after which he
sought, 'honour'. Once more, in keeping with the complexities
of human life, we are confronted by an antithesis, but an
antithesis drawn from a deeper level of observation than
before; the addition of the spiritual dimension alters everything. Abimelech was ignorant of the true nature of honour.
He sought the lesser good with a passion appropriate only to
the greater, and in doing so lost both. He was therefore
'unworthy' in both the temporal and the spiritual sense. The
great antithesis leads to a 'sentence' of a higher calibre than
the former; that was the policy of men, but this—a conflation
of two biblical verses—is the policy of God: 'The violent
obtaine heaven, onely the meeke are worthy to inherit the
earth.'[80]

The *Contemplations* abound in such 'sentences'. They are
one of the principal features of Hall's style carried over from
the *Meditations and Vowes* and the *Characters of Vertues and
Vices*. Here, however, no longer thrown out in the hasty or
disjointed Baconian manner, they derive an added strength
from all that precedes them and serve in their turn to 'distance'
us from the narration they summarize. They are Hall's way of
making us stand back from the flux of the action to view the
scene with detachment:

Faire words have won his brethren; they the Shechemites; the
Shechemites furnish him with money, money with men; His men
begin with murder, and now *Abimelec* raignes alone; Flattery, bribes
and blood, are the usuall staires of the Ambitious.
Gideons Ephod is punished with the bloud of his sons; the bloud of
his sons is shed by the procurement of the Shechemites: the bloud of
the Shechemites is shed by *Abimelec:* the bloud of *Abimelec* is spilt by
a woman. The retaliations of God are sure and just, and make a more
due pedigree, than descent of nature.[81]

Such a technique is typical of the entire work. Scenes,
actions, and characters are powerfully evoked, but the purpose

of it all is to provoke us into thought. Seldom, if ever, is narration unqualified by comment; we are always examining, probing, and comparing, always rising from the human to the divine. Antithesis, a figure whereby one mode or system of life can conveniently and effectively be contrasted with another, is a characteristic feature of the prose. In this respect the opening sentences set the pattern for all that follows:

What can I see, O God in thy creation, but miracles of wonders? Thou madest something of nothing, and of that something, all things. Thou which wast without a beginning, gavest a beginning to Time, and to the World in time. It is the praise of us men, if when we have Matter, we can give fashion: thou gavest a being to the Matter, without forme; thou gavest a forme to that Matter, and a glory to that Forme. If wee can but finish a slight and unperfect Matter according to a former patterne, it is the height of our skill: but to begin that which never was, whereof there was no example, whereto there was no inclination, wherein there was no possibilitie of that which it should be, is proper onely to such power as thine: the infinite power of an infinite Creator: with us, not so much as a thought can arise without some Matter; but here with thee, all Matter arises from nothing.[82]

We begin with an exclamation of wonder evoked by the greatness of God, and not 'wonder' merely, but 'miracles of wonders'. This passionate opening is immediately justified by two perplexing paradoxes: through divine power everything derives from nothing; and having no beginning himself, God gave what he had not got first to 'Time', which alone makes the term 'beginning' meaningful, and then to the world in Time. The self-perplexing quality of the thought is reflected in the strangely repetitious nature of the language which seems to be constantly turning back upon itself as if inadequate to its task: 'something'/'nothing'/'something'/'all things'; 'without a beginning'/'beginning to Time'/'World in time'. From this point on the 'miracles' are celebrated through antithesis; man is relentlessly contrasted with God, and the syntax displays how heavily the scales dip in the divine favour. The 'praise of us men' is dependent on an 'if'. 'If' we have matter we may fashion it, and 'if' we 'can' fashion it we are praised. But on the other side there are no qualifications. God created all matter, or in other words all that is the foundation of man's 'praise'.

Man's 'if' is conditional on the acts of God. But God has gone further still, for he outdoes man at his own work by becoming a 'fashioner' himself, and giving 'Glory' to his 'forme' rather than extracting praise from it. Nothing in the universe is exclusive to man, almost everything is exclusive to God. Syntactically the sentence is uneven: God's tricolon outweighs man's single conditional affirmation, and one section of that tricolon contains all that man boasts.

As the passage proceeds man is once more impeded by an 'if', and the 'height' of his skill is qualified by such associations as 'slight', 'unperfect', and 'former'. The fourfold balance, or rather imbalance, on the opposite side suppresses any notion of emulation: 'to begin that which never was, whereof there was no example, whereto there was no inclination, wherein there was no possibilitie of that which it should be'. The thoughts spiral outwards as the miracle grows more unfathomable phrase by phrase until language becomes almost incapable of bearing the strain of description and takes refuge in the twice repeated 'infinite'. And then follows the ultimate blow: 'with us, not so much as a thought can arise without some Matter; but here with thee, all Matter arises from nothing.' Even man's ability to think—to frame the antithesis —is dependent not directly upon God but on things which God has made out of nothing. The shape of Hall's thought is an unbalanced antithesis.

The intellectual toughness of the *Contemplations* largely accounts for the force of the prose yet is by no means self-sufficient. As always, the process of analysis paves the way for emotion; love is an act of the informed Will. The direction of the inquiry is towards things spiritual and the deity is directly addressed in numerous colloquies. Yet few of the individual contemplations display the total meditative structure of composition, understanding, and colloquy, although there are some striking exceptions such as the passage on the building of Solomon's temple.[83] The reason is that the form of the commentary has not been abandoned. Since Hall has chosen to follow the biblical account chronologically, his freedom is curtailed by the requirements of the text. He is pioneering yet another new English genre, that of the meditative commentary. It should also be remembered that many of the contemplations, especially those on the New Testament were originally delivered as sermons and then reworked in such a way that the critical and textual character of the homily disappeared, and the meditative and contemplative elements were either added (in the case of the soliloquies, etc.) or expanded.[84] As a result few such Contemplations deal with single topics, but take the points of the text (often minute ones) as they arise. Their titles denote their major theme not their sole concern. Yet it remains true that many of the individual points thus raised themselves pass through all three stages of meditation proper. A good example of all these features is *The Begger that was borne blinde, cured.*[85] The subjects in this section range from a consideration of the nature and significance of human suffering, to the benefits derived from 'inquisition', or the habit of intelligent questioning. But the central theme is the miracle itself. First of all its occurrence is described in detail: the empty sockets being filled with cold clay; the feelings of the blind man while it was happening; the actions of Christ in performing it. Then comes the questioning: why did Christ do all this when he need only have 'said but the word'? When the matter has been satisfactorily resolved the meditator turns to God in thanks. This arrangement is typical of what the reader of the *Contemplations* can expect to find.

On a wider level it would seem that in writing this work Hall was following an over-all plan for his labours in the meditative genre. According to St. Bonaventure, there were three basic subjects of meditation: the humanity of Christ centred on the New Testament; the Heavenly Court; and the Majesty of God. In this system one rises progressively from the first to the third.[86] A further subject, of course, not mentioned by Bonaventure was the 'Book of the creatures' whereby one accustomed oneself to 'reading' the world as a divine lesson. Taking this extra dimension into account one can see that Hall's work developed quite closely along Bonaventure's lines. Beginning with the 'creatures' he proceeded to the Bible, broadening the interest under Calvin's influence from an exclusive study of the New Testament to the historical books of the Old as well. After that, in his later period, while reviving his practice of incidental meditation, he moved on to the

'Heavenly Court' motif in such compositions as *The Invisible World* (1652),[87] and to the theme of the 'Majesty of God' in his *Great Mysterie of Godliness* (1652). A link between the two types of meditation, the biblical and the 'mystic', was forged in 1647 with the publication of *Christ Mysticall* a treatise on the 'blessed union of Christ with his members', a fitting sequel to the *Contemplations* which conclude with *The Ascension* and the promise of the Second Coming.[88] This is not to say, of course, that Hall could foresee the total scope of his devotional writing from the outset of his career, but rather to appreciate the logic and order of his progress, from the 'creatures' to the Bible, and from there to more purely 'spiritual' or other-worldly themes. He was ascending in carefully ordered stages after the true meditative fashion. By recognizing this we can at once understand the position and function of the *Contemplations* in the wider context of Hall's work, and also appreciate the almost inevitably 'mystical' quality of the later writings.

At the beginning of this study I discussed the rather complex motivations underlying the writing of biblical commentary in the seventeenth century, and to this subject, in conclusion, I now wish to return, for writings such as the *Contemplations* exist not merely as part of a literary tradition, but also in the context of the society of which their author himself forms a part. We have already examined Hall's emphasis on 'history' in some detail. We have seen how he dramatizes the affairs of the Jews in order to make that history come to life for contemporary readers, and how he analyses and interprets it in the light of his understanding of 'policy' both human and divine. Having gone so far he could hardly fail to appreciate the logical extension of his own methods, the discussion of real contemporary problems in the history of Judah and Israel. What is in question here is not the detection of hidden references or allusions—Hall was above such methods—but the sensitive and intelligent use of biblical commentary to analyse and comment upon problems of pressing interest to contemporary readers. This was surely one of the reasons for the work's amazing popularity. Hall's audience did not want a scholarly disquisition upon Jewish history, or a patchwork of

anagrams and riddles making cryptic allusion to this or that
great personage, but a sensible, reflective account of the
enduring and recurrent problems of the chosen race. They
regarded themselves as the new Jews, and what they were
seeking was a providential account of God's people journeying
often slowly and laboriously towards the Promised Land.

One of the major shifts in biblical exegesis caused by the
Reformers' interest in typology was the ever-increasing
tendency to interpret contemporary events as antitypes of
scriptural occurrences. In one sense this was not really a new
idea at all. On the contrary it may even be regarded as
returning typology to its very origins. The earliest Christians
were themselves Jews who regarded the Old Testament as part
of their heritage, so for them its assimilation into the new
covenant was relatively easy: the coming of the Messiah was
the fulfilment of their own history. But as Christianity spread
among Gentile peoples the position became far more difficult.
To say the least, the significance of Old Testament history was
not immediately obvious to non-Jewish converts. The desire to
make it so was one of the principal reasons why Church
Fathers such as St. Augustine became interested in the
typological interpretations of Philo of Alexandria and his
school.[89] According to this view, the characters and events of
the Old Testament could be interpreted as 'types' of the
characters and events of the New Testament. For example, the
ceremonial bread and wine of the priest-king Melchizedek
(Genesis 14: 17–20) find their antitypes in the bread and wine
of the Last Supper. As Donne put it:

The *institution* of thy whole *worship* in the *old Law*, was a continuall
Allegory; types and *figures* overspread all; and *figures* flowed into
figures, and powred themselves out into *farther figures; Circumcision*
carried a *figure* of *Baptisme*, and *Baptisme* carries a figure of that
purity, which we shall have in *perfection* in the *new Jerusalem*.[90]

In other words, since the Church itself was to be regarded as
Christ's 'Mystical Body' and the providential plan for creation
was still in the process of unfolding towards the ultimate
fulfilment of the Second Coming, it proved possible to extend
the typological method to the interpretation of contemporary
history. After Revelation the historical books of the Old

Testament provided by far the most promising material for this sort of analysis. This explains why Calvin was so fascinated by these writings while Erasmus clung so tenaciously to the ethical books of the Bible. As one modern editor has put it,

> Calvin appropriated the sufferings of God's people depicted in the *Bible* for the evangelicals in Europe and for himself. It is hardly possible, as we read his comments on Noah, David, Job, Jeremiah, or on the disciples of Jesus, to escape the truth that they all are vivified by their profound appropriateness to his condition.[91]

Perhaps the best example of this procedure in English literature is Dryden's *Absalom and Achitophel.*

Part of the fascination of typology has always been its powerful didactic force. By convincingly demonstrating a recognizable pattern in contemporary affairs the preacher can claim to understand and even predict the implications of any given situation. For instance, one entire sermon of Hall's is devoted to uncovering ominous correspondences between the old Israel and the new—England.[92] The various disasters of English foreign policy in the 1620s are examined in the light of the highly similar disasters inflicted as punishment for the sins of the original chosen people, people now completely abandoned to the hands of their enemies. In the preacher's mind at least the conclusion is clear. Again, in the *Common Apologie of the Church of England,* the religious policy of Elizabeth and James is shown to correspond closely to that of the two great reforming kings of the Old Testament, Manasseh and Josiah.[93] Readers of the *Contemplations* would therefore be quite familiar with typological methods of interpretation. Their experience of Protestant homiletics would have accustomed them to analyse their own society in the light of biblical types and antitypes. But whereas Calvin is usually quite explicit in drawing such correspondences—especially with regard to Rome—in the *Contemplations,* at least, Hall prefers to leave much of the work of discovery to the reader. He does, however, take full advantage of his dedications to alert them to the need for such labour. When dedicating this work to Prince Henry in 1612, for example, he declares that his meditations are particularly relevant for someone in the young prince's position for, 'Here your Highnesse shall see how the great patterne of Princes, the King of Heaven, hath ever ruled the World, how his Substitutes, earthly Kings, have ruled it under him, and with what successe either of glory or ruine. Both your Peace and Warre shall finde here holy and great examples.'[94] Many years later, when bringing the work to conclusion, he tells Prince Charles that it is 'not so fit for any eyes as Princely' for, 'what doth it else but comment upon that, which God hath thought good to say of Kings; what they have done, what they should have done; how they sped in good, in evill? Certainely there can be none such miror of Princes under heaven, as this, which God hath made for the faces of his Deputies on earth.'[95] The same note is maintained throughout. Each book is dedicated to someone in a position of influence and authority, and they are frequently reminded that the scriptural account has a particular relevance to persons such as themselves—a far from idle assertion.

One of the principal themes of the Old Testament account is, of course, the development and preservation of the Jewish religion, a theme inseparable from that of Jewish politics since the kings of Israel and Judah invariably determine their people's religious attitudes. Like the prophets, they stand in a unique position between God and man. Their power is paramount. They may either repel idolatry like Hezekiah, or import it, along with a foreign wife, like Ahab. Now since many of Hall's readers would have also heard him preach at Whitehall, the Spittal, or Paul's Cross, and many more would have been eagerly following the course of his religious debates with the Brownists, the Papists, and the Protestant opponents of the Synod of Dort, they would easily have recognized key terms and identifications. To find him referring to his countrymen as 'all our Israelites' would have occasioned them little surprise, nor indeed would the context of the reference, a discussion of Samson's marriage to a 'daughter of the Philistines', a foreign bride. The effect on Samson's parents is portrayed, as usual, dramatically, but remembering the time of composition (1615) it is a very pertinent topical drama: 'Shall our deliverance from the Philistims begin in an alliance? Have we bin so scrupulously carefull, that he should eate no uncleane thing, and shall we now consent to an heathenish match?'[96] The 'inconveniences' of the marriage are then listed in full: 'corruption in Religion, alienation of affections, distraction of thoughts, connivence at Idolatry, death of zeale, dangerous underminings, and lastly, an unholy seed: Who can blame them, if they were unwilling to call a Philistim daughter?'[97]

Who indeed? But Gondomar was active in the English court from 1613, and by 1615 it was quite clear that James was seriously considering a marriage alliance with Catholic Spain. To all who opposed such schemes, and the author of *No Peace with Rome* was among the foremost,[98] the point of the passage could hardly pass unnoticed, especially since the account continues as follows:

I wish *Manoah* could speake so loud, that all our Israelites might heare him; *Is there never a woman among the daughters of thy brethren, or among all Gods people, that thou goest to take a wife of the uncircumcised Philistims?* If Religion be any other than a cypher, how dare we not regard it in our most important choice?[99]

In such a context the significance of 'corruption in Religion', 'dangerous underminings', and most of all 'unholy seed' could not but evoke a powerful response from Hall's readers, and the sequel provides a perfect illustration of the points being raised. Samson is betrayed by his foreign wife:

I doe not wonder, that a Philistim woman loved herselfe and her Fathers family, more than an Israelitish Bride-grome; and if she bestowed teares upon her husband, for the ransome of them.... *Samson* never bewrayed infirmity but in uxoriousnesse: What assurance can there be of him that hath a Philistim in his bosome?[100]

And foreign fathers-in-law are not to be trusted either:

Now *Samsons* father in law shewes himselfe a Philistim, the true parent of her that betraied her husband; for no sooner is the Bride-groome departed, then he changes his son: What pretence of friendship soever he made, a true Philistim will soone be weary of an Israelite.[101]

When the context is particularly topical Hall's generalizations have a powerful effect.

Solomon too is led astray by foreign wives and the result not surprisingly is the perversion of true religion, for while

refraining from the worship of heathen abominations himself
yet 'so farre was the uxorious King blinded with affection, that
he gave not passage onely to the Idolatry of his heathenish
wives, but furtherance':

So did he dote upon their persons, that he humoured them in their
sins: Their act is therefore his, because his eyes winkt at it; his hand
advanced it: He that built a Temple to the living God, for himselfe
and Israel in Sion, built a Temple to Chemosh in the mount of
Scandall, for his Mistresses of Moab, in the very face of Gods House:
No hill about Jerusalem was free from a Chappell of Devils: Each of
his dames had their Puppets, their Altars, their Incense; Because
Salomon [sic] feeds them in their superstition, he drawes the sinne
home to himselfe, and is branded for what hee should have
forbidden. Even our very permission appropriates crimes to us: Wee
need no more guiltinesse of any sinne, than our willing toleration.[102]

This was in 1622 when the Spanish marriage was more
probable than ever before, and when it was becoming quite
obvious that the Penal Laws were being relaxed.[103] Equally
obvious was the likelihood that a Catholic queen would
demand special provision for her religion at court, a demand
soon to be made though not, as it happened, by the Infanta.
'Altars', 'incense', and winking at 'superstition' (the received
term of abuse for Roman Catholicism) have a special
appropriateness.

In 1623 Prince Charles and the Duke of Buckingham
departed for Spain to the dismay of thousands throughout
England. The following passage occurs in the section of the
Contemplations published that year:

Israel sojourned in Egypt, and brought home a golden calfe:
Ieroboam sojournes there, and brought home two; It is hard to dwell
in Egypt untainted; not to savour of the sins of the place we live in, is
no lesse strange, then for wholesome liquor tunned up in a musty
vessell, not to smell of the cask: The best body may be infected in a
contagious ayre: Let him beware of Egypt that would be free from
Idolatry.[104]

It is a guarded comment at a time when royal proclamations
were curbing the freedom of pulpit, press, and even conversation. But it is a comment nevertheless: when Charles returned
on 6 October 1623 the Psalm sung in celebration at St. Paul's

was, 'When Israel came out of Egypt, and the house of Jacob
from amongst the barbarous people' (Psalm 114).[105] 'Idolatry'
had always been one of the key terms in Hall's attack on
Rome, nor did he scruple to associate Popery with the worst
excesses of paganism: was it not scandalous, he asks,
'That ... the Churches of Christians should bee no lesse
pestered with Idols, than the Temples of the Heathen?
That ... the native beautie of the Church should bee polluted
with the filth of Paganisme?'[106]

The number of satiric remarks, supposedly directed against
the practices of biblical heathens, but actually applying
themselves by way of generalization to Rome, are far too
numerous to catalogue, but each and every one of them has
some tell-tale word such as 'innovation', 'pomp', or 'idol'
designed to alert the reader to the real target of abuse: 'And
why seven Altars? What needs all this pompe? ... It hath
beene ever seene, that the false worshippers of God have made
more pompous shewes, and fairer flourishes of their peity
[sic], and religion, than the true.'[107] Only very occasionally do
the *Contemplations* revert to explicit denunciation: David
spared the life of Saul thereby inspiring a direct attack on the
self-professed 'Ring-leaders of Christianity' who openly encourage the violation of majesty.[108] But this is uncommon and
usually unnecessary.

It was no secret that Hall was a 'puritan' in the sense that,
even after his elevation to the episcopal bench, he remained,
like Archbishop Abbot, strongly opposed to the over-empha-
sizing of ceremony and ritual, and openly hostile to the
encroachments of the 'Arminian faction'. This is why he was
distrusted by Laud, why spies were sent into his diocese, and
why the *Contemplations* take every opportunity of discourag-
ing all tampering with the received forms of divine service.
Ahaz builds a new altar to the glory of the Lord, but the Lord
rejects it:

It is a dangerous presumption to make innovations, if but in the
circumstances of Gods worship. Those humane additions which
would seeme to grace the institution of God, deprave it ... That
heart which can for the outward homelinesse despise the ordinances
of God, is alreadie aliened from true Religion, and lies open to the
grossest superstition.[109]

As a result Hall holds extremely rigid views on the duty of
kings, the upholders of Church and State. The support of the
magistrate is of the utmost importance for the furthering of
the work of God, and the work of God in seventeenth-century
terms is the protection of the Reformed religion:

Where the Temporal and Spiritual State combine not together, there
can follow nothing but distraction in the people: The Prophets
receive and deliver the will of God, Kings execute it: The Prophets
are directed by God, the people are directed by their Kings. Where
men doe not see God before them in his Ordinances, their hearts
cannot but faile them, both in their respects to their superiours, and
their courage in themselves.[110]

What this means in effect is that 'nothing is more odious,
than to make Religion a stalking horse to Policy.'[111] There can
be no compromise with Gondomar or his master. The godly
ruler is a man of unremitting zeal. It was the crime of the
otherwise laudable King Asa that while he rid Judah of the
plague of foreign religions he acquiesced in the perversion of
his own. In 1626, when the danger of the Spanish match had
finally passed, Hall took the opportunity of the last section of
his work, dedicated to Charles, to put forward his views on the
subject of the godly king. Lurking just below the surface are
all the anxieties of recent years: 'what doth it else but comment
upon that, which God had thought good to say of Kings?' The
characters may be from the *Old Testament*, but their acts have
a direct application to his own day:

Neither doth penitent *Manasseh* build God a new altar, but he
repaires the old, which by long dis-use lay waste, and was mossie and
mouldred with age and neglect.
    God loves well his owne institutions; neither can he abide
innovations, so much as in the out-sides of his services. It is an happie
worke to vindicate any ordinance of God from the injuries of times,
and to restore it to the originall glory.
    What have our pious Governors done other in Religion? had we
gone about to lay a new foundation, the worke had bin accursed;
now wee have onely scraped off some superfluous mosse, that was
growne upon these holy stones, we have cemented some broken
peeces, we have pointed some crazie corners with wholesome morter,

in stead of base clay, wherewith it was disgracefully patched up. The altar is old, it is Gods altar: It is not new, not ours: If we have laid one new stone in this sacred building, let it flye in our faces, and beat out our eyes.[112]

This is a strongly worded passage and one of Hall's rare explicit pronouncements, preparing the way for what comes next. It alerts the reader to the presence of a dual frame of reference. Manasseh was a convert and achieved only a partial reformation through lack of knowledge. But in the reign of his son the 'booke of the Law', long hidden and forgotten, was rediscovered:

How God blesses the devout indeavours of his servants? Whiles *Helkijah* was diligently survaying the breaches and the reparation of the Temple, he lights upon the booke of the Law: The authentick and originall Booke of Gods Law was by a speciall charge appointed to be carefully kept within a safe shrine, in the Sanctuary: In the depraved times of Idolatry, some faithfull Priest (to make sure work) had locked it fast up in some corner of the Temple, from the reach of all hands, of all eyes ... Some few transcripts there were doubtlesse, (parcels of this sacred Book) in other hands ... but the whole body of these awfull Records, since the late night of Idolatrous confusion and persecution, saw no light till now; this precious treasure doth *Helkijah* find, whiles he digs for the Temple: Never man laboured to the reparation of Gods Church, but he met with a blessing more than he looked for.[113]

This is analogous, of course, to the sixteenth-century 'rediscovery' of the Bible by the Reformers: the Hebrew sources are studied anew and the many faults of the Vulgate ('some few transcripts ... parcels of this Sacred Book') deservedly exposed. After centuries of ignorance the truth is finally revealed and the finders, unlike the Catholic clergy, do not 'ingrosse' the discovery to themselves, nor 'suppresse these more than sacred roles, for their owne advantage' but 'transmit them, first to the eares of the King, then by him, to the people'. 'Woe be to them that hide Gods Booke from the people, as they would doe rats-bane from the eyes of children.'[114] 'Then *by him* to the people': what Hall has chosen to emphasize is the central role of the king in the work of reformation. As soon as he hears the directions of the book, Josiah responds passionately to their message:

So soone as the good King heares the words of the book of the Law, and in speciall, those dreadfull threats of judgment, denounced against the Idolatries of his Judah, he rends his cloathes, to shew his heart rent with sorrow, and fearfull expectation of those plagues; and washes his bosome with teares.[115]

Thereafter he makes his own the cause of reform by purging his kingdom of its former corruptions:

what ever monuments were yet remaining of wicked Paganisme, he defaces with indignation, he burnes the vessels of *Baal*, and puts downe his *Chemarim*, destroyes the houses of the Sodomites, strawes the powder of their Idols in the brook *Kedron*, defiles *Topheth*, takes away the horses of the Sun, burnes the charets of the Sun with fire, and omits nothing that might reconcile God, cleare *Judah*, perfect a reformation.[116]

Not content with the cleansing of Jerusalem, he extends the work as far as Bethel, site of the altar of Jeroboam who dwelt in Egypt and led his people into idolatry—as so many were predicting of another prince in 1623. That altar was set up, as we have been informed in a particularly Machiavellian soliloquy, in the pursuance of political aims, and in despite of true religion:

he will be working out his owne ends by prophane policies ... Wicked men care not to make bold with God in cases of their owne commoditie: If the Lawes of their Maker lye in the way of their profit or promotion, they either spurne them out, or tread upon them at pleasure: Aspiring minds will know no God but honor.[117]

This altar King Josiah now destroys with the result that for the first time since the days of Samuel the Passover (traditionally the equivalent or 'type' of the Eucharist) is celebrated properly.

The message, or rather the intention, is clear. In 1626 Charles had escaped the coils of Spain. He had indeed married a Catholic bride but not the Infanta. The 'daughter of France' posed far less of a threat—or so it seemed at the time—and even the Puritans, judging from the output of the pamphlet-eering press, seemed relatively satisfied.[118] Moreover, the new anti-Spanish policies of the monarchy allowed Charles to pose as a 'Defender of the Faith' in good earnest. Give or take a few blemishes—and even Josiah was not perfect—the godly king had reappeared, and Hall's book is exactly what it declared itself to be in its dedication to that king: 'a miror of Princes . . . which God hath made for the faces of his Deputies on earth'. Yet in so far as circumstances may change again, the situation is still dangerous, and the alternatives remain the same. Jeroboam—or Samson or Solomon—is what Charles may well become. Josiah is the hope for the future, but his people still live under God's curse. In the biblical account they did not escape.

Part III

Homiletics: 'I have both censured and directed'

6.

THE SERMONS

Despite their almost total neglect at the hands of most of his critics, Hall's sermons remain essential to any study of his literary career.[1] So widely was he recognized by his contemporaries as one of the greatest and most influential preachers of the time, that when Abraham Wright set out in 1656 to demonstrate the five principal homiletic styles of the century, he chose those of Andrewes, Cartwright, the Presbyterians, the Independents, and Joseph Hall.[2] Today when Hall's sermons still remain central to any study of seventeenth-century homiletics, we can hardly dismiss them from an examination of his own work. Indeed of all the genres to which he turned his attention, he cultivated none so consistently as this. The forty-six extant sermons spanning almost his entire career as a minister allow us to follow the development of his style from his early years as an honoured court preacher to the last decade of his life spent in humble retirement at Higham.[3] As the duty of preaching was central to his concept of the priesthood, these sermons comprise an essential part of his religious and devotional writings. Throughout his career he assailed the 'dumb dogs' of the non-preaching ministry, 'those *Sigalion*-like statues, who taking up a room in Gods Church, sit there with their fingers upon their mouthes, making a trade of either wilful or lazy silence; smothering in their breasts the sins and dangers of Gods people'.[4] Though Hall may have pushed the *Virgidemiarum* aside, he never ceased to be a satirist. On the contrary, the sermons provided him with a new and, in his opinion, more suitable vehicle for the relentless condemnation of vice: his satires were banned, but his sermons were royally patronized. Yet as he was only too well aware, most of these sermons, being purely oral exercises, were destined for oblivion. Desiring 'a more publike and more enduring good', he both welcomed and encouraged the publication of the others.[5] He recognized too that the written word, though seldom as dramatic as the spoken, was nevertheless an equally important instrument of salvation affording greater leisure for private contemplation: 'The sound of the word spoken pierceth more; the letter written endureth longer: the eare is taught more suddenly, more stirringly; the eye with leisure and continuance. According to my poore abilitie, I have desired to doe good both wayes.'[6]

One further point. Although it is often difficult to ascertain the exact relationship between extant homiletic texts and the original spoken versions, in Hall's case they seem to have been extremely close for he never preached unprepared. 'Never durst I climbe into the Pulpit, to preach any Sermon', he tells us, 'whereof I had not before in my poor, and plain fashion, penned every word in the same Order, wherein I hoped to deliver it, although in the expression I listed not to be a slave to Syllables.'[7] The implication would seem to be that Hall's preliminary notes encapsulated not merely the entire 'order' of the sermon but a good deal else besides. Yet oral delivery also contributed much, and in preparing the sermons for the press every effort was made to recapture the inspiration of the impassioned moment. In the dedication to *An Holy Panegyricke* (1613), for example, Hall writes: 'I have caused my thoughts, so neere as I could, to goe backe to the very tearmes wherein I expressed them, as thinking it better to fetch those words I have let fall, than to follow those I must take up.'[8] As they have come down to us, the sermons are perhaps more accurate and polished than those heard in Whitehall or Exeter or Higham, but in other respects it seems fair to suppose that they differ very little.

I. Theory

According to St. Augustine, the foremost patristic authority on the art of homiletics, the purpose of preaching was entirely 'affective'. For him, it was the function of the preacher to drive the Christian message home so forcefully as to alter the course of his listeners' lives.[9] Yet in order to affect people emotionally and permanently, it was first necessary to work upon their reason, since an audience was more likely to surrender their feelings willingly to a speaker whose ideas they found intellectually satisfying. The art of the preacher was the art of divine persuasion, and with this formulation almost everyone, Puritan, Catholic, and Anglo-Catholic alike, was in general agreement. Upon the question of method, however, they differed violently. *How* was the audience to be persuaded? This in turn led to the vexed question of the relationship between homiletics, learning, and rhetoric: Exactly what sort of oration was a sermon? Was it bound by any laws other than theological? Was it proper to introduce into a discussion on the word of God the words and opinions of mere men—in many cases mere pagans? Was not the *Word* itself sufficient? Such problems were greatly exacerbated by the sharply conflicting preoccupations of the times: on the one hand it was an age of humanistic fervour deeply committed to the revival of scholarship, while on the other extreme theories of inspiration and grace tended to render all theological learning and scholarship redundant. As was usual in seventeenth-century controversies, answers were even more plentiful than problems. In the hands of opposing factions the sermon was reduced to either a confusing patchwork of classical and patristic allusion, or a dull exercise in cumbersome 'methods' eventually losing itself amid a welter of 'divisions' and 'subdivisions'. Attempts at reaching some form of compromise were frustrated by the failure to define adequately the terms at issue, or rather the key term, 'plain'.

Whereas all the Puritan preachers insisted repeatedly on the need to be 'plain', there was little agreement even among themselves as to what this actually meant. What it did not mean, however, is clear from their surviving works, for the cultivation of plainness by no means necessitated the rejection of imagery, sound effects, humour, or anecdote. On the contrary, the Puritan style has most accurately been described as 'an intensely imaginative hortatory prose' making full use of almost all the usual rhetorical devices with the possible exception of metaphor.[10] It is in the work of the Puritan preachers, for instance, that we can trace the growth and development of the tradition which finally culminated in the composition of *The Pilgrim's Progress*. Even 'Decalogue' Dod, one of the plainest and most methodical of them all, produced a prose 'intermixed with such variety of delightfull expressions and similitudes as would take with any man'.[11]

It is clear, therefore, that while the Puritans rejected the fivefold divisions of the Ciceronian oration and the elaborate periodic sentences which accompany them, they developed in their place a style remarkable for its richness of texture and emotional appeal. Yet such developments were by no means exclusively radical. Hall too was a noted 'anti-Ciceronian'. When addressing Convocation in 1624 in an extremely learned and allusive Latin sermon—and according to Dod 'so much Latin was so much flesh in a sermon'—he too declared his allegiance to the plain style: 'I speake plaine truth', he tells us, 'in a plaine fashion.'[12] His declaration, however, is itself an acknowledged borrowing from St. Bernard of Clairvaux, one of the favourite writers of the Anglo-Catholics. Furthermore, despite his undoubted respect for William Perkins, the chief Puritan authority on the 'plain' style, Hall, as we shall see, totally ignores Perkins's views on the proper relationship between scholarship and homiletics.

It is hardly surprising, in view of these apparent contradictions, that Hall's position has caused his critics a good deal of confusion. For Douglas Bush, for example, he is one of a small, awkward group of 'miscellaneous Anglicans', while W. F. Mitchell sets him among the 'other Anglicans' who remained apart from Andrewes, Laud, Donne, and the Anglo–Catholics.[13] M. W. Dewar goes even further when he frankly declares that Hall must have seemed a 'puzzle' to his contemporaries.[14] Yet this is so only when we attempt to ally him to either of the two allegedly 'major' parties, Radicals and Laudians, without taking into account the considerable body of episcopalian Calvinists with whom his sympathies undoubtedly lay. It is true, of course, that Hall was the product of an extremely 'Puritan' background. His first patron, the third Earl of Huntingdon, has become known to history as 'the Puritan Earl', and Emmanuel College was admittedly the centre of Cambridge Puritanism. But it is no less true that the term 'Puritan' is anything but precise, and is certainly not synonymous with either Presbyterian or Independent: Laud himself was only too well aware of the presence of 'Puritan' sympathizers on the episcopal bench. Yet Hall appears to have harboured few reservations about entering the Anglican ministry, for his was a pathway between extremes. While he attacked the anti-episcopal views of the Brownists, he opposed himself equally to the encroachments of Arminianism. In this he was at one with such notable Elizabethan churchmen as Bishop Jewel, whose sojourn in Zurich with Bullinger did not prevent his assumption of the rochet under Elizabeth. Archbishop Whitgift was also an episcopalian Calvinist, as was the unfortunate Archbishop Abbot, to whom Hall dedicated his first defence of the Anglican ministry, and whose homiletic style bears distinct resemblances to his own.[15] Style in fact was invariably dictated by theological outlook, and Hall's style is no exception. By no means anomalous, it gives a clear indication of his position in the Church. Having affinities with both Puritans and Anglo–Catholics, he was neither, nor could he adopt either style. His Senecanism bespeaks his religious stance, for even allowing for the distortion of generalizations, it remains true that it was among episcopalian Calvinists and moderate Puritans that the style enjoyed its greatest vogue.[16]

Hall's fundamental disagreement with Puritan theorists such as Perkins centres upon the introduction of allusion, quotation, and scholarship into the body of the sermon. Whereas this is quite characteristic of Hall's style, in *The Arte of Prophecying* Perkins is totally against it. Yet the two have more in common than at first appears. All differences of religious outlook notwithstanding, the educational background of most Jacobean divines was very similar, [17] and it is not learning but the *display* of learning to which Perkins is opposed:

If any man thinke that by this means barbarisme should be brought into pulpets; hee must understand that the Minister may, yea and must privately use at his libertie the arts, Philosophy, and variety of reading, whilest he is in framing his sermon: but he ought in publike to conceale all these from the people, and not to make the least ostentation. *Artis etiam est celare artem: it is also a point of Art to conceale Art.*[18]

'A point of *art* to conceal art': there lies the crux of the matter. A sermon by Perkins is no more 'artless' than a sermon by Hall, although it labours to appear so. Nor does it exclude borrowings; it simply fails to acknowledge them in an attempt to remain sympathetic to those who do not share the preacher's educational background. As William Haller puts it: 'The primary objection to metaphysical wit, learned allusions, tags of Greek and Latin, snatches from the heathen poets and philosophers, and all figures of speech depending upon recondite knowledge was that many members of the audience were sure to miss the point.'[19] Such an objection, however, can hardly be said to arise when the preacher is addressing the court of a king who is himself a classically educated writer and theologian. That a great many of Hall's sermons were written under just such conditions goes far to explain his choice of style. Indeed it was one of the ironies of the rigidly Puritan position that when divines such as John Preston refused to alter their style to suit the court, they violated one of their own strongest principles: that of careful attention to the nature of their audience.[20] Hall, on the other hand, *does* vary his style when addressing the less informed. His display of 'learning' is just as much of a rhetorical device as are the simple anecdotes of his later period which we shall shortly examine. The word for such learning, I would suggest, is neither 'ostentatious' nor 'obtrusive' but 'rich'. With the general conclusions of Perkins's treatise Hall would undoubtedly have agreed, yet in matters of detail they differed greatly, partly no doubt because Hall was a court preacher, but mostly because his interest in Perkins represented only one side of his outlook. With the school of Andrewes and the Anglo–Catholics he had connections which were not merely the result of attempted compromise, but sprang from his own fundamental convictions.

Theologically speaking, these divines were of the opinion that the Church of England was in fact 'Catholic'. It was not the Reformers who had departed from Rome, but Rome that had departed from itself. The Church Fathers, proscribed along with the classics by Perkins, could therefore be quoted profusely, since along with the Gospels they comprised the basis of the Catholic faith.[21] But this opinion, it will be remembered, is central to almost every work of controversy Hall wrote. He emphasizes his Catholicism just as strongly as do the Arminians:

What is it which maketh a Church? . . . Is it not one holy Catholicke Apostolick faith? But which is that? Is it not the same which was delivered by Christ, and the Apostles, to the whole world, and was alwaies and every where approved through all Ages, even unto our times? Wherefore are the Scriptures, wherefore the Creeds, wherefore were the primitive Councells, but that there might be certaine marks, whereby Catholicks might be undoubtedly discerned from Hereticks? . . . Did wee ever deny or make doubt of any Article, or clause of that Ancient Divinity? Either then Christ himselfe, the Apostles, Councels, Fathers, erred from the Catholick truth; or we yet remain Catholicks.[22]

It is hardly surprising, therefore, that Hall's sermons are rich in patristic allusion, or that Bernard of Clairvaux is one of his favourite authorities. Yet one could never mistake a sermon by Hall for one by Andrewes or Laud. The sermons of the Anglo–Catholics are more properly orations than those of their contemporaries, and the dominant influence upon their work would seem to have been Aristotle, via Bartholomaus Keckermann and the other Aristotelian theorists.[23] To compare Hall's *Passion Sermon* for example, with Andrewes's second sermon *Of the Passion* is to explore two wholly different religious experiences. Andrewes's sermon, despite its many divisions and subdivisions, falls more easily into the standard oratorical form than does that of Hall, and there are no digressive attacks on Rome (a feature of almost every one of Hall's sermons), no insistence upon the extraction of a specific 'doctrine' and 'use' from each individual phrase, and no series of *ad hominem* 'applications' designed to bring the text within the realm of what Hall understood by 'practical' divinity. In short, there is a greater homogeneity in Andrewes's sermon, for whereas he concentrates upon the *words* of the text and follows them closely, Hall concentrates upon the *issues* that arise from it. As a result, Hall's sermon divides more easily into a number of semi-autonomous sections. Hall's practice is best illustrated by his handling of the text of *The Righteous Mammon* (1618), 1 Timothy 6: 17:

I never held it safe to pull Scripture in peeces: these words fall alone into their parts. *Timothy* is set upon the spirituall Bench, and must give the charge. A charge, to whom? Of what? To whom? To the rich. Of what? what they must avoid, what they must indevour. What must they avoid? High-mindednesse and trust in wealth: what are the duties they must labor unto? Confidence in God; Beneficence to men: And every one of these is backed with a reason to inforce it: Why should they not be high-minded? Their wealth is but in this world ... Here is worke enough, you see, for my discourse, and your practice: The God of Heaven blesse it in both our hands.[24]

The contrast with Andrewes should not imply that Hall's sermons are in any sense disorganized, or that he is not equally endeavouring to paint a complete picture; he is, but it is a picture composed of several distinct panels. In Andrewes one senses that to some extent at least, the divisions are set up in order to collapse; in Hall they are far more enduring. Andrewes would never have written the *Passion Sermon* produced by Hall, but neither, of course, would John 'Decalogue' Dod, for Hall has no pre-arrangement, no mechanical checklist of headings against which the sermon must be examined to see if anything has been left out.[25] His divisions arise naturally from a consideration of the various 'meanings' of the text. As in the quotation above, he is at pains to demonstrate just how natural they are.[26] His style has features in common with both Puritans and Anglo–Catholics not because he was on both sides but because he was on neither. His was the independent position of episcopalian Calvinism, and his style, quite fittingly, is equally distinct.

II. Practice

Unlike those of the Anglo–Catholics, Hall's sermons seldom begin with long elaborate exordia, but plunge *in medias res* with some striking phrase designed to capture the attention immediately. 'Who knowes not that *Simon Peter* was a Fisher?' is a good example of this type of opening.[27] Hereupon two or three brief paragraphs lead almost invariably to a curt and clear division of the text supplying the various 'heads' of the homily, and the progress from this point onwards is logical and orderly. All the transitions from one heading to the next are clearly marked by a plain statement of the many subheadings and subdivisions with which the preacher is about to deal. Yet digression is frequent, usually in the form of moral complaints or exhortations addressed directly to the audience on some issue of pressing importance suggested by the main theme.

Over two-thirds of the sermons fall into either bipartite or tripartite divisions, perhaps reflecting on a larger scale Hall's tendency to construct his sentences in balancing 'pairs' or tricola. But regularity of structure is never purchased at the price of argumentative distortion. The message is the important thing and it alone dictates the number of divisions and subdivisions. While a high degree of patterning is detectable in such sermons as *The True Peace-Maker* (1624) or *The Public Fast Day Sermon* (5 April 1628), the most notable feature of Hall's method is his thoroughness, his determination to analyse every facet of his chosen theme. From this point of view the programme he sets before himself at the outset of *The Righteous Mammon* is typical of his usual practice and tone. Similarly the straightforward and precise layout of a sermon such as *Pharisaisme and Christianitie* may be taken as representative of the bulk of his work:

Text. Matthew 5: 20. 'Except your righteousnesse exceed the righteousnesse of the Scribes and Pharises, ye shall not enter into the Kyngdome of heaven.'

Opening. Three short paragraphs on the Law, the Jews, and Christ.

Division. 'What were the men? What was their righteousnesse? What wanted it? Follow me, I beseech you, in these three . . .'

1. *The men.* Discussion of the term 'pharisee'.
2. *Their righteousness.*
   1. Their devotion.
   2. Their holy carriage.
   3. Strict observance of the Law.
3. *Their unrighteousness.*
   1. Ridiculous traditions.
   2. Evil Practice.
      1. 'Hypocrisie': 'Fashionablenese'.
         'Ostentation'.
      2. 'Worldlinesse': 'Covetousnesse'.
         'Ambition'.

Exhortation. The righteousness of the audience must exceed
　　　the righteousness of the Pharisees.
(Throughout the sermon frequent digressions elaborate on
the subtheme: the relationship between the Pharisees and the
Roman Catholics.)[28]

Related to this concern for order and method is Hall's
insistence upon precise and meticulous definition. The structural order and clarity of his sermons is reflected also in their
language, and passages such as the following are therefore
frequent:

We speak of Justice first as a single vertue. Habits are distinguished
by their acts; acts by their objects. The object of all morall vertue is
good, as of all intellectuall, is True. The object of this vertue of
Justice is the good of men in relation to each other; Other vertues
order a man in regard to himselfe; Justice, in regard to another. This
good being either common, or private; common of all, private of
some; the acts and vertue of justice must be sutable; either, as man
stands in an habitude to the whole body, or as he stands to speciall
Limbs of the body: The former of these is that which Philosophers
and Casuists call a legall and universal Justice. The latter is that
particular Justice, which we use to distinguish by *Distribution* and
Commutation; the one consisting in matter of Commerce, the other in
Reward, or Punishment.[29]

Verbal analysis or philology is also common, but there is
nothing in the entire canon to compare with the great
'Immanuel' passage in Lancelot Andrewes—Hall never sought
such effects. His philology is solidly functional, not witty. He
has recourse to the Latin when the English is unclear, and to
the Hebrew when the Latin is unclear. The presentation of
such detail in the sermons themselves is intended both as a
compliment to the intelligence of the courtly or gentle listener,
and as a practical demonstration of one of the central aims of
homiletics: the correct expounding of the Scriptures through
learning and scholarship. Hall had as little sympathy as Donne
with the extreme sectarian ideal of an unlearned but inspired
ministry. As far as he was concerned, all arts, including
rhetoric, were subservient to divinity and ought therefore to
be employed in its cause.[30] While rhetoric and eloquence could
never become an end in themselves, they were nevertheless of
great importance in conveying the preacher's moral message.[31]

Their employment, however, was to be strictly controlled both by the requirements of the theme, and more important still, by the nature of the congregation. Indeed Hall's insistence upon the latter factor is one of the distinguishing features of his homiletic art. Although fully aware of the various criticisms levelled against the contemporary pulpit, and of the impossibility of suiting all tastes, he remains determined to address his listeners in their own terms, to present the Word of God in the manner most calculated to appeal to their particular worldly interests.[32] So it is, for example, that *The Righteous Mammon*, a sermon preached before the 'solemne assembly of the city' abounds in merchant imagery, while the elaborate heraldic lore of *The Imprese of God* is purposely designed to appeal to courtiers: 'What now is more fit for Courtiers to heare of, than an Imprese of honour.'[33] On the one occasion upon which Hall uses what is recognizably 'merchant' imagery at court, he defends his apparent breach of decorum by referring to the more liberal outlook of foreign aristocrats who often engaged in trade.[34] Again, when addressing the assembly of Gray's Inn in 1623 he establishes an immediate rapport with his audience by putting his message in familiar terms:

I know where I am; in one of the famous Phrontisteries of Law, and Justice: wherefore serves Law and Justice, but for the prevention or punishment of fraud and wickednesse? Give me leave therefore to bring before you, Students, Masters, Fathers, Oracles of Law and Justice, the greatest Cheator and Malefactor in the world, our owne Heart.[35]

The sermon is entitled *The Great Imposter*, and quite appropriately much of its imagery is drawn from the world (and vocabulary) of law and detection:

Call at the doore, and aske if such a one host not there; They within make strange of it, deny it, forsweare it; Call the officers, make privie search, you shall hardly find him: Like some Jesuite in a Popish dames chamber, hee is so closely contrived into false floores, and double walls, that his presence is not more easily knowne, than hardly convinced, confessed.[36]

Here, in the space of a few lines, is evoked a whole drama of villany, detection, pursuit, and concealment—a 'popish plot' within the heart.

But quite apart from this use of 'professional' imagery Hall
will often make direct appeal to his listeners' broader
experience by introducing his similes with such phrases as 'so
have we seen', 'have you seen?', 'we see', and so on, all highly
reminiscent of his *Occasional Meditations*.[37] He tells the
audience of *The Righteous Mammon* how some of them are
'like the Pageants of your great solemnities, wherein there is
the shew of a solid body, whether of a Lion, or Elephant, or
Unicorn: but if they be curiously lookt into, there is nothing
but cloth, and sticks, and ayre'.[38] Similarly we hear how the
will, 'Water-man-like lookes forward, and rowes backward'
while great men are likened to 'hailestones, that leape up on
the Tiles, and straight fall downe againe, and lye still, and melt
away'.[39]

This aspect of Hall's style is complemented by his considerable descriptive and narrative powers usually employed in the
presentation of some powerful image from public experience
calculated to produce a predictable emotional reaction. Such,
for example, is his excellent account of the plague which
captures so well not merely its dreadful physical effects but
also its even more terrifying psychological aspects:

What slaughter, what lamentation, what horror was there in the
streets of our mother City? More than twentie thousand families run
from their houses, as if those had beene on fire over their heads, and
seeke shelter in Zoar, and the mountaines. Some of them are overtaken by the pursuer, and droppe downe in the way, and lye there as
wofull spectacles of mortality, till necessity, and not charity, could
find them a grave: Others passe on, and for friends find strangers:
Danger made men wisely, and unwillingly unhospitall; The Cozen,
the Brother forgets his own blood; and the Father looks shiely upon
his own child, and welcomes him with frownes, if not with repulses;
There were that repaid their grudged harbour with infection; and
those that sped best; what with care for their abandoned houses, and
estate; what with griefe for the miserie of their forsaken neighbours,
what with the rage of those Epidemiall diseases, which they found
abroad, (as it is well observed by one, that in a contagious time all
sicknesses have some tincture of Pestilence) wore out their daies in
the deepest sorrow and heavinesse: there leave we them and returne
to the miserable *Metropolis* of this Kingdome, which they left. Who
can expresse the dolefull condition of that time and place. The armes
of London are the *Red Crosse,* and the *Sword;* what house almost

wanted these? Heere was the *Red Crosse* upon the doore, the Sword
of Gods judgement within doores, and the Motto was, *Lord have
mercy upon us.*[40]

This powerful evocation of an image both so horrific, and
so deeply ingrained in the minds of his listeners can hardly
have failed to produce its desired effect. All the terrors of the
recent crisis are here: the pervasive contagion, the distortion
of basic human emotions, the intense ugliness of the will to
survive, and brooding above them all, the remorseless,
vengeful God of the Old Testament. It is another Sodom and
Gomorrah, and the refugees fly like Lot to Zoar. By forcing
his listeners to relive the experiences of the recent plague
Hall hopes to channel their relief at its abatement into
Christian devotion. Having experienced God's anger they
must be grateful for his mercy. He is their only sure refuge. It
is interesting too that the ominous image with which the
passage ends, that of the red cross daubed upon the infected
doors, provided the subject for an occasional meditation
written apparently at the height of the pestilence.[41] Like the
blood sprinkled upon the doors of the Israelites many ages
before, it is one of God's less hidden emblems. The correspondence serves to remind us of the close connection
between the two genres, just as the intense concentration
upon the image of the cross in the sermon upon Galatians 2:
20 is directly equivalent to the methods of the short
meditations (particularly the later ones) we have previously
considered. Here it takes the form of a rigorous analysis of
the meaning of the image—indeed the sermon deals with
little else—followed by a thorough application of its various
aspects (such as one might find in a metaphysical poem) to
the spiritual requirements of the meditator:

In all these must we have our part with Christ; In the transverse of
his Crosse, by the ready extension of our hands to all good works of
piety, justice, charity. In the Arrectary, or beame of his Crosse, by
continuance, and uninterrupted perseverance in good; In the head of
his crosse, by an high–elevated hope, and looking for of glory; In the
foot of his crosse, by a lively and firme faith, fastening our soules
upon the affiance of his free grace, and mercy; And thus shall we be
crucified with Christ, upon his owne Crosse.[42]

Not surprisingly at this point, Hall acknowledges his indebtedness to St. Augustine, the first great patristic expounder of the meditative art.

Generally speaking Hall's homiletic prose style is of a strong, vibrant and 'plain' variety, at once both witty and concise:

The heart of man lies in a narrow roome, yet all the world cannot fill it; but that which may be said of the heart, would more than fill a world.
But if Truth be the mother of Hatred, shee is the daughter of Time, and Truth hath learn't this of Time, to devoure her owne brood.[43]

Such sentences are obviously influenced by the Senecan tendencies of Hall's early writings—the meditations in particular—yet they should not lead us to conclude that the prose of his sermons comprises a series of abrupt *sententiae* or quips. However distorted the modern concept of Senecanism may be, the seventeenth century recognized its flexibility. According to Fuller, one remembers, Hall 'was commonly called our *English Seneca,* for the purenesse; plainesse, and fulnesse of his style'.[44] It was not merely the clarity or simplicity but the 'fullness' of Hall's manner that made him a Senecan, for despite the brevity of many of his sentences his style is by no means disjointed or chopped. Passages such as the following, for instance, move with a clear, untrammelled orderliness:

Our life flyes hastily away, but many times our riches have longer wings, and out-fly it. It was a witty observation of *Basil,* that wealth roles along by a man, like as an heady streame glides by the bankes: Time will molder away the very banke it washeth, but the current stayes not for that, but speeds forward from one elbow of earth unto another: so doth our wealth, even while we stay, it is gone. In our penall lawes, there are more wayes to forfeit our goods, then our lives; On our high wayes, how many favourable theeves take the purse, and save life? And generally, our life is the tree, our wealth is the leaves, or fruit; the tree stands still, when the leaves are falne, the fruit beaten downe: Yea many a one is like the Pine-tree, which (they say) if his barke bee pulled off, lasts long, else it rots: so doth many a man live the longer for his losses: if therefore life and wealth strive whether is more uncertaine, wealth will sure carie it away. *Iob* was yesterday the richest man in the East; to day he is soo needy, that hee is gone into a proverbe, *As poore as Job: Belisarius* the great and famous Commander, to whom Rome owed her life twice at least, came to *Date obolum Belisario;* one halfe-peny to *Belisarius.*[45]

Here the initial sentences give a new twist to a well-worn theme, for the passage begins as if it were about to develop yet once more the age-old motif of the shortness of human life. Our expectations, however, are quickly overturned when a new point surprisingly develops the metaphor latent in the verb 'flies'—wealth is a swifter bird than life. This contention is immediately supported by the introduction of a suitably 'witty' patristic authority, and once again the point of the passage depends on the reversal of the highly standardized 'river of life' image: time 'moulders' the bank upon which the rich man stands, but he may well be a poor man by the time it crumbles. While the style of the passage is admittedly concise and brisk, the over-all movement is none the less controlled and taut. The ideas proceed in a clear consecutive line, even though the formal 'links' may sometimes be omitted. We hear in precise order what time does, what the current does, and what it all means: 'so doth our wealth, even while we stay, it is gone.' The insistent ring of the almost unbroken series of monosyllables presses the point home to advantage, as does the sudden shift in tense: 'while we stay' (continuous), 'it *is* gone' (immediate). From a purely informative point of view, of course, this whole second sentence tells us nothing that was not already plain from the first. It simply introduces the same basic thought in a new, more graphic way, yet this device of 'theme and variation' is itself an integral feature of the Senecan style producing much of the 'fullness' of which Fuller speaks. The framework of the argument may be logical, but it holds us imaginatively.

Continuing the note of pressing immediacy in the sudden declaration 'it is gone', reference is now made to the experience of the audience. Everyone present knows only too well how fleeting wealth can be, and in one short sentence, 'In our penall lawes ... On our high wayes', Hall embraces the entire spectrum of economic disaster, from ruin at the hands of the authorities to ruin at the hands of outlaws. The patterning of the clauses renders the theme insistent:

more wayes . . . forfeit goods . . . then our lives
many theeves . . . take the purse . . . and save life.

Whether the responsibility be ours or theirs the result is the
same. And now, after this brief excursion into public mores,
the general rule is summed up by the somewhat unusual
development of yet another archetypal image, that of the tree
of life. Clause patterning is again in evidence: first we learn the
significance of the tree, the leaves, and the fruit, then in the
same careful order we learn their fate. But at this point the
argument becomes suddenly more complex with the introduction of a completely new line of thought suggested by the
image of the tree—another example of the imaginative
progress of which I have spoken. It now transpires that the
stripping of the bark may be necessary to the tree's survival,
and the point of this observation is quickly made clear: 'so
doth many a man live the longer for his losses.' The argument
needs little further development: not only is wealth more
fleeting than life, but from a spiritual point of view it is often
necessary that this should be the case. All that is now required
is illustration, and this is swiftly supplied by two highly
apposite *exempla*, one biblical, the other classical. Upon these,
however, there is little need to linger, for Hall is addressing an
audience of merchants and tradesmen whose personal experience provides better 'illustration' than anything he might
devise: 'What do I instance? This is a point, wherein many of
you Citizens that are my Auditors this day, might rather reade
a lecture unto me . . . '.

I have examined this passage in some detail because it is
typical of Hall's homiletic style, and demonstrates all the most
characteristic features of his prose, with the exception of the
list, an example of which follows almost immediately as he
proceeds to jumble together all the probable instances of
sudden economic disaster which 'you could reckon up to me'.
If anything, the passage is somewhat restrained. Meticulous
clause patterning and word arrangement are even more
prevalent in other sermons. In fact there are hundreds of
examples of chiasmus, tricolon, antithesis, and balance
throughout the homilies. Witness, for instance, this carefully
structured passage from *Divine Light and Reflections* (1640):

The Earth yields us fruit, but it is onely perhaps once a year, and that not without much cost and angariation, requiring both our labour, and patience; The Clouds do sometimes drop fatnesse, but at great uncertainties; other whiles they pour down famine upon our heads; the Sea yields us commodities both of passage and sustenance, but not without inconstancy and delaies and oft-times takes more in an hour than it gives in an age; his favours are locall, his threats universall; But the Light is bountifull is bestowing it self freely with a clear, safe, unlimited largesse upon all Creatures at once, indifferently, incessantly, beneficially.[46]

This desire to achieve a patterned prose can be explained partly no doubt by the influence of Senecanism, but should also be evaluated in the light of two other formative factors, the first being the influence of the Authorized Version of the Bible. In a passage such as the following, for example, it is extremely difficult not to be reminded of the parable of the sower and his seeds:

Some passe by it [the truth], and doe not so much as cheapen it; Others cheapen it, but bid nothing; Others bid something, but under-foot; Others bid well, but stake it not; Others lastly stake downe, but revoke it. The first that passe by and cheapen it not, are carelesse unbeleevers . . . [47]

The second, and perhaps even more important point to remember is that Hall's written word is always attempting to recapture something of the force and power of the spoken voice. To give but one example, it is necessary to read the superb conclusion to *The Fashions of the World* aloud in order to appreciate the cumulative force of the repetitions and patterning:

The world makes a God of it selfe, and would be serving any God, but the true one; hate yee this cursed Idolatry, and say with *Ioshua, I, and my house will serve the Lord.*

The world would bee framing Religion to policy, and serving God in his owne formes, hate ye this will-worship, superstition, temporizing, and say with *David, I esteeme all thy precepts to be right, and all false waies I utterly abhorre, Psalm* 119.128.

The world cares not how it rends, and teares the sacred name of their Maker, with oathes and curses, and blasphemies: Oh hate yee this audacious prophannesse, yea, this profane divelisme, *and tremble at the dreadfull Maiesty of the name of the Lord our God, Micah* 5.4.

The world cares not how it sleights the ordinances of God, violates his daies, neglects his assemblies: Hate yee this common impiety. Say with the Psalmist, *Oh how sweet is thy Law, how amiable thy Tabernacles.*[48]

Here the force of the insistent repetitions serves to beat home the preacher's message. In clause upon clause the point is relentlessly hammered out: 'The world ... hate yee ... The world ... hate ye ... The world ... Oh hate yee ... The World ... Hate yee'. Nor is this the end; the passage continues in exactly the same manner for another four paragraphs. At the end of all eight there falls the same powerful emphasis upon the biblical word: 'say with *Ioshua* ... say with *David* ... Say with the Psalmist ... say ... How beautifull are the feet of them that preach the Gospell of peace'. It is an extreme example of verbal indoctrination. The sins of the world are rejected in a series of powerful, imprecatory tricola: 'will-worship, superstition, temporizing ... oathes and curses and blasphemies ... sleights the ordinances of God, violates his daies, neglects his assemblies'. The cacophonous sound effects reinforce the sense of revulsion: 'cursed Idolatry ... rends, and teares ... audacious profanenesse, yea, this profane divelisme'. The strong, uncompromising rhythms of the prose are attempting to stamp upon the minds of their hearers the equally uncompromising patterns of Christian thought.

Everywhere throughout the sermons we detect this same highly developed sense of control ordering, positioning, and arranging everything from the over-all structure of the sermons themselves to the syntactical shape of individual sentences. Yet it would be quite incorrect to imagine that Hall is always the precise, calculating logician. The sheer emotional force of his imagery argues otherwise, as does his considerable skill in modulating mood and tone in order to produce passages of great beauty such as the following:

In vain therefore shall we look for constancy upon earth; look how possible it is for a man that stands fortune-like, upon a round rolling stone in a smooth floor, to be steddy in his posture, so possible it is for us to be settled in an unchangeable condition, whiles we are upon this sphere of variablenesse. Can we think that the world shall move, and we stand still? Were the Sun the center of motion, and the earth whirled about in this vast circumference, could we make account of rest? And if in our own particular we could either stay our foot, or shift it at pleasure, notwithstanding that insensible rapture (as the Ant may creep the contrary way to the violent circumvolution of the wheel) yet we must necessarily be swayd with that universall swinge of mutability wherewith all creatures are carried forcibly about. The most lasting Kingdomes therefore have had their periods, and of the most setled government, Gods hand-writing upon the wall goes so farre as to say, *Mene, mene, thy dayes are numbred*. Oh the fickleness of this earthly glory and prosperity! Oh the glassy splendor of all humane greatnesse, crackt with a touch, with a fall broken![49]

Here once more we notice the concern with emblems, in this case the ancient emblem of Fortune standing upon her twirling globe with a possible recollection of the other 'round rolling stone upon a smooth floor' in the land of Variana which symbolized the notorious inconstancy of Lipsius and his like.[50] Emblems, of course, are intended to suggest universal truths, but here the inevitability of the conclusions is further reinforced by the patterning of the clauses: 'look how possible it is ... so possible it is'. Concessions are made only to be snatched away more forcibly: 'Were the Sun the center ... could we make account of rest? And if in our own particular ... yet we must necessarily be swayd ...' As clause is balanced against clause, all avenues of escape are effectively closed. Simultaneously the futility of the very attempt at escape is underlined by the sobering imagery: an ant creeping in the wrong direction on a violently revolving wheel, and the 'cracking' of the world's 'glassy' splendour. In the last line the careful modulation of the more strict *schemata* allows the passage to conclude poignantly on what is obviously a key term, 'broken': '*cprakt* with a touch' but 'with a fall *broken*'. The tone is far less severe and less obviously dogmatic than that of *The Fashions of the World*. Here we are invited to examine the evidence and conclude for ourselves, although of course, given the terms of reference there can be but one conclusion. It is a more subtle and imaginative form of persuasion and one well suited to the court in which it was delivered: 'The most lasting Kingdomes therefore have had their periods ...'.

As I have previously suggested, this attempt to cultivate a

courtly or gentle manner lies behind much of Hall's homiletic style, and not least his introduction of the quotations and allusions so hated by the Puritans. The heavy emphasis on mythological themes in *The Estate of a Christian,* (preached at Gray's Inn, 1626?), for example, is doubly functional.[51] In the first place it is directly in keeping with the text, 'be ye changed (or transformed) by the renewing of your minds' (Romans 12:2), which provides a splendid opportunity for a witty reversal of the Ovidian metamorphoses. Secondly in centring upon Ovid it focuses upon an author intimately related to contemporary popular literature, and one with whom everyone present could be expected to be well acquainted. In this manner, while immensely enriching his own work with so many colourful and interesting classical allusions, Hall is also exploiting the purely secular literary experience of his listeners in order to win assent for his spiritual message. The stories of Ovid were merely fables, but he will tell of truly miraculous changes, of animals changed into men. Even in his oration before the Synod of Dort he cites not only Suetonius and other 'serious' Latin authors, but Plautus and Terence as well.[52] In his own defence he was quick to point out elsewhere that St. Paul had quoted from the works of Menander.[53]

The range of Hall's quotation and allusion (the former always given first in the original and then immediately afterward in translation) reflecting the extent of his reading, is extremely wide, and goes far beyond the classics and Church Fathers, sources which in themselves provide abundant material for independent study.[54] The reader of the second part of *Saint Paul's Combat* (1627?), for example, encounters a fascinating account of ancient British chivalry drawn from the 'History of Ingulphus'.[55] *The Mischiefe of Faction* (1641) embraces a long account of the miseries of civil war illustrated with reference to the Guelphs and Ghibellines, the Albigensians, the Great Schism, the Barons' Wars, the Wars of the Roses, and the Gunpowder Plot.[56] Similarly *The True Peace-Maker* (1624) introduces us to the opinions of such worthies as St. Louis of France and Queen Isabel of Spain.[57] But perhaps most interesting of all for the light which they shed on the continuity of Hall's literary interests, are the constant allusions to the literature of discovery and travel which provide some of his sermons' most exotic and fascinating anecdotes.[58] Such diverse and wide-ranging allusion immeasurably enriches the texture of Hall's prose, and even if, upon occasion, an over-elaborate list or series of *exempla* remind us too obviously of the commonplace-books from which they derive, the general effect is highly successful, and very much in keeping with the less radical tastes of the age. It was not without good reason that Hall's sermons found early acceptance in the court of Prince Henry, and that he was so widely praised for his skill in public address.

Not all of Hall's extant sermons, however, were preached at court or before cultivated audiences in London. Fortunately some later examples have also survived and these furnish striking evidence of his concern for the composition of his congregation. Ironically it may well be that such simple works delivered during his retirement at Higham (1644–56) afforded him greater personal satisfaction than the splendid rhetorical productions of earlier years. Expounding the basic tenets of Christianity in plain straightforward terms to ordinary people, in other words the work of catechizing, had long been one of his major concerns: Not without good cause did Thomas Fuller, one of his successors at Waltham, pay generous tribute to the impact of his efforts upon the local inhabitants.[59] In his preface to *The Olde Religion* (1625) Hall himself emphasizes the importance of such pastoral duties revealing as he does so a very telling sense of dissatisfaction with some of his own homilies. 'There is no one thing, whereof I repent so much', he writes,

as not to have bestowed more houres in this publicke Exercise of Catechisme; In regard whereof, I could quarrell my very Sermons, [sic] and wish that a great part of them had beene exchanged for this Preaching conference: Those other Divine discourses enrich the braine and the tong; this settles the heart; those other are but the descants to this plainsong.[60]

Not only do the themes of these late sermons revert to the more basic issues of predestination, election, and personal devotion, but their style also becomes simpler and more relaxed:

I remember our witty Countryman *Bromiard*, tels us of a Lord in his time that had a fool in his house (as many great men in those dayes had for their pleasure) to whom this Lord gave a staffe and charged him to keep it till he should meet with one that were more fool then himself; and if he met with such a one, to deliver it over to him.

Not many years after this Lord fell sick, and indeed was sick unto death: His fool came to see him, and was told by his sick Lord that he must now shortly leave him; And whither wilt thou go said the fool? Into another World said his Lord; and when wilt thou come again; within a moneth? No; within a year? No: when then? Never. Never? and what provision hast thou made for thy intertainment there whither thou goest? None at all: No, said the fool, none at all? Here, take my staffe; Art thou going away for ever, and hast taken no order nor care how thou shalt speed in that other World whence thou shalt never return? take my staffe, for I am not guilty of any such folly as this.[61]

The tone quite obviously has changed, and the speaker now presents himself less as the witty man of letters than the wise old village parson, the aged mentor of the *Balme of Gilead* (1646). His anecdotes have a new 'once upon a time' flavour, and he is far more willing to indulge in personal reminiscence. Indeed there is a singularly poignant intimacy about his allusions to his great age and approaching death:

It is a true observation of *Seneca, Velocitas temporis,* (saith he) the quick speed of time is best discerned when we look at it past, and gone, and this I can confirm to you by experience. It hath pleased the providence of my God so to contrive it, that this day, this very morning fourscore years ago I was born into the World: a great time since, ye are ready to say; and so indeed it seems to you that look at it forward, but to me that look at it as past, it seems so short that it is gone like a tale that is told, or a dream by night, and looks but like yesterday.[62]

In these sermons there are far fewer classical allusions than ever before, and those that do appear tend to be of a simpler variety, such as references to Ulysses, Ithaca, and so on. But the Latin, Greek, and Hebrew tags remain, and surprisingly enough remain without any real inconsistency, for it was one of the great ironies of the century that in certain circles at least, such scholarship tended to be in demand even among those who were quite incapable of understanding it.[63] The appearance therefore of a certain amount of 'learning' in Hall's Higham sermons can be explained partly by the popular objection to clerical condescension, and partly by his own commitment to the ideal of an *obviously* scholarly ministry. It was not sufficient that the laity should respect their pastors as fellow cobblers or carters who happened to be 'inspired', but as men whose education and study singled them out from the rest and lent an added importance to their opinions.[64] Hall's conception of Church organization was fundamentally hierarchical, and his style, even in his last sermons, reflects this outlook.

III. Meditation and Satire in the Sermons

Logicality of argument and clarity of spiritual direction are the hallmarks of Hall's sermons. Their structure is wholly subordinate to their relentlessly didactic and 'practical' function. There is no room for either hesitancy or ambiguity. They are works of which his own 'wise man' would have thoroughly approved: 'in materiall and weighty points he abides not his mind suspended in uncertainties; but hates doubting, where he may, where he should be resolute.' Precision of language is set off by a scrupulous precision of order and arrangement designed to present both 'doctrines' and 'uses' in the most clear and forthright manner possible. The implicit assumption behind such a method can only be that human reason functions as a major agent in the process of salvation. Many of Hall's contemporaries, however, while by no means rejecting reason, approached the problem in a different manner. A sermon such as Donne's *Death's Duell*, for example, would seem to demonstrate the weakness of human reason rather than its strength. Its emphasis falls on the importance of vision and irrational faith—faith against all the logical odds. Contrasting Donne's methods with those of contemporary Puritan preachers, Stanley Fish has concluded that,

the Puritan sermon is not self-consuming, but self-sufficient, in two directions. Its forms are sufficient to its pretensions—they open and make plain the points of Scripture—and its auditors are sufficient unto the occasion—they are able to understand that which is made plain. In its unfolding the sermon promises not only that you *shall* know the truth, but that you *can* know the truth, and it keeps both promises.[66]

Much of this is directly applicable to Hall, and goes far towards explaining the sense of completeness and sound good sense that we experience both in his sermons and his devotional treatises. Even later in his career, when his outlook became more other-wordly and 'mystical', his 'eye of reason' continued to complement his 'eye of faith', and there was little tension between his still powerful logic and his beliefs. Rational criteria were simply adopted or suspended at will in accordance with the needs of the argument. Yet despite the pertinence of Mr Fish's remarks, Hall as we have seen, had much in common with the Anglo-Catholics also, and was indebted to the same authorities.

The foremost influence on Donne's homiletics was undoubtedly St. Augustine, but Mr Fish believes that the vital Augustinian text, the fourth book of *De Doctrina Christiana,* was itself what he would term a 'self–consuming artifact'. That is to say it is a work which is, 'continually pointing away from itself, calling attention to what it is not doing . . . proclaiming not only its own insufficiency, but the insufficiency of the frame of reference from which it issues, the human frame of reference its hearers inhabit'.[67] Yet Hall no less than Augustine or Donne is a writer of vision, a writer capable of losing himself in an 'O altitudo'.[68] But his approach to the mysteries of Christianity is different. He works through reason not despite it. Whereas in *Death's Duell* the message seems to emerge at the expense of the structure—and certainly at the expense of rationality—in a sermon by Hall the structure itself becomes part of the message, its order and precision being designed to reflect the order and precision of the disciplined Christian mind. The method is that of enlightened reason, and enlightened reason is the exclusive privilege of the elect. Nevertheless, Augustine remained as important to Hall as he was to Donne or Lancelot Andrewes.

The matter is not really as perplexing as might at first

appear. What is essential to realize is that almost every shade of theological opinion found something in the *De Doctrina* to serve its own particular purposes. As the work contains one of the best appreciations of the Pauline style that has ever been written, it could of course be interpreted as a strong argument in favour of homiletic eloquence, as an encouragement to the most flamboyant of the Anglo-Catholics.[69] On the other hand its insistence upon the need for perspicacity and clarity could be taken as an argument in support of methodical arrangement, precise definitions, and tightly controlled structure.[70] It was presumably in this capacity that the work appears at the end of *The Arte of Prophecying* in the list of Perkins's major sources.[71] Hall's emphasis upon emotion and mystery is just as strong as that of Augustine, but he chose to express the emotion and approach the mystery within a controlled, methodical framework. Such a practice, of course, was in complete harmony with his general religious outlook. As we have seen, *The Arte of Divine Meditation* is carefully structured to facilitate the movement from reason to emotion, from this world to the next, and the same basic pattern pervades almost all of Hall's other devotional works. His tastes in this area are probably to be traced to his logical and rhetorical training in Emmanuel College, one of the principal centres under the mastership of Chaderton for the dissemination of the new approach to both of these subjects. Ramus, one remembers, was a Protestant martyr, and Talon frequently applied his rhetorical theories to homiletics.[72] Another, and perhaps even more potent factor was the Protestant conception of sin as a fundamentally irrational lapse from the guidance of enlightened reason, the faculty whereby the elect were enabled to perceive and seek their ultimate good: the centre of Terra Australis is Pazzivilla, the City of Fools, the inhabitants of which have blinded 'the right eye of their understanding'.[73] Properly interpreted, the prevalence of sin indicates a serious intellectual perversion that can be rectified only by the employment of enlightened reason on the part of the godly. Hence the emphasis on logic, order, and method, and the insistence that doctrine and exhortation (reason and emotion, respectively) are of equal importance:

Those that are all in exhortation, no whit in doctrine, are like to
them that snuffe the candle, but powre not in oyle. Againe, those
that are all in doctrine, nothing in exhortation, drowne the wike in
oyle, but light it not; making it fit for use, if it had fire put to it; but
as it is, rather capable of good, than profitable in present. Doctrine,
without exhortation, makes men all braine, no heart. Exhortation,
without doctrine, makes the heart full, leaves the braine emptie.
Both together make a man: One makes a man wise; the other good.
One serves that we may know our duty; the other, that we may
performe it. I will labour in both: but I know not in whether more.
Men cannot practise, unlesse they know; and they know in vaine, if
they practise not.[74]

Although this passage might well stand as an epigraph to
the collected sermons, it is taken from the *Meditations and
Vowes*. This need occasion little surprise once we remember
that the 'extemporal' meditations, no less than the more
elaborate 'deliberate' ones, are planned along exactly the same
lines as are the homilies. They were all intended to 'reduce
Christianity to practice' by moving from rational understanding, through emotion, to action. Hence their similarity in
structure and method.[75]

Examination of Hall's meditative prose has already demonstrated that the later meditations are actually 'soliloquies' in
which the speaker preaches to himself, as Baxter agreed he
should, much in the way in which a minister was expected to
'apply' his doctrines to the particular circumstances of any
given audience.[76] For Hall, preaching and meditation were
inextricably linked, and the art of the homily no less than that
of divine meditation necessitated the employment of both
reason and emotion. The result is that he is always 'logical',
but seldom cold. His intentions are just as 'affective' as
Donne's although his methods are dissimilar, and his emphasis
upon Augustinian emotion is equally strong although the
effects it produces are usually quite different:

I remember holy *Augustine* speaking of his own Sermons, saith, that
when he saw the people did show contentment and delight in their
countenances, and seemed to give applauses to his preaching, he was
not satisfied with his own pains, but when he saw them break forth
into tears, then he rejoyced, as thinking his labours had sorted to
their due effect.[77]

Donne would undoubtedly have agreed, yet he moves his listeners to a different kind of a grief, perhaps in one sense a more intimate one, exploiting the personal histories of Jack and Doctor Donne, pushing his own personality vividly to the fore. There is none of this in Hall; his tears are of a different nature:

Let others celebrate St. *Peters* tears; I am for St. *Pauls;* both were precious, but these yet more; Those were the tears of penitence, these of charity; those of a sinner, these of an Apostle; those for his own sins, these for other mens... Oh blessed tears, the juice of a charitable sorrow, of an holy zeal, a gracious compassion.[78]

Hall's tears are not personal but righteous, the tears of a prophet bewailing the sins of his people. But 'prophets' must describe the sins they lament, and as a satirist Hall was very well equipped to do so. When he says that his sermons offer 'plain truth in a plain fashion' he is alluding to their content as well as their style. His 'rational' attacks on vice invariably involve its exposure as madness and folly in terms reminiscent of the *Virgidemiarum,* and throughout his career his homiletic voice tends frequently to blend with that of Jeremiah or one of the other great denouncing prophets of the *Old Testament.* As Thomas Drant had pointed out, they too were satirists: 'Complaints, I know, are unpleasing, how ever just; but now, not more unpleasing, than necessarie; *Woe is mee, my mother, that thou hast borne mee a man of contention. I must cry out in this sad day, of the sins of my people.'*[79]

This tendency is perhaps not surprising in view of Hall's interest in typology, his habit of identifying the 'chosen people' of England with the chosen people of Israel, and of seeking out correspondences between contemporary happenings and scriptural events, but it was undoubtedly strengthened by his eminent public position and connection with the court. The last quotation comes from a highly important public sermon delivered on 5 April 1628. The text was the ominous passage 'What could have beene done to my Vineyard that I have not done in it? Wherefore when I looked that it should bring forth grapes, brought it forth wilde grapes? And now goe to, I will tell you what I will doe to my Vineyard; I will take away the hedge thereof' (Isaiah 5: 4–5); the place of delivery was 'the High Court of Parliament'; and the occasion was the public fast called by Charles I in an attempt to appease the divine anger to which he attributed the disastrous failure of his foreign policy. In such circumstances it was easy for Hall to assume the mantle of the prophet. As his advice to other preachers bears witness, 'hellfire and brimstone' came easily to a man of his temperament:

And ye, my holy brethren, the messengers of God, if there be any sons of Thunder amongst you, if ever you ratled from heaven the terrible judgements of God against sinners, now do it; for (contrary to the naturall) the deep winter of iniquity is most seasonable for this spirituall thunder. Be heard above, be seene beneath. Out-face sin, out-preach it, out-live it.[80]

The transition from formal verse satirist to inspired 'son of Thunder' was an easy one. The satirist had to fight for his place in the turbulent literary scene of the 1590s. He was attacked, ridiculed, and finally banned. But the preacher had an acknowledged right to speak. His complaints were licensed, his platform erected by royal authority, and his audience, to some extent at least, captive. Something of the tone of Hall's homiletic satire may be surmised from his disapproval of 'merry' preachers:

I have heard some preachers that have affected a pleasantness of discourse in their Sermons, and never think they have done well, but when they see their hearers smile at their expressions; But here, I have said of laughter, thou art mad, and of mirth what doest thou? Surely jiggs at a Funeral, and laughter at a Sermon, are things prodigiously unseasonable: It will be long (my beloved) ere a merry preacher shall bring you to Heaven.[81]

Despite this, however, Hall's own sermons are enlivened by a sharp satiric wit which *does* allow laughter of a sort, if only, as in the *Characters*, 'laughter of disdaine'. The difference between a preacher such as Thomas Adams, who introduced full 'characters' into his sermons, and Hall, is that Hall's humour is seldom, if ever, indulgent.[82] In *The Righteous Mammon*, for example, he introduces a splendid *prosopopoeia* passage (undoubtedly modelled on a famous section of Cicero's *Pro Caelio*) in which 'one of our forefathers' returns to assail female vanity.[83] Should such a personage see 'one of these his gay daughters walke in Cheape-side before him; what doe you thinke he would thinke it were?':

Here is nothing to be seene but a verdingale, a yellow ruffe, and a periwig, with perhaps some fethers waving in the top; three things for which he could not tell how to find a name: Sure, he could not but stand amazed, to thinke what new creature the times had yeelded since he was a man: and if then he should run before her, to see if by the fore-side he might ghesse what it were, when his eyes should meet with a poudred frizle, a painted hide shadowed with a fan not more painted, brests displayd, and a loose locke erring wantonly over her shoulders, betwixt a painted cloth and skinne; how would he yet more blesse himself to thinke, what mixture in nature could be guilty of such a monster? Is this (thinks he) the flesh and blood? is this the hayre? is this the shape of a woman? or hath nature repented of her worke since my dayes, and begunne a new frame?[84]

Understandably the passage became quite celebrated. The Smectymnuans quoted it in their attack upon the supposedly anonymous 'Remonstrant', but unlike them we must not take it out of context. Almost immediately it is abruptly qualified, in the manner of the satires, by rigorous moral denunciation:

Let me therefore say to these dames, as *Benet* said to *Totilaes servant, Depone, filia, quod portas, quia non est tuum;* Lay downe that ye weare, it is none of your owne...But if none of our perswasions can prevaile, Heare this, ye garish Popingayes of our time, if you will not bee ashamed to cloath your selves in this shamelesse fashion, God shall cloath you with shame and confusion: heare this yee plaister-faced *Iezabels*, if you will not leave your dawbing, and your high washes, God will one day wash them off with fire and brimstone.

This movement is typical of the sermons as a whole, and another excellent example occurs in *Christian Liberty* (1628), where a sinner boldly expounds his worldly philosophy only to be greeted by an outburst of righteous indignation reminiscent of that produced by the opinions of the wealthy but ignorant squire in the *Virgidemiarum*.[85] Similarly the elaborate lists of vice and folly so common in the later satires are also used to great effect throughout the sermons where we encounter truly panoramic depictions of all sorts of moral evil.[86] Juvenal and the Old Testament prophets have much in common.

The chief target of satiric attention in the homilies is

undoubtedly Rome. In striking contrast to the works of
Andrewes and Laud, there is scarcely a sermon of Hall's which
does not, at some point, launch a vigorous attack on Popery
but this was the result of skilful policy not obsession. It was
Hall's hope that the broken ranks of Protestantism would
eventually close against the common enemy. Opposition to
Rome was the one issue upon which everyone was agreed, or
so it seemed for a time. During the period of Laud's
ascendancy, however, it became increasingly difficult to
maintain anything that even resembled a united front, and it is
no coincidence that for the five years between 1634 and 1640
Hall received no invitation to preach before his king.[87]
Generally speaking, however, the theme was surprisingly
serviceable. In the *Exeter Burial Sermon*, for example, it is even
pressed into action against those who oppose the opening of a
new cemetery thereby enabling the bishop to have his own
way in diocesan affairs.[88]

Explicit attacks upon the Papacy are launched in such
sermons as *The True Peace-Maker, Noah's Dove*, and *Christ and
Caesar*, but perhaps the most effective blows are the more
subtle ones.[89] *Pharisaisme and Christianity* (1608), for example, begins with an apparently straightforward discussion of
the Pharisees themselves, but after a series of implied and
suggested similarities, it comes as no great surprise to learn
that they were really 'Cappucine-like', or to be told that their
emphasis upon ecclesiastical law and tradition has been
exceeded only by the Papists.[90] In the third section of the same
sermon the unfortunate remark of the Jesuit Fr. Serarius to
the effect that 'the Pharises may not unfitly be compared to
our Catholikes' is turned to full advantage by the clever
marshalling in its support of all the previously noted
correspondences and similarities.[91] This sort of approach won
widespread acclaim, enlivened as it was by such witty
observations as that the Pope was '*Peters* successor in nothing,
but in denying his Master'.[92] Best of all, however, were the
reductio ad absurdum passages which followed the mazes of
Jesuit thought to their 'logical' conclusions. Their own
commentaries unwittingly provided an unfailing source of
satiric material and were scourged quite remorselessly: '*Ergo
adeo stolidi opifices ab se fabrefieri Deos credunt*, saith our Jesuite

Lorinus of these *Ephesians; These so foolish workemen think they can make their Gods;* And why not of Gold as well as of Graine; why not the Smith as well as the Baker? Change but the name; the absurdity is but one.'[93]

Similarly had the text of *The Imprese of God* ('in that day shall be written upon the bridles of the Horses, Holinesse unto the Lord', Zachariah 14:20), actually read 'bels' for 'bridles' as had once been suggested, how the Jesuits would have rejoiced:

What comparisons would have beene; If *Holinesse to the Lord* must be written on the Bells of Horses, much more on the Bells of Churches. What a colour would this have beene for the washing, anointing, blessing, christening of them? What a warrant for driving away Devils, chasing of ghosts, stilling of tempests, staying of thunders, yea delivering from Tentations, which the Pontificall ascribes to them?[94]

But in this case the devotees of Trent have been hoist with their own petard, for the Vulgate—according to Rome the only authoritative source—'bridles them'. We have returned yet again to the *Virgidemiarum.* Could Juvenal but return what a world of matter would he find:

> When once I thinke if carping *Aquines* spright
> To see now Rome, were licenc'd to the light;
> How his enraged Ghost would stampe and stare
> That *Caesars* throne is turn'd to *Peters* chayre.[95]

In these sermons Hall is indeed a 'man of contention' crying out 'in this sad day, of the sins of my people', but he is more than just this. He aspires to both 'censure and direct'. As a result, satire alone cannot sustain his homiletic works, they are equally indebted to the practice of divine meditation and to this influence I now wish to return my attention.

Hall himself explains the relationship between homiletics and meditation most clearly in *The Devout Soul* (1644), where he counsels the reader to meditate privately before coming to church in order to prepare himself spiritually for the experience that lies ahead. 'Our eye', he writes, 'is our best guide to God our Creator, but our ear is it that leads us to God our Redeemer . . . Our meditation first, sequesters the heart from the world, and shakes off those distractive thoughts,

which may carry us away from these better things.'[96] Among
the qualities expected of a devout man's behaviour during
service is 'application', a virtue which concerns his attitude
towards the sermon. The very term is extremely suggestive
since it also denotes the process whereby moral lessons are
derived from the natural universe in the *Occasional Meditations*. Essentially it has the same meaning here, for the listener
is expected to 'apply' each thought, as it falls from the lips of
the preacher, to his own spiritual condition, very much in the
manner to which a reading of the *Meditations and Vowes* might
have accustomed him. He is described as bringing all he hears,

home to his heart, by a self-reflecting application; like a practiser of
the art of memory, referring every thing to its proper place ... Thus
in all the variety of the holy passages of the Sermon, the devout
minde is taken up with digesting what it hears; and working it self to
a secret improvement of all the good counsell that is delivered.

All of this, both in tone and vocabulary, is familiar from a
study of the meditations; merely substitute 'sees' for 'hears'
throughout, and the passage could well stand as a preface to
the *Holy Observations*.

Hall intended his sermons to have the effect of an
immediate and spontaneous religious experience, like impassioned prayer or occasional meditation. Because of this, even
though his sermons employ the methods of discursive reason-
ing quite freely, he opposed himself to the common contemporary habit of note-taking since this was destructive of the
immediate emotional effect:

neither can the braine get so much hereby, as the heart loseth. If it be
said, that by this means, an opportunity is given for a full rumination
of wholesome Doctrines afterwards: I yeeld it, but withall, I must say
that our after-thoughts can never doe the work so effectually, as
when the lively voice sounds in our ears, and beats upon our heart.[98]

Convictions not notes were to be the reward of the listener.
What was required of him was not an agility at shorthand, but
a willing surrender to the emotional experience of the
moment. His 'memory' of the sermon would be its enduring
effect upon his way of life.

Although a relatively late work, *The Devout Soul* adds

nothing new to Hall's theory of homiletics. It simply
comments upon the practice of the past forty years. An
insistence upon meditation runs throughout his entire homiletic canon. The text of *The Righteous Mammon* (1618), for
example, is so profound that 'every word would require not a
severall houre, but a life to meditate of it.' It is therefore
reduced to a few principal 'heads'. 'It shall content us onely to
top these sheaves, since wee cannot stand to thresh them out.'[99]
The Great Imposter (1623) advises us that 'it were now time for
our thoughts to dwell a little upon the meditation, and
deploration of our owne danger and misery, who are every way
so invironed with subtilty.'[100] It then proceeds with that
meditation. Introducing one of Hall's most horrific accounts of
Hell, *The Hypocrite* (1629) suggests that sermons must
compensate for the lack of private contemplation for 'the way
not to feele an Hell, is to see it, to feare it. I feare we are all
generally defective this way; we doe not retyre our selves
enough into the Chamber of Meditation, and thinke sadly of
the things of another world.'[101] One remembers that Ignatius
of Loyola made a similar point in the first 'week' of the
Spiritual Exercises.[102] Some years later the *Exeter Burial Sermon*
(1637) offered another 'two heads of meditation': Abraham's
purchase of a burial place for Sarah, and his employment of
that purchase.[103] The *Easter Sermon* of 1648 opens with a long
consideration of the biblical imagery of leaven as applied to
sin—itself highly reminiscent of the similar meditations which
appeared that same year in the *Select Thoughts*—before moving
on to the more complex issues arising from the text:

Thus long have we necessarily dwelt upon the inference, and
contexture of this scripture, we now come to scan this divine
proposition as it stands alone in it self: wherein our meditation hath
four heads to passe thorough: 1. That Christ is a passover: 2. Our
Passover. 3. Our Passover sacrificed. 4. sacrificed for us.[104]

On this occasion, however, Hall ran out of time, and finding
his hour passed he contented himself with setting out the
'plan' of the remaining meditations for the benefit of anyone
who might wish to continue it privately:

Two particulars follow yet more in the manner; then the persons
allowed to this banquet, no uncircumcised might eat thereof: Then

in the next place we should descend to the second head of our discourse that Christ is our Passover. Then that he is our Passover sacrificed; and sacrificed for us. Ye see what a World of matter yet remains and offers it self as in a thronge to our meditations.[105]

The Mourner in Sion (1654?) opens with an appreciation of the meditative wisdom of Solomon whose 'observation was Universal of times, things, persons, actions, events: neither did he lock his experiments up in the closet of his own brest'. Its theme, the need for private mourning in a time of divine retribution, is handled after the meditative manner since the grief springs from a consideration of our sins, dangers, and punishments, and we are reminded how preferable it is 'for a man to have his heart kept in order by the meditation of death, then to run wild after worldly vanity'.[106] Similarly *Life a Sojourning* (1655), one of Hall's latest sermons, invites us to 'meditate upon the modification of this passage of our time'.[107]

In view of this insistence upon the sermon as a form of divine meditation it is hardly surprising that meditative techniques reminiscent both of the short meditations and the *Contemplations* are in evidence everywhere throughout Hall's homiletic canon. A passage such as the following, for example, might well be taken straight from Bonaventure:

As Christ therefore on his Crosse lookt towards us sinners of the Gentiles; so let us look up to him; Let our eyes be lift up to this brazen Serpent, for the cure of the deadly stings of that old serpent: See him, O all yee beholders; see him hanging upon the tree of shame, of curse, to rescue you from curse, and confusion, and to feoffe you in everlasting blessednesse: see him stretching out his armes to receive and embrace you; hanging downe his head to take view of your misery, opening his precious side to receive you into his bosome, opening his very heart to take you in thither, pouring out thence water to wash you, and blood to redeeme you . . . But this, though the summe of the Gospel, is not the main drift of my Text: I may not dwell in it, though I am loath to part with so sweet a meditation.[108]

It may perhaps be argued that Hall could have found elements such as these in the native homiletic tradition quite independently of the new vogue of meditation, and to some extent, of course, this is true. But as the author of *The Arte of*

Divine Meditation and one of the acknowledged leaders in this devotional field, Hall was surely in a position to be far more conscious of the affinities between the two genres than most other preachers. He would also remember that the greatest patristic and medieval meditators, St. Augustine and St. Bernard, were equally celebrated for their sermons. As well as this, as the last quotation demonstrates, he infused consciously meditative passages into his sermons even when the rigid exposition of the text did not strictly require them. He is 'loath to part with so sweet a meditation' although the sermon demands that he move on. Such 'meditative' elements as he found to hand in the homiletic genre he used to advantage—indeed the pre-established suitability of the sermon for this type of writing goes far to explain his success—yet there remain several distinct marks of meditative influence which cannot be explained without reference to the new genre. In *The Farewell Sermon* (1613), for example, we ascend in six stages from grief at the death of Prince Henry to the joy of Christian consolation:

My speech therefore shall as it were climbe up these six staires of doctrine.
1. That here our eies are full of tears: how else should they be wip't away? how all, unlesse many?
2. That these teares are from sorrow; and this sorrow from death, and toyle, out of the connection of all these.
3. That God will once free us, both from teares which are the effect of sorrow, and from toyle and death, which are the causes of it.
4. That this our freedome must be upon a change; for that the first things are passed.
5. That this change shall be in our Renovation. *Behold I make all things new.*
6. That this renovation and happy change shall be in our perpetuall fruition of the inseparable presence of God, whose Tabernacle shall be with men.[109]

It seems clear that this structure of six interlocking 'heads' (the pattern of the language somewhat resembles that in Herbert's 'The Wreath') is not representative of the usual homiletic technique, but it does resemble the 'points' of the continental meditation, and the notion of gradual ascent strongly suggests the 'mountain of contemplation' motif upon which, as we shall shortly see, a later sermon heavily depends. Here we have all the elements of a formal meditation—occasion, analysis, and issue—and the movement as usual, is from rational argument to religious emotion. We end in a rapturous meditation upon the glories of heaven:

> Beloved, there is no losse, no misery, which the meditation of heaven cannot digest . . . But open your eyes and see the new Jerusalem, the Citie of the great King of Saints, and all these sublunary vanities shall be condemned. Here you shall see a foure square Citie; the wals of Jasper, the foundations garnished with all precious stones, Twelve gates of twelve pearles, The houses and streets of pure gold, like shining glasse: A Crystall river runs in the midst of it; and on the banks of it growes the tree of life; ever greene, ever fruitfull; this is for the eye. The eare shall be filled with the melody of Angels, ever singing, Holy, holy, holy, Lord God Almightie. The taste shall be satisfied with Manna, the food of Angels, with the fruit of the tree of life, with that new wine which our Saviour hath promised to drinke with us in his Kingdome . . .[110]

The passage is particularly striking for the way in which it introduces the characteristically Ignatian 'application of the senses' (eye, ear, taste, etc.), a technique Hall also employs in the *Passion Sermon*, though he rarely follows it through completely.

Perhaps the most striking indication of the relationship between the two genres is that contrived by Hall himself in deliberately choosing to publish three of his sermons in the middle of the fourth book of the *New Testament Contemplations*. His comments on this occasion are particularly revealing:

> The Reader may be pleased to understand, that my manner hath still beene, first, to passe through all these divine histories by way of Sermons, and then after, to gather the quintessence of those larger discourses, into these formes of Meditations, which he sees; Onely I have thought good, upon these two following heads (for some good reasons) to publish the Sermons in their owne shape, as they were delivered, without alteration; It seemed not amisse that some of those metalls should be showne in the oare, whereof so great a quantity was presented in the wedge.[111]

This provides a perfect illustration of what Baxter meant when he spoke of the sermon as a model for private contemplation.[112]

Indeed in *The Arte of Divine Meditation* Hall himself particularly encourages the duty of meditating on the Sabbath for 'the plentifull instruction of that Day stirreth thee up to this action, and fills thee with matter.'[113] The passage also raises a host of quite fascinating questions, for not only does it establish the close connection between the two genres, but it more than suggests that Hall was in the habit of delivering what we might call 'thematic' rather than strictly 'textual' sermons. Of the three sermons appearing in the *Contemplations*, for example, none has a 'text' as such, but all are based on some biblical *incident:* one on the miracle at Bethesda, and two on the Transfiguration. Quite appropriately the division of these sermons is in keeping with their 'thematic' nature. In the *Pool of Bethesda*, for instance, Hall invites King James and his court to 'bee content to spend this houre with me in the porches of Bethesda, and consider with me, the Topography, the Aitiology, the Chronography of this miracle: These three limit our speech, and your patient attention.'[114] Each division is then subdivided into various 'heads', the 'chronography', for example, offering us two: '1. A Feast of the Jewes; 2. Christ going up to the Feast'. Similarly the first *Transfiguration* sermon sets out to consider the time, place, attendants, and company of the miracle, while the second proposes to itself the sole circumstance still undiscussed: 'what *Moses* and *Elias* did with Christ in their apparition'. But this sort of thematic division is by no means confined to these 'contemplative' sermons. As we have seen, *The Fashions of the World* can best be described as a sermon on an emblem than on a biblical text. Its divisions relate not to the words of Romans 12:2 but to the significance of an emblem depicting a naked man, shears in hand, about to design his own clothes. It proceeds by examining the various 'fashions' of the world in relation to the parts of the body they particularly affect: the head (subdivided into eye, ear, tongue, palate, etc.), the back, the neck, the shoulders, and so on.[115]

It is also of considerable interest to note the way in which the three chosen sermons are introduced among the *Contemplations*. The first *Transfiguration* sermon, for instance, appears as 'The First Part of the Meditations upon the Transfiguration of Christ. In a Sermon preacht at Havering-Bower before K.

James of blessed memory'.[116] In other words the Contemplation is a meditation and the meditation is a sermon. This being the case, it is not at all difficult to pick out the elements of the sermon which would have remained virtually unchanged in the transformation from 'oare' to 'wedge'. Passages such as the following are exactly of the type discussed in the preceding chapter: 'me thinks I see how enviously these Creeples looke, one upon another, each thinking other a lett, each watching to prevent other, each hoping to be next; like *Emulous* Courtiers ... Oh that we could wait at the Bethesda of God.'[117]

Even more significant, however, is the use throughout the *Transfiguration* sermon of the 'mountain of meditation' motif suggested, of course, by the occurrence of the miracle on Mt. Tabor:

There is not in all Divinity an higher speculation then this of Christ transfigured: Suffer me therefore to lead you up, by the hand, into mount *Tabor* (for nearer to heaven ye cannot come while yee are upon earth) that you may see him glorious upon earth ... The circumstances shall be to us, as the skirts of the hill, which wee will climbe up lightly; the time, place, attendants, company ... which when we have passed, on the top of the hill shall appeare to us, that sight, which shall once make us glorious, and in the meane time happie.[118]

Hereupon follows a lengthy account of the scriptural use of the mountain symbol providing a clear indication of its importance in Hall's thought:

doubtlesse this hill was a Symbole of heaven, being neare it as in situation, in resemblance: Heaven is expressed usually by the name of Gods hill ... *Aaron* and *Hur* were in the mountaine with Moses, and held up his hands: *Aaron* (say some Allegorists) is mountainous; *Hur*, fiery; heavenly meditation, and the fire of charity must lift up our prayers to God. As Satan carryed up Christ to an high hill, to tempt him, so he carries up himselfe to be freed from temptation and distraction: if ever we would be transfigured in our dispositions, we must leave the earth below, and abandon all worldly thoughts, *venite, ascendamus, oh come, let us climbe up to the hill, where God sees, or is seene*, saith devout *Bernard*.[119]

As the second sermon begins we are still 'climbing', in one sense quite literally, since the consideration of the 'circum-

stances' is effectually leading us stage by stage to the higher
consideration of the miracle at the summit. Only now, having
gone through all the necessary preparations, can we approach
the mystery itself:

It fals out with this discourse as with Mount Tabor it self; that it is
more easily climbed with the eye, then with the foot: If we may not
rather say of it, as *Iosephus* did of *Sinai*, that it doth not onely *ascensus
hominum*, but *aspectus fatigare*, wearie not onely the steps but the
very sight of men: wee had thought not to spend many breaths in the
skirts of the hill; the circumstances; and it hath cost us, one houres
journey already: and we were glad to rest us, ere wee can have left
them below us; One pause more (I hope) will overcome them; and
set us on the top.[120]

A short while afterwards the summit is reached: 'Wee are now
ascended to the top of the hill: Let us therefore stand, and see,
and wonder at this great sight.' Only now comes the
description of the Transfiguration itself.[121]

As one might expect, Hall's sermons are often deliberately
designed to popularize the devotional practices upon which
they themselves so heavily rely. One of them, *The Pacification
Sermon* (1641), is actually another *Arte of Divine Meditation* in
miniature.[122] Appropriately enough, in view of what has been
said of them in a previous chapter, the text is drawn from the
Psalms, 'Come, behold the Works of the Lord, what Desola-
tions He hath made in the Earth. He maketh warrs to cease
unto the ends of the Earth' (Psalms 46: 8). The first section of
the sermon deals at some length with the centrality of
meditation to the devout life, and particular emphasis is placed
on the need for periodic withdrawal from public engagements
in favour of 'serious and fixed contemplation'. As before, the
scope of such meditation is unlimited for 'there is not one act
of either his creation or administration wherein there is not the
footsteps of an omnipotence, and an infinity of providence' (p.
50). Furthermore the practice holds a particular appeal for
Calvinists since its adoption may be interpreted as a sign of
election: 'hence it is that the most contemplative have been
noted for most eminent in grace . . . for they should be the best
acquainted with God' (p. 52). This section concluded, the
sermon immediately proceeds to follow its own advice by

considering God's works of judgement and mercy. As always, the order is extremely significant, and one recalls the careful pattern of alternating emotions in *The Arte of Divine Meditation* where 'complaint' preceded 'desire' and 'humble confession' preceded 'confidence'. Here once again Hall alerts his listeners to what is happening:

> as in the very being of both, judgment leads the way to mercy; so in the meditation and view of both: As it was in the Creation; *The Evening and the Morning were the first day;* The darknesse of the night led in the brightness of the morning; and as the Prophets word was *post tenebras lucem;* when we are humbled, and astonished with the consideration of Gods vengeance upon sinners, then, and not till then are we meet for the apprehensions of his wonderfull mercies.   (p. 53)

As will soon become apparent, this method is closely related to the practices of contemporary continental meditation. Having established its own structure the sermon then considers the 'tragical sight' of God's vengeance as manifested in the horrors of war, before passing on to a discussion of his mercy as revealed in the blessings of peace—a suitable theme for a sermon designed to celebrate the truce between the Scottish and English armies. Only when both judgements and mercies have been fully examined can the meditation arrive at its moral application: 'wherefore serves all this, but for the direction of our recourse, for the excitation of our duty and imitation; for the challenge of our thankfulnesse?'   (p. 59). After some characteristically frank and 'practical' discussion of the contemporary situation the sermon then ends in the manner deemed appropriate in *The Arte of Divine Meditation*—in 'thanksgiving' and 'recommendation of our soules and wayes to God'.

We have now considered the many structural affinities between the homily and the meditation, the importance of satire to Hall's homiletic technique, and the more particularized influence of his own meditative writings upon his style. Still to be examined are the rhetorical and structural devices whereby these apparently disparate elements achieve within the homiletic genre a degree of fusion never quite attained in either the *Characters* or the *Meditations*. Let us therefore turn to *The Character of Man,* a sermon delivered and published in 1634 at the height of Hall's powers (the last of the *Contemplations* appeared that year) and quite unsurpassed for the quality of its prose.[123] The very title is significant, for the sermon actually is a 'character' in the sense that what it attempts is an exact delineation of the essential elements of human nature. We have already considered the relationship between meditations, Characters, and self-analysis at some length. Exactly the same relationships are found here. 'My Text, and so my Sermon too, is the just Character of Man; A common, and stale theme, you will say; but a needfull one: we are all apt to mis-know or to forget what we are.' (p. 106.)

The text, yet again, is from the Psalms: 'Lord what is man that thou takest knowledge of him; or the son of man, that thou makest account of him? Man is like unto vanity, etc.' (Psalms 144:3). Since David's wonder and gratitude stem from a consideration of the contrasting nature of God and man, the theme, not surprisingly, had long been a central concern of divine meditation. By emphasizing man's corruption it fostered humility; by emphasizing God's greatness and mercy it fostered devotion and hope. In this respect *The Pacification Sermon* and *The Character of Man* have much in common, for in both the meditation is structured around a central antithesis, a method fundamental to the various contemplative systems of the time. As Juan de Avila puts it,

They who are much exercised in the *knowledge* of themselves (in respect that they are continually viewing their defects so neer at hand) are wont to fall into great sadnes, and disconfidence, and pusillanimity; for which reason, it is necessary that they do exercise themselves also in another *knowledge,* which giveth comfort, and strength, much more then the other gave discouragement . . . It is therefore fit for thee, after the exercise of the *knowledge of thy selfe* to imploy thy mind, upon the *knowledge of Christ Iesus our Lord.*[124]

Such ideas led quite naturally to the composition of contrasting meditations or whole series of meditations such as occur, for example, in the third and fourth points of Loyola's meditation on sin or in Nicholas Breton's *Divine Considerations of the Soule* (1608). In the latter we find two series of seven meditations each, the first on the greatness of God, the second on the vileness of man, the powerful contrast being designed to produce in Breton's readers David's response to the same issue: 'Oh Lord what is man . . .'[125] But this is also the text of the sermon under discussion and its structure, not surprisingly, reproduces the familiar pattern:

My Text then, ye see, is *Davids* rapture, expressed in an extaticall question of sudden wonder; a wonder at God, and at man; Mans vileness: *What is man?* Gods mercy and favour, in his knowledge, in his estimation of man: Lo, there are but two lessons that we need to take out here, in the world, God and man; and here they are both: Man in the notion of his wretchednesse; God in the notion of his bounty: Let us (if you please) take a short view of both, and in the one see cause of our humiliation, of our joy and thankfulnesse in the other, and if in the former there be a sad Lent of mortification, there is in the latter, a cheerful Easter of our raising and exaltation.

(p. 107)

The Lent–Easter reference is entirely fitting since it roots the sermon firmly in the period of the ecclesiastical year in which it was delivered. Hall reminds us of it again at the point of transition from grief to joy, and the language then employed recalls St. Paul's description of the resurrection: 'This grain after a little frost-biting will sprout up the more' (p. 113). This image bespeaks the intended effect of the sermon's structure. The listener is expected to experience first a depression and then an elevation of the spirit, and both intensely.

Turning first to consider 'man as he is in himself' Hall quickly adopts the satiric vein, but, as he immediately explains, it is a religious and constructive satire, and must therefore be viewed as an integral part of the meditative process. In effect, the first meditation, that on the vileness of man, is to be made through the medium of satire:

Surely, as *Nazianzen* observes, in one kind, that nothing is more pleasing to talk of then other mens businesses, so, there is nothing more easie, than for a man to be wittily bitter in invectives against his own condition; who hath not brain, and gall enough to be a Timon, *depreciari carnem hanc* (as *Tertullian* speaks,) to disparage humanity;

and like an angry Lion to beat himself to blood with his own stern; Neither is it more rife for dogs to bark at men, than men at themselves. Alas, to what purpose is this currish clamor? We are miserable enough though we would flatter our selves; To whose insultation can we be thus exposed but to our own? I come not hither to sponge you with this vinegar and gall, but give me leave a little, though not to aggravate, yet to deplore our wretchednesse; There can be no ill blood in this: *Amaritudo sermonum medicina animarum*, This bitterness is medicinall saith St. *Ambrose;* I doe not fear we shall live so long as to know our selves too well: *Lord then what is man?* (pp. 108–9)

This is perhaps the most brilliant defence of satire Hall ever wrote, and reads like a point by point response to the objections traditionally raised against it. There can be no doubt that the author was as interested in the theory of satire as in the practice. He is aware of every aspect of the problem, every probability of rejection. He has no desire to be 'wittily bitter' merely for the sake of being so. The point lies not in the wit but in its purpose. His genius is St. Ambrose not Timon, and, as in the 'Post-script' to the *Virgidemiarum,* he is anxious that his audience should not misinterpret his intentions. He is moreover part of his own theme. He has come to 'deplore' not to 'aggravate' 'his own condition'. He is not a prey to melancholy; there is no 'ill blood' in his nature. His bitterness is 'medicinall'. Its aim is self-knowledge, and the method it employs is both simple and devastating. Man's life is considered in the light of its three major divisions: ingress, progress, and egress. As the sermon proceeds the focus shifts from the development of the individual to that of the species in an attempt to demonstrate that the pattern in both cases is exactly the same.

We begin with the stages of birth and infancy, described in a wholly anti-sentimental way designed to highlight their most unpleasant and unattractive aspects. Juvenal, one recalls, had done much the same for old age:

What should I fetch the poor wretched infant out of the blind caverns of nature, to shame us with our conceptions, and to make us blush at the substance, nourishment, posture of that which shall be a man; There he lies senselesse for some moneths (as the heathen Oratour truly observes,) as if he had no soul. When he comes forth

into the large womb of the world, his first greeting of his Mother is
with cries and lamentations, and more he would cry if he could know
into what a world he comes recompensing her painfull throws with
continuall unquietnesse; what sprawling, what wringing, what
impotence is here? There lyes the poor little Lording of the world,
not able to help himself, whiles the new yeaned Lamb rises up on the
knees, and seeks for the teats of her damme, knowing where and how
to find reliefe so soon as it begins to be. Alas, what can man do if he
be let alone, but make faces, and noises, and dye? *Lord what is man?*
This is his ingresse into the world.   (p. 109)

And his 'progresse' we are quickly informed 'is no better':

From an impotent birth he goes on to a silly childhood; If no body
should teach him to speak what would he doe ... And if a mother or
nurse did not tend him, how soon would he be both noysome, and
nothing; where other creatures stand upon their own feet, and are
wrapt in their own naturall mantles, and tend upon their Dams for
their sustenance, and find them out amongst ten thousand ... As
soon as age and nurture can feoffe him in any wit, he falls to shifts;
all his ambition is to please himself in those crude humours of his
young vanity ... Neither is he yet capable of any other care, but how
to decline his own good, and to be a safe truant: It is a large time that
our Casuists give him, that at seven years he begins to lie.   (p. 109)

We are to experience what Lear experienced in the storm, the
stripping away of all that is artificial and false to reveal
underneath the 'poor, bare, forked animal', the 'thing itself'.
The 'little Lording' of the world, 'sprawling', 'impotent', and
'noysome' is heir to corruption. Such is man, or to be more
exact, such is one man, but his condition is representative of
his race, and his progress is that of his species. To emphasize
the point Hall now turns with a Lucretian starkness to
reconstruct the equally squalid infancy of the race itself. The
result is reminiscent of the *Contemplations*:

How wofully do we think they did scramble to live? they had water
and earth before them, but fire, an active and usefull element, was
yet unknown ... Here was *Adam* delving with a jaw-bone, and
harrowing with sticks tyed uncouthly together, and pairing his nails
with his teeth: there *Eve* making a comb of her fingers, and tying her
raw-skin'd breeches together with rindes of trees, or pinning them
up with thorns ... Here Adam the first midwife to his miserable
consort, and *Eve* wrapping her little one in a skin lately borrowed

from some beast... Their fist was their hammer, their hand their dish, their armes and leggs their ladder... And now... *What is Adam?* (p. 109)

Man's progress, however, banished physical hardship but only at the price of further spiritual degeneracy:

In time Art began to improve nature; Every dayes experiments brought forth something; and now man durst affect to dwell, not safe, but fair; to be clad, not warm, but fine; and the palate waxt by degrees wanton and wilde; the back and the belly strove whether should be the more luxurious; and the eye affected to be more prodigall then they both; and ever since the ambition of these three hath spent and wearied the world, so as in the other extreme we may well cry out, *Lord what is man?* (pp. 109–10)

The full force of such a passage can be truly appreciated only when we recall the place of delivery, the court of Charles I, the court whose grand, pretentious figures, 'silken Courtiers' as Hall terms them, stare out in their stiff, artificial poses from the portraits of Van Dyke. Hall's satire was not merely verbal but visual. His depiction of the common ancestry of both high and low and his emphasis upon the essential squalor of the human condition were intended for an audience which sought, as far as possible, to push such considerations aside. The very place of delivery set his words in a contrasting context. Their force and effectiveness sets their speaker among the foremost preachers of the seventeenth century.

As the account of man's progress proceeds we are presented with a panoramic survey of human vanity:

Wo is me, how is this time spent? In hollow visits, in idle courtings, in Epicurean pamperings, in fantastick dressings, in lawlesse disports... ones is a starved vanity, anothers a pampered one; ones a joviall vanity, anothers a sullen one; ones a silken vanity, anothers a ragged one; ones a carelesse vanity, anothers a carking. (p. 110)

We are not far in such passages from the turbulent, cluttered surveys of the *Virgidemiarum* but the pathos of these satires is also in evidence. We too are tenants-at-will:

Surely we cannot make account of one minute: besides the vanity of unprofitablenesse here is the vanity of transitorinesse. How doth the momentarinesse of this misery add to the misery; what a flower, a vapour, a smoke, a bubble, a shadow, a dream of a shadow our life is? We are going, and then a carelesse life is shut up in a disconsolate end ... Alas, this worm-eaten apple soon falls, *vitreum hoc corpusculum* (as *Erasmus* termes it) is soon crackt and broken. (pp. 110–11)

One moment we feel ourselves in motion, the next, feeling itself has gone. We have scarcely time to become aware of our own condition: 'we *are* going, and then a carelesse life *is* shut up in a disconsolate end.' The worm-eaten 'apple' returns us to Eden, thereby facilitating the transition to our 'egress', death:

Well, he dyes, saith the Psalmist, and then all his thoughts perish; Lo, what a word here is? *All his thoughts perish.* What is man but his thoughts? ... each one is taken up with severall thoughts, when he dies all those thoughts perish; all those castles in the aire (νεφελοκοκκυγία as *Aristophanes* his word is) vanish to nothing; only his ill thoughts stick by him, and wait on his soul to hell. (p. 111)

The allusion to Aristophanes, the genius of Old Comedy, shows us that we are still in the realm of satire.[126] According to George Wither the Psalmist himself was 'sometime satyricall'.[127]

We have come far but the mills of God must grind finer still. Having now reviewed man's life from the point of view of his 'times', Hall proceeds to examine his 'parts': body and soul:

What is this body of mine but a piece of that I tread upon, a sack of dust (if not *saccus stercorum,* as *Bernard*) a sewer of ill humours, a magazine of diseases, a feast of wormes; And as for that better part, the inmate of this ragged cottage, though as it proceeds from thee, it is a pure immortal spirit, a spark of thine heavenly fire, a glimpse of that divine light, yet as it is mine, how can I pitty it. Alas, how dark it is with ignorance? (p. 111)

One might have thought that man had at last reached his nadir, but there is worse to come as the startling opening of the next passage suggests: 'Such is nature now in her best dresse, but if ye look upon her in the worst of her depravation, ye shall not more wonder at her misery than her ugly deformity ... If then man be such as man, what is he as a sinner? when his eyes are the burning-glasses of concupiscence, his tongue a razor of detraction ...' (pp. 111–12). Having performed its disconcerting function extremely well, the first meditation nears its close.

The time has come to apply the moral lesson. His audience is in no position to object and Hall strikes while the iron is hot: 'Is there any of you now that hears me this day that finds cause to be in love with, or proud of himself as a man? Let me see him and blesse myself' (p. 112). In Zeno's phrase we must 'put off the man' ('hominem exuere') and become something more, but that 'more' can only be constructed on the ashes of vanity and pride:

Down then dust and ashes, down with those proud plumes of the vain misconceits of thine own goodlinesse, beauty, glory: Think thyselfe but so vile as thou art, there will be more danger of thy self-contempt ... Why then doth the rich Landlord grate upon his poor scraping Tenant; Why doth the *silken Courtier* [my emphasis] brow-beat his russet Countryman? (p. 112)

The satire has been keen but functional. It has informed our consideration of man 'as he is in himself' in order to produce the desired 'Lent' or abasement of our feelings. Its real target is not man but man's pride, the root of all moral and social evil. For this reason it has presented a purposely distorted view of human life by focusing solely upon the squalid and the disgusting. And this after all is the essence of meditation: to concentrate totally and exclusively on one aspect of a spiritual problem until it is completely and exhaustively understood; to allow no extraneous matter to dilute the effect—as Ignatius forbade any thoughts of joy, even of Christ's resurrection, in the 'week' devoted to the Passion.[128] Even in method satirist and meditator have much in common. Here the audience has been brought low partly for the moral value which is to be derived from humiliation, and partly in preparation for the contrasting meditation which is soon to follow. The second half of the text, 'that thou takest knowledge of him' has still to be considered:

Doe not think now what I have all this while done, as I have seen some in a throng, or as hood-winkt boyes in their sport struck my friends. The regenerate man is an Angelical creature; And man, whatever he be in other regards, yet, as he comes out of Gods mold, is the great master-piece of his Creator ... Turn your eyes then from mans vilenesse, to the more pleasing object of God's mercy; and, as you have seen man in the dust of his abasement, so now, see him in the throne of his exaltation. (p. 113)

The contemplation of the regenerate man centres upon his 'parts'. The subject, in effect, is the same as before, except that now everything is totally transformed by the addition of grace. This is the meaning of 'regeneration': 'Even this very outside wants not his glory: The matter cannot disparage it. If thou madest this body of earth, thou madest the Heavens of nothing; what a perfect symmetry is here in this frame? what an admirable variety (as Zeno noted of old) even of faces, all like, all unlike each other' (p. 114). Wonderful as the body is, however, it is nothing in comparison with 'the inside of this exquisite piece':

Surely this reasonable soul is so divine a substance, and the faculties of it, invention, memory, judgement so excellent, that it self hath not power enough to admire its own worth, what corner of earth, what creek of sea, what span of Heaven is unsearcht by it? How hath it surrounded this globe, and calculated the stars, and motions of the other?   (p. 114)

There follows a survey of man's intellectual activity ending with his powers of speech, the expression of his noble mind, and then in a new sense the preacher asks 'what is man that thou makest this high account of him?[129] As it was the plan of the first meditation to follow a sloping path to its nadir, so it is the intention of the second to climb an ascending path to its zenith: 'But, what is all this, yet, in comparison of what thou hast done for our souls? I am now swallowed up, O God, with the wonder and astonishment of thy unconceivable mercies. What shall I say, that ere the world was, thou lovedst man that should be' (p. 114). After the experience of the first meditation this cannot but produce the desired effect: 'Lo I, that even now could have been sorry that I was a man, begin now to be holily proud of my condition; and know not whether I may change the man for the Angel ... How justly doe we now exult in the glory of man-hood, thus attended, thus united?' (p. 115.) Hall has now reached the point at which he may bring the two contrasting meditations together and harmonize their respective outlooks. This he does in the very next sentence in a manner characteristic of his famed 'moderation': 'But soft, that our rejoycing be not vain, whiles our nature is thus glorious, our person may be miserable enough. Except we be in Christ, united to the Son of God, we are never the better for the uniting of this man-hood to God' (p. 115). Little now remains to be done except for the rehabilitation of ambition and 'self-estimation' so effectively demolished earlier on: man, it transpires, must be both too proud to sin, and too ambitious not to desire heavenly honour. The sermon then concludes in the accepted meditative way, like *The Pacification Sermon*, with thanksgiving and 'recommendation of our wayes to God':

O God, thou mightest have made me a beast, yea the ugliest of crawling vermin, that I run away from... *I will praise thee for I am fearfully and wonderfully made*... Oh let not us be wanting unto thee, who has thus superabounded unto us. But this is not all. Thanks is a poor windy payment. Our returns to God must be reall; *Quid retribuam?* what should we render to our God lesse than all?... Oh that our bodies, souls, lives, actions could be wholly consecrated to thee. (pp. 115–16)

This is a conclusion made possible not merely by the second meditation but by the interaction of the two, for it was first necessary to see what man was in himself before the greatness of God's mercy could be fully appreciated. As in the ecclesiastical year, Lent had to precede Easter, mortification joy, and satire praise. The sermon had to follow the progress of the psalm in order to arrive at the psalmist's conclusion. In this way the gratitude of the ending is born not of complacency but of tension. The forceful denigration of the 'natural' man forms as integral a part of the meditative process as does the following consideration of the 'regenerate' spirit. The homiletic genre has provided Hall with a uniquely adaptable vehicle for the fusion of his meditative and satiric habits of mind, and this fusion goes far to account for his success as a preacher.

EPILOGUE: TOWARDS MYSTICISM

> Being to remove from my earthly Tabernacle, wherein I
> have worn out the few and evill dayes of my pilgrimage,
> to an abiding City above, I have desired to acquaint my
> self with that Invisible world, to which I am going: to
> enter-know my good God, and his blessed Angels and
> Saints, with whom I hope to passe an happy eternity.
> (Preface to *The Invisible World*)

Since contemplation and mysticism have always gone hand in
hand it was virtually inevitable that Hall should tend towards
what Evelyn Underhill terms a form of devotional mysticism
in his later years.[1] His retirement to Higham sequestered him
sufficiently from the doings of the world to foster the
development of such mystical elements as had always been
present in his thought. As he practised it, the purpose of
meditation was to keep the idea of God as constantly and
effectively before the mind as was humanly possible, to make
the world to come as real to the meditator as the world in
which he lived.[2] To read the great 'book' of creation with a
spiritual awareness was to attempt to 'admit of all material
objects, as if they were so altogether transparent, that through
them I might see the wonderfull prospects of another world.'[3]
The state of mind to which Hall aspired was one of remarkable
detachment, one that rendered both satire and contemplation
easy. For him, the providential aspects of life were paramount:
Nature was a mirror of its creator's power, and history was the
account of God's persistent intervention in the progress of his
chosen race. He had read and rejected Machiavelli, preferring
instead the outlook of John Foxe.[4] In such public calamities as
the death of Prince Henry he saw the vengeance of an angry
God, and was equally quick to attribute the turmoil of the civil

wars to the decay of devotional religion.[5] In the collapse of the
Anglican Church and the proliferation of the sects he detected
the sure signs of approaching dissolution. 'Who can say other',
he asks, 'upon the view of these wild thoughts, then *Gerson*
said long since, that the world now growne old, is full of
doting fancies; if not rather that the world now near his end,
raves, and talks nothing but fancies, and frenzies?'[6] From the
time of his undergraduate days 'mundus senescit' had been
one of his constant themes.[7] He expected the world to end, if
not in his own lifetime, at least in that of his children.
'Nothing appears', he tells us, 'why we should not make full
account that the world is near to it's last period; and that our
Lord Jesus is at hand for his finall judgement.'[8] As a result, he
saw everything in purely moral terms. There was little
complexity in his social outlook, all centred upon the
individual: 'What should be done then? Except wee would
faine smart, each man amend one, and we all live . . . Let every
man pull but one brand out of this fire, and the flame will goe
out alone. What is a multitude, but an heap of unities?'[9] His
two autobiographical tracts are really accounts of God's
intervention in his own affairs, of *Specialities of Divine
Providence in the life of Joseph Hall,* a life which has followed a
carefully predetermined, or rather predestined, pattern. He
was meant to become a bishop, to defy Laud on matters of
ceremony, to enter the Smectymnuan debate, to be sent to the
Tower, and to endure all the personal losses of old age. This
belief was the source of his comfort; this was the inspiration of
the *Songs in the Night* (1654) sung upon the occasion of his
wife's death. His was a life without loose ends, a life in which
chance played no part. In his later writings he himself becomes
an *object* of meditation, one of the creatures in whom God's
power is made manifest.

As their writings demonstrate, Protestants of Hall's temperament vigorously opposed themselves to all forms of 'superstition'—it was part of their strategy in the battle against Rome.
Yet for all their rationalism they remained far closer to
medieval habits of thought than to modern. Indeed the
modern reader finds all sorts of unresolved conflicts in the
writings of an author such as Hall. For example, in the self-
same letter in which he ridicules the Blessed Virgins of Halle

and Sichem, the Lourdes and Fatima of the time, he asserts his own confirmed belief in 'witch-wolves' (female werewolves). These he had all but seen himself during his tour of the Ardennes (1605): 'we saw a boy there, whose halfe–face was devoured by one of them neere the village . . . Not many dayes before our comming, at *Limburgh* was executed one of those miscreants, who confessed on the wheele to have devoured two and fortie children in that forme.'[10] Hall's attitude towards the supernatural is just as 'superstitious', if we may use the word, as any contemporary Roman Catholic's, and just as partisan. 'Miracles', he asserts, 'must be judged by the doctrine which they confirme; not the doctrine by the miracles.'[11] It is, therefore, with striking equanimity that he rejects as damnable the claims of such Counter-Reformation mystics as Teresa of Avila and Philip Neri while at the same time encouraging belief in allegedly miraculous happenings in the life of Melanchthon.[12] It is characteristic of this mode of thought that the Catholic claims are by no means rejected outright. Hall does not doubt that such events have happened, he simply questions their source. On such occasions reason is kept firmly in its place; the third most perceptive eye is the eye of faith. 'Humane reason', we are told, 'is apt to be injuriously saucie, in ascribing those things to an ordinary course of naturall causes, which the God of Nature doth by supernaturall agents.'[13] The quotation comes from a work appropriately entitled *The Invisible World* published along with *The Great Mysterie of Godliness* in 1652. Here, as the title suggests, Hall attempts to contemplate the spiritual universe of angels and demons, the tripartite universe of earth, heaven, and hell.

This work, which may best be considered as the culmination of a life devoted to rectifying the evils of the present world and to focusing attention upon the joys of the world to come, provides a fascinating insight into the range of Hall's reading. He is familiar with the writings of Dionysius the Areopagite, John Gerson's sermon on angels, and *De Variis Diaboli Tentationibus,* an incredibly wide range of Roman Catholic legends both medieval and contemporary, and Jean Bodin's *De La Demonomanie des Sorciers* (1580). In many respects his own account of the spiritual world is highly traditional and, of course, works such as this are a staple of devotional literature.

What is unusual, however, is the author's personal involvement in the account he sets forth. Among other such incidents we hear, for example, of a 'miraculous cure' wrought at 'S. Madernes in Cornwall ... upon a poor Cripple whereof (besides the attestation of many hundreds of the neighbours) I took a strict and personall examination.'[14] 'This man', the account continues, 'that for sixteen years together was fain to walk upon his hands, by reason of the close contraction of the sinews of his legs, was, (upon three monitions in his dream to wash in that well) suddainly so restored to his limbs, that I saw him able both to walke, and to get his own maintenance; I found here was neither art nor collusion, the thing done, the Author invisible.' How far we are here from the celebrated cures of Hall and Sichem it is perhaps unfair to inquire.

The divine inspiration of certain dreams is further attested by the experience of a certain Mr Cook of Waltham who was 'informed in his dream, in what hole of his dove-cote' he would find important missing documents—Hall himself can vouch for the truth of the matter.[15] One cannot read an account such as this without recalling the very similar description of how his mother was assured of her election after a long period of spiritual doubt by having the symbols of a recurrent dream expounded by Anthony Gilby, the Marian exile who was the incumbent of Ashby-de-la-Zouch.[16] Hall came to reject Gilby's radical views concerning the method of Church government, but never outlived, nor wished to outlive, his devotional influence. What was involved here was a view of life that emphasized the direct intervention of God in the history of his people, and Hall was prepared to maintain it despite the cost. Alone of all the Caroline bishops, he was vocal in his support for the highly controversial Puritan exorcist John Darrell, who first came to prominence while Hall himself was still a fellow of Emmanuel College. The importance of this cannot be overstressed. The Darrell affair was quite notorious and the ecclesiastical authorities laboured might and main to discredit the whole business. Samuel Harsnett, the future Archbishop of York, wrote what was generally considered to be a damning account of Darrell's activities implicating a number of highly respected Puritan clergymen and sympathizers including William Bradshaw, Hall's contemporary at Ashby Grammar

School, and his brother-in-law, John Brinsley. In Cambridge
the Vice-Chancellor forbade the sale of Darrell's books and
Bradshaw had to withdraw temporarily from the university. A
special canon was even inserted in the new Church Canons of
1604 with the intention of preventing all such activities in the
future.[17] Yet despite all this, here is how Hall recalled the
episode in 1652:

Upon the ground of this Scripture [James 4.7] it was (as my self was
witnesse) that in our age Mr. Dayrel, a godly, and zealous preacher,
undertook and accordingly (through the blessing of God upon his
faithfull devotions) performed, those famous ejectments of evill
spirits both at *Nottingham* and *Lancashire,* which exercised the press,
and raised no small envie from the gainsayers.[19]

Actually events came much closer home than either
Nottingham or Lancashire. Darrell lived for several months in
Ashby-de-la-Zouch and much of Harsnett's tract centres upon
his stay in that town. To anyone interested in the evolution of
Hall's particular brand of Anglicanism it is fascinating to
remember that Harsnett regarded the affair as a part of a
Puritan plot to undermine episcopacy by suggesting a greater
efficacy of the Spirit in disaffected circles—and Hall's brother-
in-law and mentor were certainly disaffected.[20] Yet Hall
rejected both Harsnett (for there can be little doubt that he is
one of the most envious 'gainsayers' mentioned) and the
radicals. He never saw the events of the 1590s as part of a plot,
and even when raised to the episcopal bench, completely
refused to turn his back on those early, exciting days when, as
he believed, he first came face to face with the forces of the
world beyond. It was this conviction that lay behind his
disputation in Brussels with the Jesuit Fr. Costerus, the
substance of which is recounted in *Some Specialities.*[21] This is
how he could assure Costerus that the work of exorcism was
proceeding as normal in the Reformed Church, thereby
affording tangible proof of God's endorsement of the Reformation. There is a wilful element in all religious faith and Hall
desperately wanted to believe such things. It seems highly
probable from the frequent references to witches in the later
meditations that he also accepted the reports of the self-
appointed witch-finder Matthew Hopkins whose activities led

to so many convictions and executions in the late 1640s.[22] In *Resolutions and Decisions of Divers Practicall Cases of Conscience* (1649) he deals with such questions as 'whether upon the appearance of Evill Spirits we may hold discourse with them' and 'how farre a secret pact with evill spirits doth extend',[23] while *Satan's Fiery Darts Quenched* (1647) consists of a series of challenges and responses addressed to Satan himself.

As he grew older, Hall's concern with such matters deepened. He even came to regard his lack of attention to angels as 'a great sin'. He has been slack he confesses,

in returning praises to my God, for the continual assistance of those blessed and beneficent spirits, which have ever graciously attended me, without intermission, from the first hour of my conception to this present moment; neither shall ever (I hope) absent themselves from my tutelage, and protection, til they shall have presented my poor soul to her final glorie: Oh that the dust and clay were so washed out of my eyes, that I might behold, together with the presence, the numbers, the beauties and excellencies of those ever-present guardians.[24]

In *The Invisible World* he amply recompenses former omissions (if omissions there had ever been) by the assertion that 'there are many thousand events, wherein common eies see nothing but nature, which yet are effected by the ministration of Angels.'[25] Any attempt to work in the opposite direction, to diminish the intervention of spiritual forces by extending the role of nature is instantly cried down. A certain Master of Philosophy, we are reminded, who attempted to quell the fears of his fellow passengers during a thunderstorm by explaining to them 'the naturall reasons of that uprore in the clouds' was instantly 'strucken dead with that dreadful eruption which he sleighted.' 'What could this be', Hall asks, 'but the finger of that God, who will have his works rather entertained with wonder, and trembling, then with curious scanning.'[26] For Hall, nothing of any importance had been called in doubt by the 'new philosophy', and even if the element of fire had been extinguished, its disappearance was of little consequence—it might well appear again as theories changed. To his way of thinking the matter was quite detached from spiritual affairs;

only Millenarians such as John Archer founded their beliefs
upon the shifting sands of human learning:

But what if there be no element of fire? such Tenets surely the
Schools afforded our younger days... that if there be an excesse of
heat in those upper Regions under the concave of the Moon, yet it is
neither fire, nor elementall. But if upon some new Principles he shal
make the substance of the starry heaven (which we had wont to call
quintessentiall) to be the element of fire, I shall choose rather to
wonder at that strange Philosophy, then to wrangle about it; wishing
that it were no more unsafe to broach our own singular imaginations
in these points of Divinity, then in these harmles speculations of
Nature.[27]

'Harmles speculations of Nature'—whenever Hall speaks of
human knowledge he asserts its limitations. He quotes Bacon
not on the subject of the advancement of learning nor the
coming of the New Atlantis, but to the effect that 'do we hear
but a Bee humming about our ears, the greatest Naturalist
cannot know whether that noise come from within the body,
or from the mouth, or from the wings of that flye.'[28] His
attitude towards what he himself admits to be staggering
advances in the state of scientific knowledge is exactly the
same as his attitude towards travel discussed in Chapter 2.
Even the wording and syntax are remarkably similar. He will
have no Utopias either physical or intellectual:

Oh vain affectation of wild, and roving curiosity! If their desires
cannot be bounded, yet their motions must; When they have the full
sight of heaven above them, they cannot climbe up into it; they
cannot possibly see that whole glorious contignation; and when the
whole earth lies open before them, they can measure but some small
peeces of it. How can they be quiet till they have purchased *Tycho
Brahe* his prospective trunk of thirty two foot long, whereby they
may discover a better face of heaven; some lesser Planets moving
about the Sun, and the Moonets about Saturn and Juppiter, and the
mountains, seas and vallies in the Moon? How can they rest til
having acquainted themselves with the constellations of our Hemisphere, they have passed the Equinoctiall, and seen the triangle, the
crosse, and the clouds, and the rest of the unknown stars that move
above the other Pole? And when all this is done, they are but who
they were, no whit better, no whit wiser, and perhaps far lesse happy
than those, who never smelt any but their own smoak; never knew

any star, but Charls-wayn, the morning star, and the seven.[29]

Hall turns from unsatisfying knowledge to absorbing mystery, from 'prospective glasses' to the invisible world. 'It is our illumination', he tells us 'that perfects reason; and that illumination is from the Father of lights; without whose divine light naturall reason is but as a dyall without the Sun, eyes without light.'[30] It is one of the devil's temptations that he should be, 'no other then thy self, a man; and follow the light and guidance of that which makes thee so, right Reason; and whatsoever disagrees from that, turn it off as no part of thy beliefe, to those superstitious bigots which are willing to lose their reason in their faith.'[31] But the reply is determined and clear,

it is from nature that I am a man; it is from grace that I am a man regenerate; Nature holds forth to me as a man, the dim and weak rush-candle of carnall reason; The grace of regeneration shows me the bright torch-light, yea, the sun of divine illumination ... it is true, that reason is the great gift of my Creator ... but where is it in the originall purity to be found under heaven? ... as it is marred by thee, even naturall truths are too high for it; as it is renued by God, it can apprehend and imbrace supernaturall verities: It is regenerate reason that I shall ever follow.[32]

In his later meditations Hall turns to the contemplation of subjects which defy natural reason. Indeed in *The Great Mysterie of Godliness* he comes to regard faith itself as the greatest mystery of all.[33] Where we cannot 'comprehend' we are urged to 'wonder and adore'. We are lost 'betwixt a God and a Man; betwixt finite, and infinite'.[34] More and more, as so often happens in mysticism, we are moving towards ideas which ultimately cannot be expressed at all. Hall's reason is reserved for his moderation, for working out a pathway between extremes, but in *An Holy Rapture; or Patheticall Meditations of the Love of Christ* (1647) 'extreams meet without a mean.'[35] Such emotions cannot be rationalized. The love of God 'were not infinite if it could bee uttered; Thoughts goe beyond words; yet even these come far short also; He that saw it, says; Eye hath not seen, nor ear heard, neither have entred into the heart of man, the things which God hath prepared for them that love him.' No 'conceits' or 'affections'

can be 'in the least sort answerable to so transcendent mercy'.[36]
The movement is towards ecstasy, and the entire meditation
proceeds on the level of the colloquy: 'I am swallowed up, O
God, I am willingly swallowed up in this bottomlesse abysse of
thine infinite love; and there let me dwell in a perpetuall
ravishment of spirit.'[37]

Yet here we encounter a strange paradox. The movement is
towards ecstasy, yet ecstasy is never achieved. Hall is torn
between conflicting forces. The unitive life, the third stage of
meditative ascent after purgation and illumination, both
attracts and repels him.[38] Although he uses the characteristic
terminology of 'rapture' and 'ravishment', he never once
employs the term 'contemplation' in the sense of 'ecstasy', and
his 'raptures' are far different from those of Teresa of Avila.[39]
Like Jeremy Taylor, he remains suspicious and fearful of the
voices, visions, and trances of the great Counter-Reformation
mystics. For him the stage of illumination is sufficient.[40] But
this is essentially a preparatory stage, a 'way of opening the
door', a stage in which the personality and will, though ready
to surrender, are never fully 'swallowed up'. The violent,
involuntary rape of the senses so powerfully captured in
Bernini's Teresa was never to be Hall's. A passage from *Satans
Fiery Darts Quenched* (1647) explains why. Beyond the
ascending stair of sense, reason, and faith it places ecstatic
vision, but only by dying can we take that final step:

The wise and bountifull God hath vouchsafed to hold forth four
severall lights to men; all which move in four severall orbes, one
above another; The light of sense, the light of reason, the light of
faith, the light of ecstaticall, or divine vision; and all of these are
taken up with their own proper objects: Sense is busied about these
outward and materiall things; reason is confined to things intelligible; faith is imployed in matters spirituall and supernaturall; divine
vision in objects celestiall, and infinitely glorious; None of these can
exceed their bounds, and extend to a sphere above their owne; What
can the brute creature, which is led by meer sense, do, or apprehend
in matters of understanding and discourse? What can meer man who
is led by reason, discerne in spirituall and supernaturall things?
What can the Christian, who is led by faith, which is the evidence of
things not seen, attain unto in the clear vision of God, and heavenly
glory? That God, who is a God of order, hath determined due limits

to all our powers, and faculties . . . I will therefore follow my sense so far as that will lead me; and not suffer my self to be beaten off from so sure a guide; Where my sense leaves me, I will betake my self to the direction of reason, and in all naturall and morall things, shall be willingly led by the guidance thereof; but when it comes to supernaturall and divine truths; when I have the word of a God, for my assurance, farewell reason, and welcome faith; as when I shall have dispatcht this weary pilgrimage, and from a Traveller shall come to be a Comprehensor, farewel faith, and welcome vision.[41]

Even in Hall's latest, most passionate works the very order and clarity of the outlay still bespeak the controlling influence of reason and logic. Teresa attempts to describe her experiences in a myriad of different ways, many of which are mutually conflicting, but there are no such contradictions in Hall. He has not been rapt up into heaven with St. Paul, his eye has not seen nor his ear heard. In *An Holy Rapture* he asks to be allowed to 'dwell in a perpetuall ravishment of spirit, till being freed from this clog of earth, and filled with the fulnesse of Christ, I shall be admitted to enjoy that, which I cannot now reach to wonder at . . .'[42] The limitations of meditation impress him as much as its benefits: 'if at any time during this pilgrimage, thine eye-lids have been some little raised [sic] by divine Meditations, yet how narrowly, how dimly art thou wont to see?' Only in death can the eyes be 'broadly' and 'fully' opened.[43] This is surely one of the most fascinating aspects of Protestant mysticism for St. Bernard's intense desire for spiritual vision is there in all its force though constantly frustrated by an awareness of spiritual blindness—'what blinde light looks in here at these scant loopholes of my soul?':[44]

Had I been in the streets of *Jericho*, sure, me thinks, I should have justled with *Zacheus* for the Sycomore [sic], to see Jesus; and should have blessed my eyes for so happy a prospect . . . And why should not the eyes of my faith behold the same object which was seen with *Stephens* bodily eyes? I see thee, O Saviour, I see thee, as certainly, though not so clearly.[45]

'Though not so clearly': there is something extremely poignant in the qualification. But this is the characteristic Protestant mode. For them there is expectation not fruition.

Their autobiographical tracts leave them in a state of embattled preparation. It remains for the funeral sermon to describe the ultimate fulfilment—hence the great importance of that genre among such circles. In *The Free Prisoner* (1640) and *The Souls Farewell to Earth, and Approaches to Heaven* (1651) Hall imagines the freeing of the soul from the body, the journey upwards through the spheres, and the approach to heaven. But that is as far as he can go. He describes himself as Moses on Mt. Nebo glimpsing, but not entering, the promised land: 'Doe thou but say, Die thou on this Hil, with this prospect in mine eye'—a provocative reversal of 'say but the word and my servant shall be healed.' 'All the few daies therefore of my appointed time', he concludes, 'will I wait at the threshold of grace untill my changing come; with a trembling joy, with a longing patience, with a comfortable hope.'[46] This waiting at the threshold is the way of illumination, 'an essentially transitional state, introducing the self into a new sphere of activity.'[47] The autobiographical tracts end in much the same way.[48] When the great mystics lapse into silence it is because they cannot explain their experiences or their visions, when Hall counsels silence it is because he has not yet either experienced or seen.

This helps to explain his hostile reaction to the Millenarian revival of the 1650s, even though he remained just as sure as the Millenarians themselves that the world was near its end. 'I am perswaded in my soul', he tells us, 'that the coming of our Saviour is neer at hand ... But, for the particularities of the time, and manner, I both have learn'd, and do teach silence.'[49] In reply to John Archer's startling predictions in *The Personal Reigne of Christ upon Earth* (1643) he produced his last great controversial work, *The Revelation Unrevealed* (1650). Here he strongly objects to seeing 'Evangelicall promises thus carnally drained into a wrong channell'.[50] On the question of assessing God's intentions he is at one with Lancelot Andrewes who 'when a plaine man came seriously to him, and asked his opinion concerning an obscure passage in that Book [Revelation], answered, *My friend, I am not comme so far*'.[51] His message, as always, is that 'modest Christians' must learn to 'rest in revealed Truths, and to leave the unlocking of the secret Cabinets of the Almighty, to the onely key of his Divine

Wisedome, and Omniscience.'[52] Nor will he allow the sort of
typology which I have examined in Chapter 4 to degenerate
into a form of fortune-telling. Instead he recognizes that the
very perplexity of Revelation subjects it to all sorts of polemic
interpretations:

Mr. *Brightman,* a learned and godly Divine, thinks to find not
England only, but *Cecill,* and *Walsingham* there; A Belgick Doctor in
the Synod of *Dort* thought to find *Grave Maurice* there; *Joannes
Brocardus* thinks to finde *Venice* there; and a grave Divine (whose
name I will spare) was so confident to finde the *Palatinate* there,
both in the losse and recovery of it, as that he would needs present
his thoughts to the judicious eyes of King *James* himselfe, with small
thanks for his labour; neither wanted there some that made full
account to finde the late Victorious *Gustavus Adolphus* therein
plainly designed; as if the Blessed Apostle, now in his *Pathmos,* overlooking all the vast Continent betwixt us, should have had his
thoughts taken up with our petty Occurrences in this other side of
the World.[53]

As this passage amply suggests, Hall recognized the
importance of keeping abreast of the Apocalyptic tradition
even if only to refute it. The very title of his work constitutes
an attack upon Thomas Brightman's nine hundred-page
commentary, *A Revelation of the Revelation* (1615), a work
which first appeared in Latin four years earlier under the no
less striking title *Apocalypsis Apocalypseos.*[54] Always popular,
this work was brought more forcibly to public attention in
1641 by the publication of the anonymous tract, *A Revelation
of Mr. Brightman's Revelation,* and the same year saw the
appearance of *Reverend Mr. Brightman's Judgement on Prophecies,* eight editions of which had passed the press by 1650. *A
Revelation of the Revelation* is remarkable for the detail with
which it professes to apply the prophecies of St. John to
contemporary history. In fact it would seem that it was here,
rather than in Foxe, that the notion of an elect nation as
distinct from an international elect Church first took shape.[55]
That Brightman was a 'learned and godly Divine' Hall never
attempted to deny, but by 1650 it was clear to all but the most
partial that his predictions had been overtaken by events. He
could only be regarded as a discredited prophet 'by whose
accompt the Turkish Tyranny should have lasted but seven

yeares after he wrote his *Revelation,* where as now near forty yeares are since passed, and the Empire holds up still'.[56]

But quite apart from his interest in Brightman, Hall moved in circles much concerned with the unravelling of the Apocalypse. In *The Revelation Unrevealed* he refers to the writings of the celebrated Joseph Mede (1586–1638), one of the most meticulous and sane of its English interpreters, who appears to have exercised a considerable power of restraint upon his more radical supporters.[57] Nor was Hall's knowledge limited to published works for he tells us that one of Mede's Latin manuscripts has recently come into his hands.[58] Mede, it should be noted, was a close friend and frequent correspondent of John Dury, that tireless apostle of Protestant unity ordained by Hall while Bishop of Exeter—though significantly with the laying on of presbyters' hands. Dury was intensely interested in Mede's work on Revelation and may well have communicated his enthusiasm to Hall.[59] Another contact, however, was Archbishop Ussher, one of Hall's oldest friends and one of the few scholars to receive several copies of Mede's great *Clavis Apocalyptica* when it was first published for private circulation in 1627.[60] Ussher was himself engaged upon solving the problem of universal chronology and sent Hall a copy of the first instalment of his *Annales Veteris et Novi Testamenti* in 1650. In his letter of thanks Hall declares that the chronology is awaited with longing by Christians all over the world ('toti Christiano orbi exoptatissimum').[61] When he received the last instalment of the *Annales* in 1654, Hall wrote back to ask whether Simon Magus could be identified with the Antichrist of St. Paul's prediction (Thessalonians 2: 1–12). 'I must confess', he writes, 'if the times may accord, there may seem to be some probability in casting antichrist upon an age not so far remote from the apostolic as hath been commonly reputed.'[62] This is a striking and important assertion and may well indicate a growing interest in the so called 'New Way' of interpretation pioneered by Hugo Grotius and his English disciple Henry Hammond. According to their view, the Reformation is not mentioned in Revelation the historical predictions of which extend only to the coming of Constantine.[63] Hall refers to the works of Grotius and Hammond in his letter to Ussher in terms which suggest complete familiarity with their ideas.[64] Moreover, he had written to Hammond some three years previously commending his opinion regarding the Antichrist but recognizing the many problems still to be solved.[65] It should be noted, however, that the identification of Simon Magus with the Pauline 'man of sin' by no means removes the label of Antichrist from the Papacy. What is at question here is the identification of the specific individual with whom 'the ordinary Christians of Thessalonica were well acquainted'.[66] Hall himself points out that St. John refers to many Antichrists and the texts in question afford scope for the identification of any apostate movement or individual in this way (I John 4: 3).

Hall's exhaustive knowledge of Apocalyptic and Millenarian literature combined with his friendship with some of the leading authorities upon the subject perfectly equipped him to answer and criticize John Archer's startling predictions, but he also had one other important qualification. Although seventy-six years old at the time of composition, his satiric eye remained quite undimmed. By the simple device of gathering together the dozens of mutually exclusive Millenarian interpretations—of which Archer's was but one—he discredits them all. The thirteen 'paradoxes' abstracted from Archer's own theory effectively reduce both theory and theorist to absurdity:

Oh happy Kingdome, where there is no taint of hypocrisie! But shall men have hearts then?...But what news is it that no person excommunicate shall be there? what place can there be possibly imagined for an excommunication in a Kingdome (after a sort) heavenly...Neither shall the persons onely of the then-living Saints be freed from depravation by sin, but all their children in all the succeeding generations; none of them shall prove bad, none reprobate; all shall be called the seed of the blessed; what though they be begotten and conceived in sin? what though they propagate sin to the fruit of their loynes? yet their issue shall not prove sinners; As much as to say, as there shall be fire, but neither heat, nor smoke; There shall be a poysonous fountain, but it shall yield no unwholsome water.[67]

Yet for all its polemic power it is essential to realize that *The Revelation Unrevealed* is far more than a controversial tract. It represents a vindication of the devotional mysticism of all

Hall's later work. Because his own thoughts were becoming
increasingly more other-worldly and spiritual, because he was
preoccupied with thoughts of his own approaching death, he
was shocked by the gross materialism of Archer's claims, by
seeing 'evangelical promises ... carnally drained'. Rather like
Augustine after the fall of Rome, he had lost all trust in human
institutions. He exhorts his readers to 'fix not their belief upon
any Kingdome of Christ our Saviour, but spirituall and
heavenly'.[68] He will not see religion pressed into the service of
yet another attempt to establish a fool's paradise.[69] Written just
two years before *The Invisible World, The Revelation Unrevealed* reasserts the mystery of the spiritual life against the
presumptions of human speculation. It emphasizes the limits
of even enlightened reason. The devotional 'mysticism' of
Hall's Higham days was the inevitable outcome of the
composition in 1606 of *The Arte of Divine Meditation,* of the
persistent bending of the mind on some spiritual object until
the thoughts come to an issue. Rightly considered *The
Revelation Unrevealed* is the defence of that mysticism, a
vindication of the purely spiritual emphasis of *Christ Mysticall*
(1647), and a preface to *The Great Mysterie of Godliness*
(1652) and *The Invisible World* (1652). That the defence
should have been conducted in such an eminently rational,
and not infrequently satiric, manner was entirely appropriate.

APPENDIX A

The Relationship of The Discovery of a New World to Mundus Alter et Idem

In 1609 John Healey produced a complete translation of Hall's *Mundus Alter et Idem* entitled *The Discovery of a New World* and the work was reissued with a new preface around 1614.[1] Very little is known about the translator, who may have been the son of a Catholic recusant named Richard Healey, a servant of Lord Sheffield. If so, he is thought to have been implicated in the Gunpowder Plot.[2] Our only sure information, however, is that gleaned from the dedications to his other translations. From this source we learn that he was a favourite of William Herbert, third Earl of Pembroke, whose patronage he gained on the recommendation of John Florio.[3] The dedicatory epistle to his translation of St. Augustine's *Of the Citie of God* (1610), written by the Publisher Thomas Thorpe, speaks of him as having left England for Virginia —a statement which seems probable enough in view of the fact that the Earl was at that time a member of the King's Council for the Virginia Company.[4] Thorpe also wrote the dedication for the second edition of Healey's version of Epictetus's *Manuall* (1616), and there he declares that the translator is dead.[5]

The Discovery was Healey's 'apprentises essay' in translation,[6] and part of his difficulty in undertaking the task must have lain in choosing between the different styles of translation then popular. On the one hand, for example, descending from John Cheke and Nicholas Grimald, there was a tradition of scholarly accuracy favouring close rendering of the substance, and where possible the style, of the parent text. John Stradling's version of Lipsius's *De Constantia* was of this type.[7] On the other hand, regarding the translator primarily as a popularizer, others favoured a freer, less restricting mode. Among the members of this school there was much talk of making the classics speak English—hence, for example, the peculiarly English flavour of Philemon Holland's Livy. The finished work is intended to represent what the ancient author might have written had he been a sixteenth- or seventeenth-century Englishman. It was therefore essential that such translations should reflect the prevailing manner of contemporary composition. So, in translating Montaigne, Florio drew upon the vocabulary and style of *Euphues* and, that naturalized classic, Sylvester's Du Bartas, itself one of the most popular translations. Hence his work became an integral part of English letters, rather than just an English version of a French author. When we recall the personal interest that Florio took in Healey and the *Mundus*, it is not surprising to find that *The Discovery of a New World* belongs entirely to this second mode of translation.[8] Much to Hall's disgust, therefore, when the work appeared in the vernacular in 1609 it did so in the loose, racy idiom of Nashe and Dekker:

No, I will bee as good as my word and iustifie, that if *Hercynia* keepe ten thousand theeves (as lightlie it doth alwayes,) *Booty-forrest* shall keepe a thousand thousand: Baw waw! *Hercynia*? why 'tis a blanket for a Catte, a petty Cock-pitte, nay a very Tobacco–boxe in respect of *Booty-forrest*.[9]

Energetic and striking as this undoubtedly is, it preserves little of the learned university wit and subtle nuance of phrasing intended by Hall:

Butinia sylva, prae qua illa Germanorum Hircynia, decem latronum millibus stipata, pomariolum angustius, aut mera quasi sepes videtur.[10]
(Booty Forest, in comparison with which the German Hercynia, bristling with ten thousand brigands, seems like a narrow little orchard, or a mere hedge.)

In Hall the imagery is of a homogeneous nature and stands in a decreasing sequence (forest, orchard, hedge) emphasized by positioning and syntax. The effect in Healey is entirely different. Volubility rather than subtlety characterizes *The Discovery*.

Healey had an eye to the contemporary market and was trying to relate *The Discovery* to the popular literary trends of the day. In Lavernia (Chapter II), for example, we are told of the thieves' speech that,

In istorum sermone quaedam Wallica vocabula notavi, quod ego ex ignotis nostratium peregrinationibus factum iudicarim.   (pp. 194–5)
(I noted certain Welsh words in their conversation, and this I took to be the result of hitherto unknown travels in the area by our country-men).

Healey renders it as follows, complete with a highly revealing marginal note:

Their (a) language is very crabbed, I could not possibly learne it; onely I observed some Welsh words, taught them as it seemes by some ancient travellers of our Westerne Brittons.
(a) Of this language there is an excellent exact discoverie made in *Thomas Deckers Bellman*, but in his *Lanthorne and Candle-light*, he hath outstript all the world for variety of knowledge in Canting.   (p. 125)

That both works here referred to were published as recently as 1608 attests to Healey's interest in popular contemporary literature. Tales of cheats and rogues, couched in their own canting language, were still very popular, and it was to this type of literature that Healey sought to relate *The Discovery*. In describing the solemn inanity of the Fool's Paradise (Moroniae Felicis Paradisium), for example, he renders the phrase 'Illusum est singulis probe' ('They are all brought to utter ridicule', p. 178), as 'They are all singularlie, and ingeniously *coni-catcht*' (p. 115, my emphasis), and in the list of Moronian words appended to the description of Variana he inserts, 'A male cony, Ircub', among the Paracelsian terms (p. 88). Again, in describing the life-style of the Ucalegonians, where the *Mundus* reads simply, 'coenant, dormiunt, surgunt, prandent, recumbunt' (p. 44; 'They sup, they sleep, they rise, they lunch, they recline at table'), Healey gives the following, far more elaborate, version, 'They sup, they sleepe, they rise, they dine, and they sup, and so round in a ring, (unless a little whoring now and then chance to adde one dance more to the round)' (p. 34). He also takes the opportunity of associating Hall's account with the epigrams of Sir John Davies by giving a marginal reference to epigram 39, 'In Fuscum', a poem not merely similar in theme, but undoubtedly the source of the sentence in brackets, his own addition to Hall's text.[11]

With alterations such as these occurring on almost every page, it comes as no surprise to find a passage like the following in the middle of the description of Pazzivilla: 'Here indeed (saith hee) dwell the Cocatrices, the *Roffianaes*, the *Makquerells*, and all those ancient fish wives that sell *Ruffes*, *Mackrell* and *Whiting-mops* whatsoever.' (p. 102.) Needless to remark, this is neither what Hall wrote nor intended, and consequently the major flaw of *The Discovery*, considered *solely* as a translation—for one can only admire its vigour and fluency—is that it suppresses some of the original's finest effects, while substituting others of a nature totally incompatible with the author's intentions. In the translation we are reading Healey not Hall.

That this should have been the case was inevitable from the moment Healey adopted the second mode of translation discussed above. Noting that the *Mundus* was written in an apparently simple and even conversational style of Latin, he chose as his medium the then popular colloquial style of English rogue literature. Addressing Hall (whose displeasure he evidently anticipated) in the highly disingenuous epistle 'I.H. the translator, unto I.H. the Author', he declares, 'Sir, if the turning of your witty worke into our mother tongue doe distast you, blame not any but your selfe that wrote it: *Language doth not alter the sense of any thing.*' (My emphasis; p. 5.)

But 'sense' *is* dependent on 'language'. The style of the *Mundus* is an integral component of its total effect and cannot be altered without altering the whole character of the work. Whereas Hall's Mercurius is restrained, academic, and subtle, the speaker in Healey is loud, verbose, and not infrequently coarse. Whereas Hall draws on the language of Roman satire and comedy, Healey draws on the dialect of bell-men, and fish-wives, the language of the boisterous characters who populate the world of *Bartholomew Fayre*: 'There are two select persons bound by the law to attend the bodie all the way with two blacke silke fannes, to drive away the flies from it, be it in winter when the flies are all dead, and *the carcasse not a fart the sweeter*, all's one for that, law is law, and must bee allowed.' (My emphasis; p. 120.)

The Latin of the *Mundus* was too refined for Healey who wished to reinterpret the work to a completely different audience. For him the emphasis fell on *Mundus Idem* rather than on *Mundus Alter*. He wanted to make the satire explicit. His version of the Crapulian elections, for instance, employs terminology more appropriate to an urban council than to the senate of Hall's description:

The more that each mans rotundity of corpulence is found to bee enlarged; unto the higher place is hee presently advanced: so that I have seene some come sneaking out of the fagge end of the suburbes, who had held their *Shoppikins* in the verges of the Cities Podex, God knowes how many winters, iustle notwithstanding at length, into an honourable place in the Citty, and at last come to be a principal *Syre* of this famous Common-weale. But now you shall heare: If either sicknesse, (as it often falleth out) or age, doe chance to make these *Alder-guts* cast their Colloppes afterward, they are immediately put off the Bench and loose both greace, and grace at one clap: this is hard now, but it's true as hard as it is I can tel yee that.   (pp. 26–7)

In its own way this is quite excellent, and once again one must applaud the translator's linguistic facility, but it is not Hall's work. Healey is laughing at the rather inglorious rise of low-born, upstart aldermen, or 'alder-guts' as he terms them. Such phrases (drawn from their own social background) as 'fagge end of the suburbes', 'shoppikins', 'cities podex', 'cast their Colloppes', 'God knowes how many', and 'greace and grace', provide all the humour he has to offer.

In the Latin, however, the emphasis is entirely different. The elections, we are told, are not such as you would find 'alibi' (elsewhere), and though the denial is certainly a spur to speculation, no further clue is given, and the reader is left to draw his own conclusions. The emphasis, brought out by the order and structure of the sentence, is upon the rapid and fantastic rise and fall, and the humour stems as much from the imaginative qualities of the scene itself as from the implied comparison:

Et quo quis magis crescit, illo provehitur altius; ita quosdam vidi ab infimae et obscurissimae urbeculae moenibus, suo quidem merito nobiliore adhuc donatos civitate tandemque in urbium celeberrima, Senatoria dignitate auctos; qui tamen ubi vel morbo (quod saepe fit) vel aetate, statuto macilentiores evaserint, una cum carne pristinum honorem amiserunt. (p. 32)
(The bigger a man grows, the further is he advanced. So I have seen natives of lowly and obscure little towns solely through their own merit presented with far more eminent citizenship, finally achieving the dignity of senatorial rank in the foremost of cities; yet these same men becoming leaner than the law allows through sickness (a common cause) or old age have lost both office and obesity together).

The movement of the Latin sentence is part of the sense, rising to its climax at 'Senatoria dignitate auctos', and then suddenly, like the senators themselves, falling away to its close. We note also the irony of 'suo quidem merito'—this is a fair community, corpulence, not favour, ensures success.

The difference between the *Mundus* and *The Discovery* stretches even to the marginal annotations. In Hall these are part and parcel of the over-all satiric intent, but in Healey they are often no more than bona fide annotations intended to aid his readers' comprehension. For example, when we are told that 'the Eat-allians have unreconcileable warres with two other nations, the Hunger-landers ... and the Trivingers', the allegorical point is made clear by a note explaining that 'Gluttony is a deadly enemy both to hunger and good husbandry' (p. 32). This is something Hall does only at the outset and then merely as a guide to how the rest of the work should be read. Later on he introduces the subjects of sceptical philosophy (p. 131) and lycanthropy (p. 141) and passes by without comment, whereas Healey feels the need to explain both terms (pp. 87, 93).

Also, in keeping with his emphasis on *Mundus Idem*, Healey uses the notes to draw explicit correspondences between the real and imaginary worlds. He informs us, for example, that the inhabitants of Moronia treat their friends, 'Iust as our Citizens use a man as long as hee hath cash, you have him, brow and bosome, but that fayling, my maister is not within sir' (p. 84). To Hall's note on bribe-taking, the disease of Demosthenes (p. 208), he adds, 'It raignes here in England, at some seasons of the yeare, very powerfully, God knowes, and to the wrack of many an upright cause' (p. 133). A large proportion of the translator's hundred or more additional notes are of this nature. On the other hand, however, Hall's intentionally monstrous, pseudo-scholarly note on the etymology of Crapulia (p. 19) is completely deleted. It was far too abstruse for the type of audience Healey had in mind. Yet his methods are by no means consistent. The tone and content of his annotations vary widely, some being comprised of basic explanatory material, while others repeat Hall's meticulous scholarly lore. It is hardly likely, for instance, that a reader to whom the term 'sceptic' has to be explained will want to consult the *Bibliotheca Historica* of Diodorus Siculus to examine a reference to Eurydice (p. 96). This same inconsistency is found with notes incorporated into the text; with such phrases as 'ut cum Apuleio loquar' (p. 25), he deals erratically, sometimes using them, sometimes omitting them.[12]

Yet important as the notes are, to my mind the most significant change of all, and the most total departure from the Latin, comes in the treatment of proper names. That this should be so is rather ironic, for Healey himself emphasized their importance in an epistle prefixed to the second issuing of *The Discovery* where he says that the work must be read three times: 'Once for *Strabo*, once for *Socrates*, and once for *Merlin Cocaius*; The first for the *Geography*, the second for the *Morality*, and the third for the *Language*, and *Etymology*' (p. 149). One may note in passing that a further irony arising from this statement is the complete omission of all of Hall's elaborate maps and charts, one of the work's most original features and surely essential to its 'geography'.[13] There can be no doubt whatsoever that fictitious names with learned etymologies form part of the very texture of the *Mundus*, permeating the entire narrative from beginning to end. Since they span seven languages—Latin, Greek, French, German, Spanish, Italian, and Hebrew—Healey was perfectly correct in associating the work with Merlin Cocaius (Teofilo Folengo) author of the *Macaronicon*, but what he apparently did not appreciate was that his remarks are applicable only to the Latin text. Having chosen to reduce all the names, whatever their linguistic origin, to his own brand of Nashean English, he forfeited the whole seven-tiered effect. Hence, for example, the point of Hall's list of Morosophi (Phoolosophers), is entirely lost:

Alij se (ni male memini) *Morello scurras* vocant, alii *Cluniachos*, et *Latrinenses*: Alij *Licetanos, Zoccolantos, Cercosimios, Matteobassos, Scelestinos,*

Della mercede, Della vita commune. (p. 117.)[14]

Whereas Hall wrote with reference to various orders of Catholic monks, some of which are named in marginal notes and all of which are easily decipherable, Healey opted for the less difficult device of *reductio ad absurdum*: 'There was one sort called *Browne–backs*, and another called *Clunches*: besides (as I remember) there are the *Quadricornes*, the *Barly-faces*, the *Greene-geese*, the societies of *Saint Patch del Culo*, Saint *Gynny come home at noone*, and many more.' (p. 79.) Here only two names have any definite significance, the rest are coinages inserted purely for sound effect. Hall's is a subtle joke depending upon his reader's ability to detect the witty changes in naming, and to follow the not over-difficult clues; Healey's is one of broad humour, all on the surface, depending on the ludicrous sound. Once the macaronic element has vanished we return to plain name-calling in the old satiric tradition of the English pamphlet. There needs no explanation of 'Fooliana', 'Swash-buckliero', 'Gossipingoa', and the rest, and so all the accompanying marginal comments, and the painstakingly elaborate etymological index are of necessity dispensed with. Yet even here Healey found consistency impossible for there are passages in the Latin which remain completely intractable. Heavily indebted to St. Augustine's *De Haeresibus*, for example, the description of Doxia becomes unintelligible if either proper names or descriptive details are altered, for the whole point is that these things actually happened, that truth is stranger than fiction. All Healey can do in such circumstances is to drop the more pronounced features of his style, incorporate almost all of Hall's elaborate notes, and give a rather pedestrian version which jars with the general tenor of his narrative (p. 121).

In our sense of the term, *The Discovery* is more properly an adaptation of the *Mundus* than a translation. Indeed some passages have been either altered or amplified to such a degree as to become unrecognizable. In his letter 'I.H. the Translator, unto I.H. the Author' Healey defends this practice by claiming that, 'where I varye from your Originall, it is eyther to expresse your sence, or preserve your conceit' (p. 5). But the additions go far beyond this avowed purpose, and become increasingly obtrusive, from the point of view of the Latin, as the work proceeds. The fact that they fit in so well with Healey's own version is in itself an indication of how far this has diverged from the original. Early on the additions are relatively minor, serving to introduce new images or observations which occurred to Healey as he wrote. For example, in the description of Crapulia where Hall says simply 'viri ad miraculum crasso corpore, obesoque' ('the men were incredibly corpulent and paunchy', p. 36),

Healey writes, 'The whole sort of al these citizens are generally of an unmeasurable grosenesse (and seemed to mee when I sawe them walke iust like so many tunnes, moving each upon two pottle pots).' (p. 29.) Occasionally, too, he will run on in places where Hall knew just when to stop, and this particularly in passages introducing physical imagery of a nauseating kind. Where Hall remains content with saying, 'paulum calidae imbibit, vomitat, et purgatur illico; quodque egeritur hoc modo, res fisci est.' (p. 39; 'He drinks a little hot water, vomits, and is instantly purged, the matter driven out in this manner going to the treasury'), Healey goes much further:

[He] drinkes a little hott water, spewes a while, and within a quarter of an houre, *Viah*, he lets flie upon *Aiax*, and rises from his roast as sound as a bell. Now all the what you wil, that he voids at either end during this purging time, is immediately confiscate unto the Dukes treasurie, and *strained* upon in such a case, by certaine surveyors, especially appointed for such commodities. (p. 31.)

Hence it is that no study of Hall's imagery can be based on Healey's translation, the only authoritative source is the original Latin text.

This is equally true of some of the most vividly descriptive passages of *The Discovery*, many of which are attributable solely to the translator. A comparison of the Fool's Paradise sections illustrates the point very well. Of the palace servants the *Mundus* says, 'experrectum salutant Regem, faustumque diem apprecantur: quodque mavelit hodie vestis genus officiose percontantur' (p. 180; 'They hail the newly-awakened king, wish him a fortunate day and dutifully inquire what type of outfit he would prefer today'). The style here is typical of Hall: simple, clear, and impeccably under-stated. But when we turn to Healey we find something far different:

Health and happie daies to thy Sacred Maiestie, great King. King thinks hee? masse this is brave. What apparell will it please your Maiestie to weare to day? your sute of Gold-smiths worke, your suite of tissue embrodered with Rubies, your cloth of gold doublet with the Carbuncle buttons ...Heyda! my man's an *Endymion* indeede now, and will not change states with the man in the moone, he, for al his fulgid throne he sittes in. (p. 116)

By the time we reach Lavernia in the fourth book these additions have grown to the proportions of original composition. The mere mention of 'Itali et Germani insidiatores' ('Italian and German brigands', p. 196) evokes the rendering, 'the damned, soulelesse, fiend-bred, hell-borne *Italian* theeves ... and those durty, gut-swolne, toad-sprung *Germaines*' (p. 127). Yet the same year in which *The Discovery* was published, Hall was preaching to the court against the 'profane tongue' which walked abroad through the land.[15] Again, the simple introduction of the word 'Hercynia' serves as a springboard for,

> put Schwartzwaldt, Odenwaldt, Steigerwaldt, Westerwaldt, Behemerwaldt, waldt quoth you? nay put all the waldts, welts and gards in *Europe* to it; I tell yee, let one word suffice, they all make but a dayes iourney for an Irish Lowse, (bee shee never so speedie) if you measure it with this. (p. 126)

In this case I cannot quote the Latin text for comparison—it does not exist.

What Hall, as a master of decorous Senecan prose, must have thought of Healey's style is easy to determine. In the first century of his *Meditations and Vowes* (1605) he declares,

> The praise of a good speech standeth in words and matter: Matter, which is as a faire and well-featur'd body; Elegance of words, which is as a neat and well-fashioned garment. Good matter, slubbered up in rude and carelesse words, is made lothsome to the hearer; as a good body mis-shapen with unhandsome clothes.[16]

It would seem that he made his feelings on the issue fully known to Healey himself, for in the epistle to the reader appended to the second issue of *The Discovery*, the translator retracts all he had previously said of the importance of 'language'. Now it appears that the English version does differ, and that radically, from the Latin:

> But as touching this present pile of *English*, it is mine, it hath no further alliance to his, then chalke hath to cheese, for as those have no cohaerence in their nearest proprieties (which translations should never want) but onely in their generall kind of essence as they are both corporeall substances; no more doth this worke any way resemble his in fashion, stile, or discourse, but onely in the invention and proiect. (pp. 146–7)

Though it might be objected that this is merely a fabricated argument designed to suit the needs of the occasion, it may actually represent the fruits of reconsideration, for Healey's ideas on the art of translation seem to have altered after he completed *The Discovery*. In the preface to his translation of Theophrastus, for example, he states that the translator should observe a mean between servility and looseness, and that, 'to swerve too much from the Author, implieth a secret disabling, as if the Original might be bettered; which cannot but savour of much self-opinion and singularity, yet if there were a necessity to erre in either, I had rather be over-strict, then any whit too bold.'[17] This shift in attitude may well have been caused by a study of the methods of Isaac Casaubon, 'the Magazine or Storehouse of all learning', upon whose Latin translation of Theophrastus's *Characters* Healey based his own English version. A comparison of this with Hall's *Characters* demonstrates Healey's ability to adopt the restrained Senecan style when he so chose. He was undoubtedly a stylist of some versatility.

It is quite clear from Healey's remarks that Hall suffered from the attribution of *The Discovery* to himself, an attribution possibly occasioned by the coincidence of their initials I.H. and I.H. Quite understandably the tone and style of *The Discovery* were entirely out of keeping with the image of the dignified clergyman Hall had become. In order to stem this tide of criticism Healey declares,

But that these weakenesses (for so I confesse they are) in mee, should be made as staines to the reputation of another, of one whose learning, life, and workes now extant may serue as purging fires whereat all those that hence haue taken occasion to wrong him thus, might long agoe haue lighted their ignorance were it neuer so immense; that my lightnesses should bee reputed as births of his worthines! Oh that my pen (whereby since I haue ignorantly iniur'd him, I doe thus willingly and freely cleare him) could but make them see what an uniust construction they haue made of an ignorant (and I protest vtterly vnwilling) offence! But since mine owne unwarinesse gaue first occasion of those unkinde, and more then foolish callumniations which ignorance draweth from mine error, to staine his goodnesse with; all the satisfaction I can giue him, is to shew my selfe willing to make a faire way againe for his deserts, in the bosomes of such as hence take their occasion of dislike, by proclaiming this truth to all that shall read it, that this present *Discouery of the South-Indies* is none of his, but had this forme giuen it, without his knowledge, by one who will euer acknowledge his worth & grauity to haue beene utterly ignorant of any vnfit phrase whatsoeuer included in the whole booke.   (pp. 147–8)

With this explicit statement of the facts the issue of *The Discovery* closed. The *Mundus* itself was virtually disowned by Hall and deliberately excluded along with the *Virgidemiarum* from all editions of his collected works. It was, however, frequently brought to public attention by a formidable gallery of enemies ill-disposed to accept Healey's generous appraisal. Apart from two pirated adaptations which appeared in 1669 and 1688, *The Discovery* did not reappear after 1614 until the present century.[18] Nor was it superseded by a new translation, for with the sole exception of a somewhat uninspired rendering of the first six chapters of *Crapulia* by Swift's friend, Dr. William King, no other English version was produced until 1981.[19]

APPENDIX B

The Authorship of Mundus Alter et Idem

Both the Frankfurt (1605?) and the Hanau (1607) editions of the *Mundus* appeared anonymously but the authorship of the work soon became known and proved a constant source of embarrassment to Hall throughout his career, despite the reassurances of its editor William Knight. The early publishing history of the *Mundus* is fraught with difficulties and it would now appear that only some of the extant copies were actually produced on the Continent. Furthermore in the index (and only the index) to a number of these the title of Book II, Chapter 2, 'Quid mihi a Gynaecopolitis factum fuerit', reads 'Quid Alberico Gentili a Gynaecopolitis factum fuerit'. Understandably this insertion led to some confusion. Alberico Gentili (1552–1608), an Italian refugee living in England, had been Regius Professor of Civil Law at Oxford since 1587 and was known and respected throughout Europe. His eminence in the field of international law is second only to that of Grotius, and much of the famous *De iure Belli et Pacis* is indebted to his writings. As a result, when a German translation of the *Mundus* appeared in 1613 (second edition, 1704) under the title *Utopiae Pars II. Mundus Alter et Idem*, the translator ascribed the work to Gentili himself, unlikely though it was that an anonymous author would insert his own name in the 'index capitum'.[1] Significantly the Utrecht edition of the *Mundus* which appeared in 1643 makes no mention of Gentili, contenting itself with the pseudonym Mercurius Britannicus.[2] Two years previously in France, Gabriel Naudé, Cardinal Mazarin's librarian, said that the Mundus had been written by an Englishman whose name was unknown to him.[3] Hall would not seem to have had any reason to satirize Gentili, and it may well be that the insertion was a mistake by the German printer Wilhelm Antonius who was also publishing works by Gentili at the same time.[4]

In a recent study of almost all the copies of the early editions of the *Mundus* which are known to survive, Mr John Millar Wands has pointed out that the 'Frankfurt' edition, though undoubtedly sold at the Frankfurt Book Fair of 1606, was in fact published in England, probably by Henry Lownes, for John Porter, the bookseller under whose name the work was entered in the *Stationers' Register* on 2 June 1605. Four months earlier Porter had also been assigned Hall's *Meditations and Vowes*. Furthermore Wilhelm Kip, the engraver responsible for the title-page, is known to have been active in England from 1597 to 1610. In fact he seems to have worked exclusively in England during this period. Mr Millar conjectures that there were actually three early editions of the *Mundus*, not two. They were the 'Frankfurt' edition of 1605 (or perhaps early 1606); the Hanau edition of 1606 (until now always dated 1607); and a reissue composed from the gatherings of both which appeared in 1607. He draws particular attention to the fact that in five copies of this reissue which were apparently made up in England, or imported *into* England (where Hall's authorship was, of course, known to Porter), the name *Alberico Gentili* is crossed out and the word 'mihi' is inserted in the margin. All of the alterations are in the same hand.[5] The same is true of the copy of the Frankfurt edition in the library of Pembroke College, Cambridge, an edition apparently unknown to Mr Wands.[6]

Some further points concerning the publication of the *Mundus* must also be borne in mind. First of all, the editor William Knight was a personal friend of Hall's and is so addressed in one of his *Epistles* (1611).[7] In that same work Hall virtually acknowledges the *Mundus* when he puns on the name of the Eburones—which should be Ebriones (drunkards)—'after all the ruins of my neglected Philologie'. One immediately recalls Knight's reference to 'nonnulla alia sua commenta *Philologa* luce et laude dignissima' entrusted to him at the same time as the *Mundus* but deemed 'levia aut vana' by their author.[8] Furthermore in another letter to William Bedell, Hall urges his addressee not to be discouraged from writing by 'the inundations of *Francford*'. 'Indeed', he adds,

we all write; and while we write, cry out of number. How well might many be spared, even of those that complaine of too many? whose importunate babbling cloyes the world, without use. My suspition gives mee, that some may perhaps reflect this censure upon my selfe. I am content to put it to hazzard, and (if need be) beare it. But certeinly (mee thinks) of profitable writings store is an easie fault: No man is bound to read; and he that will spend his time and his eyes where no sensible profit drawes him on, is woorthie to lose his labour.[9]

This passage occurs *only* in the 1608 edition of the *Epistles*. In *A Recollection of such Treatises as have beene severally published* (1615) it is completely deleted and does not reappear in any of the other collected editions.[10]

The *Mundus* is dedicated to Henry Hastings, fifth Earl of Huntingdon. After what has been said in the introduction to the present work, it is unnecessary to labour the significance of this point. Hall's debt to the Hastings family cannot be over-emphasized, and it was one of which he remained acutely aware. To the fifth Earl he also dedicated *Heaven upon Earth* (1606) and the fifth book of the *Contemplations* (1614) where he describes him as 'the first patrone of my poore studies'.[11] Considered in order of composition, the *Mundus* is in fact the earliest of Hall's works to bear any dedication.

The only critic seriously to question Hall's authorship of the *Mundus* was Mr Edward Petherick who, in an article of the 'Bacon is Shakespeare' type published in 1896, decided that the author was probably Gentili.[12] This conclusion, which has since been universally rejected, is all the more surprising in view of the contrary evidence produced by Petherick himself, but leaving aside for the moment the convolutions of the argument and the complete failure to mention the scores of verbal echoes between the *Mundus* and Hall's other works—not to mention the evidence of the Latin style—there is one major factual flaw in the discussion.[13] This is the statement that the *Mundus* was first attributed to Hall by Thomas Hyde, Bodley's Librarian, in 1674, eighteen years after the bishop's death.[14] If this were so, it might well give us pause for doubt. Fortunately for us, though perhaps unfortunately for Hall, it is completely erroneous. The work was correctly identified without contradiction several times during the bishop's own lifetime by people who were in a position to know the truth, foremost amongst them being John Milton.

When John Healey translated the *Mundus* in 1609 he addressed himself as 'I.H. the Translator, unto I.H. the Author' thereby giving a sound indication to anyone who did not already know that the work was indeed to be attributed to Hall.[15] In the orthography of the day 'i' and 'j' were interchangeable and the initials 'I.H.' or 'J.H.' had already appeared on a number of Hall's other works. Originally the *Virgidemiarum* too had come out anonymously, but the 1599 edition of the *Byting Satyres* bore the initials 'I.H.'—there was little point in preserving the fiction when Francis Meres had revealed the identity of the author in 1598. After this everyone knew that I.H. was 'Hall of Imanuel Colledge in Cambridge'.[16] Again, just a year before the publication of Healey's translation, the text of Hall's first Paul's Cross sermon, *Pharisaisme and Christianity*, appeared with no other attribution than I.H. The authorship, of course, was beyond question. In 1609, the very year in which *The Discovery of a New World* was first published, Hall's anti-Catholic treatise, *The Peace of Rome*, appeared under the initials J.H. to be followed the next year by the similarly ascribed *Common Apologie of the Church of England*. Little doubt could remain in anyone's mind as to who Healey's 'I.H.' was. Moreover, when he declares 'your gravity and place, *Envie* as well as I must reverence', he is undoubtedly alluding to the 'Defiance to Envie' with which I.H.'s *Virgidemiarum* opens.[17] In every edition of the *Mundus*, one remembers, the tomb of Vortunius is said to have been set up by 'H.I.'—the same initials reversed.[18]

Having made the startling changes which we have examined in Appendix A, Healey thought it advisable to pre-empt criticism by assuring Hall that 'if the turning of your witty worke into our mother tongue doe distaste you, blame not any but your selfe that wrote it... if you but rest unmoov'd, let any man else kicke, Ile scorne him' (p. 5). Hall, however, did not rest 'unmoov'd'. Unless Knight was lying, he had not even approved the publication of the *Mundus* itself, but *The Discovery* was completely unacceptable—and all the more so because of its popularity. When it was reissued in 1614, therefore, it was accompanied by a new preface written in a far different tone (pp. 145–9). It appears from this that the coincidence of the initials I.H. (John Healey) and I.H. (Joseph Hall) had led some readers to believe that Hall himself was responsible for the translation. Had not Donne translated his own *Conclave Ignatii*? The result was that many had taken the occasion to tax him with 'divers (in their judgement) immodest, light, scurrilous, and ridiculous passages therein' (p. 146). This being the case, Healey now sets out to make a clear distinction between the author and the translator. 'I doe here absolutely averre and give notice', he declares, 'to all that shall hereafter take view hereof, This worke was neuer his, he neuer saw it, neuer dreamed of any such matter, untill hee met it in the hand of another man' (p. 146). But this was only part of the problem. There remained the question of the *Mundus* itself concerning which Healey continues:

There was indeed a little booke some 8. or 9. yeares agoe that came from *Franckford*, which some few (I know not upon what illumination more then ordinary) affirmed to haue passed the file of his muse, which if it be true, it can be no way in the world either preiudiciall to his learning, (seeing it hath all perfection fitting an absolute poeme) nor to his grauity or profession, seeing it was a birth of his youth.   (p. 146)

The very tone of this passage demonstrates beyond all doubt that Healey himself is to be numbered among the 'few' who attribute the work to Hall, and with good reason. It is clear from the preface that the author has complained to Healey in the strongest possible terms about the translation. If he had not written the *Mundus* either this was the place to make the fact publicly known. All that needed to be said was that 'some few' were completely wrong, and that Healey himself had been misinformed concerning I.H. No such assertion, however, can be made. Instead the laboured defence of the work in view of the 'gravity or profession' of '*that Reverend man* that long agoe laid the first proiect of this *Discovery*' (p. 145) constitutes all the evidence we need. In Healey's opinion the *Mundus* is a work in which Hall,

hath towred aboue the capacities (at least aboue the imitation) of all those ouer-weening iudgements that dare any way presume to traduce his originall. In iust defence of which worthy worke, I cast defiance in the teeth of all that malice or traduce him, that it is neither any way scurrilous, immodest, light, nor ridiculous. (p. 146)

Concerning the translation, however, we read that,

There is no man in the whole world, who hath either conuersed with himselfe in person, or his workes in print, that euer will surmise this present copy to haue had any testimony of his acknowledgement, or approbation to bee any way befitting his place, or (which is more) his profession. (p. 146)

It is perhaps worth noting at this point that Gentili died in 1608, at least six months before the publication of Healey's *first* preface.

The next attribution of the work to Hall would appear to be by the epigrammatist John Owen who published the following couplet in 1612:

> Mercurius Britannicus
> Optima descripsit Morus, Tu pessima Mundi:
> Tu nobis narras vera; sed ille bona.

This, of course, is quite non-committal as to the question of authorship, but in 1622 the title was altered to read 'Mercurius Britannicus. Ad I.H.' Owen obviously admired the work but its later critics did not.

In 1619, in reply to a letter which first appeared in his *Epistles* (1608),[20] the Jesuit Edward Coffin assailed Hall at great length in *A Refutation of M. Ioseph Hall His Apologeticall Discourse, For The Marriage of Ecclesiasticall Persons*. Throughout the body of this work Coffin displays an amazing familiarity with Hall's writings to which he makes frequent snide allusion. For example, at one stage he remarks, 'this is indeed *et satyrae*, and *sat irae*, to use your owne words' (p. 62)—a quotation from a short Latin epigram published with the *Virgidemiarum*. Later on, and this time without any explicit attribution, he says, 'Alas (poore M. Hall) I pitty your ignorance, but condemne your malice, fayne you would byte, but wanting teeth you can but only barke' (p. 365). The reference, of course, is to the *Tooth-lesse Satyrs* at which Milton was later to poke such cruel fun. In a work such as Coffin's one would not expect the *Mundus* to pass unmentioned, nor does it. Discussing the freedom of the clergy to marry, for example, he asks, 'whence then commeth this *freedome?* in what places and persons? ... I feare M. *Hall* in the end wil runne to *Terra Virginea, Guiana, Chyna, Mexico,* or some other regions under the Antarticke Pole to find it out.' (p. 225.) Towards the end of the *Refutation* 'M. *Halls* travells' (p. 355) are again called to our attention, and in reply to his remark 'there left our liberty, there began their bondage' Coffin enquires, 'where M. *Hall* do you meane? in *Terra Florida, Virginia,* or *Utopia?*' (p. 371). But the most telling allusion of all comes in Coffin's description of the conclusion to the letter which began the whole controversy: 'At the end of the Epistle M. *Hall,* as a man weary of his travells abroad, returneth home to *England.'* (p. 317.) We have read these words before—at the end of the Mundus itself: 'itineris tanti laboribus fractus in patriam redii.'[21]

Hall's opponents in theological controversy were understandably unwilling to allow him to forget the productions of his secular youth, but no-one made quite so much ado about them as did John Milton. The Smectymnuans themselves were relatively restrained and would appear to make only one allusion to the *Mundus* when they find that 'the limits of this Prelaticall Church extend as farre as from the high and lofty Promontory of Archbishops [the promontory of Crapulia?] to the *Terra incognita* of an etc.'—a glance at Laud's so-called 'etcetera oath'.[22] Hall's laconic reply is 'witty again'.[23] It was therefore left to Milton to rake up the ashes of the scandal of which we hear echoes in Healey's second preface.

In his *Animadversions upon the Remonstrants Defence against Smectymnuus* (July, 1641), Milton alludes in passing to both the *Virgidemiarum* and the *Mundus:*

Ans. You love toothlesse Satyrs; let me informe you, a toothlesse Satyr is as improper as a toothed sleekstone, and as bullish.
Remon. I beseech you brethren spend your Logick upon your own workes.[24]
Remonst. Alas we could tell you of *China, Japan, Peru, Brasil, New England, Virginia,* and a thousand others that never had any *Bishops* to this day.
Answ. O do not foile your cause thus, and trouble *Ortelius,* we can help you, and tell you where they have bin ever since *Constantines* time at least, in a place call'd *Mundus alter & idem,* in the spacious, and rich Countries of *Crapulia, Pamphagonia, Yvronia,* and in the Dukedome of *Orgilia,* and

Variana and their *Metropolis* of *Ucalego-nium*. It was an oversight that none of your prime *Antiquaries* could think of these venerable Monuments to deduce *Episcopacy* by: knowing that *Mercurius Britanicus* had them forth-comming.[25]

Reaction was not long delayed for in *A Modest Confutation of A Slanderous and Scurrilous Libell, entituled Animadversions upon the Remonstrants Defense against Smectymnuus* (February, 1642) an anonymous supporter of Hall, possibly his son Robert, saw fit to reply to the first of these sallies with a detailed defence of the term 'tooth-lesse satyrs', and indeed of satire in general. Wisely he omits to make any mention of the *Mundus*, apparently believing that his blanket condemnation of Milton's methods constitutes sufficient reply:

You begin therefore with his youth; the sport and leisure of his youth, even that must be raked up out of the dust, and cited to witnesse against him, as it were to disparage the holinesse of his Age and Calling. [*When my early sinnes are done away as a morning cloud, they shall never obscure or darken my setting Sun: God will never impute them to me, man may*] hath been the comfort of many a dying Saint, in the day of evill, when the iniquity of their heels have encompassed them (p. 8).

However nobly motivated, this was undoubtedly a tactical error, and one of which Milton took immediate advantage. Hall's early writings had now become a major issue in the controversy, and the Confuter himself had prepared the way for further attacks by declaring that an author's moral character can invariably be deduced from his writings. Predictably, Milton responded in *An Apology Against a Pamphlet call'd A Modest Confutation* not merely with a renewed onslaught upon the *Virgidemiarum* (ample material for which had been supplied by the recent defence), but by a direct challenge concerning the work which had not been defended, the *Mundus*. Seizing upon the use of the word 'mime' he declares,

Could he not beware, could he not bethink him, was he so uncircumspect, as not to foresee, that no sooner would that word *Mime* be set eye on in the paper, but it would bring to minde that wretched pilgrimage over *Minshews* Dictionary call'd *Mundus alter & idem*, the idlest and the paltriest Mime that ever mounted upon banke. Let him ask *the Author of those toothlesse Satyrs* who was the maker, or rather the anticreator of that universall foolery, who he was, who like that other principle of the *Maniches* the *Arch evill one*, when he had look't upon all that he had made and mapt out, could say no other but contrary to the Divine Mouth, that it was all very foolish ... Let him go now and brand another man injuriously with the name of *Mime*, being himselfe the loosest and most extravagant *Mime*, that hath been heard of; whom no lesse then almost halfe the world could serve for stage roome to play the *Mime* in.[26]

A few pages after this, recalling the aspersions so liberally bestowed upon his own character in the Confutation, he asks,

What if I had writ as your friend the author of the aforesaid *Mime, Mundus alter & idem*, to have bin ravisht like some young *Cephalus* or *Hylas*, by a troope of camping Huswives in *Viraginia*, and that he was there forc't to sweare himselfe an uxorious varlet, then after a long servitude to have come into *Aphrodisia* that pleasant Countrey that gave such a sweet smell to his nostrils among the shamelesse Courtezans of *Desvergonia*? surely he would have then concluded me as constant at the Bordello, as the gally-slave at his Oare.[27]

It is clear from these precise allusions that Milton was working with a copy of the *Mundus* readily available for his inspection. And it was the *Mundus* itself, not Healey's translation, which he used; all of the fictional lands and peoples are given their appropriate Latin names.

Hall was not one to allow any kind of libel to slip by unnoticed. In controversy after controversy he was noted for the vigour with which he repelled false attributions of all sorts, and even in the last years of his life we find him still valiantly defending his works against all calumnies.[28] In 1642, for the second time in less than thirty years, he had a perfect opportunity to reject the *Mundus* once and for all. What better argument could he have adduced against Milton than that he was a liar? But no such answer appeared, and for the time being the episcopal party remained silent. In 1652, however, four years before Hall's death, Peter Heylyn, that arch-champion of all things Anglican, produced his *Cosmographie,* a serious geographical work to which he added a witty survey of fictional worlds. One of these is *Mundus Alter et Idem* and it is quite obvious that as Heylyn wrote his account of it he bore Milton's words in mind. Had the attribution been false he would have said so. As it is, he must be understood as supplying the defence which the *Confutation* failed to make. The *Mundus,* he tells us, is

a witty and ingenious invention of a learned *Prelate,* writ by him in his younger dayes (but well enough becoming the austerity of the gravest head), in which he distingusheth [*sic*] the *Vices, Passions; Humours,* and ill *Affections* most commonly incident to mankind, into several *Provinces;* gives us the *Character* of each, as in the descriptions of a Country, People, and chief Cities of it: and sets them forth unto the eye in such lively colours, that the vitious man may see therein his own *Deformities,* and the well-minded man his own *imperfections.* The Scene of this design laid by the Reverend Author, in this *Terra Australis;* the *Decorum* happily preserved in the whole *Discovery;* the style acutely clear, the invention singular. Of whom and his *New World* I shall give you that *Eulogie,* which the *Historian* doth of *Homer,*

Nec ante illum quem ille imitaretur, neque post illum qui eum imitari posset, inventus est.[29]

With Hall's death in 1656 'envie', as he had predicted so long before, died too.[30] He was universally admired during the Restoration period and the *Mundus* was finally catalogued under the proper name by Thomas Hyde, Bodley's Librarian, in 1674. The appropriate epitaph to the whole affair was provided by Henry Hare, second Baron Coleraine, in *The Situation of Paradise Found Out* (1683) when, defending the use of allegory, he wrote that 'what hath been done this way by *Bishop Hall,* (under the name of Mercurius Britannicus) . . . is, I think well enough approved of' (p. 31).[31]

I A CHRONOLOGICAL LIST OF JOSEPH HALL'S PRINCIPAL WORKS

Virgidemiarum, Sixe Bookes (1597-8)

The Kings Prophecie: or Weeping Joy (1603)

Meditations and Vowes, Divine and Morall (1605-6)

Mundus Alter et Idem (Frankfurt, 1605?)

Heaven upon Earth: Or, Of True Peace and Tranquillitie of Minde (1606)

The Arte of Divine Meditation (1606)

Holy Observations... Also Some fewe of Davids Psalmes Metaphrased, for a taste of the Rest (1607)

Characters of Vertues and Vices (1608)

Epistles (1608-11)

Salomons Divine Arts... with an open and plaine Paraphrase, upon the Song of Songs (1609)

The Peace of Rome... whereto is prefixed A Serious Disswasive from Poperie (1609)

A Common Apologie of the Church of England: Against the uniust Challenges of the over-iust Sect, commonly called Brownists (1610)

Polemices Sacrae Pars Prior: Roma Irreconciliabilis (1611)

Contemplations on the Principall Passages of the Holy Storie (1612-34)

Quo Vadis? A Iust Censure of Travell as it is commonly undertaken by the Gentlemen of our Nation (1617)

The Honor of the Married Clergie, Maintayned Against the malicious Challenges of C.E. Masse-Priest (1620)

The Olde Religion (1628)

An Answer to Pope Urban His Inurbanitie (1629)

The Reconciler. An Epistle Pacificatorie of the seeming—differences of opinion concerning the truenesse and visibility of the Roman Church (1629)

Occasional Meditations (1630-3)

A Plaine and Familiar Explication (by way of Paraphrase) of all the hard Texts of the whole Divine Scripture of the Old and New Testament (1633)

Propositiones Catholicae (1633)

αυτοσχεδιάσματα *Vel, Meditatiunculae Subitaneae* (1635)

Henochismus: Sive, Tractus De modo ambulandi cum Deo (1635)

The Remedy of Prophanenesse. Or, Of The true sight and feare of the Almighty (1637)

Certaine Irrefragable Propositions worthy of Serious Consideration (1639)

An Humble Remonstrance to the High Court of Parliament (1640)

Christian Moderation (1640)

Episcopacie by Divine Right (1640)

A Defence of the Humble Remonstrance, Against the frivolous and false exceptions of Smectymnuus (1641)

A Short Answer to the Tedious Vindication of Smectymnuus (1641)

A Letter Lately sent by A Reverend Bishop from The Tower to A private Friend (1642)

The Devout Soul, or, Rules of Heavenly Devotion, Also, the Free Prisoner, or The Comfort of Restraint (1644)

The Peace-Maker (1645)

The Remedy of Discontentment. Or A Treatise of Contentation (1645)

The Balme of Gilead: Or, Comforts for the Distressed, Both Morall and Divine (1646)

Christ Mysticall; or The Blessed union of Christ and his Members. Also, An Holy Rapture ... Also, The Christian laid forth in his whole Disposition and Carriage (1647)

Satans Fiery Darts Quenched, or, Temptations Repelled (1647)

Pax Terris (1648)

Select Thoughts ... Also, The Breathings of the Devout Soul (1648)

χειροθεσία *or The Apostolique Institution of Imposition of Hands, for Confirmation, revived.* (1649)

Resolutions and Decisions of Divers Practicall Cases of Conscience in continuall Use amongst men, very necessary for their Information and Direction (1649)

The Revelation Unrevealed (1650)

Susurrium cum Deo: or Holy Self-Conferences of the Devout Soul ... Together with The Souls Farewell to Earth, and Approaches to Heaven (1651)

The Great Mysterie of Godliness, Laid forth by way of affectuous and feeling Meditations. Also, The Invisible World, Discovered to spiritual Eyes, and Reduced to usefull Meditation (1652)

The Holy Order; or Fraternity of the Mourners in Sion. Whereunto is added, Songs in the Night: or, Cheerfulnesse under Affliction (1654)

The Shaking of the Olive-Tree, The Remaining Works of that incomparable Prelate Joseph Hall ... with Some Specialities of Divine Providence in his Life Noted by His own Hand. Together with His Hard Measure: Written also by Himself (1659)

II *MODERN EDITIONS*

Brown Huntington, ed., *The Discovery of a New World* (Cambridge, Mass., 1937)

Davenport, A., ed., *The Poems of Joseph Hall* (Liverpool, 1949)

Grosart, A.B., ed., *The Complete Poems of Joseph Hall* (Manchester, 1879)

Hall, P., ed., *The Works of Joseph Hall*, 12 vols. (Oxford, 1837–9)

Huntley, Frank Livingstone, ed., *Bishop Joseph Hall and Protestant Meditation* (New York, 1980)

Kirk, Rudolf, ed., *Heaven upon Earth and Characters of Vertues and Vices* (New Brunswick, N.J., 1947)

Pratt, J., ed., *The Works of Joseph Hall*, 10 vols. (London, 1808)

Schulze, Konrad, ed., *Die Satiren Halls* (Berlin, 1910)

Wands, John Millar, ed. and trans., *Another world and yet the same: Bishop Hall's Mundus Alter et Idem* (New Haven, 1981)

Wynter, Philip, ed., *The Works of The Right Reverend Joseph Hall*, 10 vols. (Oxford, 1863)

BIBLIOGRAPHY

I PRIMARY SOURCES

(Place of publication is London unless otherwise stated)

Adams, Thomas, *Works* (1630)

Andrewes, Lancelot, *Opuscula Quaedam Posthuma* (Oxford, 1852)

Anonymous, *A Survey of That Foolish, Seditious, Scandalous, Prophane, Libell, The Protestation Protested* (1641) (sometimes wrongly ascribed to Hall)

—— *A True Relation of The Life and Death of the Right Reverend Father in God William Bedell*, ed. Thomas Wharton Jones (1878)

—— *Everyman*, ed. A. C. Cawley (Manchester, 1961)

—— *Philadelphus Vapulans Theophili Iscani Ad calumniosam Irenaei Philadelphi Epistolam Responsio. Qua Anglicanae Ecclesiae sana fides, Pietasq:, et Episcopalis ὑπεροχῆς Institutio Apostolico-Divina, A Do Jos: Hallo Exon. Episcopo pridem defensa, asseritur* (1641)

—— *The Marriage of Wit and Wisdom*, ed. J. O. Halliwell (1846)

—— *The Three Parnassus Plays*, ed. J. B. Leishman (1949)

—— *The Whipper Pamphlets*, ed. A. Davenport, 2 pts. (Liverpool, 1951)

Archer, John, *The Personal Reigne of Christ Upon Earth* (1643)

Aston, Sir Thomas, *A Remonstrance against Presbitery* (London, 1641)

Augustine, Aurelius, *A Pretious Booke of Heavenlie Meditations; whereunto is annexed Saint Augustines psalter*, trans. Thomas Rogers (London, 1581)

—— *A right Christian Treatise Entituled S. Augustines Praiers*, trans. Thomas Rogers (London, 1581)

—— *Works*, ed. Marcus Dods, 15 vols. (Edinburgh, 1871–6)

Avila, Juan de, *The Audi Filia, or a Rich Cabinet Full of Spirituall Iewells* (St. Omer, 1620)

Bacon, Francis, *Essayes. Religious Meditations. Places of perswasion and disswasion* (1597)

—— *The Philosophical Works*, ed. John M. Robertson (1905)

Baillet, Adrien, *Jugemens des Sçavans sur les principaux ouvrages de auteurs*, 6 vols. (Amsterdam, 1725)

Bayle, Pierre, *The Dictionary Historical and Critical*, 5 vols. (London, 1734–41)

Baxter, Richard, *The Saints Everlasting Rest* (1650)

Bedell, William, *The Copies of Certaine Letters which have passed betweene Spaine and England in matter of Religion* (1624)

Bonaventure, St., *The Life of Christ*, trans. W. H. Hutchings (1881)

Bosius, Johannes Andreas, *De Comparanda Prudentia iuxta et Eloquentia Civili* (Jena, 1679)

Boyle, Robert, *Works*, 5 vols. (1744)

Breton Nicholas, *Works*, ed. A. B. Grosart, 2 vols. (Edinburgh, 1879).

Brinsley, John, *Ludus Literarius, or The Grammar Schoole*, ed. E. T. Campagnac (1917)

Bryskett, Lodowick, *Literary Works*, ed. J. H. P. Pafford (Farnborough, Hants. [Germany pr.], 1972)

Burton, Henry, *Apologia Pro Epistola Quae Nupere prodiit sub nomine Irenaei Philadelphi Adversus Argutias Theophili Iscani* (1641)

—— *Babel no Bethel That is, The Church of Rome no true visible Church of Christ* (1629)

—— *The Seven Vials Or A briefe and plaine Exposition upon the 15: and 16: Chapters of the Revelation* (1628)

Burton, Robert, *The Anatomy of Melancholy*, ed. Holbrook Jackson, 3 vols. (1932)

Butterfield, Robert, *Maschil, or, A treatise to give instruction, touching the state of the Church of Rome... For the vindication of the right Reverend Father in God, the L. Bishop of Exeter* (1629)

Calvin, John, *Commentaries*, trans. Joseph Haroutinian and Louise Pettibone Smith, The Library of Christian Classics (1958)

—— *Commentaries on the Four Last Books of Moses arranged in the form of a harmony*, trans. Charles William Bingham, 4 vols. (Edinburgh, 1852–5)

—— *Commentaries on the Twelve Minor Prophets*, trans. John Owen, 5 vols. (Edinburgh, 1846–9)

—— *Commentaries: The Gospel according to St. John 11–21 and the First epistle of John*, trans. T. H. L. Parker (1961)

—— *Institutes of the Christian Religion*, ed. John T. McNeill, Library of Christian Classics, 2 vols. (1961)

—— *Of the life or conversation of a Christen Man* (1549?)

Cholmley, Hugh, *The State of the Now-Romane Church, Discussed By way of vindication of the Right Reverend Father in God, the Lord Bishop of Exceter* (1629)

Cicero, Marcus Tullius, *Academics*, trans. James S. Reid (1880)

Coffin, Edward, *A Refutation of M. Ioseph Hall His Apologeticall Discourse, For the Marriage of Ecclesiasticall Persons* (St. Omer, 1619)

Donatus, Aelius, *P. Terentii Carthaginensis Afri Comoediae sex; ex recensione F. Lindenbrogii, cum ejusdem mstorum lectionibus et observationibus atque A Donati Eugraphi et Calpurnii commentariis integris. His accesserunt Bentleii et Faerni lectiones ac conjecturae... necnon selectisssimae virorum annotationes*, 2 vols. (1820)

Donne, John, *LXXX Sermons* (1640)

—— *The Elegies and The Songs and Sonnets*, ed. with an introduction and commentary by Helen Gardner (Oxford, 1965)

—— *The Poems*, ed. Herbert Grierson, 2 vols. (Oxford, 1912)

Drant, Thomas, *A Medicinable Morall, that is the two Bookes of Horace his Satyres, Englyshed accordyng to the prescription of Saint Jerome... The Wailyngs of the Prophet Heremiah, done into Englyshe verse. Also Epigrammes* (1566)

du Moulin Louis, *Irenaei Philadelphi Epistola... In qua Aperitur Mysterium Iniquitatis novissime in Anglia redivivum, et excutitur liber Iosephi Halli, quo asseritur Episcopatum esse iuris divini* (1641)

Eden, Richard, trans., *The first Three English books on America*, ed. Edward Arber (Birmingham, 1885)

Erasmus, Desiderius, *Colloquies*, trans. Craig R. Thompson (Chicago, 1965)

—— *Ioanne Frobenius Lectore, Habes iterum Morias Encomium... una cum Listrij commentarijs, et aliis complusculis libellis* (Basle, 1517)

—— *The Praise of Folly*, trans. Betty Radice, and ed. A. H. T. Levi (Harmondsworth, 1971)

Elyot, Thomas, *The Castel of Helth* (1541)

Flecknoe, Richard, *Enigmatical Characters* (1658)

Fuller, Thomas, *The Church-History of Britain* (1648)

—— *The History of the Worthies of England* (1662)

—— *The Holy State; the Profane State*, ed. Maximilian Graff Walten, 2 vols. (New York, 1938)

Galen, Claudius, *Opera Omnia*, ed. C. G. Kühn, 20 vols. (Leipzig, 1821–33)

Garzoni, Tommaso, *L'hospidale de'Pazzi incurabili* (Ferrara, 1586)

—— *The Hospitall of Incurable Foules* (1600)

Gerson, John, *Opera*, 4 vols. (Paris, 1606)

Gibbons, Richard, *An abridgement of Mediations of the Life, Passion, Death, and Resurrection of Our Lord and Saviour Jesus Christ.*

Written in Italian by the R. Father Vincentius Bruno of the Society of Jesus (St. Omer? 1614)

Gilby, Anthony, *A Pleasaunt Dialogue... between a Souldior of Barwicke and an English Chaplaine* (1581)

Granada, Luis de, *Granados Devotion*, trans. Francis Meres (1598)

—— *Of Prayer and Meditation*, trans. Richard Hopkins (Paris, 1582)

Greenham, Richard, *Works* (1599)

Hall, Robert (?), *A Modest Confutation of a Slanderous and Scurrilous Libell. Entituled, Animadversions upon the Remonstrants Defence against Smectymnuus* (1642)

Hare, Henry Baron Coleraine, *The Situation of Paradise Found Out* (1683)

Harsnett, Samuel, *A Discovery of the Fraudulent practices of John Darrel... and of his dealing with one M. Couper* (1599)

Healey, John, trans., *Epictetus his Manuall. Cebes his Table. Theophrastus Characters* (London, 1616)

—— trans., *Of the Citie of God* (1610)

Herbert, George, *Works*, ed. F. E. Hutchinson (Oxford, 1941)

Heylyn, Peter, *Cosmographie* (1652, 1670)

Howell, James, *Epistolae Ho-Elianae* (1726)

Ingulf, *The History*, ed. and trans. Joseph Stevenson, 7 vols. (1853–6)

Ignatius of Loyola, *The Spiritual Exercises*, trans. from the Spanish with a commentary and a translation of the *Directorium in Exercitia* by W. H. Longridge (London, 1919)

Jonson, Ben, *Complete Poems*, ed. George Parfitt (Harmondsworth, 1975)

—— *Works*, ed. C. H. Herford and Percy and Evelyn M. Simpson, 11 vols. (Oxford, 1925–52)

Knight, William, *A Concordance Axiomaticall: Containing a Survey of Theologicall Propositions: with their Reasons and uses in holie Scripture* (1610)

Laud, William, *Works*, ed. William Scott, Library of Anglo–Catholic Theology, 7 vols. (Oxford, 1847–60)

Lilly, William, *History of His Life and Times* (1715)

Lipsius, Justus, *Diva Virgo Hallensis* (Antwerp, 1604)

—— ed., *L. Annaei Senecae Philosophi Opera, Quae Exstant Omnia* (Antwerp, 1605)

—— *Opera* (Lyons, 1613)

—— *Two Bookes of Constancie... Englished by Sir John Stradling*, ed. Rudolf Kirk (New Brunswick, N.J., *1939*)

Marston, John, *Poems*, ed. A. Davenport (Liverpool, 1961)

Mercator, Gerard, *Historia Mundi or Mercator's Atlas*, trans. W.S. [altonstall] (1635)

Milton, John, *Complete Prose Works*, ed. Don M. Wolfe *et al.*, 8 vols.
  (New Haven, 1953–)
Montaigne, Michel, *Essayes*, ed. Desmond MacCarthy, 3 vols. (1928)
More, Sir Thomas, *A frutefull pleasant, and wittie worke, of the beste
  state of a publique weale, and of the newe yle called Utopia*, trans.
  Ralph Robinson (1556)
Naudé, Gabriel, *Bibliographia Politica* (Wittenberg, 1641)
Ortelius, Abraham, *Epitome of the Theater of the Worlde* (1603)
—— *Nomenclator Ptolemaicus* (Antwerp, 1584)
Overbury, Sir Thomas, *The Overburian Characters*, ed. W. J. Paylor
  (Oxford, 1936)
Owen, John, *Epigrammatum ... Ad Doctissimam Heroinam, D Arbel-
  lam Stuart* (London, 1612, 1622)
Patrick, Symon, *Auto-biography* (Oxford, 1839)
Perkins, William, *The whole treatise of the Cases of Conscience* (1606)
——*The Work*, intro. and ed. Ian Breward, The Courtenay Library
  of Reformation Classics, 3 (Appleford, Berks., 1970)
—— *Works*, 3 vols. (1616–18)
Prynne, William, *Canterburies Doome or the First Part of a Compleat
  History of The Commitment, Charge, Tryall, Condemnation, Execu-
  tion of William Laud Late Archbishop of Canterbury* (1646)
Quarles, Francis, *Emblemes* (1635)
—— *Enchyridion* (1639)
—— *Observations concerning Princes and States, upon Peace and Warre*
  (1642)
Rebelais, François, *Gargantua and Pantagruel*, trans. J. M. Cohen
  (Harmondsworth, 1955)
Rankins, William, *Seven Satires*, ed. Arnold Davenport (Liverpool,
  1948).
Rogers, Thomas, trans., *A Pretious Booke of Heavenlie Meditations:
  whereunto is annexed Saint Augustines psalter* (1581)
—— trans., *A right Christian Treatise Entituled S. Augustines Praiers*
  (1581)
Sarpi, Fr. Paulo, *An Apology, or, Apologeticall answere ... unto the
  Exceptions and Objections of Card Bellarmine against certaine
  Treatises and Resolutions of John Gerson, concerning the force and
  validitie of Excommunication* (1607)
Seneca, Lucius Annaeus, *Select Letters*, ed. Walter Summers (1910)
'Smectymnuus,' *A Vindication of the Answer to The Humble
  Remonstrance, from the Uniust Imputations of Frivolousnesse and
  Falsehood* (1641)
—— *An Answer to a Booke Entituled An Humble Remonstrance*
  (1641)

Spencer, Thomas, *Maschil Unmasked. In A Treatise Defending this sentence of our Church: Vidz. The present Romish Church hath not the nature of the true Church. Against the publick opposition of Mr. Cholmly, and Mr. Butterfield, two children revolted in opinion from their own subscription, and the faith of their Mother the Church of England* (1629)

Spenser, Edmund, *Works*, variorum edn., ed. E. Greenlaw et al., 11 vols. (Baltimore, 1932–57)

Starkey, Thomas, *A Dialogue between Cardinal Pole and Thomas Lupset*, ed. Kathleen M. Burton (London, 1948)

Stow, John, *The Annales or Generall Chronicle of England* (London, 1615)

Tate, Nahum, *Characters of Vertue and Vice...Attempted in Verse from a Treatise of Reverend Joseph Hall, Late Bishop of Exeter* (London, 1691)

Theophrastus, *Characteres Ethici, sive Descriptiones morum Graece. Isaacus Casaubonus recensuit, in Latinam Sermonem vertit, et Libro Commentario Illustravit* (Lyons, 1592)

—— *The Characters*, ed. R. G. Ussher (London, 1960)

—— ΘΕΟΦΡΑΣΤΟΥ ἠθικοὶ χαρακτῆρες *Notationes Morum. Isaacus Casaubonus recensuit, in Latinam Sermonem vertit, et Libro Commentario illustravit* (Lyons, 1599)

Vaughan, Henry, *Works*, ed. L. C. Martin, 2 vols. (Oxford, 1914)

Whitefoote, John, *Deaths Alarum or The Presage of approaching Death given in a Funeral Sermon... For the Right Reverend Joseph Hall* (London, 1656)

Whitlock, Richard, *Zootomia* (London, 1654)

Wotton, Sir Henry, *Life and Letters*, ed. Logan Pearsall Smith, 2 vols. (Oxford, 1907)

Wright, Abraham, *Five Sermons, in Five several Styles; or Waies of Preaching* (1656)

II SECONDARY SOURCES

Alden, Raymond MacDonald, *The Rise of Formal Satire in England under Classical Influence* (Philadelphia, 1899)

Ascoli, Georges, *La Grande-Bretagne devant l'opinion française au XVIIe siècle*, Travaux et Mémoires de l'Université de Lille, nouvelle série, 13, 2 vols. (Paris, 1930)

Atkins, J. W. H., *English Literary Criticism: The Renascence* (New York, 1947)

Auerbach, Erich, *Scenes from the Drama of European Literature*, trans. Ralph Manheim (New York, 1959)

Babb, Lawrence, *The Elizabethan Malady* (East Lansing, 1951)

Bald, R.C., *John Donne: A Life* (Oxford, 1970)

Baldwin, Edmund Chauncey, 'The Relation of the English "Character" to its Greek Prototype', *PMLA* 18 (1930)

Barker, Arthur E., *Milton and the Puritan Dilemma* 1641-60 (Toronto, 1942)

Batten, J. Minton, *John Dury Advocate of Christian Union* (Chicago, 1944)

Baugh, A.C., ed., *A Literary History of England*, 2nd edn., 4 vols. (1967)

Bechtel, Paul Moyer, *The Devotional Works of Joseph Hall* (Ann Arbor, 1965)

Bennett, Joan, *Five Metaphysical Poets* (Cambridge, 1964)

Berneri, Maire Louise, *Journey through Utopia* (1950)

Blench, J.W., *Preaching in England in the Late Fifteenth and Sixteenth Centuries* (Oxford, 1964)

Bloomfield, Paul, *Imaginary Worlds* (1932)

Boyce, Benjamin, *The Polemic Character 1640–1661* (Lincoln, Nebr., 1955)

—— *The Theophrastan Character in England to 1642* (Cambridge, Mass., 1947)

Breslow, Marvin Arthur, *A Mirror of England: Puritan Views of Foreign Nations 1618–1640* (Cambridge, Mass., 1970)

Brooks, Harold, F., 'The "Imitation" in English Poetry, especially in Formal Satire, before the Age of Pope', *RES* 25 (1949)

Brown, Huntington, *Rabelais in English Literature* (Cambridge, Mass., 1933)

Brown, John Russell and Bernard Harris, eds., *Elizabethan Poetry*, Stratford-upon-Avon Studies, 2 (1960)

Bush, Douglas, *English Literature in the Earlier Seventeenth Century 1600–1660* (Oxford, 1945)

Campbell, Oscar James, *Comicall Satyre and Shakespeare's "Troilus and Cressida"* (San Marino, California, 1938)

Caputi, A.F., *John Marston, Satirist* (Ithaca, New York, 1961)

Carruthers, S. W., 'Norfolk Presbyterianism in the Seventeenth Century', *Norfolk Archaeology*, 30 (1947–52)

Chandos, John, ed., *In God's Name: Examples of Preaching in England 1534–1662* (1971)

Chew, Aubrey, 'Joseph Hall and John Milton', *ELH* 17 (1950)

—— 'Joseph Hall and Neo-Stoicism', *PMLA* 65 (1950)

Clausen, Wendell, 'The Beginnings of English Character-Writing in the Early Seventeenth Century', *Philological Quarterly* 25 (1946)

Collins, Joseph Burns, *Christian Mysticism in the Elizabethan Age with its Background in Mystical Methodology* (Baltimore, 1940)

Collinson, Patrick, *Archbishop Grindal 1519–83* (1979)

—— *The Elizabethan Puritan Movement* (1967)

Cohn, Norman, *The Pursuit of the Millennium* (1970)

Connolly, James L., *John Gerson, Reformer and Mystic* (Louvain, 1928)

Corthell, Ronald James, 'Joseph Hall's *Characters of Vertues and Vices*: A "Novum Repertum"', *Studies in Philology*, 76 (1979)

Croll, Morris, *Style, Rhetoric, and Rhythm*, ed. J. Max Patrick *et al.* (Princeton, 1966)

Cross, Claire, *The Puritan Earl: The Life of Henry Hastings Third Earl of Huntingdon 1536–1595* (1966)

Cullum, Sir John, *The History and Antiquities of Hawstead and Hardwick* (1813)

Curtius, Ernst Robert, *European Literature and the Latin Middle Ages*, trans. from the German by William R. Trask (1953)

D'Alton, J.F., *Roman Literary Theory and Criticism* (1931)

Davies, Godfrey, 'English Political Sermons, 1603–1640', *HLQ* 3 (1939–40)

—— *The Early Stuarts 1603–1660*, 2nd edn. (Oxford, 1959)

Dewar, M.J., 'Bishop Joseph Hall 1574–1656. An Ecumenical Calvinist Churchman', *The Churchman*, 80 (1966)

Dodd, A.H., *Elizabethan England* (1974; first pub. as *Life in Elizabethan England*, 1961)

Eddy, W.A., *'Gulliver's Travels': A Critical Study* (Oxford, 1923)

Finberg, H.P., ed., *The Agrarian History of England and Wales*, 8 vols. (Cambridge, 1967–   )

Firth, Katharine R., *The Apocalyptic Tradition in Reformation Britain 1530–1645* (Oxford, 1979)

Fisch, Harold, 'Bishop Hall's Meditations', *RES* 25 (1949)

—— 'The Limits of Hall's Senecanism', *Proceedings of the Leeds Philosophical and Literary Society*, 6 (1944–7)

Fish, Stanley E., *Self-Consuming Artifacts* (1972)

Fox, Levi, *A Country Grammar School: A History of Ashby-de-la-Zouch Grammar School through four centuries 1567 to 1967* (Oxford, 1967)

Freeman, Rosemary, *English Emblem Books* (1948)

Gay, Edwin F., 'The Midland Revolt of 1607', *Transactions of the Royal Historical Society*, New Series, 18 (1904)

Gonner, E.C.K., *Common Land and Enclosure* (1966)

Gordon, G.S., ed., *English Literature and the Classics* (Oxford, 1912)

Gransden, W.K., ed., *Tudor Verse Satire* (1970)

Greenough, Chester, *A Bibliography of the Theophrastan Character in England* (Cambridge, Mass., 1947)

Haller, William, *The Rise of Puritanism* (New York, 1938)

Harrison, G.B., ed., *The Elizabethan Journals* (Ann Arbor, 1955)

Hertzler, Joyce Oramel, *The History of Utopian Thought* (New York, 1923)

Highet, Gilbert, *The Anatomy of Satire* (Princeton, 1962)

Hill, Christopher, *Milton and the English Revolution* (1977)

Holden, William P., *Anti-Puritan Satire 1572–1642* (New Haven, 1954)

Hoskins, W.G., *Provincial England* (1963)

—— 'The Leicestershire Farmer in the Sixteenth Century', *Transactions of the Leicestershire Archaeological Society*, 22 (1941–5)

Howell, Wilbur Samuel, *Logic and Rhetoric in England 1500–1700* (New York, 1961)

Huntley, Frank Livingstone, *Bishop Joseph Hall 1574–1656; A biographical and critical study* (Cambridge, 1979)

Jensen, E.J., 'Hall and Marston: The role of the satirist', *Satire News Letter*, 4 (1967)

Jevons, H. Stanley, 'Contemporary Models of Sir Thomas More: Utopia and the Socialist Inca Empire', *TLS* 2 Nov. 1935

Jewson, C.B., 'Return of Conventicles in Norwich Diocese 1669-Lambeth MS No. 639', *Norfolk Archaeology*, 33 (1962–5)

Johnson, A.B.J., 'The earlier seventeenth century sermon and the beginnings of the plain style in English prose with reference to Joseph Hall' (unpublished doctoral dissertation, University of London, 1972)

Jones, J., *Bishop Hall: His Life and Times* (1826)

Kaufmann, U. Milo, *The Pilgrim's Progress and Traditions in Puritan Meditation* (New Haven, 1966)

Keil, Heinrich, ed., *Grammatici Latini*, 7 vols. and supplement (Leipzig, 1857–78)

Kernan, Alvin, *The Cankered Muse* (New Haven, 1959)

—— *The Plot of Satire* (New Haven, 1965)

Ketton-Cremer, R.W., *A Norfolk Gallery* (1948)

—— *Norfolk in the Civil War* (1969)

Kinloch, T.F., *The Life and Works of Joseph Hall* (1951)

Kirk, Rudolf, 'A Seventeenth-Century Controversy: Extremism vs. Moderation', *Texas Studies in Literature and Language*, 9 (1967–8)

Knappen, Marshall Mason, *Tudor Puritanism* (Chicago, 1939)

Lacassagne, Claude, 'La Conception de la Vérité dans les œuvres de Joseph Hall', *Recherches Anglaises et Américaines*, iii (1970), 29–37.

—— 'La Satire religieuse dans *Mundus Alter et Idem* (1605) de

Joseph Hall', *Recherches Anglaises et Americaines,* iv (1971), 141–56.

Lanham, Richard A., *A Handlist of Rhetorical terms* (1968)

Lecocq, Louis, *La Satire en Angleterre, de 1588 à 1603* (Paris, 1969)

Lederer, Josef, 'John Donne and Emblematic Practice', *RES* 22 (1946)

Lee, Sidney, 'The Beginnings of French Translation from the English', *Transactions of the Bibliographical Society,* 8 (1907)

Legg, J. Wickham, *A Bibliography of the Thoughts of Marcus Aurelius Antoninus* (1910)

Lewalski, Barbara, *Donne's 'Anniversaries' and the Poetry of Praise; The Creation of a Symbolic Mode* (Princeton, 1973)

—— *Protestant Poetics and the Seventeenth-Century Religious Lyric* (Princeton, 1979)

Lewis, George, *A Life of Joseph Hall* (1886)

Leyburn, Ellen Douglas, *Satiric Allegory: Mirror of Man* (New Haven, 1956)

Lovejoy, Arthur O., *The Great Chain of Being* (Cambridge, Mass., 1936)

McCabe, Richard A., 'Elizabethan Satire and the Bishops' Ban of 1599', *The Yearbook of English Studies,* 11 (1981)

—— 'Fulke Greville and Joseph Hall', *Notes and Queries,* 28 (1981)

—— 'The Form and Method of Milton's *Animadversions upon the Remonstrants Defence against Smectymnuus'*, *ELN* 18 (1981)

McClung, William Alexander, *The Country House in English Renaissance Poetry* (1977)

Mack, Maynard, 'The Muse of Satire', *Yale Review,* 41 (1951–2)

Major, R.H., *Early Voyages to Terra Australis* (1859)

Manuel, Frank E., ed., *Utopias and Utopian Thought* (Boston, 1967)

Marshall, Emma, *Winifrede's Journal of her Life at Exeter in the days of Bishop Hall* (1892)

Martz, Louis L., *The Paradise within. Studies in Vaughan, Traherne and Milton* (New Haven, 1964)

—— *The Poetry of Meditation.* rev. edn. (1962)

Masson, David, *The Life of Milton,* 7 vols. (London, 1859–94)

Matthiessen, F.O., *Translation an Elizabethan Art* (Massachusetts, 1931)

Merchant, Frank Ivan, 'Seneca the Philosopher and his Theory of Style', *American Journal of Philology,* 26 (1905)

Miller, Perry, *The New England Mind: The Seventeenth Century* (New York, 1939)

Milligan, Burton, 'Sixteenth- and Seventeenth-Century Satire against Corn Engrossers', *Studies in Philology,* 37 (1940)

Mitchell, W. Fraser, *English Pulpit Oratory from Andrewes to Tillotson* (1932)
Moore, Philip S., *The Works of Peter of Poitiers* (Notre Dame, Indiana, 1936)
Morley, Henry, ed., *Ideal Commonwealths* (1896)
Morall, John B., *Gerson and the Great Schism* (Manchester, 1960)
Morton, A.L., *The English Utopia* (1952)
Muddiman, J.G., ed., *Trial of King Charles the First* (Edinburgh, 1928)
Mueller, William R., *John Donne: Preacher* (Princeton, N.J., 1962)
Muller-Schwefe, Gerhard, 'Joseph Hall's "Characters of Virtues and Vices". Notes towards a Revaluation', *Texas Studies in Literature and Language*, 14 (1972–3)
Mumford, Lewis, *The Story of Utopias* (1923)
Owst, G.R., *Literature and Pulpit in Medieval England* (Cambridge, 1933)
Parker, L.A., 'The Depopulation Returns for Leicestershire in 1607', *Transactions of the Leicestershire Archaeological Society*, 23 (1946–7)
Parker, T.H.L., *Calvin's New Testament Commentaries* (1971)
—— *John Calvin* (1975)
Parker, William R., *Milton's Contemporary Reputation* (Columbus, Ohio, 1940)
Patch, Howard R., *The Goddess Fortuna in Medieval Literature* (Cambridge, Mass., 1927)
Paulson, Ronald, ed., *Satire: Modern Essays in Criticism* (Englewood Cliffs, N.J., 1971)
Peter, John, *Complaint and Satire in Early English Literature* (Oxford, 1956)
Petherick, Edward A., *'Mundus Alter et Idem'*, *The Gentleman's Magazine*, 281 (1896)
Pourrat, Pierre, *Christian Spirituality*, trans. W. H. Mitchell, 3 vols. (1922–7)
Praz, Mario, *Seventeenth-Century Imagery* (Rome, 1964)
Price, Lawrence Marsden, *The Reception of English Literature in Germany* (Berkeley, 1932)
Randolph, Mary Claire, 'The Structural Design of Formal Verse Satire', *Philological Quarterly*, 21 (1942)
—— 'Thomas Drant's Definition of Satire, 1566', *Notes and Queries*, 180 (1941)
Rebholz, R., *The Life of Fulke Greville* (Oxford, 1971)
Rowse, A.L., *The England of Elizabeth* (1950)
Salyer, Sandford M., 'Joseph Hall as a Literary Figure' (unpublished doctoral dissertation, Harvard, 1921)

—— 'Renaissance Influences in Hall's *Mundus Alter et Idem*', *Philological Quarterly*, 6 (1927)

Schleiner, Winfried, *The Imagery of John Donne's Sermons* (Providence, 1970)

Seaton, Ethel, *Literary Relations of England and Scandanavia in the Seventeenth Century* (Oxford, 1935)

Selden, Raman, *English Verse Satire, 1590–1750* (1978)

Seznec, Jean, *The Survival of the Pagan Gods* (Princeton, 1953)

Shuckburgh, E.S., *Emmanuel College* (1904)

Sloan, Thomas O., 'Rhetoric and Meditation: three case studies', *JMRS* 1–2 (1971–2)

Smith, Charlotte Fell, *Mary Rich, Countess of Warwick (1625–1678)* (1901)

Smith, G. Gregory, ed., *Elizabethan Critical Essays*, 2 vols. (Oxford, 1904)

Smith, Hallet, *Elizabethan Poetry* (Cambridge, Mass., 1952)

Smith, Philip A., 'Bishop Hall, "Our English Seneca"', *PMLA* 63 (1948)

—— 'The Limits of Hall's Senecanism', *Proceedings of the Leeds Philosophical and Literary Society*, 6 (1944–7)

Stein, Arnold, 'Joseph Hall's Imitation of Juvenal', *MLR* 43 (1948)

Stone, Lawrence, *An Elizabethan: Sir Horatio Palavicino* (Oxford, 1956)

Stout, Gardner D., 'Sterne's Borrowings from Joseph Hall's *Quo Vadis?*', *ELN* 2 (1965)

Summers, J.H., *George Herbert, His Religion and Art* (London, 1954)

Sutherland, James, *English Satire* (Cambridge, 1958)

Tawney, R.H., and E. Power, eds., *Tudor Economic Documents*, 3 vols. (London, 1924)

Taylor, E.G.R., *Late Tudor and Early Stuart Geography, 1583–1650* (London, 1934)

Teager, Florence S., 'Patronage of Joseph Hall and John Donne', *Philological Quarterly*, 15 (1936)

Thomas, Keith, *Religion and the Decline of Magic* (London, 1971)

Trevor-Roper, H.R., *Archbishop Laud* (London, 1940)

Trimpi, Wesley, *Ben Jonson's Poems. A study of the Plain Style* (Stanford, California, 1962)

Tuve, Rosemund, *Allegorical Imagery* (Princeton, N.J., 1966)

Underhill, Evelyn, *Mysticism*, 12th (rev.) edn. (London, 1930)

Wallerstein, Ruth Coons, *Studies in Seventeenth-Century Poetic* (Madison, Wis., 1950)

Wands, John Millar, 'The Early Printing History of Joseph Hall's *Mundus Alter et Idem*', *Publications of the Bibliographical Society of America*, 74 (1980)

Waterhouse, Gilbert, *The Literary Relations of England and Germany*, (Cambridge, 1914)

Welsby, Paul, ed., *Sermons and Society* (London, 1970)

Wendel, François, *Calvin*, trans. Philip Mairet (London, 1963)

White, Helen C., *English Devotional Literature, 1600–40*, University of Wisconsin Studies in Language and Literature, 29 (Madison, 1931)

White, Harold Ogden, *Plagiarism and Imitation in the English Renaissance*, Harvard Studies in English, 12 (Cambridge, Mass., 1935).

Wilcox, John, 'Informal Publication of Late Sixteenth-Century Verse Satire', *Huntington Library Quarterly*, xiii (1949–50)

Williams, Arnold, *The Common Expositor* (Chapel Hill, 1948)

Williamson, George, 'Senecan Style in the Seventeenth Century', *Philological Quarterly*, 15 (1936)

—— *The Senecan Amble* (1948)

Worman, Ernest James, *Alien Members of the Book-Trade during the Tudor Period* (London, 1906)

Wright, Celeste Turner, 'The Usurer's Sin in Elizabethan Literature', *Studies in Philology*, 35 (1938)

Yates, Frances, *John Florio: The Life of an Italian in Shakespeare's England* (Cambridge, 1934)

—— *The Art of Memory* (1966)

—— *The Rosicrucian Enlightenment* (1972)

NOTES

INTRODUCTION (pp. 1–6)

1. John Jones, *Bishop Hall: His Life and Times* (London, 1826); George Lewis, *A Life of Joseph Hall* (London, 1886); Emma Marshall, *Winifrede's Journal of her Life at Exeter and Norwich in the Days of Bishop Hall* (London, 1892).
2. T. F. Kinloch, *The Life and Works of Joseph Hall* (London, 1951); Paul Moyer Bechtel, *The Devotional Works of Joseph Hall* (Ann Arbor, 1965); Frank Livingstone Huntley, *Bishop Joseph Hall 1574–1656; A Biographical and Critical Study* (Cambridge, 1979).
3. *Works*, i, sig. A3ʳ⁻ᵛ.
4. *The Olde Religion* (1628), π 5ᵛ.
5. 'It is the warrantable and necessary duty of S, *Peter*, and all his true Evangelical successors, when they meet with a froward generation to call it so.' *Works*, ii, 341.
6. *Poems*, p. 47.
7. *Works*, i, 322.
8. Ibid., p. 322.
9. Ibid., p. 253.
10. *The Best Bargaine* (1623) in *Works*, i, 473.
11. *Poems*, p. 11.
12. *Noahs Dove* (1624) in *Works*, i, 515.
13. *Meditations and Vowes* (1605) in *Works*, i, 48.
14. William Haller, *The Rise of Puritanism* (New York, 1938), pp. 34–48.
15. *Observations of Some Specialities of Divine Providence in the Life of Joseph Hall* in *Olive-Tree*, pp. 41–2. Hereafter *Specialities*.
16. Ibid., p. 2; For an excellent account of the life of Hastings see Claire Cross, *The Puritan Earl: the Life of Henry Hastings Third Earl of Huntingdon 1536–1595* (London, 1966).
17. *Specialities*, pp. 2–3; *Episcopacie by Divine Right* (1640), Part III, p. 39.
18. *Specialities*, p. 4.
19. 'Since I saw you, I saw my father die: How boldly and merrily did he passe thorow the gates of death, as if they had no terror, but much pleasure! Oh that I could as easily imitate, as not forget him!' *Epistles* (1610) in *Works*, i, 288.
20. Cross, p. 124; For a full account of the school during Hall's time there see Levi Fox, *A Country Grammar School: A History of Ashby-de-la-Zouch Grammar School through four centuries 1567–1967* (Oxford, 1967), pp. 1–43.

21. *History of His Life and Times* (London, 1715), p. 4.

22. *Cheirothesia* (1649), pp. 71-3.

23. Cross, pp. 41, 99, 122-3.

24. *Resolutions and Decisions of Divers Practicall Cases of Conscience* (1649), pp. 446, 448; *Resolutions* (1650), p. 412.

25. Cross, p. 27.

26. *Works*, i, 73; *Poems*, pp. 103, 263-4.

27. *Works*, i, 262; *Christian Moderation* (1640), Book II, p. 43. Cf. *Resolutions and Decisions*, 2nd edn. (1650), sig. A3ʳ⁻ᵛ: 'Of all Divinity that part is most usefull, which determines cases of Conscience; And of all cases of Conscience the Practicall are most necessary; as action is of more concernment then speculation: And of all practicall Cases those which are of most common use are of so much greater necessity and benefit to be resolved, as the errors thereof are more universall, and therefore more prejudicall to the society of mankinde.'

28. For Greenham see Haller, pp. 27-8. Perkins's *The whole treatise of the Cases of Conscience* appeared posthumously in 1606, an incomplete version having appeared two years previously. It is interesting to note that it is dedicated by Thomas Pickering to Lord Denny, Hall's patron from 1607 to 1627. Apparently Denny had patronized Perkins also, and after his death lent assistance to his widow and children. For an excellent discussion of the importance of 'case' divinity in Puritan thought see *The Works of William Perkins*, intro. and ed. Ian Breward, The Courtenay Library of Reformation Classics, 3 (Appleford, Berks., 1970), pp. 58-80.

29. *Specialities*, pp. 10-11.

30. Ibid., pp. 15-22.

31. *Polemices Sacrae Pars Prior: Roma Irreconciliabilis* (1611) trans. as *No Peace with Rome* in *Works*, i, 599-632.

32. *A Sermon of Publique Thanksgiving* (1625), in *Works*, ii, 302; *Epistolae Ho-Elianae* (1726), p. 83.

33. *Specialities*, pp. 23-4, 25-6.

34. For Hall's relationship with Burton see Lewis, pp. 147-53; See also Ronald A. Rebholz, *The Life of Fulke Greville* (Oxford, 1971), p. 232; Richard McCabe, 'Fulke Greville and Joseph Hall', *Notes and Queries*, 28 (1981), 45-6.

35. *Specialities*, p. 25. Hall married Elizabeth Winniff (or Wenyeve) by whom he had 9 children, one of whom, George, later became Bishop of Chester. Lewis, pp. 68-9, 426-7.

36. *Specialities*, pp. 31-3.

37. Ibid., p. 41.

38. For Hall's letter to the Drurys upon leaving Hawstead see *Works*, i, 265. See also *Poems*, pp. 145-8; R.C. Bald, *John Donne: A Life* (Oxford, 1970), 238-40, 243-4, 487; Florence S. Teager, 'Patronage of Joseph Hall and John Donne', *Philological Quarterly*, 15 (1936), 408-13.

39. *Deaths Alarum, or The Presage of approaching Death: given in a Funeral Sermon... For the Right Reverend Joseph Hall* (London, 1656), p. 74.

40. This is one of the major faults of Kinloch's study. See the excellent review by Harold Fisch in *RES* 4 (1953), 178–9.
41. Christopher Hill, *Milton and the English Revolution* (London, 1977), pp. 154, 268–78; Arthur E. Barker, *Milton and the Puritan Dilemma 1641–1660* (Toronto, 1942), pp. 308–13.
42. *A Pleasaunt Dialogue... betweene a Souldior of Barwicke and an English Chaplaine* (place uncertain, 1581), sigs. H1ʳ-H2ᵛ, L7ʳ, M3ʳ⁻ᵛ.
43. *Episcopacie by Divine Right*, Part II, 103–9; *A Defence of the Humble Remonstrance, Against the frivolous and false exceptions of Smectymnuus* (1641), pp. 125–7.
44. *The Elizabethan Puritan Movement* (London, 1967), pp. 185, 307, 313.
45. Paul Welsby, *George Abbot: The Unwanted Archbishop* (London, 1962), pp. 147–54.
46. *Works*, ed. P. Hall, xi, 448.
47. *The Remedy of Prophanenesse. Or, Of the true sight and feare of the Almighty* (1637), pp. 229–31.
48. Ibid., pp. 231–2.
49. *Christ Mysticall; or The Blessed union of Christ and his Members* (1647), p. 106.
50. *Works*, ed. P. Hall, xi, 460.
51. *Works*, i, 1000.
52. *Common Apologie*, in *Works*, i, 574, 582.
53. Ibid., p. 574.
54. *Works*, ed. P. Hall, xi, 428.
55. *The Olde Religion* (1628), p. 195.
56. Morton (1654–1659) was a close friend of John Donne and successively Bishop of Chester, Lichfield, and Durham. Davenant (1576–1641) was the uncle of Thomas Fuller and Bishop of Salisbury. Primrose (1580?–1641) was minister of the French Church in London. Prideaux (1578–1650) was Regius Professor of Divinity at Oxford and later (1641) Bishop of Worcester. All were 'low Church' clerics of the same outlook as Hall.
57. *The Olde Religion... with an Advertisement now Added*, 3rd edn. (1630), pp. 191–2. The 'Advertisement' first appeared in the 2nd edn. (1628).
58. 'As if preferment had changed my note, and taught mee to speake more plausible language concerning the Roman Church, then I either did, or ought.' Ibid., pp. 189–90. For a full account of this controversy and its importance see Rudolf Kirk, 'A Seventeenth-Century Controversy: Extremism vs. Moderation', *Texas Studies in Literature and Language*, 9 (1967–8), 5–35.
59. *Works*, i, 559.
60. *A Defence*, , p. 134.
61. pp. 128–9.
62. *Canterburies Doome or the First Part of a Compleat History of The Commitment, Charge, Tryall, Condemnation, Execution of William Laud Late Arch-bishop of Canterbury* (London, 1646), pp. 227–38, 273 (mispag. 263)–6. Laud was also accused of censoring the letters

between Hall and Davenant which were published in the enlarged edition of *The Olde Religion*. The censored material concerned the upholding of the Calvinist doctrines of predestination and grace at the Synod of Dort. See pp. 165–6, 508–9.

63. *Works*, ed. William Scott, Library of Anglo-Catholic Theology, 7 vols. (Oxford, 1847–60), v (1853), 325. But see also pp. 343, 352. For Laud's own account of the writing of *Episcopacie by Divine Right* see iv (1854), 308–12.

64. *Specialities*, p. 34.

65. *Olive-Tree*, p. 316.

66. *Holy Decency in the Worship of God* in *Olive Tree* pp. 253–64.

67. 'I finde no just place for an oath to be administered to a man for his owne accusation; which certainly is altogether both illegal, and unreasonable; If a man will voluntarily offer to cleare himselfe by an Oath, out of the assurednesse of his own innocence, he may be allowed to be heard, but this may neither be pressed to be done, nor yet conclusive, when it is done ... It was ever therefore lawfull (even when Ecclesiasticall Inquisitions were at the highest) for a man to refuse answer to such questions upon oath, or otherwise, which tended to his owne impeachment; as unjustly, and unwarrantably proposed.' *Resolutions and Decisions* (1649), pp. 150–1. For Hall's other statements on the issue see *Common Apologie* in *Works*, i, 564–5; *A Defence of the Humble Remonstrance*, pp. 81–4; *A Speech in Parliament* (May 1641), in *Works* ed. Wynter, viii, 282.

68. *Specialities*, pp. 41–2.

69. *A Letter*, p. 10.

70. *Works*, ed. Wynter, x, 534, 535.

71. *A Vindication of the Answer to the Humble Remonstrance, from the Uniust Imputations of Frivolousnesse and Falsehood* (London, 1641), p. 204.

72. *Works*, ed. Wynter, x, 536. Bedell was a particularly close friend. He was Hall's contemporary at Emmanuel College and was rector of St. Mary's, Bury St. Edmunds during Hall's time at nearby Hawstead. Hall wrote a commendatory poem for Bedell's pastoral on the Gunpowder Plot *(Poems*, p. 123) in which he compares him to Spenser. In 1624 Bedell published *The Copies of Certaine Letters which have passed betweene Spaine and England in matter of Religion*, an exchange between Hall, himself, and another College contemporary named Jacob Wadsworth who had converted to Roman Catholicism. The work is interesting in that Wadsworth, to whom Hall addressed a public letter of expostulation in 1608 (*Works*, i, 251–2), persistently casts Hall as an extremist, but sees in Bedell the perfect model of Christian charity and moderation. Bedell later became Provost of Trinity College Dublin (1627–9) and Bishop of Kilmore and Ardagh (1629–42). His style of episcopacy greatly resembled Hall's and he too was accused of being a Puritan. *A True Relation of The Life and Death of The Right Reverend Father in God William Bedell*, ed. Thomas Wharton Jones (London, 1872), pp. 31, 42, 47, 53, 58.

73. *Works*, ed. Wynter, x, 541.
74. Ibid., p. 540.
75. Ibid., p. 543.
76. *Works*, vi, 577.
77. Ibid., p. 576.
78. Ibid., p. 575.
79. *The Peace-Maker* (1645), p. 50.
80. *A Short Answer to the Tedious Vindication of Smectymnuus* (1641), pp. 19-20.
81. Ibid.,p.89.
82. *Olive-Tree*, p. 82.
83. *Animadversions upon The Remonstrants Defence against Smectymnuus*, p. 18.
84. *Susurrium cum Deo: or Holy Self-Conferences of the Devout Soul* (1651), p. 65. In *Pax Terris* (1648) he tells us that 'forasmuch as a latitude, though not incompatible with safety (tuta quaedam latitudo), must necessarily be allowed both to men and doctrines, there will be the greatest need of Christian charity, in examining and determining the judgements of other people.' *Works*, ed. P. Hall, xi, 255.
85. *Susurrium*, p. 287.
86. The Adiaphorists are those of whom Melanchthon prophesied 'that in the last age of the world this errour will raigne amongst men, that either Religions are nothing, or differ onely in words'. *The Olde Religion* (1628), p. 4.
87. *Christian Moderation*, Book II, pp. 25-6.
88. *Peace-Maker*, pp. 207-8, 223-4.
89. *Olive-Tree*, p. 294.
90. *Cheirothesia* (1649), sig. A3^{r-v}.
91. *Holy Decency*, in *Olive Tree*, pp. 257, 262.
92. *Resolutions and Decisions* (1649), pp. 283, 327.
93. *Works*, ed. P. Hall, xi, 255.
94. *Christian Moderation*, Book I, pp. 4-6.
95. *Olive-Tree*, pp. 353-4.
96. In *Cheirothesia*, for example, the 'elegant and solid termes of learned *Hooker*' alternate with the opinions of Calvin 'the just glory' of the French Church. See pp. 59-60, 69, 71, 77.
97. *Christian Moderation*, Book II, pp. 142-3.
98. Works, ed. P. Hall, xi, 261, 267.
99. The best statement of Hall's attitude towards the state of the Church is *The Holy Order; or Fraternity of the Mourners in Sion* (1654).
100. *Works*, ed. Wynter, x, 533.
101. For an excellent account of Hall's time at Norwich see R.W. Ketton–Cremer, *Norfolk in the Civil War* (London, 1969), pp. 128-33, 224-37; *A Norfolk Gallery* (London, 1948), pp. 15-36.
102. One of those who sought Hall out to receive ordination at his hands was Symon Patrick, future Bishop of Ely and author of *The Parable of the Pilgrim* (1664). In his autobiography he tells how he was 'received with great kindness by that reverend old Bishop, who examined us and

then ordained us in his own parlour at Higham, about a mile from Norwich, April 5th, 1654.' *The Auto-biography of Symon Patrick, Bishop of Ely* (Oxford, 1839), p. 24.

103. *Works*, ed. Geoffrey Keynes, 6 vols. (London, 1928–31), v (1931), p. 159.

104. *Christ Mysticall*, sig. A6ᵛ; *Susurrium*, sig A12ᵛ. Hall greatly respected 'the reverend, and learned Mr Downame' and had read *The Christian Warfare. Satans Fiery Darts Quenched* (1647), sig. A3ᵛ.

105. *Resolutions* (1650), sig. A12ʳ.

106. Whitefoote, p. 66. The doctor was honoured far beyond his native shores. Regarding his reputation in France Georges Ascoli writes 'Plus que Dyke, plus que Bacon, Hall a excité l'esprit de nos grands moralistes', *La Grande-Bretagne devant l'opinion française au XVIIe siècle*, Travaux et Mémoires de l'Université de Lille, nouvelle série, 13, 2 vols. (Paris, 1930), ii, 96–101 (p. 100). One of his most dedicated translators was the Swiss Protestant Theodore Jaquemot who translated a great number of his works at Geneva including the *Epistles* (1627), the *Contemplations* (Old and New Testament, 1628–29), *The Arte of Divine Meditation* (1632), the *Occasional Meditations* (1632), and *The Remedy of Discontentment* (1664). In Germany Hall was 'by far the most popular of the English Theologians', Gilbert Waterhouse, *The Literary Relations of England and Germany in the Seventeenth Century* (Cambridge, 1914), pp. 41–7, 63, 102–6 (p. 102). For the continental reputation of Hall's most popular work, the *Characters of Vertues and Vices* (and also of the *Meditations and Vowes* and *Heaven upon Earth*), see *Heaven upon Earth and Characters of Vertues and Vices*, ed. Rudolf Kirk (New Brunswick, N.J., 1947), pp. 52–63; Gerhard Muller-Schwefe, 'Joseph Hall's *Characters of Vertues and Vices*. Notes Toward a Revaluation', *Texas Studies in Literature and Language*, 14, (1972–3), 235–51 (pp. 247–51).

CHAPTER 1

1. *The Poems of Joseph Hall*, ed. Arnold Davenport (Liverpool, 1949), p. 11. All references given in the text are to this edition.

2. Patrick Collinson, *The Elizabethan Puritan Movement* (London, 1967), pp. 417–31.

3. *A Literary History of England*, ed. A. C. Baugh, 2nd edn., 4 vols. (London, 1967), ii, 437–8.

4. Collinson, p. 424. See Also Richard Hooker, *Works*, ed. John Keble, 3 vols. (Oxford, 1888), ii, 4–5.

5. For the identification of Penry as Marprelate see Donald J. McGinn, *John Penry and the Marprelate Controversy* (New Brunswick, N.J., 1966).

6. *The Elizabethan Journals*, ed. G. B. Harrison (Ann Arbor, 1955), Part II, pp. 147, 148, 150, 154–5.

7. For an interesting social and literary survey see Oscar James Campbell

Comicall Satyre and Shakespeare's 'Troilus and Cressida' (San Marino, California, 1938), pp. 15–24.

8. M. M. Knappen, *Tudor Puritanism* (Chicago, 1939), p. 200. In later years, during the Smectymnuan controversy, Hall was to recall the work as 'that bitter Dialogue betwixt *Miles Monopodius*, and *Bernard* Blinkard' written by 'one of the hotest and busiest sticklers in these quarrels at Frankfurt'. *Episcopacie by Divine Right* (1640), Part III, p. 39.

9. Raman Selden, *English Verse Satire, 1590–1765* (London, 1978), p. 68.

10. *A Fig for Momus,* sig. A3ᵛ.

11. R. C. Bald, *John Donne: A Life* (Oxford, 1970), p. 240.

12. *Sermons and Society,* ed. Paul Welsby (London, 1970), p. 12. For an account of the ancient and traditional relationship between sermons and satire see G. R. Owst, *Literature and Pulpit in Medieval England* (Cambridge, 1933), pp. 210–470.

13. Drant, sigs. aiiᵛ–aiiiʳ.

14. *Contemplations upon the Principal Passages of the Holy Storie,* vol. vii (1623) in *Works,* i, 1196. (located here in vol. vi).

15. *Saint Pauls Combat* II (1627?) in *Works,* ii, 448: 'It is the charge of God, *Crie aloud, spare not, life up thy voyce like a trumpet, and show my people their transgressions, and the house of Iacob their sins. Es. 58. 1* The words are Emphaticall, whereof the first signifies a straining of the throat with crying; and the next (the trumpet) implies a sound of warre; this same (bellum cum vitiis) war with sins must be... uncapable of so much as a truce, yea as a respiration.'

16. *Pharisaisme and Christianitie* (1608) in *Works,* i, 376.

17. Robert Hall (?), *A Modest Confutation of a Slanderous and Scurrilous Libell, Entituled, Animadversions upon the Remonstrants Defence against Smectymnuus* (London, 1643), pp. 8–9.

18. Kernan, pp. 14–30; *Satire: Modern Essays in Criticism,* ed. Ronald Paulson (Englewood Cliffs, N.J., 1971), p. xiii.

19. Kernan, p. 28.

20. Ibid., p. 114; For a more balanced view see Campbell, pp. 24–34.

21. Kernan, p. 89.

22. Mary Claire Randolph, 'The Structural Design of Formal Verse Satire', *Philological Quarterly,* 21 (1942), 368–84.

23. *The Plot of Satire* (New Haven, 1965), pp. 95–104.

24. *The Anatomy of Satire* (Princeton, New Jersey, 1962), *p. 3.*

25. *Grammatici Latini,* ed. Heinrich Keil, 7 vols. and supplement (Leipzig, 1857–78), i (1857), 485–6.

26. Mary Claire Randolph, 'Thomas Drant's Definition of Satire, 1566', *Notes and Queries,* 180 (1941), 416–18.

27. On the divergence of opinions in the 1590s see John Peter, *Complaint and Satire in Early English Literature* (Oxford, 1956), pp. 301–3.

28. *P. Terentii Carthagiensis Afri Comoediae sex ex recensione Frid. Lindenbrogii cum ejusdem mstorum lectionibus et observationibus atque Aelii Donati, Eugraphii et Calpurnii commentariis integris. His accesserunt Bentleii et Faerni lectiones ac conjecturae... necnon selectissimae virorum doctorum annotationes,* 2 vols. (Londini, 1820), i, p. xxvi.

29. Ibid., p. xxvi.
30. *Elizabethan Critical Essays*, ed. G. Gregory Smith, 2 vols. (Oxford, 1904), i, 176, 294; ii, 32–3, 209.
31. *Seven Satires*, ed. Arnold Davenport (Liverpool, 1948), pp. 6, 8,, 13, etc.
32. Drant, sig, aivᵛ.
33. *Poems*, pp. 9, 10, 51.
34. *A Modest Confutation*, p. 9.
35. The Confuter quotes loosely from memory. See *Poems*, p. 10. The Confuter's assertion that Hall employed the terms 'tooth-lesse' and 'byting' metaphorically is undoubtedly correct. In a discussion of usury in *Heaven upon Earth* (1606), for example, he refers to a 'nice distinction' between 'toothlesse, and biting Interest' whereas in reality 'Iustice pleads even the most toothlesse usury to have sharp gummes.' *Works*, i, 84.
36. *Satires*, I. iv. 78–9, Loeb edn., pp. 54–5. Drant makes the same point: 'Who bites his lip, when his folly is bitten, hath either envy in his heart, or suspition in his head.' *Seven Satires*, p. 3.
37. Highet, pp. 63–4.
38. Kernan, p. 10.
39. Was Hall remembering *Everyman?*': 'Everyman, I wyll go with the and be thy gyde,/In thy moost nede to go by thy syde.' *Everyman*, ed. A. C. Cawley (Manchester, 1961), p. 16.
40. 'God never made man such as he is; It is our sin that made our soule to grovell.' *Saint Pauls Combat*, I, in *Works*, ii, 434.
41. For half-lines see Davenport, pp. 13, 16, 33, 59, 80, 82, 87. Marston imitated Hall in this. See *The Poems of John Marston*, ed. Arnold Davenport (Liverpool, 1961), pp. 144, 145, 146 etc. For the appropriateness of the half-line to the epic see Torquato Tasso, *Discourses*, trans. Mariella Cavalchini and Irene Samuel (Oxford, 1973), p. 143.
42. The 18th century responded favourably to this aspect of Hall's satires. Gray said, 'they are full of spirit and poetry; as much of the first, as Dr. Donne, and far more of the latter.' Peter Whalley asserted that 'the Verses of Bishop *Hall* are in general extremely musical and flowing, and are greatly preferable to Dr. *Donne*'s, as being of a much smoother Cadence.' *The Works of Thomas Gray*, ed. Edmund Gosse, 4 vols. (London, 1884), ii, 233; *An Enquiry into the Learning of Shakespeare* (London, 1748), p. 42.
43. 'As a true friend is the sweetest contentment in the world: so in his qualities he well resembleth hony, the sweetest of all liquors. Nothing is more sweet to the taste nothing more sharpe and cleansing, when it meets with an exulcerate sore. For my selfe, I know I must have faults; and therefore I care not for that friend, that I shall never smart by. For my friends, I know they cannot be faultlesse; and therefore as they shall finde me sweet in their praises and encouragements, so sharpe also in their censure. Either let them abide me no friend to their faults, or no friend to themselves.' *Meditations and Vowes* (1605-6) in *Works*, i, 46. See also ibid., p. 48 and Collinson, pp. 172–3, 215.

44. *Works,* i, 320–1.

45. Ibid., pp. 321–2.

46. *Characters of Vertues and Vices* (1608) in *Works,* i, 172.

47. One of the Sermons Preacht to *The Lords of the High Court of Parliament, in their solemne Fast on Ashwednesday, Febr. 18.* (1628), in *Works,* ii, 341–2.

48. For Hall as a literary critic see Davenport, pp. xxxv–lx, and J. W. H. Atkins, *English Literary Criticism: The Renascence* (London, 1947), pp. 210–12.

49. *Works,* i, 670.

50. See esp. 11, 66–86. *Ben Jonson: The Complete Poems,* ed. George Parfitt (Harmondsworth, 1975), p. 189.

51. *Complete Prose Works of John Milton,* ed. Don M. Wolfe *et al.,* 8 vols. (New Haven, 1953–), i (1953), p. 915.

52. Arnold Stein, 'Joseph Hall's Imitation of Juvenal', *MLR* 43 (1948), 315–22 (p. 321). On the general question of Hall's debt to the classics see Raymond MacDonald Alden, *The Rise of Formal Satire in England under Classical Influence* (Philadelphia, 1899), pp. 117–23.

53. *The Whipper Pamphlets,* Part I, ed. Arnold Davenport (Liverpool, 1951), pp. 36, 38.

54. 'Hall of Imanuel Colledge in Cambridge' is singled out as one of the foremost English satirists in Francis Meres' *Palladis Tamia, Wits Treasury* (1598)—the year the *Byting Satyres* first appeared. Smith, ii, 320.

55. John Wilcox explains the satires in terms of their young authors' desire to attract court attention. 'Informal Publication of Late Sixteenth-Century Verse Satire', *Huntington Library Quarterly,* 13 (1949–50), 191–200; See also James Sutherland *English Satire* (Cambridge, 1958), p. 31.

56. Davenport supplies notes to all the supposed or alleged personal allusions but it is interesting to note in this connection that there was a rule of Emmanuel College to the effect that 'no fellow nor Pensioner, upon anie cause or private occasion, shall either in sermon, common-place, or probleme in the Chappell, use any speech or speeches which tend to the disgraceinge of any particular person, or noting private faults disgracefullie, which can have no sound spirituall use of edification, or at least not any good use without that ill. And besides our agreement we doe promise before God that we will never use [nor] intend to use any such in our exercises hereafter.' Hall denies that his satires make personal allusions, and his thinking may well have been influenced by this rule. E.S. Shuckburgh *Emmanuel College* (London, 1904), p. 33.

57. For the relationship between this satire and the whole genre of country house poetry—the genre to which belongs Jonson's 'To Penshurst'— see William Alexander McClung, *The Country House in English Renaissance Poetry* (London, 1977), pp. 42–5.

58. See *Works,* ed. P. Hall, xii, p. 137.

59. Davenport points out that Hall's immediate source was Scaliger's *Teretismata,* 'Satyra' (p. 251).

60. Bernard Harris, 'Men like Satyrs', in *Elizabethan Poetry*, ed. John Russell Brown and Bernard Harris, Stratford-upon-Avon Studies, 2 (London, 1960), p. 193.
61. Wilcox, p. 199.
62. *English Satire* (Cambridge, 1958), p. 30.
63. *Statutes of the Realm*, IV, Part 2, p. 894.
64. 'In summary, one may point out that the satire against grain speculators rested upon a firm foundation of real abuses; that examination of the satirists' principal accusations reveals little exaggeration.' Burton Milligan, 'Sixteenth- and Seventeenth-Century Satire against Grain Engrossers', *Studies in Philology*, 37 (1940), 585–97 (p. 597).
65. *Contemplations upon the Principall Passages of the Holy Storie*, vol. iii (1615), in *Works*, i, 946.
66. *CSPD (Eliz. I) 1595–97*, p. 343.
67. Ibid., p. 343.
68. Ibid., p. 344.
69. *Acts of the Privy Council*, 26 (1596–7), p. 455.
70. *Statutes of the Realm*, IV, Part 2, pp. 891–3.
71. Ibid., pp. 893–6.
72. *Acts of the Privy Council*, 27 (1597), p. 129.
73. *Works*, i, 500.
74. 'The Leicestershire Farmer in the Sixteenth Century', *Transactions of the Leicestershire Archaeological Society*, 22 (1941–5), 61.
75. 'Leicestershire was at its highest in 1598–1602.' Edwin F. Gay 'The Midland Revolt and the Inquisitions of Depopulation of 1607', *Transactions of the Royal Historical Society*, New Series, 18 (1904), 195–244 (p. 236).
76. *Observations of Some Specialities*, in *Olive-Tree*, p. 8.
77. *One of the Sermons Preacht at Westminster On the day of the publike Fast (April 5, 1628) To the Lords of the High Court of Parliament*, in *Works*, ii, 315.
78. Hoskins, p. 50.
79. For an illustration of such a dwelling see A. H. Dodd, *Elizabethan England* (London, 1974; first pub. as *Life in Elizabethan England*, 1961), p. 39.
80. *A Sermon Preacht at Higham near Norwich, on Sunday July 1, 1655*, in *Olive-Tree*, p. 205.
81. *Statutes of the Realm*, IV, Part 2, p. 891.
82. *Tudor Economic Documents*, ed. R. H. Tawney and E. Power, 3 vols. (London, 1924), i, 87.
83. A. L. Rowse, *The England of Elizabeth* (London, 1950), pp. 227–8; McClung, pp. 28–35.
84. Claire Cross, *The Puritan Earl* (London, 1966), pp. 105, 260.
85. *Acts of the Privy Council*, 26 (1596–7), p. 405.
86. 'The Depopulation Returns for Leicestershire in 1607', *Transactions of the Leicestershire Archaeological Society*, 23 (1946–7), 234.
87. *Tudor Economic Documents*, i, 89.

88. *Common Land and Inclosure* (London, 1912), p. 136.
89. Parker, pp. 231, 234-5, 241.
90. If Hall had any literary model for this it was probably More's *Utopia*: 'thei inclose al into pastures: thei throw doune houses: they plucke downe townes, and leave nothing standynge, but only the churche to be made a shepehowse...those good holy men turne all dwellinge places and all glebeland into desolation and wildernes.' *A frutefull pleasaunt, and wittie worke, of the beste state of a publique weale, and of the newe yle, called Utopia,* trans. Ralph Robinson (London, 1556), fols. 14ᵛ-16ʳ (fol. 15ʳ).
91. *The Marriage of Wit and Wisdom,* ed. J.O. Halliwell (London, 1846), pp. 140-1.
92. *The Annales or Generall Chronicle of England, begun first by maister Iohn Stow, and after him continued...unto the ende of this present yeere 1614. by Edmond Howes* (London, 1615), p. 889.
93. *A Sermon Preach'd in the City of Excester At the Consecration of a new Burial-place there, on Saint Bartholmews day, Aug. 24 1637,* in *Works,* iii, 94. See Also *Contemplations upon the...Holy Storie,* vol. ii (1614) in *Works,* i, 863: 'Whence are our depopulations, and inclosures, but for that men cannot abide either fellowes or neighbours?...The more a man can leave himselfe behinde him, and aspire to a care of community, the more spirituall he is. Nothing makes a man so good a patriot as Religion.'
94. *Works,* i, 57-8.
95. 'In Leicestershire during the period 1578 to 1607 enclosure was predominantly the work of the upper classes though it was accompanied by the more modest enclosures of those lower in the social scale.' Parker, p. 238.
96. Ibid., p. 238.
97. The rise of the Furse family in Devon began with the admittance of John Furse to the Inns of Court. He remained a clerk, but his grandson, Robert, became a squire. Rowse, pp. 232-4.
98. *Works,* ed. C. H. Herford and Percy and Evelyn M. Simpson, 11 vols. (Oxford, 1925-52), iii (1927), 529.
99. Rowse, p. 244.
100. Parker, pp. 239, 240.
101. Ibid., p. 240.
102. Ibid., p. 238.
103. *CSPD (Eliz. I) 1595-97,* pp. 458-9.
104. Among the victims whom Steer's group had intended either to kill or plunder was one 'Rabone, the yeoman'. The 1607 depopulation returns for Leicestershire declare that a certain Bennet Smith of Wymondham converted and enclosed 70 acres of arable, while Roger Orton of Swepston enclosed 60 acres. *CSPD (Eliz. I) 1595-97,* p. 345; Parker, p. 237.
105. Though it may seem odd to us, Hall's use of the term 'usurie' was technically correct. The objection to usury was that it attempted to make dead matter 'breed'; husbandry was the natural usury blessed by

God. Celeste Turner Wright, 'The Usurer's Sin in Elizabethan Literature', *Studies in Philology*, 35 (1938), 178–94 (p. 185).

106. The textbook example of this technique was the case of Cotesbach, the Leicestershire village involved in the revolt of 1607. See *The Agrarian History of England and Wales*, ed. H.P.R. Finberg, 8 vols. (Cambridge, 1967–), iv (1967), 233–4, 253–4.

107. *Tudor Economic Documents*, i, 87.

108. *The Poems of John Marston*, ed. Arnold Davenport (Liverpool, 1961), p. 116.

109. 'Neither doth this pride raise a man more above others, then above himselfe: And what wonder is it if hee will not know his poore neighbours, which hath forgotten himself?...according to our ordinary Proverb, Their good and their blood rises together; Now it may not be taken as it hath beene; Other cariage, other fashions are fit for them; their attire, fare, retinue, houses, furniture displease them, new must be had; together with coaches, and lacquies, and all the equipage of greatnesse: These things (that no man mistake me) I mislike not: they are fit for those that are fit for them...it is the heart that maketh all these evill: when that is puft up with these windy vanities, and hath learned to borrow that part of the devils speech, *All these things are mine*...Now all these turne into sinne.' *Works*, i, 669–70.

110. Ibid., pp. 160–1.

111. Ibid., p. 160.

112. Richard A. McCabe, 'Elizabethan Satire and the Bishops' Ban of 1599', *The Yearbook of English Studies*, 11 (1981), 188–93.

CHAPTER 2

1. *Mundus Alter et Idem* (Frankfurt, 1605?), 'Prefatio ad Lectorem', fol. 5^r. All references (including page numbers given after quotations and citations in the text) are to this edition. For the date of composition see also n.5. On the question of authorship see Appendix B.

2. The Frankfurt edition is undated, but the work was entered in the *Stationers' Register* on 2 June 1605. Since a 2nd edition which appeared at Hanau in 1607 was apparently advertised in 1606, the conjectural date of the 1st edition is 1605. Gilbert Waterhouse, *The Literary Relations of England and Germany in the Seventeenth Century* (Cambridge, 1914), p. 42; John Millar Wands, 'The Early Printing History of Joseph Hall's *Mundus Alter et Idem*', *Papers of the Bibliographical Society of America*, 74 (1980), 1–12.

3. *Mundus*, fol. 5^r. This was probably the William Knight (dates unknown) listed in the *DNB* who graduated from Christ's College Cambridge, held the living of Little Gransden, and wrote *A Concordance Axiomaticall: Containing A Survey of Theologicall Propositions: with their Reasons and uses in holie Scripture* (1610). Hall wrote him a letter in 1611 encouraging him to persevere in his ministry. *Works*, i, 343–4.

4. *Complete Prose Works of John Milton*, ed. Don M. Wolfe *et al.*, 8 vols. (New Haven, 1953–), i, 697, 880–2, 887, 914. See below Ch. 3, sect. 2.

5. The best modern edition is *The Discovery of a New World*, ed. Huntington Brown (Cambridge, Mass., 1937). All quotations are from this edition. Basing his arguments on internal evidence, Brown believes that some sections of the *Mundus* were written after 1601, and possibly as late as 1605 (p. xxix). The argument, however, is far from conclusive but what seems to be a reference to the death of Queen Elizabeth (*Mundus*, p. 94) would indicate that some parts of the work were indeed either written or expanded in or after 1603. Nevertheless there is no reason to doubt the basic truth of Knight's assertions.

6. *The Discovery*, pp. 5, 145–9.

7. Frances Yates, *John Florio: The life of an Italian in Shakespeare's England* (Cambridge, 1934), pp. 284–92.

8. *Satiric Allegory: Mirror of Man* (New Haven, 1956), pp. 1–14, 71–106.

9. Ibid., p. 6.

10. *Mundus*, 'Prefatio ad Lectorum', fol. 4^r.

11. *The Discovery*, pp. 148–9.

12. *Elizabethan Critical Essays*, ed. G. Gregory Smith, 2 vols. (London, 1937), ii 160. Gabriel Naudé, Cardinal Mazarin's librarian, came closest to describing the *Mundus* when he termed it a Poneropolis, or City of Rogues (Plutarch, *Moralia*, VI (Loeb), 499): It was intended he said, as a satire 'adversus depravatos praesentis seculi mores, in quo dum singulas stationes singulis vitiis asignat, gentesque illas incolentes ac loca ipsa contorticulatis ingeniose fictisque; ex cujusque rei natura vocibus appellat; non inepte meo judicio Poneropolim instituit, quae ad hilaritatem non minus homines excitare, quam ad virtutem inflammare possit.' *Bibliographia Politica* (Wittenberg, 1641), p. 41.

13. Leyburn, p. 50.

14. Sandford M. Salyer, 'Renaissance Influences in Hall's *Mundus Alter et Idem*', *Philological Quarterly*, 6 (1972), 321–34 (pp. 327–32).

15. *The Academics of Cicero*, trans. James S. Reid (London, 1880) p. 15.

16. *Poems*, ed. Davenport, p. 71.

17. *Christian Moderation* (London, 1640), Book II, p. 71.

18. *Epistles* (1608) in *Works*, i, 256–9.

19. *Poems*, p. 71.

20. Smith, ii, 320.

21. *The Three Parnassus Plays*, ed. J. B. Leishman (London, 1949), pp. 88–92. Frank Huntley goes so far as to suggest that Hall had a hand in the composition of the *Parnassus Plays*. What his evidence actually demonstrates, however, is that Marston may have believed this to be the case. There is, of course, a crucial distinction. The verbal echoes can just as easily be explained as simple borrowings—this is Leishman's approach. See *Bishop Joseph Hall 1574–1656; A biographical and critical study* (Cambridge, 1979), pp. 29–45.

22. *Mundus*, pp. 29, 51–2. *The Discovery*, pp. 171, 173, 211. Healey's Mercurius signs himself 'The Cambridge Pilgrime' (p. 136).

23. *Tudor Verse Satire*, ed. W. K. Grandsden (London, 1970), p. 130.

24. *Mundus*, p. 21; *The Discovery*, p. 165.
25. George Williamson, 'Senecan Style in the Seventeenth Century', *Philological Quarterly*, 15 (1936), 321–51.
26. J. W. H. Atkins, *English Literary Criticism: The Renascence* (London, 1947), pp. 22–4, 46–7.
27. *Style, Rhetoric, and Rhythm: Essays by Morris W. Croll* ed. J. Max Patrick *et al.* (Princeton, 1966), pp. 124, 171, 185.
28. See, for example, *Ioannes Frobenius Lectori. Habes iterum Morias Encomium . . . una cum Listrij commentarijs, et aliis complusculis libellis* (Basle, 1517).
29. Levi Fox, *A Country Grammar School: A History of Ashby-de-la-Zouch Grammar School through four centuries 1567 to 1967* (Oxford, 1967), p. 14.
30. Croll, pp. 220–2, 224–6.
31. Peter Heylyn, *Cosmographie* (London, 1670), Appendix, p. 1093.
32. *Works*, ed. P. Hall, xii, p. xi.
33. King's translation is reprinted in *Ideal Commonwealths*, ed. Henry Morley (London, 1896), pp. 267–84. For Hall's influence on Swift see W. A. Eddy, *Gulliver's Travels: A Critical Study* (Oxford, 1923) pp. 44–5, 68.
34. E. G. R. Taylor, *Late Tudor and Early Stuart Geography, 1583–1650* (London, 1934), p. 33.
35. *Early Voyages to Terra Australis*, ed. R. H. Major (London, 1859), p. lxix.
36. Ibid., p. 16.
37. *Epitome*, fol. 1. Due to a printing error the 1605 and 1607 editions of the *Mundus* read 'Terra stashulis' which is meaningless. The Utrecht edition of 1643, for which the maps were re-engraved, restores the correct reading 'Terra Australis'. In any case the point is made explicitly in the *text* of the 1st edn., *Mundus*, p. 24.
38. In a sermon of 1628 Hall reminds his listeners that 'our Globe can tell us of a great part of the World, that hath no name but *Incognita*, not knowne, whether it have any inhabitant.' *Works*, ii, 309.
39. *Historia Mundi or Mercator's Atlas*, trans. W. S. [altonstall] (London, 1635), pp. 929–30; *Theatrum Orbis Terrarum* (Antwerp, 1584), map 5: 'Novus Orbis'.
40. *Quo Vadis?* (1617) in *Works*, i, 646.
41. *Gargantua and Pantagruel*, trans. J. M. Cohen (Harmondsworth, 1955), p. 73.
42. *Poems*, pp. 202, 225–6.
43. Richard Eden, *The first Three English books on America*, ed. Edward Arber (Birmingham, 1885), p. 300. For the Hecla legend in English literature see Ethel Seaton, *Literary Relations of England and Scandinavia in the Seventeenth Century* (Oxford, 1935), pp. 276–9.
44. *No Peace with Rome* (1609) in *Works*, i, 620.
45. *A Tale of a Tub*, ed. A. C. Guthkelch and D. Nichol Smith (Oxford, 1958), pp. 106–7.
46. *Works*, i, 620–1.

47. *Complete Prose Works,* i, 881.
48. *Mundus Alter et Idem Sive Terra Australis antehac semper incognita; longis itineribus peregrini Academici nuperrime lustrata. Authore Mercurio Britannico. Accessit propter affinitatem materiae Thomae Campanellae Civitas Solis. et Nova Atlantis Franc. Baconis. Bar. de Verulamio* (Utrecht, 1643).
49. *The Beautie and Unitie of the Church* (1626?) in *Works,* ii, 368.
50. *Christian Liberty Laid forth in a Sermon* (1628) in *Olive-Tree,* p. 20. Those who attempt to subvert the social order by founding 'temporall dominion' solely upon 'grace' are attacked in *Christ Mysticall* (1647), p. 99.
51. Desiderius Erasmus, *The Praise of Folly,* trans. Betty Radice with an introduction and notes by A. H. T. Levi (Harmondsworth, 1971), pp. 29–30.
52. Thomas Fuller, *The History of the Worthies of England* (London, 1662), Leicestershire, p. 129. In this connection see Knight's humorous reference to the age of the world, *Mundus,* $3\pi^{\text{r-v}}$.
53. *Poems,* p. 34.
54. *Works,* i, 321.
55. *The Revelation Unrevealed* (London, 1650), p. 214.
56. Maire Louise Berneri, *Journey through Utopia* (London, 1950), p. 56; H. Stanley Jevons, 'Contemporary Models of Sir Thomas More: Utopia and the Socialist Inca Empire', *TLS* (1935), *p. 692.*
57. Mircea Eliade, 'Paradise and Utopia: Mythical Geography and Eschatology'. in *Utopias and Utopian Thought,* ed. Frank E. Manuel (Boston, 1967), pp. 261, 262, 264.
58. *The First Three English Books on America,* p. 278.
59. *The Remedy of Prophanenesse* (London, 1637), pp. 195–6.
60. A. L. Morton, *The English Utopia* (London, 1952), p. 13.
61. *Quo Vadis?* (1617) in *Works,* i, 643.
62. *Gargantua and Pantagruel,* trans. Cohen, 573–4.
63. Northrop Frye, 'Varieties of Literary Utopias' in Manuel, p. 39.
64. Morton, p. 14.
65. *The Colloquies of Erasmus,* trans. Craig R. Thompson (Chicago, 1965), pp. 287–303. Hall acknowledges the debt, *Mundus,* p. 173.
66. *Quo Vadis?* (1617) in *Works,* i, 641–2, 652.
67. Berneri, pp. 88–93.
68. *The Rosicrucian Enlightenment* (London, 1972), pp. 118–29, 140–55.
69. Many sections recall the *Virgidemiarum:* Extravagance, pp. 161–2; lawyers, pp. 206–8; enclosure, pp. 212–13, etc.
70. *Poems,* p. 25. A modern example is Orwell's *Animal Farm.*
71. *Contemplations upon the Principall Passages of the Holy Storie,* vol. i, in *Works,* i, 775. The passage continues, 'the head is nearest to heaven, as in place, so in resemblance; both for roundnesse of figure, and for those divine guests which have their seat in it; There dwel those majesticall Powers of reason, which make a Man.'
72. *Christian Liberty* (1628), in *Olive-Tree,* p. 25; But see also *Occasional Meditations* (1633), pp. 120–1.

73. Juvenal, X, 11. 365–6.

74. *Susurrium cum Deo* (1651), pp. 109–24.

75. *The Peace-Maker*, p. 183. See also *Christian Moderation* (1640), Book II, p. 1: 'it would be an hard competition betwixt intellectual errors, and practicall, whether are the more hainous.' Cf. the very similar opinion attributed to Cardinal Pole in Thomas Starkey, *A Dialogue between Cardinal Pole and Thomas Lupset*, ed. Kathleen M. Burton (London, 1948), p. 44. See also Lodowick Bryskett, *A Discourse of Civil Life* in *Literary Works*, ed. J. H. P. Pafford (Farnborough, Hants [Germany pr.] 1972) pp. 180–1.

76. *Two Bookes of Constancie . . . Englished by Sir John Stradling*, ed. Rudolf Kirk (New Brunswick, N.J., 1939), pp. 107–11. Lipsius may be seen in the pose the *Mundus* illustrates in the engraved portrait opposite the title-page of *L. Annaei Senecae Philosophi Opera . . . a Iusto Lipsio emendata* (Antwerp, 1605).

77. Burton had read the *Mundus*. See, *The Anatomy of Melancholy*, ed. Holbrook Jackson, 3 vols. (London, 1932), pp. 97, 98.

78. Ibid., p. 396.

79. Ibid., p. 390.

80. Ibid., pp. 385, 386, 405.

81. Hall is indebted to Garzoni at many points. For example, his description of the Moronian intelligence (p. 116), the illusions of the Lyperians (137–8, 141), the Lisonican flatterers (p. 163), and the duke of Orgilia (pp. 146–7) were all suggested in part at least by *L'hospidale*. See the anonymous translation *The Hospitall of Incurable Fooles* (1600), pp. 17–19, 62, 95, 133. The influence, however, stretched only to descriptive detail, not to structure or arrangement. Hall's opinion of the work, which he terms 'scriptum parum feliciter' (p. 182), was not high. Another acknowledgement of indebtedness is made on p. 145.

82. *The Essayes of Michael Lord of Montaigne*, ed. Desmond MacCarthy, 3 vols. (London, 1928), i, 92–104.

83. *The Anatomy*, i, 202–6.

84. Lawrence Babb, *The Elizabethan Malady* (East Lansing, 1951), pp. 54–6.

85. *Epistles* (1608), in *Works*, i, 258.

86. *Claudii Galeni Opera Omnia*, ed. C. G. Kuhn, 20 vols. (Leipzig, 1821–33), xix (1830), 706–7.

87. *The Castel of Helth* (London, 1541), fol. 9^{r-v}.

88. See also *Epistles* (1608), in *Works*, i, 264. The theory that climate influences character was obviously one to which Hall subscribed, and is present throughout his description of *Terra Australis*. Writing to William Bedell concerning Jacob Wadsworth, a convert to Roman Catholicism, he says, 'I pity the impotent malice of the man: sure that hot region and sulphurous religion are guilty of this his choler.' *Works*, ed. Wynter, x, 501.

89. 'By how much the humane flesh is and ought to be more dear, by so much more odious is the thought of eating it, neither let them imagine they can escape the imputation of an hateful savageness in this act, for

that it is not presented to them in the form of flesh, whiles they professe to know it is so, howsoever it appeareth ... Corporally then to eat (if it were possible) the flesh of Christ, as it could (in our Saviours own word) profit nothing, so it could be no other then a kinde of religious Cannibalisme, which both nature and grace cannot but justly rise against.' *A Plain and Familiar Explication of Christ's Presence in the Sacrament of his Body and Blood, Out of the Doctrine of the Church of England* (1631), in *Olive-Tree*, pp. 289–90.

CHAPTER 3

1. The *Characters* enjoyed an enormous popularity on the Continent. They were translated into French as early as 1610 by Jean Loiseau de Torval (a French subject in the employ of the English foreign service and a good friend of the lexicographer Robert Cotgrave), and 3 further editions of this translation appeared at Paris in 1612, 1619, and 1634. There were also two Genevan editions in 1628 and 1634. More surprisingly the work was again translated by a French Catholic, Urbain Chevreau, in 1659 (possibly, however, as early as 1645). Between 1628 and 1696 there were 4 German translations. Italian versions appeared in 1628 and 1666 and a Danish version in 1689. See Sidney Lee, 'The Beginnings of French Translation from the English', *Transactions of the Bibliographical Society*, 8 (1907), 97–106; *Heaven upon Earth and Characters of Vertues and Vices*, ed. Rudolf Kirk (New Brunswick, N.J., 1948), pp. 52–73; Gerhard Müller-Schwefe, 'Joseph Hall's *Characters of Vertues and Vices*: Notes Toward a Revaluation', *Texas Studies in Literature and Language*, 14 (1972–3), 235–51 (pp. 247–51).
2. Benjamin Boyce, *The Theophrastan Character in England to 1642* (Cambridge, Mass., 1947), p. 122.
3. ΘΕΟΦΡΑΣΤΟΥ *ἠϑικοὶ χαρακτῆρες Theophrasti Notationes Morum. Isaacus Casaubonus recensuit, in Latinum sermonem vertit, et Libro Commentario Illustravit* (Lyons, 1599). This edition contained an extra 5 characters (XXIV–XXVIII) to some of which there are allusions in Hall. See Wendell Clausen, 'The Beginnings of English Character-Writing in the Early Seventeenth Century', *Philological Quarterly*, 25 (1946), 32–45 (p. 38).
4. Boyce, pp. 3–10.
5. *Characters of Vertues and Vices* (1608) in *Works*, i, 151, 154. Further references given after quotations in the text are to this edition, deemed the best in the most recent textual study. See Kirk, p. 80.
6. *Rhetoric* II. 12–18. See also *Ethics* IV. 2–3.
7. Casaubon (1599), p. 86. All references are to this edition.
8. Ibid., p. 88.
9. On the original intention of the work and the nature of the later additions see *The Characters of Theophrastus*, ed. R. G. Ussher (London, 1960), pp. 3–4, 6, 11.
10. Casaubon, p. 88–9.

11. Clausen, p. 41.
12. 'Nam ex diligenti vitae hominum observatione, confecta est haec morum depictio: ex huius veluti tabulae *contemplatione* non otiosa, vitae et morum nascetur emendatio' [my emphasis]. Casaubon, p. 93.
13. Kirk, p. 14.
14. Casaubon, p. 88.
15. Ibid., pp. 79–80. The satire (I. 9) is subtitled 'Garruli hominis character'.
16. Edmund Chauncey Baldwin, 'The Relation of the English "Character" to its Greek Prototype', *PMLA* 18 (1903), 412–23 (pp. 417–20).
17. Boyce, pp. 56–7, 128.
18. *Salomons Divine Arts, of 1. Ethickes 2. Politickes 3. Oeconomicks... With an open and plaine Paraphrase, upon the Song of Songs* (London, 1609).
19. 'These things be comely and pleasant to see, and worthy of honour from the beholder: A young Saint, an old Martyr, a religious Souldier, a conscionable Statesman, a great man courteous, a learned man humble, a silent woman, a child understanding the eye of his Parent, a merry companion without vanity, a friend not changed with honour, a sick man cheerefull, a soule departing with comfort and assurance.' *Works*, i, 125–6.
20. *The Fall of Pride* (1626?) in *Works*, ii, 401. The text is from Proverbs 29: 23.
21. *Salomons Divine Arts* in *Works*, i, 202.
22. *Poems*, ed. Davenport, p. 129.
23. Boyce, pp. 53–121.
24. Kirk, pp. 19–51.
25. *Christ Mysticall; or The blessed union of Christ and his Members. Also, An Holy Rapture... Also, The Christian laid forth in his whole Disposition and Carriage* (London, 1647), p. 268.
26. *Works*, i, 65.
27. *A Sermon Preached before his Maiestie at his Court of Thebalds, on Sunday, Sept. 15, 1622* in *Works*, i, 455.
28. Rosemund Tuve, *Allegorical Imagery* (Princeton, N.J., 1966), pp. 57–143.
29. *Poems*, p. 65.
30. Mario Praz, *Seventeenth-Century Imagery*, 2nd edn. (Rome, 1964), pp. 15–18. Hall's assertion that 'pictures have beene accounted the books of Idiots' probably derives from the often repeated *dictum* of St. Gregory the Great, 'quod legentibus scriptura, hoc idiotis praestat pictura' (Epistles, IX. 9). See Jean Seznec, *The Survival of the Pagan Gods* (Princeton, 1953), p. 273.
31. *Meditations and Vowes*, I, 21, 32, 68, 92; II. 34, 82, etc.
32. All the relevant passages are collected and quoted by Müller–Schwefe, p. 245.
33. Ibid., p. 244.
34. *Epistles* III. 10 (1608), in *Works*, i, 302.
35. *A Common Apologie of the Church of England* (1610), in *Works*, i, 553, 572–3, 578, 579.

36. *English Literature and the Classics,* ed. G. S. Gordon (Oxford, 1912), p. 71.

37. *Holy Observations* (1607), in *Works,* i, 126. In *The Invisible World* (1652), p. 152, he asks why he should attempt to 'divide' virtues which God has 'inseparably conjoyned'.

38. Perhaps Goldsmith is remembering this passage when he makes Lofty produce a similar packet of letters in *The Good Natur'd Man. Works,* ed. Arthur Friedman, 5 vols. (Oxford, 1966), v, 77–8.

39. See particularly the details of the busybody's gossip (p. 170), the inconstant's religion (p. 173), and the vainglorious' boasting (p. 176).

40. *Characters of Vertue and Vice... Attempted in Verse from a Treatise of the Reverend Joseph Hall, Late Lord Bishop of Exeter* (London, 1691).

41. *Epistles,* IV. 10, in *Works,* i, 322.

42. *The Overburian Characters,* ed. W. J. Paylor (Oxford, 1936), p. 13.

43. Ibid., p. 3.

44. *Enigmaticall Characters* (London, 1658), p. 92—the *second* p. 92 owing to mispagination.

45. *The Advancement of Learning,* ed. G. W. Kitchin (London, 1915), p. 168.

46. *A Modest Confutation,* sigs. A3^r–A4^r. For a full account of the controversy and its background see David Masson, *The Life of John Milton,* 7 vols. (1859–94); ii (1871), 213–68, 356–409.

47. *An Apology Against a Pamphlet Call'd A Modest Confutation of the Animadversions upon the Remonstrant against Smectymnuus,* in *Complete Prose Works of John Milton,* ed. Don M. Wolfe *et al.,* 8 vols. (New Haven, 1953–   ), i, 882–3. Hereafter Wolfe.

48. On the Authorship of the *Confutation* see William R. Parker, *Milton's Contemporary Reputation* (Columbus, Ohio, 1940), pp. 266–8. For the suggestion that the Confutant was Robert Dunkin a clergyman of Hall's own diocese of Exeter see Frank Livingstone Huntley, *Bishop Joseph Hall 1574–1656* (Cambridge, 1979), pp. 127–9.

49. Benjamin Boyce, *The Polemic Character, 1640–1661* (Lincoln, Nebr., 1955), pp. 26, 32, 91.

50. *Humble Remonstrance,* pp. 1–2.

51. *Animadversions.* Wolfe, i, 670.

52. *The Peace-Maker. Laying forth the Right way of Peace, in Matter of Religion* (London, 1645), pp. 169–77.

53. *A Vindication of the Answer to the Humble Remonstrance, from the Uniust Imputations of Frivolousnesse and Falsehood* (London, 1641), p. 196.

54. *A Modest Confutation,* sig. A3^r, p. 2.

55. *An Apology.* Wolfe, i, 880–2.

56. 'A Letter to Louis Crocius', in *Works,* ed. P. Hall, xi, 438–45.

57. H. R. Trevor-Roper, *Archbishop Laud* (London, 1940), pp. 307, 426.

58. *Animadversions.* Wolfe, i, 731.

59. *A Short Answer to the Tedious Vindication of Smectymnuus* (London, 1641), sig. A3^v.

60. *An Answer,* p. 5.

61. *A Vindication,* p. 184.

62. *Episcopacie by Divine Right*, Part III, pp. 31–3.
63. 'It is but arrogance therefore, and the pride of a *metaphysicall* fume, to thinke that *the mutinous rabble* (for so he calls the Christian congregation) *would be so mistaken in a Clerk of the University* that were to be their minister.' *An Apology*, Wolfe, i, 933–4.
64. *Animadversions*. Wolfe, i, 704.
65. 'He stiles himselfe, *a Dutifull sonne of the Church.* And it hath beene a Custome of late times, to cry up the holy *Mother the Church of England*, to call for absolute obedience to *holy Church*; full conformity to the orders of holy Church; Neglecting in the meane time, *God the Father, and the holy Scripture.' An Answer*, pp. 79–80.
66. *A Speech in Parliament* (1641), in *Olive-Tree*, p. 427.
67. Wolfe, i, 83–4.
68. *A Common Apologie of the Church of England* (1610), in *Works*, i, 578.
69. *Mundus Alter et Idem* (Frankfurt, 1605?), p. 189.
70. *Epistles*, III, 1 (1608) in *Works*, i, 287–8.

CHAPTER 4

1. *Works*, i, 311. Unlike many of his continental contemporaries Hall makes no distinction whatsoever between the terms meditation and contemplation. He uses them as synonyms.
2. *Poems*, pp. 24–5, 71–2.
3. *Works*, i, 88.
4. Ibid., p. 10; *Poems*, p. 36.
5. 'Thus doe thou, o my soule, when thou art raised up to this height of thy fixed Contemplation, cast down thine eyes contemptuously upon the region of thy former miseries . . .', *Susurrium cum Deo . . . Together with The Soules Farewell to Earth* (1651), pp. 333–46 (pp. 336–7); See C. S. Lewis, *The Discarded Image* (Cambridge, 1964), pp. 26, 32–3.
6. *Works*, iii, 107.
7. *Institutes*, ed. John T. McNeill, Library of Christian Classics, 2 vols. (London, 1961), i, 35.
8. Ibid., p. 251.
9. *Deaths Alarum* (1656), p. 63.
10. *Mary Rich, Countess of Warwick (1625–1678)*, by Charlotte Fell Smith (London, 1901), pp. 322–3; U. Milo Kaufmann, *The Pilgrim's Progress and Traditions in Puritan Meditation* (New Haven, 1966), pp. 131–2.
11. *Occasional Reflections upon Several Subjects* (Oxford, 1848; orig. publ. 1656), p. xiii.
12. *Works*, i, 95–6.
13. Helen C. White, *English Devotional Literature 1600–40*, University of Wisconsin Studies in Language and Literature, 29 (Madison, 1931), pp. 77–8, 84–6.
14. A. G. Dickens, *The English Reformation*, rev. edn. (Glasgow, 1967), p. 39; For the influence of meditation on Elizabethan literature see

Joseph Burns Collins, *Christian Mysticism in the Elizabethan Age* (Baltimore, 1940).

15. *Poems*, pp. 102-3.
16. Greenham, p. 37.
17. Ibid., p. 37.
18. Ibid., p. 40.
19. *Seven Treatises*, pp. 235-59. See esp. pp. 236-9.
20. *Works*, i, 22.
21. Ibid., sig. A5ʳ.
22. Ibid., p. 96. *Select Thoughts* (1648), p. 10.
23. *Remedy of Prophanenesse*, pp. 53-4. All references supplied in the text are to this edition.
24. Evelyn Underhill, *Mysticism*, 5th edn. (London, 1914), pp. 494-530.
25. *The Spiritual Exercises of Saint Ignatius of Loyola*, trans. from the Spanish with commentary and translation of the *Directorium in Exercitia* by W. H. Longridge (London, 1919), pp. 52, 56.
26. *Works*, i, 28-9.
27. Underhill, p. 559.
28. *Works*, i, 4, 20.
29. '*Remonstrant*: Wanton wits must have leave to play with their owne sterne. *Answere*: A Meditation of yours doubtlesse observ'd at Lambeth from one of the Archiepiscopall Kittens'. *Animadversions* (1641), p. 29.
30. *Works*, i, 96.
31. Ibid., pp. 96, 97.
32. Ibid., p. 96. George Estye (1566-1601), student and fellow of Gonville and Caius College, was the rector of St. Mary's, Bury St. Edmunds before William Bedell. Hall wrote a Latin inscription for his monument. Edward Dering (d. 1576), fellow of Christ's College Cambridge and renowned London 'lecturer', accused Queen Elizabeth to her face of failing to purge the Church of its many corruptions and was prohibited from preaching by her express command.
33. Ibid., p. 97.
34. *Specialities of Divine Providence*, in *Olive-Tree*, pp. 23-4.
35. Thomas Rogers's translation *A right Christian Treatise Entituled S. Augustines praiers* went through four editions between 1581 and 1604. *A Pretious Booke of Heavenlie Meditations . . . whereunto is annexed Saint Augustines psalter* (1581) by the same translator was also highly popular.
36. J. Wickham Legg, *A Bibliography of the Thoughts of Marcus Aurelius Antoninus* (London, 1910), pp. 18, 22, 28; *The Invisible World* (1652), p. 143.
37. Louis Martz, *The Poetry of Meditation* (New Haven, 1962), pp. 25, 113, 331-52.
38. *Works*, i, 22.
39. Ibid., p. 1.
40. *Five Metaphysical Poets* (Cambridge, 1964), p. 7.
41. Martz, pp. 44-53.
42. *Devotions*, ed. John Sparrow (Cambridge, 1923), p. 113.

43. Winfried Schleiner, *The Imagery of Donne's Sermons* (Providence, 1970), pp. 94–103.

44. *Works,* i, 96.

45. *Patrologia Latina,* ed. Migne, ccx, 579. See Arthur O. Lovejoy, *The Great Chain of Being* (Cambridge, Mass., 1936), pp. 24–143.

46. Ernest Curtius, *European Literature and the Latin Middle Ages* (London, 1953), pp. 138–44. See also pp. 319–26.

47. *Works,* i, 96.

48. Ibid., 774.

49. Curtius, p. 140; *The Mischief of Faction* (1641), in *Olive-Tree,* p. 77.

50. *Works,* i, 774.

51. For an account of Bellarmine's work see Ruth Coons Wallerstein, *Studies in Seventeenth-Century Poetic* (Madison, Wis., 1950), pp. 213–15.

52. *The Works of George Herbert,* ed. F. E. Hutchinson (Oxford, 1941), pp. 116–17.

53. Philip S. Moore, *The Works of Peter of Poitiers* (Notre Dame, Indiana, 1936), pp. 65–77 (p. 75).

54. *Occasional Meditations* (1633), pp. 2–4.

55. *Works,* i, 8.

56. Ibid., p. 33.

57. *Works,* ii, 368. For other emblematic lists in Hall see ibid., p. 308, and *Select Thoughts* (1648), pp. 148–9.

58. *Emblemes* (1635), sig. A3^r.

59. Freeman, *English Emblem Books* (London, 1948); Martz, *The Paradise Within* (New Haven, 1964).

60. *Protestant Poetics* (Princeton, 1979), pp. 179–212 (p. 212).

61. 'John Donne and the Emblematic Practice', *RES* 22 (1946), 182–200.

62. *George Herbert, His Religion and Art* (London, 1954), p. 124.

63. *The Minor Poems,* Variorum edn. ed. Edwin Greenlaw *et al.,* 2 vols. (Baltimore, 1943–7), ii (1947), 174.

64. *Occasional Meditations* 15, 43, 52, 110, 133, 134 refer to their images as emblems.

65. H. Fisch, 'Bishop Hall's Meditations', *RES* 25 (1949), 210–21 (p. 215).

66. *Works,* i, 151.

67. Sir John Cullum, *The History and Antiquities of Hawstead and Hardwick* (London, 1813), pp. 159–65; Freeman, pp. 90–9; *The Discovery of a New World* ed. Huntington Brown (Cambridge, Mass., 1937), pp. 112, 186–7.

68. *A Sermon Preach't to his Majesty, At the Court of White-hall* (1625?), in *Works,* iii, 194; *Emblemes,* pp. 36–9.

69. *Poems,* p. 102.

70. Ibid., p. 122.

71. *Works,* i, 96.

72. *Christ Mysticall,* p. 29.

73. Ibid., pp. 31–2.

74. *Remedy of Prophanenesse,* p. 11.

75. Martz, p. 279.
76. *Works*, i, 102.
77. *Poems*, p. 139.
78. Works, i, 96.
79. Daniel, *The Worthy tract of Paulus Iovius contayning a Discourse of rare inventions, both Militarie and Amorous called Imprese* (1585); Fraunce, *Insignium . . . quae ab Italis Imprese nominantur, explicatio* (1588); Willet, *Sacrorum Emblematum Centuria Una* (1592).
80. *Works*, i, 406–7. Hall's childhood mentor, Anthony Gilby, translated *The Testament of the Twelve Patriarchs* into English in 1575.
81. Ibid., pp. 406, 407, 414.
82. *Works*, ii, 377.
83. Praz, *Studies in Seventeenth-Century Imagery* (Rome, 1964), p. 199.
84. *Works*, i, 316.
85. *Occasional Meditations*, pp. 109–10.
86. R. C. Bald, *John Donne: A Life* (Oxford, 1970), pp. 487, 529.
87. *LXX Sermons by John Donne* (London, 1640), p. 13.
88. *Poems*, ed. Herbert Grierson, 2 vols. (Oxford, 1912), i, 246–7; *Select Thoughts* (1648), pp. 29–30. Cf. also the clock and sun imagery in 'Obsequies to the Lord Harington' 11. 131–54 (Grierson, i, 275–6) and *Select Thoughts* 6 (pp. 22–3).
89. *Poems*, p. 153.
90. Referring to Christ's 'tropicall kind of speech' in *Roma Irreconciliabilis* (*No Peace with Rome*, 1611), Hall tells us that 'the whole Reverend Senate of the Fathers cries out, and redoubles the names of Symboles, Types, Signes, Representation, Similitude, Figures, and what-ever word may import a borrowed sense.' *Works*, i, 625.
91. *The Peace-Maker* (London, 1645), pp. 80–1.
92. *Occasional Meditations*, pp. 216–17.
93. *The Works of Henry Vaughan*, ed. L. C. Martin, 2 vols. (Oxford, 1914), ii, 478–9.
94. Ibid., i, 186.
95. Ibid., ii, 497–9.
96. *Occasional Meditations*, pp. 329–31.
97. *Devout Soul*, 2nd edn. (London, 1650), pp. 100–1.
98. *The Art of Memory*, 2nd edn. (Harmondsworth, 1969), p. 130. See pp. 139, 171–2.
99. Ibid., p. 256.
100. Ibid., pp. 260–78.
101. *Ludus Literarius, or The Grammar Schoole*, ed. E. T. Campagnac (London, 1917), p. 183.
102. *Occasional Reflections*, p. xxxi.
103. *Occasional Meditations*, sigs. A7^v–A8^r.
104. *Susurrium cum Deo*, sigs. A3^v–A4^r.
105. *Christ Mysticall*, p. 2.
106. All references supplied in the text are to the edition in *Works*, i, 89–119.
107. Kaufmann, pp. 130–3.
108. Martz, pp. 331–52.

109. *Seven Treatises,* p. 242.
110. Pierre Pourrat, *Christian Spirituality,* trans. W. H. Mitchell 3 vols. (London, 1922-7), iii (1927), 1-48.
111. *Works,* i, 113.
112. *Devout Soul,* pp. 8-9.
113. *Mundus Alter et Idem* (Frankfurt, 1605?), p. 183.
114. See, e.g., the elaborate diagrammatic plan of *The Remedy of Discontentment* (London, 1645), facing p. 1.
115. *Works,* i, 27; *Remedy of Discontentment,* p. 2.
116. Frank Livingstone Huntley, *Bishop Joseph Hall 1574-1656; A biographical and critical study* (Cambridge, 1979), p. 47; A. B. Johnson, 'The earlier seventeenth century sermon and the beginnings of the plain style in English prose with reference to Joseph Hall' (unpublished doctoral dissertation, University of London, 1972), pp. 201-93, 334-51.
117. *Episcopacie by Divine Right* (London, 1640), part 3, p. 39. For the Ramist doctrine of 'method' see Perry Miller, *The New England Mind: The Seventeenth Century* (New York, 1939), pp. 138-41. The plan of *The Remedy of Discontentment* mentioned above (n.114) does *not* fully observe the Ramist division into a series of dichotomies for which see Miller pp. 125-7. Hall points out that Ramus did not support the presbyterian system of church government even though he was 'a man censured for affecting innovations in Logicke and Philosophie'.
118. Richard A. Lanham, *A Handlist of Rhetorical Terms* (London, 1968), p. 110.
119. Martz, p. 47.
120. Kaufmann, pp. 121, 127.
121. *Spiritual Exercises,* p. 53.
122. *Christian Moderation* (London, 1640), Book I, p. 171.
123. *Spiritual Exercises,* pp. 53-4.
124. Ibid., pp. 76-8.
125. Ibid., pp. 163-4.
126. For an account of Baxter's similar problems see Martz, pp. 168-75.
127. Ibid., 332-7.
128. *Works,* i, 299-300.
129. *The Great Mysterie of Godliness ... Also, The Invisible World* (1652), p. 290.
130. For an account of this work see James L. Connolly, *John Gerson, Reformer and Mystic* (Louvain, 1928), pp. 256-79.
131. *An Apology, or, Apologeticall answere, made by Father Paule a Venetian, of the order of the Servi, unto the Exeptions and objections of Cardinall Bellarmine, against certaine Treatises and Resolutions of Iohn Gerson, concerning the force and validitie of Excommunication* (London, 1607).
132. A marginal note reads: 'Saving our just quarrell against him for the Councell of Constance'. Despite his support for the General Council at the time of the Great Schism, Gerson refused to contemplate the abolition of the Papacy, and appears to have supported the burning of Huss. See John B. Morrall, *Gerson and the Great Schism* (Manchester, 1960), pp. 102, 110-11.

133. John Gerson, *Opera*, 4 vols. (Paris, 1606), iii, col. 495. In this edition *La Montaigne* appears in a Latin translation.

134. *Montaigne*, 494–5; *Arte*, 96, 110.

135. *Montaigne*, 498, 527; *Arte*, 97, 98.

136. *Montaigne*, 497, 524; *Arte*, 99.

137. *Montaigne*, 508, 509, 514; *Arte*, 100.

138. *Montaigne*, 510; *Arte*, 101.

139. *The History of the Worthies of England* (London, 1662), Leicestershire, p. 130. It is surely significant that Hall's contemporaries never refer to him as a Stoic. On the contrary, when they call him Seneca what they emphasize is the *Christian* nature of his writing. The name never stands unqualified. The first such reference would seem to be by his translator, Jean Loiseau de Torval, who published the French version of the *Meditations and Vowes* under the title *Le Seneque Ressucité Chrestien* (1610, 1614)—the *Christian* Seneca. The title-page proceeds to call particular attention to the style of the work 'œuvre et stile extraordinaire'. The Latin translation of *Heaven upon Earth* by Everhard Schuttenius which appeared at Amsterdam in 1623 is even more explicit: *Coelum in Terra, hoc est, Seneca Christianus... Authore magno illo Et vere Christiano hujus aevi nostri Seneca, D. Iosepho Hallo.* The same emphasis is found in the Puritan Henry Burton who refers to Hall in his *Seven Vials* (1628) as 'our Divine *Seneca*' (p. 52). The allusion in a letter of Sir Henry Wotton (1638) which Fuller identifies as referring to Hall, speaks of 'our spiritual Seneca' and praises him for displaying 'Christian wisdom and charity'. *The Life and Letters of Sir Henry Wotton*, ed. Logan Pearsall Smith, 2 vols. (Oxford, 1907), ii, 370. Similarly in *A Remonstrance against Presbitery* (1641), Sir Thomas Aston praises 'our English Seneca' as one of the great 'assertors of our Religion against its common enemy of Rome' (sig. b3ᵛ). Defending his own use of the curt Senecan style in *Zootomia* (1654), Richard Whitlock cites Hall in support of his position: 'take the confirmation of our english [*sic*] *Divine Seneca, Bishop Hall*, who saith, never any *Heathen* writ more *Divinely*, never any *Philosopher* more *probably.*' *Two Seventeenth-Century Prefaces*, ed. A. K. Crostan (Liverpool, 1949), p. 10. Whitlock's reference is, of course, to *Heaven upon Earth, Works*, i, 65.

140. 'Bishop Hall, "Our English Seneca"', *PMLA* 63 (1948), 1191–1204 (p. 1191).

141. *Heaven upon Earth and Characters of Vertues and Vices*, ed. Rudolf Kirk (New Brunswick, N.J., 1948), pp. 19–51 (p. 28).

142. Kirk, p. 19; Smith, pp. 1191, 1194; *The Peace-Maker*, pp. 3–4.

143. George Williamson, *The Senecan Amble* (London, 1948), pp. 130–31, 139.

144. *Works*, i, 53. All of Hall's religious works are structured to move from reason to emotion. Their principal object is to excite religious passion. Hence 'to show no passion, is too Stoicall'. On the other hand, Hall found it extremely useful to employ the negative aspects of Stoicism in his battle against the vanity of human wishes. Stoicism facilitated the

cultivation of the 'contemptus mundi'. 'I marvell then', he writes, 'that any wisemen could be other but Stoicks, and could have any conceit of life, but contemptuous.' *Works*, i, 289.

145. 'The Limits of Hall's Senecanism', *Proceedings of the Leeds Philosophical and Literary Society*, 6 (1944–7), 453–63.

146. *The Balme of Gilead* (London, 1646), p. 183.

147. Aubrey Chew, 'Joseph Hall and Neo-Stoicism', *PMLA* 65 (1950), 1130–45 (p. 1145).

148. Kirk, p. 44; *Works*, i, 81.

149. *Works*, i, 63.

150. Ibid., p. 67.

151. Ibid., p. 65.

152. *Resolutions*, p. 201.

153. François Wendel, *Calvin*, trans. Philip Mairet (London, 1963), pp. 27–37.

154. *Works*, i, 72.

155. Calvin, *Of the life or conversation of a Christen man* (London, 1549?), sigs. C3^r–C3^v. Hall too upheld Christian 'philosophy' against the philosophy of the pagans. See *Works*, i, 22.

156. *Works*, i, 71–2.

157. Ibid., p. 65.

158. *The Balme of Gilead*, p. 326.

159. T. H. L. Parker, *John Calvin* (London, 1975), p. 28.

160. *Essayes. Religious Meditations. Places of perswasion and disswasion.* (London, 1597). In this edition the meditations are in Latin, but in the edition of the same title which appeared the following year they are in English.

161. See Wesley Trimpi, *Ben Jonson's Poems, A Study of the Plain Style* (Stanford, California, 1962), pp. 28–40.

162. *Poems*, p. 99.

163. *Remedy of Prophanenesse*, p. 5; *Works*, i, 473.

164. *Works*, i, 619.

165. Williamson, *The Senecan Amble*, pp. 155–6. The importance of matter over manner is asserted succinctly in the *Meditations and Vowes*: 'Elegancie without soundnesse, is no better than a nice vanitie. Although therefore the most hearers are like Bees, that goe all to the flowers, never regarding the good herbs (that are of as wholesome use, as the other of faire shew:) yet let my speech strive to be profitable; plausible, as it happens: better the coat be mis-shapen, than the body.' *Works*, i, 9.

166. Trimpi, pp. 62–6.

167. *Works*, i, 37.

168. Ibid., sig. A5^r.

169. Ibid., p. 17.

170. *Style, Rhetoric, and Rhythm. Essays by Morris W. Croll* ed. J. Max Patrick *et al.* (Princeton, 1966), p. 208.

171. *The Philosophical Works of Francis Bacon*, ed. John M. Robertson (London, 1905), p. 125. See Also Williamson, *The Senecan Amble*, pp. 156–7.

172. *Works,* i, 10; Martz, p. 135.
173. Croll, pp. 229–30.
174. Williamson, *The Senecan Amble,* pp. 178–9. See also his 'Senecan Style in the Seventeenth Century', *Philological Quarterly,* 15 (1936), 331–3.
175. *Works,* i, 364. In *A Short Answer to the Tedious Vindication of Smectymnuus* (1641) Hall tells us that his words 'were never yet taxed for an offensive superfluitie' (p. 99). Milton describes him as a 'tormenter of semicolons' who 'makes sentences by the Statute, as if all above three inches long were confiscat'. *Complete Prose Works,* ed. Don M. Wolfe *et al.,* 8 vols. (New Haven, 1953–   ), i, 873, 894.
176. *Works,* i, 19.
177. For Seneca's style see *Select Letters of Seneca,* ed. Walter C. Summers (London, 1910), pp. xlii–xcv; Frank Ivan Merchant, 'Seneca the Philosopher and his Theory of Style', *American Journal of Philology,* 26 (1905), 44–59; J. F. D'Alton, *Roman Literary Theory and Criticism* (London, 1931), pp. 332–5.
178. *Works,* i, 56.
179. Croll, p. 213. Croll's editors point out (pp. 204–5) that his views on this issue must be modified in the light of later examinations which have revealed 'many cases of disguised symmetry which Croll overlooked'.
180. *Works,* i, 8.
181. Ibid., p. 5.
182. Ibid., p. 155.
183. *Occasional Meditations,* pp. 48–9.
184. Ibid., pp. 35–6.
185. Ibid., pp. 132–3.
186. Ibid., pp. 2–4.
187. Ibid., pp. 252–3, 295.
188. Thomas Sloan, 'Rhetoric and Meditation: three case studies', *Journal of Medieval and Renaissance Studies,* 1–2 (1971–2), p. 49.
189. *The Saints Everlasting Rest* (London, 1650), pp. 749–54.
190. Sloan, p. 51.
191. *Breathings* (1648), pp. 3–4.
192. Ibid., pp. 1–2.
193. *Confessions,* trans. R. S. Pine-Coffin (Harmondsworth, 1961), p. 231.
194. Ibid., p. 233.
195. See, e.g., *Select Thoughts* 13 and 15. Passages such as the former which concern themselves almost exclusively with expounding biblical imagery or incidents are strongly resembled by Vaughan's meditative 'text' poems which appear in the second part of *Silex Scintillans.*
196. *Breathings,* p. 47.
197. Croll, p. 224–6.
198. *Susurrium cum Deo,* pp. 2–3.
199. *Deaths Alarum,* p. 72.
200. *Susurrium* 16, 17, 18, 21, 25, 28, 59, 67, etc. For the establishing of a similar perspective in Boethius' *De Consolatione Philosophiae,* a work which strongly influenced the mystic and meditative traditions, see

Joseph Burns Collins, *Christian Mysticism in the Elizabethan Age* (Baltimore, 1940), p. 92.

201. *Susurrium cum Deo,* pp. 280–2.
202. T. F. Kinloch, *The Life and Works of Joseph Hall* (London, 1951), p. 91.
203. *Select Thoughts,* pp. 296–7.
204. *Works,* i, 95.
205. Kirk, pp. 8, 25–7; *Meditations and Vowes,* I, 77; II, 74, 75; III, 42, 43.
206. *Susurrium cum Deo,* pp. 200–4.
207. *Works,* i, 331–3.
208. Ibid., p. 151.
209. *Christ Mysticall,* sig. A6ᵛ.
210. Ibid., p. 218. See also pp. 223–4.
211. William Haller, *The Rise of Puritanism* (New York, 1938), p. 31.
212. W. Fraser Mitchell, *English Pulpit Oratory from Andrewes to Tillotson* (London, 1932), pp. 217–21.
213. Martz, p. 123; Pourrat, iii, 12, 34, 35.
214. *Spiritual Exercises,* pp. 44–66.
215. *Works,* i, 110.
216. Ibid., p. 248. All references supplied in the text are to this edition in *Works,* i.
217. Martz, p. 238; Lewalski, p. 166.
218. *Devout Soul* 2nd edn. (1650), pp. 89, 91–3, 99–106.
219. Ibid., pp. 107–9, 114–22.
220. *Works,* i, 114.
221. *Devout Soul,* pp. 127–8.

CHAPTER 5

1. The various volumes (or 'books') of the *Contemplations* were published separately, and there are minor variations in the titles. I use the general title from *Works,* i (which does not, however, contain the New Testament *Contemplations*) to designate the work as a whole. As arranged in the collected editions, the various volumes do not correspond to the order of publication. Wherever necessary, therefore, I have supplied the original date of publication even though, both for convenience and upon textual considerations, I have always quoted from the collected works. Most of the New Testament *Contemplations* appeared for the first time in *Works,* ii, and it is this text—quite obviously the first definitive one—that I have employed throughout.
2. 'More than twenty yeares are slipt away, since I entred upon this taske of sacred Contemplations ... which I rather wished, then hoped I might live to finish. The God of heaven hath beene pleased to stretch out my dayes so farre, as to see it brought, at last, (after many necessary intermissions) to an happy end.' *Works,* ii, π3ʳ⁻ᵛ.
3. The censoring of the Bible was one of Hall's foremost objections to Rome. See *The Peace-Maker* (1645), pp. 175–6.

4. Norman Cohn, *The Pursuit of the Millennium* (London, 1970), pp. 252–61.

5. Psalms 149: 6–9. Hugh Peters preached on this text on 28 Jan. 1649 in support of the execution of Charles I, drawing also upon Isaiah 14: 18–20. See *Trial of King Charles the First*, ed. J. G. Muddiman (Edinburgh, 1928), p. 135.

6. *Christian Liberty Laid forth in a Sermon Preacht to his late Majesty at White-Hall in the time of the Parliament holden anno 1628* in *Olive-Tree* p. 20.

7. *The Devout Soul* (London, 1650), pp. 88–9.

8. *The Revelation Unrevealed* (London, 1650), p. 33. For further references and tributes to Calvin see *Cheirothesia* (1649), p. 60, and *A Defence of the Humble Remonstrance* (1641), p. 52.

9. Barbara Lewalski, *Protestant Poetics and the Seventeenth-Century Religious Lyric* (Princeton, New Jersey, 1979), pp. 111–44.

10. *Scenes from the Drama of European Literature*, trans. Ralph Manheim (New York, 1959), p. 57.

11. *Institutes*, ed. John McNeill, Library of Christian Classics, 2 vols. (London, 1960), i, 429.

12. Lewalski, p. 129.

13. Ibid., pp. 129–30.

14. T. H. L. Parker, *Calvin's New Testament Commentaries* (London, 1971), p. 50.

15. Ibid., p. 64.

16. *Works*, ed. Marcus Dods, 15 vols. (Edinburgh, 1871–6), v (1872), 478–9.

17. Parker, p. 66.

18. *A Disputation on Holy Scripture*, ed. and trans. by William Fitzgerald (Cambridge, 1849), pp. 405–7.

19. *Epistles* in *Works*, i, 262. See also 'Hermae', his poem on Whitaker's death, and 'Lusus in Bellarminum' which appeared in Whitaker's *Praelectiones* (1599), *Poems*, pp. 1–4, 101–2.

20. *A Plaine and Familiar Explication of the Old and New Testament* (1632), in *Works*, ed. Wynter, iv, 442–3.

21. *Works*, i, 902.

22. Ibid., pp. 834, 847. For similar concessions to typology and 'allegorical' interpretation made by predominantly 'literal' Elizabethan preachers see J. W. Blench, *Preaching in England in the late Fifteenth and Sixteenth Centuries* (Oxford, 1964), pp. 61–3.

23. *Revelation Unrevealed*, p. 33.

24. *Resolutions and Decisions of Divers Practicall Cases of Conscience* (1649), p. 296.

25. *Works*, ii, 150.

26. *Noah's Dove* (1624) in *Works*, i, 510.

27. *Commentaries on the Four Last Books of Moses, arranged in the form of a harmony*, trans. Charles William Bingham, 4 vols. (Edinburgh, 1852–5), i (1852), p. 64.

28. *Works*, i, 832.

29. *Works,* ed. Wynter, iii, 52.
30. Ibid., p. vii.
31. Patrick Collinson, *Archbishop Grindal 1519–1583* (London, 1979), p. 42. See Ch. 4, n. 90.
32. *A Defence of the Humble Remonstrance* (1641), p. 101.
33. *Works,* ed. Wynter, iv, 190.
34. *Episcopacie by Divine Right,* ii, 44–5.
35. *Works,* ed. Wynter, iv, 617.
36. Ibid., p. 599.
37. *Revelation Unrevealed,* p. 40.
38. Ibid., pp. 200–1. Cf. Whitaker, pp. 488–95.
39. Ibid., pp. 27–34.
40. Parker, p. 67.
41. *Revelation Unrevealed,* pp. 15, 213–14.
42. *Works,* ii, 89.
43. *Works,* i, 1320.
44. *Calvin: Commentaries,* trans. and ed. Joseph Haroutunian and Louise Pettibone Smith, Library of Christian Classics (London, 1958), p. 21.
45. *Works,* i, 1134.
46. Ibid., p. 1302.
47. Ibid., p. 803.
48. *Calvin's Commentaries: The Gospel according to St. John 11–21 and the First Epistle of John,* trans. T. H. L. Parker, ed. D. W. and Thomas Torrance (London, 1961), pp. 10–11; *Works,* ii, 231–2.
49. *Works,* ii, 237; *Calvin's Commentaries,* trans. Parker, pp. 16–17.
50. *Works,* i, 1091.
51. *Calvin's Commentaries,* trans. Parker, p. 16.
52. *Works,* ii, 236.
53. Louis Martz, *The Poetry of Meditation* (London, 1962), p. 30.
54. *Works,* i, 941, 948.
55. Richard Gibbons, *An Abridgment of Meditations of the Life, Passion, Death, and Resurrection of our Lord and Saviour Jesus Christ. Written in Italian by the R. Father Vincentius Bruno of the Society of Jesus.* (St. Omer?, 1614), §2, π10.
56. *Works,* ii, 277, 281.
57. *Works,* i, 1180–1, 1310; ii, 62.
58. *Works,* ii, p. 114.
59. U. Milo Kaufmann, *The Pilgrim's Progress and Traditions of Puritan Meditation* (New Haven, 1966), p. 122.
60. *Works,* ii, 272–3; Granada, *Of Prayer and Meditation,* trans. Richard Hopkins (Paris, 1582), fol. 270ᵛ.
61. Bonaventure's work contains one of the most important statements of meditative theory in the Western tradition. See *The Life of Christ,* trans. and ed. W. H. Hutchings (London, 1881), pp. 180–216. Hall ranks both Bernard and Bonaventure among the masters of meditation, *Works,* i, 103.
62. *Works,* i, 774, 1145, 1226.
63. Ibid., pp. 796, 969.

64. Ibid., pp. 1337–53. Hereafter references to the Haman story are given after quotations in the text.
65. Kaufmann, p. 127.
66. Ibid., p. 147.
67. *Works*, i, 944–5.
68. 'I remember of old the fool that made the all sport in the play was called the Vice; and surely it is no otherwise still; vice it is, that makes the mirth in this common theater of the world.' *A Sermon Preacht at Hampton-Court to King James In Ordinary attendance in September 1624,* in *Olive-Tree*, p. 7.
69. *Works*, i, 1269, 1337; ii, 246.
70. *Works*, i, 1332; ii, 264.
71. *The Spiritual Exercises*, trans. from the Spanish with commentary and translation of the *Directorium in Exercitia* by W. H. Longridge (London, 1919), pp. 135–41.
72. Martz, pp. 71–83.
73. Bonaventure, p. 40.
74. *Works*, ii, 19–20.
75. *Works*, i, 1265.
76. Ibid., pp. 956, 958.
77. Ibid., p. 945.
78. *Works*, ii, 6,7.
79. *Works*, i, 955.
80. Matthew 5:5 'Blessed are the meeke: for they shall inherit the earth'; Matthew 11:12 'the kingdome of heaven suffereth violence, and the violent take it by force.'
81. *Works*, i, 956, 957. As far as Hall was concerned the workings of God were so regulated by divine law that even non-believers could draw forth maxims from their observations: 'What credit hath thy great name won with these barbarous nations, that they can out of all experience make maximes of thine undoubted protection of thy people, and the certaine ruine of their adversaries?' *Works*, i, 1349.
82. *Works*, i, 771.
83. *Works*, i, 1156–9. First of all the actual process of construction is pictured in detail: the raising of the money; the co-operation of the people; the material from Lebanon; the fashioning of that material (pp. 1156–7). This is all excellently done, but it is only the first stage of the meditation: 'But what doe we bend our eyes upon stone, and wood, and metals? God would never have taken pleasure in these dead materials for their owne sakes, if they had not a further intendment: Me thinkes I see foure Temples in this one.' Hereupon follows the process of understanding, and we explore the significance of the building, at first generally (p. 1157), and then in a series of fixed points: 'In proportion ... In matter ... In situation' (p. 1158). Having worked out the meaning of the spiritual lesson, we turn to address God in the colloquy: 'Behold, if *Salomon* built a Temple unto thee, thou hast built a Temple unto thy self in us ... Wheresoever thou art, O God, thou art worthy of adoration ... Sanctifie us unto thy selfe, and be thou sanctified in us' (1158–9).

84. The significance of this for the sermons is discussed in the following chapter. A comparison of *The Passion Sermon* delivered in 1608 (*Works* i, 383–402) and *The Crucifixion* (Works, ii, 265–75) provides a good illustration of the changes effected in transition. Whereas the contemplation is almost wholly affective and devotional, the sermon is a work of meticulous scholarship, set out under a series of 'divisions' and 'subdivisions', on the theological issues involved. A marginal note (p. 272) refers the reader of the Contemplation to the more extensive and technical treatment of the doctrinal points in the earlier work.

85. *Works*, ii, 207–11.

86. Bonaventure, pp. 183–4. For similar ascending stages in Augustinian meditation see Joseph Burns Collins, *Christian Mysticism in the Elizabethan Age* (Baltimore, 1940), pp. 26–9.

87. The date of 1659 assigned to this work in the *STC* is misleading. It was not a posthumous publication but appeared with *The Great Mysterie of Godliness* in 1652. The 1659 edition was the second.

88. Published along with Christ Mysticall was *An Holy Rapture: or, A Patheticall Meditation of the Love of Christ.* For the highly traditional nature of Hall's progression see Collins, pp. 36–64.

89. Auerbach, p. 52.

90. *Devotions*, ed. John Sparrow (Cambridge, 1923), p. 114.

91. Haroutunian and Smith, p. 38.

92. *One of the Sermons Preacht at Westminster On the day of the publike Fast* (April 5. 1628) in *Works*, ii, 305–17.

93. *Works*, i, 536.

94. Ibid., pp. 767–8.

95. Ibid., p. 1258.

96. Ibid., p. 968.

97. Ibid., p. 968.

98. This is made clear in his sermons also: 'Those two late blessings ... were worthy of immortall memorie, The Prince out of Spaine, Religion out of the dust; For the one, what a winter was there in all good hearts, when our Sun was gone so farre Southward? How chearefull a Spring in his returne? For the other, who saw not how Religion began (during those purposely protracted Treaties) to droope and languish, her friends to sigh, her enemies to insult, daring to brave us with challenges, to threaten our ruine; *The Lord look't downe from Heaven, and visited this poore Vine of his,* and hath shaken off these Caterpillers from her then-wasting leaves; Now we live, and it flourisheth.' *A Sermon of Publique Thanksgiving ... Preached before his Majestie ... at his Court of Whitehall Jan 29. 1625* in *Works*, ii, 302.

99. *Works*, i, 968–9.

100. Ibid., p. 971.

101. Ibid., p. 972.

102. Ibid., p. 1163.

103. In 1622, for example, James I ordered the release of a great number of Catholics from prison as a compliment to Spain. See Godfrey Davies, *The Early Stuarts, 1603–1660*, 2nd edn., (Oxford, 1959), p. 209.

Preaching before James in 1624 Hall points out that 'the late relaxation of penall laws for religion discovered many a turn-coat' and warns that even now 'if the winde should turn, how many ... would be ready to say *Canemus domino*, etc. let us sing unto the Lord a new song.' *Olive-Tree*, p. 15.

104. *Works*, i, 1176.

105. Godfrey Davies, 'English Political Sermons, 1603–1640', *HLQ* 3 (1939–40), 5–7; Thomas Middleton, *A Game at Chess*, ed. J. W. Harper (London, 1966), p. xxiv.

106. *No Peace with Rome* (1612), in *Works*, i, 631.

107. *Works*, i, 896. Rome's seven hills would not be far from the minds of contemporary readers.

108. Ibid., p. 1069.

109. Ibid., p. 1286.

110. Ibid., p. 1033.

111. Ibid., p. 1088.

112. Ibid., p. 1303.

113. Ibid., p. 1305.

114. Ibid., pp. 1305, 1306–7.

115. Ibid., p. 1305.

116. Ibid., p. 1307.

117. Ibid., p. 1176.

118. Marvin Arthur Breslow, *A Mirror of England: English Puritan Views of Foreign Nations 1618–1640* (Cambridge, Mass., 1970), pp. 107–11.

CHAPTER 6

1. See, e.g., Frank Livingstone Huntley, *Bishop Joseph Hall 1574–1656; A biographical and critical study* (Cambridge, 1979), pp. 110–11.

2. *Five Sermons, in Five several Styles; or Waies of Preaching* (London, 1656). For the imitation of Hall see pp. 23–38.

3. Hall gives some account of his preaching both early and late, and of its importance in his life in *Observations of Some Specialities* and *Bishop Hall's Hard Measure*, in *Olive-Tree*, pp. 11,26,56.

4. *A Sermon Preacht at Hampton-Court to King James. In Ordinary attendance in September 1624*, in *Olive-Tree* p. 2.

5. *The Passion Sermon* (1609), in *Works*, i, 385.

6. *Pharisaisme and Christianity* (1608), in *Works* i, 369–70.

7. *Observations of Some Specialities*, in *Olive-Tree*, p. 26.

8. *Works*, i, 433.

9. *The Works of Aurelius Augustine, Bishop of Hippo*, ed. Marcus Dods, 15 vols. (Edinburgh, 1871–6), ix (1873), pp. 139–41.

10. William Haller, *The Rise of Puritanism* (New York, 1938), pp. 129–30.

11. Ibid., p. 137.

12. *Works*, i, 515. The original Latin version reads 'Nuda nude loquor, ut fidus ille olim monitor'. *Columba Noae Olivam Adferens Iactatissimae Christi Arcae* (London, 1624), p. 23. The translation, however, which

first appeared in 1625 was made by Hall's eldest son under his own supervision. It therefore accurately reflects the sense of his Latin. Hall himself refers to his 'poor, and plain fashion' in his autobiographical tracts, *Olive-Tree*, p. 26.

13. Douglas Bush, *English Literature in the Earlier Seventeenth Century 1600–1660* (Oxford, 1945), p. 323; W. F. Mitchell, *English Pulpit Oratory from Andrewes to Tillotson* (London, 1932), p. 195.

14. M. W. Dewar, 'Bishop Joseph Hall, 1574–1656: An Ecumenical Calvinist Churchman', *The Churchman*, 80 (1966), 199.

15. See, e.g., the clipped syntax and plentiful classical allusions of Abbot's *A Sermon Preached at Westminster May 26. 1608 At the Funerall Solemnities of the Right Honorable Thomas Earle of Dorset, late L. High Treasurer of England* (London, 1608), pp. 10–11. The influence of Lyly is, however, still perceptible in Abbot.

16. Mitchell, pp. 108–9.

17. Ibid., p. 201.

18. *The Works of that famous and Worthy Minister of Christ, in the Universitie of Cambridge, Mr. William Perkins*, 3 vols. (London, 1616–18), ii (1617), 670.

19. Haller, p. 140.

20. Ibid., p. 167.

21. Mitchell, pp. 139–40.

22. *Noahs Dove* (1624), in *Works*, i, 517–18. For Andrewes's very similar account of the basis of the Anglican faith, its connections with Catholicism, and the early Church councils see *Opuscula Quaedam Posthuma* (Oxford, 1852), p. 91.

23. For the typical structure of an Anglo-Catholic sermon see J. W. Blench, *Preaching in England in the Late Fifteenth and Sixteenth Centuries* (Oxford, 1964), pp. 108–11. On the structural differences between homilies constructed after the Perkins and Keckermann fashion see Perry Miller, *The New England Mind: The Seventeenth Century* (New York, 1939), pp. 332–7. See also Mitchell, pp. 95–101.

24. *Works*, i, 663.

25. For Dod's daunting 'method' see Mitchell, pp. 112–14.

26. In *The Womans Vail* (1641?), for example, he tells the audience that his division is such that they must already have made it themselves; *Olive-Tree*, p. 237. He frequently implies that the texts divide themselves almost automatically, and tries to infuse some witty conceit or turn of phrase calculated to make his divisions all the more memorable. The division of *The Best Bargaine* (1623) is in this respect typical. 'The subject of my Text is a *Bargaine*, and *Sale*. A Bargaine enjoyned, a sale forbidden: and the subject of both bargaine and sale, is *Truth*; A bargaine able to make us all rich; a sale able to make any of us miserable; *Buy the Truth, and sell it not*; A sentence of short sound, but large extent; the words are but seaven syllables, an easie load for our memories; the matter is a world of work; a long taske for our lives.' Note the usual movement away from the 'words' to the 'matter'; *Works*, i, 473.

27. One of the Sermons Preacht to the Lords of the High Court of Parliament, In their solemne Fast held on Ashwednesday, Febr. 18 (1628) in Works, ii, 335.

28. Works, i, 371–82.

29. The True Peace-Maker (1634), in Works, i, 497.

30. Holy Observations, 50, in Works, i, 132. Hall was no more troubled by the 'artificiality' of rhetoric than by the artificiality of language itself. Referring in The Character of Man (1634) to the legend that the Egyptian king Psammetichus discovered man's natural language by having a child reared in total isolation, he rejects the idea out of hand: 'If no body should teach him to speak what would he doe? Historians may talk of, Bec, that the untaught infant said; I dare say he learn't of the goats, not of nature; I shall as soon believe that *Adam* spake Dutch in Paradise according to *Goropius Beccanus* his idle fancy, as that the child meant to speak an articulate word unbidden.' Works, iii, 109. See Herodotus, II. 2.

31. The Devout Soul, 2nd edn. (1650), pp. 5–7.

32. 'If we preach plainly, to some it will savour of a carelesse slubbering, to others of a mortified sincerity; Elaborately, some will tax our affectation, others will applaud our diligence in dressing the delicate viands of God.' Works, ii, 68.

33. Works, i, 406.

34. Ibid., p. 476.

35. Ibid., p. 461.

36. Ibid., p. 464.

37. See e.g. A Sermon ... to King James (1624), in Olive-Tree, pp. 1–2, 5.

38. Works, i, 666.

39. Ibid., pp. 463, 672.

40. A Sermon of Publique Thanksgiving: for The Wonderful Mitigation of the late Mortalitie (1626), in Works, ii, 302–3.

41. Occasional Meditations (1633), pp. 175–7.

42. A Sermon Preacht to his Maiestie, on the Sunday before the Fast, (being March 30) at White-hall; In way of preparation for that holy Exercise (1628), in Works, ii, 330; For the passage in Augustine see The Book of Grace, 26, in Letters, trans. Wilfrid Parsons, 5 vols. (New York, 1951–6), iii (1953), 113–14.

43. Works, i, 461, 475.

44. The History of the Worthies of England (London, 1662), Leicestershire p. 130.

45. The Righteous Mammon, Works, i, 672–3.

46. Olive-Tree, p. 43.

47. The Best Bargaine, Works, i, 475.

48. Works, ii, 384.

49. A Sermon Preach't to his Majesty, At the Court of White-Hall, Aug. 8. (1625?) in Works, iii, 194.

50. Howard R. Patch, The Goddess Fortuna in Medieval Literature (Cambridge, Mass., 1927), pp. 45, 61, 148; Mundus Alter et Idem (1605?), p. 129.

51. *Works*, ii, 391–2.

52. *Works*, ed. P. Hall, xi, 468, 472, 480.

53. 'Saint Paul made that verse of the Heathen Poet, Canonicall, Evill conversation corrupts good manners.' *Works*, ii, 345.

54. Hall used almost the entire range of classical authors then available. Among the Church Fathers his favourite authorities were Augustine, Tertullian, Gregory Nazianzen, Lactantius, Ambrose, John Chrysostom, and Jerome. Among the Medieval authorities he preferred Bernard of Clairvaux (very frequent), John Gerson (very frequent), Bonaventure, and Aquinas. Church history is represented by Josephus, Sozomen, Socrates, and Eusebius. He also quotes widely from such Renaissance authors as Erasmus, Luther, Calvin, Lipsius, and, of course, Bellarmine and most of the Catholic and Protestant controversialists.

55. *Works*, ii, 446. *The History of Ingulf*, ed. and trans. Joseph Stevenson, The Church Histories of England, 7 vols. (London, 1853–6), ii, Part II (1854), p. 667.

56. *Olive-Tree*, pp. 72–3.

57. *Works*, i, 498.

58. Exploratory navigation, sea-monsters, and the travels of William de Rubruquis feature in the first *Saint Paul's Combat*, while even Terra Australis itself receives mention in *The Public Fast Sermon* (5 April 1628). *Works*, ii, 309, 435, 442.

59. *The History of the Worthies of England* (London, 1662), pp. 129–30.

60. *The Olde Religion* (1628), 2^{r-v}; For Hall's support of James I's efforts to further the work of catechizing see *The Peace-Maker* (1645), p. 193. For the text of Hall's own catechism see *Works*, i,. 763–4.

61. *A Sermon Preacht at Higham near Norwich, on Sunday July 1. 1655*, in *Olive-Tree*, p. 226 (mispag. for 206).

62. Ibid., p. 205.

63. Mitchell, p. 106.

64. These opinions, of course, had to be orthodox opinions. Hall favoured rigid censorship of the pulpit and complains equally about the damage done by the illiterate and the over-clever. *Works*, ed. P. Hall, xi, 484–7.

65. Stanley E. Fish, *Self-Consuming Artifacts* (London, 1972), pp. 43–77.

66. Ibid., p. 75.

67. Ibid., p. 42.

68. Ibid., p. 66.

69. *Works*, ix, 127–35.

70. Ibid., pp. 137–9.

71. Perkins, *Works*, ii, 673.

72. Wilbur Samuel Howell, *Logic and Rhetoric in England 1500–1700* (New York, 1961), pp. 153, 182, 184, 228–9. See also Johnson, A.B.J., 'The earlier seventeenth century sermon and the beginnings of the plain style in English prose with reference to Joseph Hall' (unpublished doctoral dissertation, University of London, 1972), pp. 201–93, 334–51.

73. Miller, pp. 111–16.

74. *Meditations and Vowes*, III, 35 in *Works*, i, 47.
75. Barbara Lewalski writes: 'The basis in Protestant theory for the near-fusion of the sermon and the meditation was the supposed identity of their purposes and their parts . . . Like the sermon, meditation as the Protestants conceived it involves argument and persuasion, illustration and analysis; it may also begin with and be based upon a biblical text, and it customarily interrogates and apostrophizes an audience—the self or God. Joseph Hall's *Arte of Divine Meditation* identified as pertaining to exercises of meditation precisely the same purposes and elements which Protestant *artes concionandi* defined for the sermon—the analysis of a religious doctrine or topic by the understanding, and the stimulation of the affections and the heart.' *Donne's 'Anniversaries' and the Poetry of Praise; The Creation of a Symbolic Mode* (Princeton, 1973), pp. 85–6.
76. 'As in preaching to others, the bare propounding and opening of truths and duties, doth seldome finde that successe as the lively application: so it is also in meditating.' *The Saints Everlasting Rest* (1650), p. 749.
77. *A Sermon Preacht at Hampton Court to King James, In Ordinary attendance in September 1624*, in *Olive-Tree*, pp. 7–8.
78. Ibid., p. 6.
79. *One of the Sermons Preacht at Westminster, On the day of the publike Fast (April 5. 1628) To the Lords of the High Court of Parliament*, in *Works*, ii, 315.
80. *An Holy Panegyricke* (1613), in *Works*, i, 446.
81. *A Sermon . . . to King James* (1624), in *Olive-Tree*, p. 8.
82. *The Works of Thomas Adams* (London, 1630), pp. 440–77, 498–508.
83. *Pro M. Caelio Oratio*, 14. 33–4.
84. *The Righteous Mammon* (1618), in *Works*, i, 670.
85. *Christian Liberty* (1628), in *Olive-Tree*, pp. 21–2; *The Poems*, pp. 24–5.
86. See e.g. *Works*, ii, 315–16.
87. In *Divine Light, and Reflections* (Whitsunday, 1640) he tells us that his last court sermon was *The Character of Man* (March 1634). *Olive-Tree*, p. 34.
88. *A Sermon Preach'd in the City of Excester, At the Consecration of a new Burial-place there, on Saint Bartholmews day, Aug 24. 1637*, in *Works*, iii, 101.
89. *Works*, i, 499–500, 516–19; ii, 412–13.
90. *Works*, i, 373–4.
91. Ibid., pp. 377–8, 380–1.
92. *The Imprese of God II* (1610), in *Works*, i, 415.
93. *Saint Pauls Combat*, in *Works*, ii, 440.
94. *Works*, i, 409.
95. *Poems*, p. 72.
96. *Devout Soul*, pp. 90–1.
97. Ibid., pp. 99–101.
98. Ibid., p. 102.
99. *Works*, i, 675.
100. Ibid., p. 467.

101. *Works,* ii, 362–3.
102. *The Spiritual Exercises of Saint Ignatius of Loyola,* trans. from the Spanish with commentary and translation of the *Directorium in Exercitia* by W. H. Longridge (London, 1919), pp. 66–7.
103. *Works,* iii, 94.
104. *Olive-Tree,* pp. 191–2.
105. Ibid., pp. 198–9.
106. Ibid., pp. 155, 182.
107. Ibid., p. 208.
108. *A Sermon preached To his Majestie, on the Sunday before the Fast* (1628), in *Works,* ii, 325.
109. *Works,* i, 424.
110. Ibid., pp. 429–30.
111. *Works,* ii, 159.
112. *A Christian Directory: or, A Summ of Practical Theologie* (London, 1673), pp. 307–8.
113. *Works,* i, 101.
114. *Works,* ii, 161.
115. Ibid., pp. 375–85.
116. Ibid., p. 169.
117. Ibid., p. 166.
118. Ibid., p. 171.
119. Ibid., p. 172.
120. Ibid., p. 179.
121. Ibid., p. 180.
122. *A Sermon Preacht in the Cathedral at Exceter, upon The solemn Day appointed for the Celebration of the Pacification Betwixt the Two Kingdoms. Viz. September. 7. 1641,* in *Olive-Tree,* pp. 48–64. References in the text are to this edition.
123. *Works,* iii, 105–16. This is also one of the most allusive of Hall's sermons drawing upon Augustine, Ambrose, Lactantius, Chrysostom, Horace, Aristophanes, Seneca, Dio, Gerson, Aquinas, Suidas, Erasmus, and Sozomen, to name but some. It is also of considerable interest, in view of his connection with meditation, to note that Bernard of Clairvaux is quoted 6 times.
124. Juan de Avila, *The Audi Filia, or a Rich Cabinet Full of Spirituall Iewells* (St. Omer, 1620), pp. 336–8.
125. *Works,* ed. A. B. Grosart, 2 vols. (Edinburgh, 1879), ii, 23. Breton's whole antithetical method (the greatness of God/the weakness of man etc.) is encapsulated in an elaborate chiastic antithesis drawn by Hall in the early stages of the homily: 'Shortly, thou art all holinesse, power, justice, wisdome, mercy, truth, perfection: Man is nothing but defect, error, ignorance, injustice, impotence, corruption' (p. 108).
126. *The Birds,* 1. 819.
127. *A Preparation to the Psalter* (London, 1619), p. 77.
128. *Spiritual Exercises,* p. 142. On this aspect of contemplation see Evelyn Underhill, *Mysticism,* 5th edn. (London, 1914), p. 361.
129. Cf. the contemplation 'Of Man', *Works,* i, 774–5.

EPILOGUE

1. *Mysticism*, 5th edn (London, 1914), p. 559. See also Joseph Burns Collins, *Christian Mysticism in the Elizabethan Age* (Baltimore, 1940), p. 2.
2. *The Remedy of Prophanenesse* (1637), pp. 52–4.
3. *The Invisible World, Discovered to spiritual Eyes, and Reduced to usefull Meditation* (London, 1652), p. 356.
4. *An Holy Panegyrick* (1613), in *Works*, i, 444, 446.
5. Ibid., p. 446; *The Devout Soul* (1640), sigs. A1ᵛ–A2ʳ.
5. *Christ Mysticall or The Blessed Union of Christ and his Members* (London, 1647), pp. 119–20.
7. Thomas Fuller, *The History of the Worthies of England* (London, 1662), pp. 129–30.
8. *The Revelation Unrevealed i*(1650), pp. 226–7.
9. *Epistles*, in *Works*, i, 321.
10. Ibid., p. 258.
11. Ibid., p. 261.
12. *The Invisible World*, pp. 155–60, 163–7.
13. Ibid., p. 138.
14. Ibid., pp. 169–70.
15. Ibid., p. 143.
16. *Observations of Some Specialities*, in *Olive-Tree*, pp. 2–3.
17. Keith Thomas, *Religion and the Decline of Magic* (London, 1971), pp. 483–6.
18. *A Discovery of the Fraudulent Practises of Iohn Darrel Bacheler of Artes, in his proceedings Concerning The Pretended Possession and dispossession of William Somers ... and of his dealings with one Mary Cooper* (London, 1599). For references to Brinsley see pp. 90, 151.
19. *The Invisible World*, pp. 332–3.
20. Harsnett, pp. 14–15.
21. *Specialities*, pp. 17–19.
22. *The Invisible World*, pp. 303–4; *Susurrium cum Deo* (1651), pp. 52–6; Thomas, pp. 542, 544–5.
23. *Resolutions*, pp. 212–41.
24. *The Invisible World*, pp. 106–7.
25. Ibid., p. 133.
26. Ibid., pp. 138–9.
27. *The Revelation Unrevealed*, pp. 181–2.
28. *The Invisible World*, p. 128; See Bacon, *Sylva Sylvarum* (London, 1651), p. 43.
29. *The Devout Soul ... Also, The Free Prisoner, or The Comfort of Restraint* (London, 1640), pp. 143–5.
30. *St. Pauls Combat* I (1627?), in *Works*, ii, 436.
31. *Satans Fiery Darts Quenched* (1647), p. 29.
32. Ibid., pp. 30–1.
33. *The Great Mysterie*, p. 71.
34. Ibid., p. 9.
35. *Christ Mysticall ... Also, An Holy Rapture*, p. 160.

36. Ibid., pp. 183, 202.
37. Ibid., p. 212.
38. Underhill, pp. 427–57.
39. For Teresa rapture is a sudden, involuntary ecstasy. Ibid., p. 449.
40. For Taylor's attitude see *Works*, ed. Reginald Heber, 10 vols. (London, 1847–54), ii (1847), 139–42.
41. *Satan's Fiery Darts*, pp. 35–9.
42. *An Holy Rapture*, pp. 212–13.
43. *The Invisible World*, pp. 214–15.
44. *The Free Prisoner*, p. 168.
45. *Select Thoughts* (1648), pp. 265–7.
46. *Susurrium cum Deo . . . Together with The Souls Farewell* (1651), pp. 417–18, 419.
47. Underhill, p. 391.
48. *Specialities*, pp. 44, 64.
49. *The Revelation Unrevealed*, pp. 10–11.
50. Ibid., p. 18.
51. Ibid., p. 3.
52. Ibid., p. 233.
53. Ibid., pp. 4–5.
54. The first English translation appeared at Amsterdam in 1611 under the title *A Revelation of the Apocalyps*. Another work entitled *A Revelation of the Revelation . . . Whereby the Pope is most plainely declared and proved to bee Antichrist* was published by Thomas Mason in 1619.
55. Katharine R. Firth, *The Apocalyptic Tradition in Reformation Britain 1530–1645* (Oxford, 1979), p. 108, 164–79.
56. *The Revelation Unrevealed*, p. 232.
57. Firth, pp. 213–28.
58. *The Revelation Unrevealed*, p. 20.
59. For Hall's association with Dury see J. Minton Batten, *John Dury Advocate of Christian Union* (Chicago, 1944), pp. 16, 26, 27, 47. In response to an appeal by Dury, Hall wrote a short essay on the peace of the Church which originally appeared under the title, *De pacis ecclesiasticae rationibus inter evangelicos usurpandis* (1634). The work was reissued 4 years later in an anthology entitled *De Pace Inter Evangelicos procuranda Sententiae Quattuor* (pp. 135–72). In *Works*, xi the editor, Peter Hall, supplies his own translation which he deems the first, but an anonymous translation appeared as early as 1641 in *Good Counsells for the Peace of Reformed Churches by Some Reverend and Learned Bishops and Divines Translated out of Latine*. This includes a translation of Hall's entire contribution with the exception of his explanatory letter to the reader.
60. Firth, p. 216.
61. *Works*, ed. P. Wynter, x, 523.
62. Ibid., p. 528.
63. Firth, p. 246.
64. *Works*, ed. Wynter, x, 527.
65. Ibid., pp. 525–7.

66. Ibid., p. 528.
67. *The Revelation Unrevealed*, pp. 135–7.
68. Ibid., p. 210.
69. Archer's conception of Christ's earthly kingdom reminds Hall of 'a Jewish, or Mahumetane Paradise', pp. 139–40.

APPENDIX A

1. The work was entered in the *Stationers' Register* on 18 Jan. 1609 to Thomas Thorpe. The later edition of *The Discovery* discusses the reception of the first, and alludes to the Frankfurt edition of the *Mundus* which it says appeared some 8 or 9 years previously. *The Discovery* (1614?), $\pi 1^v$–2^r.
2. *CSPD* (James I), 1603–10, pp. 295, 301, 310–13; E. A. Petherick, '*Mundus Alter et Idem*', *The Gentleman's Magazine*, 281 (1896), 82–4.
3. *Epictetus his Manuall. And Cebes his Table* (London, 1610), sig. A3^{r-v}.
4. *Of The Citie of God* (1610), sig. A3^r. William Crashaw who wrote the dedication to the 1620 edition of the same work, and who originally encouraged Healey to undertake it, was also a promoter of the Virginia company.
5. *Epictetus Manuall. Cebes Table. Theophrastus Characters* (London, 1616), sig. A3^r.
6. *Epictetus* (1610), sig. A3^v.
7. *Two Bookes of Constancie . . . Englished by Sir John Stradling*, ed. Rudolf Kirk (New Brunswick, N.J., 1939), p. 68.
8. F. O. Matthiessen, *Translation an Elizabethan Art* (Cambridge, Mass., 1931), pp. 123–30; Frances Yates, *John Florio: The life of an Italian in Shakespeare's England* (Cambridge, 1934), pp. 284–92.
9. *The Discovery of a New World*, ed. Huntington Brown (Cambridge, Mass., 1937), p. 126. All references given after quotations and citations in the text are to this edition.
10. *Mundus Alter et Idem* (Frankfurt, 1605?), p. 196. All further references given in the text are to this edition.
11. I. D. (John Davies) and C.M. (Christopher Marlowe), *Epigrammes and Elegies* (Middleborugh?, 1595?), 'In Fuscum', sig. D1^r.
12. While Healey omits 'ut cum Apuleio loquar' (p. 22), he keeps 'Apuleiano sensu' (p. 34; *Mundus*, p. 44). However he omits 'apud Petronium legisse memini' (p. 28; *Mundus*, p. 34), etc.
13. In *The Anatomy of Satire* (1962) Gilbert Highet speaks as if this were an invention of Swift's (p. 149), but it is at least possible in view of Dr King's interest in the work that the idea came from Hall.
14. Morello scurrae, as Hall's note indicates, refers to the colour of the habit worn by the monks at Vallombrosa. *Cluniachi* refers to the monks of Cluny, whose Abbot Odilo set Purgatory under Etna. *Latrinenses*, called *Lateranenses regulares* in the accompanying note, are the Order of Canons Regular of the Lateran. *Zoccolanti* is a nickname for the

Franciscans, 'those who walk in wooden-soled shoes'. *Cercosimii* are explained by Hall as the *Certosini*, i.e. the Carthusians. 'Certosa' is an Italian verbal corruption from the name of the order's first house at Chartreux. *Matteobassi* is formed from the name of the Capuchin founder Matteo di Bassi. *Scelestinos* stands for Celestines, the clever change making the name mean criminals, from Latin 'scelus' for crime. *Della mercede* is the Order of Our Lady of Mercy and *Della vita commune* refers to the Brethren of the Common Life.

15. *The Passion Sermon* (1609), in *Works*, i, 396.
16. *Works*, i, 9.
17. *Epictetus Manuall. Cebes Table. Theophrastus Characters* (London, 1616), sig. I1ᵛ.
18. The 1688 version was entitled *The Travels of Don Francisco De Quevedo through terra australis incognita, discovering the laws, customs, manners and fashions of the south Indians; a novel originally in Spanish* and was attributed to Gomez de Quevedo y Villegas. In 1669 an adaptation of the Viraginian passages appeared under the title *Psittacorum Regio. The Land of Parrots: Or, The She-lands. With a Description of other strange adjacent Countries in the Dominions of Prince de L' Amour, not hitherto found in any Geographical Map. By one of the late most reputed wits.*
19. King's version is reprinted in *Ideal Commonwealths*, ed. Henry Morley (London, 1885), pp. 273–84. For a modern translation see *Another World and yet the Same*, trans. and ed. John Millar Wands (New Haven, 1981).

APPENDIX B

1. Gilbert Waterhouse, *The Literary Relations of England and Germany* (Cambridge, 1914), pp. 44–5.
2. *Mundus Alter et Idem Sive Terra Australis antehac semper incognita; longis itineribus peregrini Academici nuperrime lustrata. Authore Mercurio Britannico. Accessit propter affinitatem materiae Thomae Companellae Civitas Solis. et Nova Atlantis Franc. Baconis. Bar. de Verulamio* (Utrecht, 1643).
3. Naudé, *Bibliographia Politica* (Wittenberg, 1641), p. 41. Naudé's assertion was upheld in Johannes Andreas Bosius, *De Comparanda Prudentia iuxta et Eloquentia Civili* (Jena, 1679), p. 36. Similarly in the 1720 edition of his *Dictionnaire historique et critique*, Pierre Bayle ascribes the work to Hall. See the English translation *The Dictionary Historical and Critical of Mr. Peter Bayle*, 5 vols. (London, 1734–38), iii (1736), 345. A list of pseudonyms in Adrien Baillet, *Jugemens des Scavans sur les principaux ouvrages de auteurs*, 6 vols. (Amsterdam, 1725), v (part II), 545, identifies Mercurius Britannicus as Joseph Hall. Hall's authorship was universally acknowledged in France. Georges Ascoli, *La Grande-Bretagne devant l'opinion française au xviie siècle*, Travaux et Mémoires de l'Université de Lille, nouvelle série, 13, 2 vols. (Paris, 1930), ii, 105, 322, 331.

4. The only connection between Hall and Gentili which I can find is that Gentili served as secretary to Sir Horatio Pallavicino on the occasion of whose death Hall wrote no less than 3 memorial poems. Lawrence Stone, *An Elizabethan: Sir Horatio Palavicino* (Oxford, 1956), p. 38; *Poems*, pp. 103–5.

5. 'The Early Printing History of Joseph Hall's *Mundus Alter et Idem*', *Papers of the Bibliographical Society of America*, 74 (1980), 1–12 (pp. 3–4, 12).

6. Judging by Mr Wands' criteria, this is one of those copies which appear to be first editions but are not. Wands, p. 5.

7. *Works*, i, 343–4.

8. Ibid., pp. 257–9. *Mundus* (1605?), π 5^r.

9. *Epistles, The First Volume* (1608), pp. 75–7. Wynter (vi, 151) was quite wrong in suggesting that this passage first appeared in the 19th-century editions of Pratt and P. Hall.

10. *A Recollection*, p. 409.

11. *Works*, i, 63, 844.

12. Edward A. Petherick, '*Mundus Alter et Idem*', *The Gentleman's Magazine*, 281 (1896), 66–87.

13. Much of the internal evidence is to be found collected in S. M. Salyer, 'Joseph Hall as a Literary Figure' (unpublished doctoral dissertation, Harvard, 1921), pp. 222–37.

14. Petherick, p. 69.

15. *The Discovery of a New World*, ed. Huntington Brown (Cambridge, Mass., 1937), p. 5. All references are to this edition. Healey went on to produce what remained the standard translation of St. Augustine's *City of God* for over 2 centuries. Speaking of his career as a translator in 1610, the publisher Thomas Thorpe says that he has progressed from 'a devised Country scarse on earth' to 'a desired *Citie* sure in heaven'. His first subject was the 'light' but not 'lewde' work of a 'scarce knowne novice' but now he has turned to 'a famous Father'. 'Scarce knowne novice' cannot refer to the internationally famous and ageing Gentili, but well applies itself to Sir Robert Drury's chaplain whose career as a devotional writer had begun only 5 years earlier. *Of the Citie of God ... Englyshed by J.H.* (London, 1610), sig. A3^r.

16. *Elizabethan Critical Essays*, ed. G. Gregory Smith, 2 vols. (London, 1904), ii, 320.

17. *Poems*, pp. 7–10. See also Hall's reference in book six to the 'far-fetch'd language of th'-*Antipodes*' (p. 91).

18. *Mundus* (1605?), p. 128; *Mundus* (1607), p. 128.

19. *Epigrammatum ... Ad Doctissimam Heroinam, D. Arbellam Stuart* (London, 1612, 1622), epigram 248. See *Heaven upon Earth and Characters of Virtues and Vices*, ed. Rudolf Kirk (New Brunswick, N.J., 1947), p. 55.

20. *Works*, i, 271–4.

21. *Mundus* (1605?), p. 241.

22. *An Answer to a Booke Entituled An Humble Remonstrance* (1641), p. 83.

23. *A Defence of the Humble Remonstrance, Against the frivolous and false exceptions of Smectymnuus* (1641), p. 148. In a sermon of 1628 Hall had

himself reminded his listeners that 'our Globe can tell us of a great part of the World, that hath no more name but *Incognita*, not knowne, whether it have any inhabitant.' *Works*, ii, 309.

24. *Complete Prose Works*, ed. Don M. Wolfe *et al.*, 8 vols. (New Haven, 1953–   ), i, 670.
25. Ibid., p. 697.
26. Ibid., pp. 880–2.
27. Ibid., p. 887. See Also p. 914.
28. See, e.g., *Works*, ed. Wynter, x, 529–32.
29. *Cosmographie* (London, 1652), Book IV, p. 195.
30. *Poems*, p. 47.
31. The attribution of this work in the *DNB* to Hugh Hare, first Baron Coleraine, is quite clearly wrong. Hugh Hare died in 1667, but the preface refers to Joseph Glanvil's continuation of Bacon's *New Atlantis* (1676) and *The History of the Sevarites or Severambi* (1675–9).

INDEX